Encyclopedia of
Philosophers
on Religion

Encyclopedia of Philosophers on Religion

BERNARD J. VERKAMP

McFarland & Company, Inc., Publishers
Jefferson, North Carolina, and London

To all my students and colleagues over the years

LIBRARY OF CONGRESS CATALOGUING-IN-PUBLICATION DATA

Verkamp, Bernard J. (Bernard Joseph), 1938–
    Encyclopedia of philosophers on religion / Bernard J. Verkamp.
      p.   cm.
    Includes bibliographical references and index.

    ISBN 978-0-7864-3286-8
    illustrated case binding : 50# alkaline paper ∞

    1. Philosophers — Biography — Encyclopedias.
    2. Religion — Philosophy — Encyclopedias.   I. Title.
    B104.V47   2008
    210.92'2 — dc22   2008023326

British Library cataloguing data are available

On the cover: statue ©2008 Shutterstock;
stained glass window ©2008 Value Stock Images

Manufactured in the United States of America

McFarland & Company, Inc., Publishers
  Box 611, Jefferson, North Carolina 28640
    www.mcfarlandpub.com

May 2009

Table of Contents

Preface

I read somewhere recently that nowadays most philosophers and their students are atheists. Such a claim, I suspect, is true in regard to philosophers only to the extent that one thinks philosophy is being done these days only in certain schools of thought (e.g., logical positivism, materialistic naturalism), and excludes not only all those many individuals who practice philosophy within the framework of one or another particular religion (e.g., the Reformed Epistemologists, Catholic Thomists, Christian Existentialists), but also anyone who, independent of any specifically religious orientation, entertains, say, a more idealistic, albeit evolutionary, approach to philosophy (e.g., Process Philosophers). Insofar as philosophy students are concerned, I can only speak from my own experience. Of the more than six thousand students I have taught over the past thirty years, some, but certainly not most, were atheists. Be that as it may, the vast majority of current philosophers and their students I have known, read, or taught have remained deeply interested in questions of a religious sort. Furthermore, even if it were true that most philosophers and their students are nowadays atheists, what they think and say about God and religious matters in general must be weighed against the long conversation that has been going on for centuries among philosophers, most of whom certainly were not atheistic in their thinking. Having the latest word in the philosophical *dialektike* is no guarantee of having a corner on the truth. There are good reasons, therefore, for all philosophers and students to pursue their interest in religious questions within the historical context of this ongoing philosophical conversation about God and religion.

Trying to get in on that conversation, however, is no easy task, given the vast number of books and articles that have been published down through the centuries in an attempt to keep the public aware of what philosophers themselves have been thinking and saying to each other about religious matters, not to mention the innumerable commentaries on their works. As Arnold Toynbee once asserted, no human being can ever live long enough to master the amount of material relevant to such a task. And in the following biographical encyclopedia I make no pretense of having even come close to capturing all the rich nuances of religious thought that have surfaced in the centuries-long conversation among philosophers. What I have tried to provide is simply a bird's-eye view of the major points each of the many different philosophers included herein have made about God and religion. Not everything they said could be included in one-page summaries. And not every philosopher addressed the same points. Most have something to say about the existence and nature of God; many talk about human immortality; some address the problem of evil; some emphasize the nature of religious language and symbolism; some offer definitions and interpretations of religion, while others, and perhaps most, focus on an evaluation of religion. No attempt was made, therefore, to infer answers from every philosopher to every question that might today be raised in a systematic approach to the philosophy of religion. Nor did I try to trace the historical dependency of what one philosopher said on the thought of another. Many excellent works of that kind already exist. I also did not have in mind to interpret the thinking of the philosophers represented, although, admittedly, the selection and arrangement of the material could not be done without a degree of interpretation that some readers might very well find debatable. My intention was rather to let each of the philosophers speak for him or herself (albeit mostly in my own words), all the better thereby to create the impression of an ongoing conversation. Biographical information about each philosopher's own religious upbringing, practice, and beliefs, or lack thereof, has been included, not only because it is inherently important and interesting, but also because it can help explain the color or tone of what he or she has said about religion. It should not be taken to imply, however, that such information, in and of itself, can validate or invalidate the philosopher's conclusions. Following each philosopher's entry is a select bibliography of the primary and secondary sources consulted.

As any student of the history of philosophy will immediately detect, the 152 philosophers included do not comprise an exhaustive list. Many philosophers have not been included, either because they had little or nothing to say about religious matters (e.g., Quine), or because what they did say either lacked originality or was not deemed to be of much significance. Judgments of this sort are, of course, open to revision, and not a few of the philosophers excluded are still living and might yet contribute to the conversation in the future.

Readers will also notice that excluded from our list are many great theologians (e.g., Tillich, Karl Rahner, Lonergan), sociologists (e.g., Durkheim, Weber, Wach, Bellah), psychologists (e.g., Freud, Jung, Piaget, Coles), anthropologists (e.g., Geertz, Turner), historians and phenomenologists (e.g., Otto, Eliade, van der Leeuw, Biangi), and even scientists (e.g., D.T. Campbell, Theodosius Dobzhansky, Alister Hardy, E.O. Wilson), all of whom have had some very important things to say about God and religion that often bordered on or rested upon philosophical insights. I tried, however, to limit the list to only those thinkers whom most historians of philosophy have identified as being primarily philosophical in their thought and writing, although with a few (like Thomas Aquinas) the identification might very well be debated.

THE PHILOSOPHERS

Abe, Masao (1915–2006)

Abe was the third of six children born to a physician and his wife in Osaka, Japan. Although the whole family belonged to the True Pure Land (Jōdo-Shin) sect, a cheerful, world-accepting branch of Mahayana Buddhism founded by Shinran Shonin in the thirteenth century to emphasize the gratuitous nature of Amida's salvific influence, only the mother was a devout practitioner. During Abe's high school years, however, a feeling of anxiety about the way he was unconsciously hurting others prompted him to take seriously what he was reading in a collection of talks by Shinran about human sinfulness and the need for faith in Amida's loving mercy. He wanted to take up the study of philosophy, and did in fact continue his study of Buddhism at Osaka Commercial University where his family had sent him to pursue a degree in economics. He was especially troubled at the time by the question about how his religious faith could be reconciled with reason. Upon graduation, he started working for a company in Kobe, but a growing sense of emptiness soon inclined him to leave the business world.

At the age of twenty-six, four months after the Japanese bombing of Pearl Harbor, he enrolled, much to the chagrin of his supposedly more patriotic family and friends, at Kyoto University to study Western philosophy. His goal was to push his rationality beyond the breaking point into a reaffirmation of his Pure Land faith. But a protracted debate with Professor Shin'ichi Hisamatsu, who like another of his Kyoto professors (Keiji Nishitani) had been a student of the great Zen master Kitaro Nishida, eventually convinced him that his Pure Land beliefs were illusory, or as Nietzsche had put it, "holy lies." After flirting briefly with Nietzsche's own "positive nihilism," Abe struggled for some time to understand the total negation of the self implied by Hisamatsu's Zen notion of "Absolute Nothingness," before finally experiencing an awakening to the "formless, unobjectifiable True Self" or "Buddha nature."

Inspired by his subsequent association at Columbia University with the then preeminent Zen scholar, D.T. Suzuki, and with Paul Tillich and Reinhold Niebuhr at neighboring Union Theological Seminary, Abe went on to become, at least since the death of Suzuki in 1966, the leading interpreter and exponent of Zen Buddhism for the Western world. Publication of articles he has written and the multiple lectures he has delivered at universities around the world on the dynamic nature of *Sunyata* (Nothingness) and other Buddhist doctrines have stimulated, as he had hoped they would for the sake of world unity, an intense interfaith dialogue.

ABE ON RELIGION. Particular religions have been subject to criticism since ancient times. But hardly anyone throughout human history, not even during the Age of Enlightenment when religion's worldview and understanding of nature were questioned, ever doubted the fundamental significance or the

1

necessity of religion itself for the human soul. In the past few centuries, however, not only have many people become indifferent to religion or sought substitutes for religion in art and literature, but also there have arisen on a more theoretical level at least four different ideologies that deny in principle religion itself, namely: mechanistic/materialistic scientism, Marxism, traditional Freudian psychoanalysis, and Nietzschean nihilism. While the first three attack religion from without, dismissing it as being unscientific, and therefore false and illusory, the last attacks it from within, rendering it useless as an antidote to fears of meaninglessness by going "beyond" the experience of a living God, declaring the latter's "death," and depreciating all traditional religious values for the sake of reappropriating the human "will to power."

Superseding any attempts at interfaith dialogue is the most crucial task of all religions in modern times to respond to these antireligious forces. Nontheistic Buddhism, for example, must exploit its emphasis upon "dependent co-origination," "suchness," and "Emptiness" in such wise as not only to find a "new, non-teleological, non-mechanical teleology" that will reconcile religion with modern science, but also to cultivate a Self-awakening that will recapture a qualitative conception of mankind as a single, living, self-aware entity (its "Buddha-nature"), negate the sovereignty of nation-states, and help bridge the traditional gap between East and West by affording itself a genuinely qualitative sense of being a world religion. With an interpretation of its doctrine of the divine *kenosis* as a "total self-negation of God," Christianity might be in a position to respond similarly.

Sources

Abe, Masao. "Kenotic God and Dynamic Sunyata." In *The Emptying God: A Buddhist-Jewish-Christian Conversation.* Edited by John B. Cobb Jr. and Christopher Ives. Maryknoll, NY: Orbis Books, 1990. 3–65. (Ives's "Introduction" on pp. xiii–xix is an excellent biographical source.).
_____. *A Study of Dōgen: His Philosophy and Religion.* Edited by Steven Heine. Albany: State University of New York Press, 1992.
_____. *Zen and Western Thought.* Edited by William R. LaFleur. Honolulu: University of Hawaii, 1989.
Cha, John Y. "Abe, Masao." In *World Philosophers and Their Works.* Vol. 1. Edited by John K. Roth. Pasadena, CA, and Hackensack, NJ: Salem Press, Inc., 2000. 1–7.
Mitchell, Donald, ed. *Masao Abe: A Zen Life of Dialogue.* Boston, Rutland, Vermont, and Tokyo: Charles E. Tuttle Co., Inc., 1998. See esp. Abe's "Response," 371–409.

Abelard, Peter (1079–1142)

Abelard's early religious instruction in his birthplace of Pallet, Britanny, would likely have included (in addition to Sunday sermons) learning basic prayers and creeds, selections from the bible, and lives of the saints. His father (who, like his wife, would eventually enter monastic life) wanted Abelard to pursue a military career like his own, but the son became instead a wandering scholar, already at the age of fifteen. He was primarily interested in dialectics and studied the same under Roscelin, who was espousing a Nominalist denial of the reality of universals, and then in Paris under William of Champeaux, who favored the opposite view of Platonic realism. After prevailing in intermittent public debates with William, and (before a six-year bout with poor health sent him scurrying back to Brittany) attracting multiple students to his own schools, Abelard eventually turned to the study of theology under Anselm of Laon.

Astonished by Abelard's logical assaults and his skill at interpreting Scriptures, students flocked to the lectures he began giving in Paris. His affair with Heloïse compromised his position, however, and his enemies succeeded in having his views on the Trinity condemned at the Council of Soissons in 1121 and having him confined to a monastery (other than the one, St. Denis, in which he had sought refuge after being emasculated, and the identity of whose founder he had called into question). Later, after being released, setting up another school, and serving a brief, turbulent stint as abbot of St. Gildas, Abelard, with his supposedly rationalistic interpretation of Christian mysteries, incurred the wrath of Bernard of Clairvaux, who contrived to have his views condemned again at the Council of Sens in 1141.

Abelard appealed to the pope, but on his way to Rome stopped off at the monastery of Cluny. Its abbot, Peter the Venerable, convinced Abelard to reconcile with Bernard and to spend the rest of his life under Cluny's protection. Several years earlier he had confessed that he did not wish to be a philosopher or a disciple of Aristotle if it meant conflicting with the Apostle Paul or cutting himself off from Christ. Abbot Peter attested that Abelard's last years at Cluny were humble and saintly, and that before he died, he confessed his sins and received communion.

ABELARD ON RELIGION. As a universal notion, religion has no independent reality of its own. It can, however, be predicated of particular social entities (like Judaism or Christianity) to the extent that the latter, as exercises in the virtue of justice, enjoy a common state of being by way of showing to God the reverence He deserves. Although no exact philosophical or theological definition of the divine nature can be given, the New Testament reveals God, or the being of highest perfection (the *summum Bonum*), as a Triune God of Power (Father), Wisdom (Son), and Love (Holy Spirit), who became man in the person of Jesus Christ. By his death on the cross, Jesus not only redeemed fallen mankind through loving submission to the will of his Father, he also set the perfect example of how humans can best practice religion, namely, by a proper disposition toward charity: love of God above all for His own sake, and love of one's neighbor in accordance with his or her excellence.

Neither the Jews of old, nor the ancient Greek and Roman philosophers were oblivious to this doctrine of the Trinity and its ethical identification of justice, religion, and charity. The pagan and Hebrew prophets inclined their people not only to attribute to God the power, wisdom and love that any rational person would ascribe to a perfect being, but also to express an explicit faith in the redemptive value of the Incarnation, and most importantly, to live their lives in a genuinely religious manner, obeying the natural or Mosaic laws, not just because they were brought up that way, but because of their free intention to do all for the love of God. No doubt, then, many Jews and pagans living before the time of Christ were saved. By loving Wisdom, they were in effect loving Christ, and to that extent deviated little or not at all from the Christian religion. Still, it is in the Christian religion that whatever rational truth ancient Judaism and pagan philosophy contained finds its richest expression. And no philosopher, except perhaps in provocative jest, should call Christians mad.

Sources

Abelard's Christian Theology. Summarized by J. Ramsay McCallum. Merrick, NY: Richwood Publishing Co., 1976.

Abelard, Peter. *Collationes (Dialogue between a Christian, a Philosopher and a Jew)*. Edited and translated by John Marenbon and Giovanni Orlandi. Oxford: Clarendon Press, 2001.

_____. *Exposition of the Epistle to the Romans*. In *A Scholastic Miscellany*, translated by Eugene R. Fairweather. New York: The Macmillan Company, 1970. 276–87.

_____. *The Letters of Abelard and Heloïse*. Translated by C.K. Scott Moncrieff. New York: Cooper Square Publishers, Inc., 1974.

_____. *Scito Teipsum. (Ethics)*. In *A Scholastic Miscellany*, translated by Eugene R. Fairweather. New York: The Macmillan Company, 1970. 288–97.

_____. *Sic et Non (Prologue)*. Translated by Brian Tierney et al., in Brian Tierney, *The Middle Ages*. Vol. 1. *Sources of Medieval History*. 2nd ed. New York: Alfred A. Knopf, 1973. 145–48.

Gilson, Etienne. *History of Christian Philosophy in the Middle Ages*. New York: Random House, 1954. 153–63.

Luscombe, D.E. "Introduction" to *Peter Abelard's Ethics*. Oxford: Clarendon Press, 1971.

Marenbon, John. *The Philosophy of Peter Abelard*. Cambridge: Cambridge University Press, 1997.

_____, and Giovanni Orlandi. "Introduction" to Abelard, *Collationes*. xvii–cxx.

Robertson, D.W., Jr. *Abelard and Heloïse*. New York: The Dial Press, 1972.

Smith, S.R. "Abelard, Peter." In *New Catholic Encyclopedia*, Vol. 1. Edited by W.J. McDonald. New York: McGraw-Hill, 1967. 15–17.

Starnes, Kathleen M. *Peter Abelard: His Place in His-*

tory. Washington, D.C.: University Press of America, Inc., 1981.

Williams, Paul L. *The Moral Philosophy of Peter Abelard*. Lanham, MD: University Press of America, 1980.

Adorno, Theodor W. (1903–1969)

Adorno's father (Oscar Wiesengrund) was of Jewish descent but had converted to Christianity. Though assimilated to the Christian environment, he retained a Jewish sense of history (with its notions of a non-mythological God, a chosen people, and the traditional hermeneutic role of the Jewish outsider) that may have helped shape his son's eventual outlook. Adorno's mother (Maria née Calvelli Adorno), an accomplished musician, was Catholic. At her insistence, Adorno was baptized and brought up a Catholic. He received a Catholic elementary education and participated in many of the Church's liturgical services. At about the age of ten, however, he began taking instructions from a teacher (Reinhold Zickel) of strong Protestant convictions, who not only introduced him to poetry and literary criticism, but apparently also persuaded him to be confirmed and to take religious instruction in Frankfurt's Protestant Saint Catherine's Church. He would later be tempted to convert back to Catholicism, but after reading Thomas Mann's *The Magic Mountain,* gave up thinking that a medieval Catholic theocracy might be the solution for a disjointed world.

After finishing university studies in philosophy, literature, and music, Adorno wrote a doctoral thesis criticizing Husserl's phenomenology on grounds that it failed to do what his *Doktorvater* (Hans Cornelius) felt was necessary, namely, the freeing of science from all dogmatic preconditions. He was clearly moving away from any positive religious philosophy that would posit meaning as given prior to investigation. Under the direction of the Christian theologian, Paul Tillich, he presented a *Habilitationschrift* on Kierkegaard, in which, while praising the Danish theologian

for his refusal to accommodate his religious convictions to bourgeois society, he also strongly criticized his "monotheistic disguise of myth" and his absurdist vindication of sacrifice (such as, in the case of the crucified Christ, would magically reconcile civilization and nature). It has been suggested that this was Adorno's way of bidding farewell to Christianity and distancing his own ideas from its beliefs.

Even while concentrating on his sociopolitical concerns of the Frankfurt Institute, he would remain deeply interested in, and respectful of, religion. But for his personal religion, he would increasingly look, as a "man of the mountains," to the realm of nature where, along with "all the unconscious things around him," he could best experience himself as a "heavy piece of fruit" on "the tree that is God."

ADORNO ON RELIGION. Enlightenment had aimed at liberating human beings from fear and installing them as masters. But in the attempt to control nature, and make progress at any cost, rationality was reduced to instrumental reason and the "whole enlightened earth" became radiant with triumphant calamity, climaxing in the horror of Auschwitz. Although Nazi anti–Semitism claimed to disregard religion on the assumption that people no longer cared about eternal salvation, religious tradition remained deeply embedded in the party's racist ideology.

While the moment of truth in religion had been debarred in the alliance between enlightenment and power, its reified forms (e.g., unchanneled yearning and zealotry) had been conserved and was eventually exploited by the fascists. It is imperative upon religion also, therefore, to try to rearrange its thinking and action so that nothing similar to Auschwitz will ever happen again. This cannot be done by trying to exploit the crisis of reason through substituting questions about the need of religion (e.g., obligations) for concern about its truth. For the religious origin of anti–Semitism can be located precisely in the bad conscience of those Christians who felt obliged to confirm their eternal salvation by the worldly ruin of those (e.g., Jews) who refused to make the murky sacrifice of reason required by the Christian attempt to reconcile nature and the supernatural in the death of the God-man, Jesus. Nor will it help to concoct demythologized, Existentialist or Romantic, versions of fideism that reduce faith to an irrational feeling. Accepted for anything other than its own truth content, religion undermines itself and evaporates into pure symbolism. What religion needs is not less, but more reasoning — not to rationalize irrational dogmas or to defend a turn toward transcendence as a screen for societal hopelessness, but to think critically about what, in the face of modern history and science, the existence of God, as that which is absolutely other than what this world appears to be, can possibly mean.

Sources

Adorno, Theodor W. "Elements of Anti-Semitism." In Theodor Adorno, *Can One Live After Auschwitz*, edited by Rolf Tiedemann; translated by Rodney Livingstone and others. Stanford, CA: Stanford University Press, 2003. 391–426.

_____. *Kierkegaard: Construction of the Aesthetic*. Translated by Robert Hullot-Kentor. Minneapolis: University of Minnesota Press, 1989.

_____. *Metaphysics: Concept and Problems*. Stanford, CA: Stanford University Press, 2000.

_____. "Offenbarung oder autonome Vernunft." In *Frankfurter Hefte* 13/6 (June): 392–402; 484–498. Adorno's contribution to the first part of this discussion was also published in Adorno, Theodor W., *Stichworte, Kritische Modelle* 2. Frankfurt, 1969, and has been translated as "Reason and Revelation" and published in Theodor W. Adorno, *Critical Models: Interventions and Catchwords*. New York: Columbia University Press, 1998. 135–42.

Jäger, Lorenz. *Adorno: A Political Biography*. Translated by Stewart Spencer. New Haven and London: Yale University Press, 2004.

Küng, Hans. *Does God Exist?* Translated by Edward Quinn. Garden City, NY: Doubleday and Company, Inc., 1980. 323–39; 489–91.

Siebert, Rudolf J. *The Critical Theory of Religion: The Frankfurt School*. Berlin, New York, and Amsterdam: Mouton Publishers, 1985. See esp. 156–64.

Zuidervaart, Lambert. "Theodor W. Adorno." *Stanford Encyclopedia of Philosophy*. http://plato.stanford.edu/. 1–20.

Alexander, Samuel (1859–1938)

In accordance with the Jewish tradition of the family into which he was born, Alexander experienced *bar mitzvah* at the age of thirteen. After receiving a broad education in the Classics, Mathematics, Science, and Foreign Languages at Wesley College in Melbourne, he went to England and won a scholarship at Oxford's Balliol College that allowed him to pursue further his interest in empirical science. Five years later, in 1882, he was elected to a Fellowship at Lincoln College (Oxford), an event which, as noted in the May 5 issue of the *Jewish Chronicle*, made him the first Jew ever to be elected a fellow of an Oxford or Cambridge college.

Except for a year abroad at a German university for the sake of acquainting himself with the latest developments in the new field of psychology, he spent the next decade studying and teaching philosophy (mainly metaphysics and ethics) and psychology at Lincoln and other colleges, before being appointed in 1893 to the chair of philosophy at the University of Manchester that he would hold until his retirement in 1924. While there he carried on extensive correspondence with many of the leading scholars of the day, but especially with F.H. Bradley and Bernard Bosanquet, whose Idealist views he tried to transpose onto a more realist base. Called upon to deliver the Gifford Lectures during the years 1916–1918, he took the occasion to expound his rather Spinozistic and Ottomanian (Rudolf Otto's) conception of religion as a cognitive feeling of dread, fascination, and humility toward an object of experience that embodies all the emerging highest possibilities of Nature (namely, the Deity). The lectures were published in 1920 under the title: *Space, Time and Deity*.

Although he had become deeply attached to Jewish tradition from his early youth and was proud of his Jewish identity, he did not maintain very close ties with the local Jewish community in Manchester. But having ceased believing in the possibility of Jewish assimilation, he had become an early, wholehearted supporter of Zionism, contributing regularly to the Palestine Foundation Fund and collaborating in a variety of ways with the Hebrew University of Jerusalem and the Inter-University Jewish Federation. He made significant financial contributions to the support of Jewish refugees from Nazi persecution. Following his death in 1938, the ashes of his cremated body were buried in the section of Manchester's cemetery reserved for the British Jewish Reform Congregation.

ALEXANDER ON RELIGION. Religion consists of the experience of something divine in the world, of a mysterious object, called God, which evokes an emotional attitude of worshipful dependency, love, and devotion. In the experience itself no question is ever raised about whether the object experienced exists or not. For the religious person its existence is as much a fact as is a green leaf for a dispassionate observer. It would never dawn on the worshiper to suspect that God is a mere figment of his imagination. And were this native passion towards God not already lit, no speculative reflection about the existence and nature of the religious object would render it worshipful.

On the other hand, the religious sentiment itself is not enough to prove the reality of God, and must, therefore, be supplemented by a metaphysical inquiry into what place, if any, the religious object of worship occupies in a universe consisting of things, including our finite selves, evolving within the matrix of Space-Time. To satisfy the mature religious sentiment, its object must be shown to be something greater than man and independent of him while at the same time being close and personal enough to evoke a loving response. Neither traditional pantheism nor theism can meet such demands. Nor can the Christian attempt to reconcile divine transcendence and immanence through its doctrine of the Incarnation succeed. The solution is rather to conceive of God as a creature of time who, far from being already the perfect Prime Mover,

First Cause, or Creator, is constantly in the making to the extent of being one with the whole of the present world insofar as it is straining toward Deity (i.e., the next higher level in emergent evolution). Only a God so conceived coincides with the object of the religious sentiment which inclines us to reach out toward something higher and greater than ourselves, and to work with It toward the future, ideal actualization of Deity through the conversion of evil to good, and preservation of, if not the individual, at least the human species.

Sources

Alexander, Samuel. *Philosophical and Literary Pieces.* London: Macmillan and Co., Ltd., 1939.

_____. *Space, Time, and Deity.* 2 vols. London: Macmillan and Co., Ltd., 1927.

Brettschneider, Bertram D. *The Philosophy of Samuel Alexander.* New York: Humanities Press, 1964. 143–70.

Emmet, Dorothy. "Foreword to the 1966 Reprint Edition" of Alexander, *Space, Time and Deity*, Vol. 1. New York: Dover Publications, Inc., 1966. v–xx.

Hartshorne, Charles, and William L. Reese. *Philosophers Speak of God.* Chicago and London: The University of Chicago Press, 1963. 365–72.

Laird, John. "Memoir (Life of Alexander)." In Alexander, *Philosophical and Literary Pieces.* 1–96.

_____. "Samuel Alexander's Theism." *The Hibbert Journal* 40 (January 1942). 146–55.

Wright, William Kelley. *A History of Modern Philosophy.* New York: The Macmillan Company, 1941. 578–95.

Alston, William P. (1921–)

Alston was raised a Methodist in Shreveport, Louisiana. But his practice of religion while growing up had left him rather cold, and already, in his early teens, exposure to atheistic arguments and attitudes had inclined him to abandon his faith. He would remain unchurched for the next decade. During his post–high school years of military service (1942–1946) he happened to read Jacques Maritain's *Introduction to Philosophy* and was inspired to begin a self-study of all the major philosophers that eventually got him admitted to the University of Chicago's Ph.D. program without ever having taken a formal course in philosophy. But it was only after completing his doctoral program and being appointed a professor of philosophy at the University of Michigan that his personal interest in religion revived. By his own account, it had little to do with any philosophical, theological, or historical arguments about the truth of Christianity.

He joined and was confirmed in Ann Arbor's Episcopal Church of St. Andrew's only because he felt something missing in his life and was attracted by the liturgy and moderate intellectual climate of the Anglican religion. Sensing, however, that he was only using religion to escape problems he was having in his relations with other people, and fearing along Freudian lines that his religious faith was nothing but a childish exercise in wish-fulfillment, he once again jumped ship in the late fifties, and for the next fifteen years, while still teaching at Michigan and making a name for himself with major publications (e.g., *Philosophy of Language*), lived a purely secular life. But he was "never an enthusiastic atheist," and after getting some psychotherapy and inspiration from a reconverted daughter, a group of charismatic Christians, and an Episcopal preacher, he returned to the Episcopal Church in 1975 and has remained an active member ever since, taking professorial positions at the University of Illinois in Urbana-Champaign and Syracuse University in New York.

He admits that his ongoing philosophical endeavors, publishing multiple books and articles about logic, epistemology, metaphysics and religion, directing seminars, and founding scholarly journals (e.g., *Faith and Philosophy*), have greatly influenced his religious life. But he also insists that it was his intuitive attraction to an undogmatic, religious communal way of life, and not any philosophical reflection, that ultimately moved him from unbelief to belief.

ALSTON ON RELIGION. Although divine-human dialogue is incompatible with divine omni-determination of His creation, a timeless, omniscient God can enter into genuine dialogue with human beings, even to the point of sharing His own true beliefs and loving inclinations with them through divine commands, prayer, and so on. The religious experience resulting therefrom can occur at three different grades of immediacy. At one level, God's presence is perceived through the awareness of another object of perception like the beauty of nature or the word of the Bible. At the opposite end of the spectrum is the extreme grade of "absolute immediacy," in which one's awareness of God's presence is so direct that all distinctions between object and subject are transcended in an undifferentiated unity. In between is the grade of "mediated immediacy," in which the presence of God is perceived, not through any other object, but directly, through a specifiable mode of consciousness. It is this latter type of religious experience that is most like sense perception, to the extent that it consists of an object presenting itself independent of conceptualization, belief, or judgment by the knowing subject. This proves nothing about the existence of God, but it does say that if God exists, makes a causal contribution to one's current experience, and gives rise to beliefs about Himself, the direct experience of His presence can properly be thought of as religious perception, and not be dismissed as a purely subjective feeling to which is superadded a culture-based explanation.

Although there can be only one true religion and there is no insuperable obstacle to speaking literally about God, the doxastic practice of any one religion resulting from such direct or indirect experience of God's presence cannot be proven to be superior to that of any other religion. But if one's particular religion meets one's spiritual needs, one would be wise to stay with it, adhering to its distinctive beliefs, even while acknowledging the right of individuals within other traditions to do the same.

Sources

Alston, William P. *Divine Nature and Human Language: Essays in Philosophical Theology*. Ithaca and London: Cornell University Press, 1989.

_____. *Perceiving God*. Ithaca and London: Cornell University Press, 1991.

_____. "A Philosopher's Way Back to the Faith." In *God and the Philosophers*. Edited by Thomas V. Morris. New York and Oxford: Oxford University Press, 1994: 19–30.

_____. "Religious Experience and Religious Belief." *NOUS* 16 (1982): 3–12.

_____. "Religious Diversity and Perceptual Knowledge of God." *Faith and Philosophy* 5.4 (October 1988): 433–48.

"Alston, William Payne." In forthcoming *The Dictionary of Modern American Philosophers*. n.p.: Thoemmes Press, n.d. http://www.ac.wwu.edu/~howardd/alston/alstonforthoemmes.pdf. 1–7.

Hick, John. "A Concluding Comment." *Faith and. Philosophy* 5.4 (October 1988): 455.

Swinburne, Richard. "Review (of Alston's *Divine Nature and Human Language*)." *Faith and Philosophy* 9.1 (January 1992): 116–20.

Verkamp, Bernard J. *The Sense of Religious Wonder: Epistemological Variations*. Scranton, PA: University of Scranton Press, 2002. 67–78.

Anselm of Canterbury (c. 1033–1109)

Consistent with his parents' plans to prop up the family's declining fortunes by having their son seek ecclesiastical preferment, Anselm early on became a clerk in the church of his hometown, Aosta. After the death of his mother and a quarrel with his father, he fled from Aosta in 1056, hoping somehow to find a way to combine dual interests in learning and spirituality. He had earlier contemplated becoming a monk, and it is possible that during the next few years he spent some time at the famous Benedictine abbey of Cluny. Dissatisfied by it and other Burgundian and French schools, and having heard of the renown of Lanfranc of Pavia as a teacher, Anselm followed the latter to the Abbey of Bec, where, under Lanfranc's direction, he undertook a program of religious and intellectual development and decided to become a Benedictine monk himself.

Three years later, in 1062, he succeeded Lanfranc as the Abbey's prior, and then, in 1078, was elected its Abbot. It was during this period that he wrote, in addition to a study of Aristotelian logic, an early batch of letters extolling among other things the value of friendship, and a set of *Prayers and Meditations*, his famous *Monologion* and *Proslogion*. Several more treatises concerning truth and spiritual liberty were written in the subsequent decade before he reluctantly accepted an appointment as Archbishop of Canterbury in 1093.

For the next fifteen years he was embroiled in the battle between the pope and England's king over lay investiture, with frequent trips to Rome and back, but still managed to write a number of important treatises on the Incarnation (*Cur Deus Homo*), the Procession of the Holy Spirit, the Immaculate Conception, Predestination, etc. Despite a lack of administrative skill in the world outside the monastery that compounded the grief and affliction of his years as Archbishop, he never lost his monastic zeal for eternal life and applied it dutifully toward the pastoral reform of the English Church. Within half a century of his death in 1109, at the prompting of Thomas Becket, he came to be included among the English saints. Six hundred years later he was declared a Doctor of the Church.

ANSELM ON RELIGION. Whoever wishes to be saved must hold the Catholic faith. There are many practical differences which do not compromise the unity of love and can be peaceably tolerated in the Church. But there is no room for diversity on the Scriptural-based fundamentals of faith. Individuals claiming to be Christians who deny them ought, therefore, be anathematized until they recant. It is pointless to try soliciting from them an explanation of their error, or to try explicating for them the truth. They should simply be required to adhere to their baptismal vows. For no Christian ought to question the truth of what the Catholic Church wholeheartedly believes and confesses.

Still, those who love the Christian faith and live by it ought also to seek humbly and as best they can to discover the reason why it is true. This ought to be done both for the joy that comes from understanding the faith and for the rational defense of the faith it provides against the impious pagans and heretics. It does not mean, however, that one should seek to understand in order to believe. Quite the contrary, one should believe in order to understand. And although the mysteries of faith will never be fully understood prior to the beatific vision, the reason of fallen man can, when cleansed by faith, lend rational support to what one believes. Observing the degrees of perfection in the goodness, wisdom, and being of creatures, for example, reason can come up with many arguments for the existence of God as the absolutely good and wise Being that causes everything to exist. Or, starting with the definition of God as that than which nothing greater can be thought, it can be demonstrated that God must necessarily exist, not merely in the mind (like the idea of a perfect island), but in reality. Reason can also help believers understand the triune nature of God or why, in order to restore fully the honor and satisfaction owed by man to God, God became man in the person of Jesus Christ, thereby offering salvation to Jews and Gentiles alike.

Sources

Anselm of Canterbury. *Basic Writings: Proslogium; Monologium; Gaunilon's "On Behalf of the Fool;" Cur Deus Homo.* Translated by S.N. Deane, with an introduction by Charles Hartshorne. LaSalle, IL: Open Court, 1962.

_____. *(Complete treatises) Volume Three: Two Letters concerning Roscelin; the Incarnation of the Word; Why God became a Man; the Virgin Conception and Original Sin; the Procession of the Holy Spirit; Three Letters on the Sacraments.* Edited and translated by Jasper Hopkins and Herbert Richardson. Toronto and New York: The Edwin Mellen Press, 1976.

_____. *The Major Works.* Edited by Brian Davies and G.R. Evans. Oxford: Oxford University Press, 1998.

_____. *Three Philosophical Dialogues. On Truth; On Freedom of Choice; On the Fall of the Devil.* Translated by Thomas Williams. Indianapolis: Hackett Publishing Company, Inc., 2002.

Copleston, Frederick, S.J. *A History of Philosophy.* Vol. 2, pt. 1. Garden City, NY: Doubleday and Company, Inc., 1962–77. 177–86.

Gilson, Etienne. *History of Christian Philosophy in the Middle Ages.* New York: Random House, 1954. 128–39.

Pelikan, Jaroslav. *The Growth of Medieval Theology (600–1300).* Chicago and London: The University of Chicago Press, 1978.

Schmitt, F.S. "Anselm of Canterbury, St." *New Catholic Encyclopedia.* Vol. 1. Edited by W.J. McDonald. New York: McGraw-Hill, 1967. 581–83.

Southern, R.W. *Saint Anselm: A Portrait in a Landscape.* Cambridge: Cambridge University Press, 1990.

Arendt, Hannah (1906–1975)

Arendt's parents were well-educated socialists who had little taste for religion. But they did allow Hannah to accompany her Reform-Jewish, Arendt-grandparents to Königsberg's synagogue, whose Rabbi Vogelstein was a leader of liberal German Jewry. It was from this same rabbi that several times a week the seven-year-old Arendt received religious instruction, the only formal religious training she would ever get (apart from the mandatory Christian Sunday school she attended while in kindergarten). Later, when Arendt announced to the rabbi that she had lost her belief in God, he replied with the curt comment, "And who asked you?," suggesting to the young woman that being a Jew transcended personal religious convictions, or lack thereof. Against the occasional anti–Semitic accusation she heard at school about Jews being guilty of murdering the Lord Jesus, her mother had taught her to defend her Jewish identity with vigor, and never to humble herself.

Expelled from Königsberg's girls' *Gymnasium* because of her rather independent and rebellious spirit, Arendt was sent by her mother to the University of Berlin, where she attended lectures in Christian theology being given by the leading Christian existentialist in Germany at the time, Romano Guardini. He introduced her to the writings of Kierkegaard, which excited her so much that she decided to major in theology, first at Marburg under the tutelage and adoring eye of Heidegger, then for a semester with Husserl at Freiburg, and finally at Heidelberg with Jaspers, under whom she wrote her doctoral dissertation on Augustine's threefold concept of love, tapping (as had also Heidegger) their temporal implications.

During subsequent years of involvement in Zionist politics, Nazi internment, flight to and life in America, and writing about totalitarianism, Eichmann, the banality of evil, etc., she would downplay Augustine's emphasis upon transcendent love (between man and God) and insist upon the separation of religion and politics. But she retained a deep, nondogmatic, religious faith, admiring religious leaders and thinkers like Pope John XXIII and Paul Tillich, and regretting attempts by some Jews to identify themselves as a people apart from their traditional trust and love of God. When her non–Jewish husband, Heinrich Blücher, died, she expressed a desire for a Jewish funeral service, with its Hebrew *Kaddish* (or death prayer) giving expression to the holiness of God. Although friends debated whether to include Jewish prayers in her own funeral service in 1975, a Hebrew psalm was in fact recited.

ARENDT ON RELIGION. Never doubting the existence of God and making one's way through life with a kind of childish, unquestioned trust in God, is quite different from a dogmatic faith that must constantly deal with the difficulty of reconciling the existence of God with a thousand years of philosophical reflection on problems of causality, radical evil, and so on. Traditional religions to which such faith has given rise have little value. True, the self-forgetfulness exemplified by the historical Jesus was a paradigm of human goodness, exceeding by far the Socratic preoccupation with personal integrity. And there have been good men, like John XXIII, who in dark times have lived up to the teaching of Jesus. But being of a hidden sort, such goodness was by nature not only anti-institutional but also antipolitical, and all the more so after Jesus' message was converted by traditional Christianity into a doctrine of personal salvation or damnation. This spawned an ascetical attitude of otherworldliness that reversed the early Greek vision of mortal human life in an eternal universe, perpetuated beastly slave labor, demeaned this-worldly, creative work that lays

the foundation of political life, and undermined political action — i.e., the freedom to take initiative, to begin ever anew in the thoughtful, judicious pursuit of unpredictable, miraculous events.

The medieval, Platonically derived doctrine of Hell had lent support to political authority, and might — had it been exploited by Pius XII and other religious authorities — have helped head off Nazi and other forms of modern totalitarianism. But with the majority of people having lost all fear of Hell, institutional religion (discounting any notion of a secular religion) no longer has any political clout. This is best anyway. For, although an imaginative retrieval of certain religious values (e.g., Augustinian love of neighbor) might be helpful, the injection of religious passion into political life would likely pervert both religion and politics into detestable exercises in ideological fanaticism.

Sources

Arendt, Hannah. *The Human Condition*. Chicago: The University of Chicago Press, 1958.

_____. *The Life of the Mind: Thinking and Willing*. 2 vols. New York: Harcourt Brace Jovanovich. 1978.

_____. *The Origins of Totalitarianism*. New York: Harcourt Brace Jovanovich, 1973.

_____. "Religion and Intellectuals." *Partisan Review* XVII.2 (February 1950): 113–16.

_____. "Religion and Politics." *Confluence: An International Forum*. (September 1953): 105–26.

Bernauer, James W., S.J. *Amor Mundi: Explorations in the Faith and Thought of Hannah Arendt*. Boston, Dordrecht, and Lancaster: Martinus Nijhoff Publishers, 1987.

Canovan, Margaret. *Hannah Arendt: A Reinterpretation of Her Political Thought*. Cambridge: Cambridge University Press, 1992.

Hinchman, Lewis, and Sandra Hinchman, eds. *Hannah Arendt: Critical Essays*. New York: State University of New York Press, 1994.

Kristeva, Julia. *Hannah Arendt*. New York: Columbia University Press, 2001.

Wanker, William Paul. *Nous and Logos: Philosophical Foundations of Hannah Arendt's Political Theory*. New York and London: Garland Publishing Inc., 1991.

Young-Bruehl, Elizabeth. *Hannah Arendt: For Love of the World*. New Haven and London: Yale University Press, 1982.

Aristotle (384–322 B.C.)

Both of Aristotle's parents were from Ionia, the birthplace of not only western philosophy, but also, earlier, of Homer, whose poetic, anthropomorphic representation of the Olympian pantheon dominated popular religion and its festive celebration of divine power for centuries to come. As a physician, his father belonged to the guild of the "sons of Aesculapius," the Greek god of healing who himself was thought to intervene in the therapeutic treatments priests would prescribe to patients seeking cures. Although little is known of Aristotle's childhood, it is likely that the Macedonian court in which he grew up, and would later work as the tutor of soon-to-be-apotheosized Alexander the Great, was predominantly religious in belief and practice.

Whatever religious sentiments Aristotle may have imbibed from such an environment, they would certainly have been reinforced by his admission at the age of seventeen to, and his twenty-year-long stay at, the Athenian Academy being run by Plato, who by that time was showing increasingly religious proclivities and made no secret of his affection for religious storytelling. Later in his life Aristotle himself would remark to a friend that "the lonelier and the more isolated I am, the more I have come to love myths." Elsewhere, in his *Metaphysics*, he would link this love of myth with a love of wisdom and the sense of wonder which he saw as the source of all philosophizing. This has inclined some scholars to conclude that, alongside his lifelong devotion to science and its empirical methodology, Aristotle was also a profoundly religious man who had a deeply sensitive, mostly hidden life of piety based upon his personal, intuitive experience of wonder at the godlike nature of man and the awesome beauty of the visible universe.

The charge of impiety (*asebeia*) brought against him for having erected a statue and penned a poem in honor of Hermias, a former student of Plato's Academy who had become the ruler of Assos and whose niece he had married, was no doubt politically motivated by anti-Macedonian sentiment in Athens following the death of Alexander in 323 B.C. In his last will, he claims to have prayed for the preservation of his adopted son, Nicanor, and asks that he set up in Stagira, the town of Aristotle's own birth, life-size statues of the divine saviors, Zeus and Athena. This need not be taken to mean, however, that he ever thought of the metaphysically conceived Prime Mover as a personal Being whom one might worship or to whom one might pray in any genuinely religious sense.

ARISTOTLE ON RELIGION. Nowhere should we be more modest than in discussions about the gods. But all men have some conception of the nature of the gods. They imagine the form and ways of the gods as being like their own, and ascribe to them many different names. Their conception of the gods springs ultimately either from the experience of a soul in dreams and death, or from observation of the orderly movement of the sun and stars. Experience of the soul and its intellectual capacity as being better than the body inclines humans to think that there is a best — a supremely intelligent being, whose actuality consists of eternally thinking of itself. Such a Being has no knowledge of the material universe, and to that extent is responsible neither for its creation, nor its care.

Being itself eternal, the material universe requires no temporal impetus to initiate its constant evolution. But, ontologically speaking, the eternal movement of material entities toward realization of their specific forms requires some moving cause like the heavenly bodies. To explain the movement of the latter, however, there must be posited the existence of a First Mover which moves everything, but which itself is immutable. Such a First Mover is God.

In the pure act of knowing itself as the supremely intelligent substance, God, as the Final Cause, draws all entities, and especially man, toward the actualization of their potential by inspiring love and desire for itself. While humans have no way of befriending such a self-absorbed God, they can and should strive to become like God through virtuous living and especially through the contemplative pursuit of wisdom, which, by tapping man's innate sense of wonder, goes beyond empirical observation or ratiocination and finds expression in a love of mythology. Although prayer and worship can evoke no response from the Supreme Being, the practice of religion contributes to political harmony, and it is the proper function of the state to look after its maintenance.

Sources

Aristotle. *The Works of Aristotle. Great Books of the Western World*. Vols. 8 and 9. Edited by R.M. Hutchins. Chicago: Encyclopædia Britannica, Inc., 1952.

Adler, Mortimer J. *Aristotle for Everyone*. New York and London: Macmillan Publishing Co., Inc., 1978. 185–90.

Barnes, Jonathan, ed. *The Cambridge Companion to Aristotle*. Cambridge: Cambridge University Press, 1995.

Chroust, Anton-Hermann. *Aristotle; new light on his life and on some of his lost works*. 2 vols. London: Routledge and K. Paul, 1973. See esp. 221–31.

Copleston, Frederick, S.J. *A History of Philosophy*. Vol. 1, pt. 2. Garden City, NY: Doubleday and Company, Inc., 1962–77. 9–120.

Lear, Jonathan. *Aristotle: The Desire to Understand*. Cambridge: Cambridge University Press, 1988. See esp. 8–10; 293–320.

Pieper, Josef. *Leisure, The Basis of Culture*. New York and Toronto: The New American Library, 1963. See esp. 112–16.

Verkamp, Bernard J. *The Sense of Religious Wonder: Epistemological Variations*. Scranton, PA: The University of Scranton Press, 2002. 94–102.

Augustine of Hippo
(A.D. 354–430)

Though determined to have his son acquire literary and rhetorical learning, Augustine's hardworking father had little interest in the boy's religious education. A nominal catechumen who did not yet believe in Christ, the father probably held religious sentiments closer to those of his pagan fellow Numidians who worshiped the dreadful Supreme Father of the sky, Saturn. On the other hand, Augustine's mother, who had been raised in a Christian family and was deeply committed to Tagaste's pre-Donatist, traditional form of Catholicism, had every intention of bringing her son up in the Catholic faith. Having had him signed with the Cross of Christ at the moment of his birth, she promptly began instructing him about the eternal life promised by Jesus and would gladly have honored his plea to be baptized several years later during a near-death illness had he not recovered so quickly.

It was also his mother's piety, reinforced by conversations with some men of prayer he had met while growing up, that influenced him to remain loyal to the Catholic church and to look to the Bible in search of the wisdom, toward which, after enduring the harsh discipline of his early pagan schooling and the sexual turbulence and concubinage of his later teens, his reading of Cicero's *Hortensius* had inclined him at the age of nineteen. And when, disappointed by the "inelegant earthiness" of the biblical stories, he converted for nine years to the Manichaean spiritual brand of Christianity and fled to Milan to advance his career in teaching rhetoric, she followed him there, and with no little help from his reading of Plotinus and Paul and listening to the preaching of Milan's great bishop, Ambrose, gently coaxed him back into the true fold. Following his baptism, Augustine was initially determined to pursue a monastic version of the philosopher's "cultured retirement," celebrating and writing about the happy life his newly recovered Catholic faith had afforded him and his companions. But his popularity soon resulted in his being ordained, first in 391 as a priest, and then, four years later, as bishop of Hippo.

During the remaining thirty-five years of his life he would insist upon maintaining a quasi-monastic lifestyle with the priests of his diocese, but much of his own time and energy would be taken up in travel and administrative activities. All the while, he managed to write hundreds of treatises, letters, and sermons in an attempt to exonerate the Church of any blame for Rome's collapse, and to challenge the Manichaean, Donatist, Pelagian, Semi-

Pelagian, and Arian "heresies" that he thought threatened to undermine the Catholic truths he had, thanks mainly to his mother's incessant prayers, rediscovered to his own lasting joy.

AUGUSTINE ON RELIGION. When people hear the word "God" they are all inclined to imagine that than which there is nothing higher. The essence of religious piety, therefore, is to think about God in the highest possible way. But different religions have various opinions about what really is that than which there is nothing higher. The Manichaeists, for example, imagine that the highest principle eternally at war with the force of evil is a luminous, corporeal substance. To prove them wrong, we might, as the Platonists encourage us to do, turn inward to discover within our illuminated minds certain eternal, immutable, and, therefore, incorporeal, intelligible objects (the principle of contradiction, mathematical truths, etc.), and, upon reflection, discover further that common to all such truths is Truth or Wisdom itself.

This still leaves somewhat open, however, the question about whether this Truth, which is more sublime than reason, is actually that than which nothing is higher. For only through the eyes of Christian faith can we catch a glimpse of the inner nature of God as the Supreme Being, who, because He alone truly is, is the immutable, incorruptible, eternal source of all else that is. Though One, this God is also revealed as the Father, Son, and Holy Spirit, in whose triune image man was freely created out of nothing and through whose love (expressed preeminently in the humble life of Jesus) sinful mankind (or at least the elect) is given the chance to return to the source of its being. Faith, however, is more than a desire to assent intellectually to such propositions; it is, rather, a mode of loving God that translates into a love of neighbor, creating a mind-set in the context of which revealed truths begin to make sense. Those who, by divine grace, have such love belong to the City of God, and in the end will rise body and soul to the happiness of eternal peace and glory. The atheistic and skeptical rest, who love themselves and their carnal pleasures more than God, will be left to their just damnation.

Sources

Augustine. *An Augustine Synthesis*. Arranged by Erich Przywara. New York: Harper, 1958.
_____. *The City of God*. Translated by Marcus Dods. New York: The Modern Library, 1950.
_____. *Confessions*. Translated by J.J. O'Donnell. Oxford: Clarendon Press, 1992.
_____. *On Free Choice of the Will*. Translated by Anna S. Benjamin and L.H. Hackstaff. Indianapolis: Bobbs-Merrill Company, Inc., 1964.
_____. *The Political Writings*. Edited by Henry Paolucci. Chicago: Henry Regnery Company, 1962.
_____. *The Trinity*. Translated by E. Hill. Brooklyn, NY: New City Press, 1990.
Brown, Peter. *Augustine of Hippo: A Biography*. New York: Dorset Press, 1967.
Copleston, Frederick, S.J. *A History of Philosophy*. Vol. 2, pt. 1. Garden City, NY: Doubleday and Company, Inc., 1962–77. 55–105.
Du Roy, O.J.-B. "Augustine, St." *New Catholic Encyclopedia*. Vol. 1. Edited by W.J. McDonald. New York: McGraw-Hill, 1967. 1041–58.
Gilson, Etienne. *The Christian Philosophy of Saint Augustine*. Translated by L.E.M. Lynch. New York: Random House, 1960.
Portalié, Eugène, S.J. *A Guide to the Thought of St. Augustine*. Translated by Ralph J. Bastian, S.J. Chicago: Henry Regnery Company, 1960.
Stump, Eleonore, and Norman Kretzmann, eds. *The Cambridge Companion to Augustine*. Cambridge: Cambridge University Press, 2001. See esp. the articles by John Rist, "Faith and Reason," 26–39; Scott MacDonald, "The Divine Nature," 71–90; Mary T. Clark, "De Trinitate," 91–102.

Averroës (Ibn Rushd) (1126–1198)

Averroës was born into a learned Cordoban family of judges only a few years after the death of al-Ghazālī, the Iranian ex-philosopher who wrote *The Incoherence of the Philosophers* in which philosophers are severely criticized for contradicting not only themselves, but more seriously, the obvious teaching of the *Qur'an*. In addition to receiving an education in medicine, science and poetic literature as a young man, Averroës also studied

Islamic law, philosophy and theology, and would no doubt have gained familiarity early on with al-Ghazālī's writings. If he did, it did not deter him from pursuing further his interest in philosophy. A friend, the philosopher and court physician Ibn Tufayl, encouraged him to write a commentary on Aristotle so that Abū Ya'qūb Yūsuf, the "Prince of the Believers" ruling the Almohad dynasty then in control of Northwest Africa and Muslim Spain, might find his reading of the Greek philosopher less confusing. Averroës responded by writing a summary of the Aristotelian *corpus*, and was rewarded by eventually being appointed to several judgeships and named the ruler's personal physician.

Except for a brief period of exile toward the end of his life, he stayed on at the court to write the many more commentaries on Aristotle and other philosophical treatises that would have such an influence on Christian thinking in medieval Europe. Especially significant of his own independent thought were the two works *On the Harmony of Religion and Philosophy* and *The Incoherence of the Incoherence*, which he wrote to defend philosophy against the attacks launched by al-Ghazālī and other conservative theologians. While admitting that philosophy should not be taught to the masses, he insisted that it pointed to the same truth preached in symbolic form by religion, and that, being no more a post–Qur'ānic innovation than Islamic law, philosophy is no less than the latter a permissible expression of Muslim faith.

A conservative majority of theologians succeeded in convincing the ruling caliph (al-Mansur) to declare Averroës something of a heretic in his latter years and to order all his books banned and burned. Within a couple of years, however, the caliph relented and allowed Averroës to return to the court in Morocco. Notwithstanding the abuse he took from Islamic theologians, there is little doubt that he went to his grave a devout and committed Muslim.

AVERROËS ON RELIGION. The Islamic religion is divine and true. It consists of two parts: external and interpreted. Its external core is found in the text of the Qur'an, whose miraculous nature is indicated by the fact that both its literary excellence and its theoretical and practical prescriptions (far superior to those of Jewish and Christian scriptures) are beyond the human ingenuity of an illiterate Prophet. As with religion in general, the Qur'an is primarily concerned with the majority, and addresses them in accordance with their own temperament and nature. To that extent, its doctrines are couched in rhetorical arguments and corporeal symbolization. It is incumbent upon the masses to accept their apparent meaning at face value. But there is also an interpretive dimension to religion, for the Qur'an did not neglect trying to arouse the assent of the philosophers, who, in obedience to religious law itself, use demonstration as the highest form of logical deduction to investigate existing entities for evidence of their divine Maker.

The truth they discover (e.g., the identity of existence and essence, the hierarchy of Intelligences, the eternity of the world, etc.) does not conflict with the truth revealed by religion. It is incumbent upon these learned elite to interpret ambiguous passages of the Qur'an and to identify those doctrines around which rational consensus can be achieved (e.g., existence of a provident and inventive God). But the allegorical hidden meaning they discern should not be divulged to the masses. In trying to do so, the dialectical theologians corrupt both faith and philosophy, destroy the belief of the masses, and spawn heretical sects. While, therefore, it is permissible to interpret, for example, the doctrine of immortality common to all religions (including Islam, whose Precious Book identifies death with sleep) spiritually to mean reabsorption of the human material intellect into the Agent Intellect, it would not be right to impose such talk upon the masses, for whom corporeal symbolization is a much stronger stimulus to pursue a life beyond.

Sources

Averroës. *Faith and Reason in Islam: Averroës' Exposition of Religious Arguments*. Translated by

Ibrahim Y. Najjar. Oxford: One World Press, 2001.

_____. *The Incoherence of the Incoherence.* Translated by Simon van den Bergh. 2 vols. London: Luzac, 1969.

_____. *On the Harmony of Religion and Philosophy.* Translated by George F. Hourani. London: Luzac and Co., 1976.

Davidson, Herbert A. *Proofs for Eternity, Creation and the Existence of God in Medieval Islamic and Jewish Philosophy.* New York and Oxford: Oxford University Press, 1987.

Fakhry, Majid. "Introduction" to Averroës, *Faith and Reason in Islam.* 1–15.

Gilson, Etienne. *History of Christian Philosophy in the Middle Ages.* New York: Random House, 1954. 216–25.

Glassé, Cyril. "Ibn Rushd." *The Concise Encyclopedia of Islam.* San Francisco: Harper and Row, Publishers, Inc., 1989. 174–75.

Hourani, George F. "Introduction" to Averroës, *On the Harmony of Religion and Philosophy.* 1–43.

Ivry, Alfred. "Averroës." In *Medieval Philosophy*, edited by John Marenbon. London: Routledge, 1998. 49–64.

Urvoy, Dominique. *Ibn Rushd (Averroës).* Translated by Olivia Stewart. London and New York: Routledge. 1991.

Vaux, Carra de. "Ibn Rushd." *First Encyclopaedia of Islam.* Vol. 3. Edited by M. Th. Houtsma et al. Leiden: E.J. Brill, 1987. 410–13.

Zedler, B.H. "Averroës (Ibn Rushd)." *New Catholic Encyclopedia.* Vol. 1. Edited by W.J. McDonald. New York: McGraw-Hill, 1967. 1125–27.

Avicenna (Ibn Sīnā) (980–1037)

At the time of Avicenna's birth in the tenth century near Bukhārā (Uzbekistan), the Islamic world was marked by both political and religious heterogeneity, with Shī'ism being in the ascendancy as a result of the rise of the Fâtimid dynasty. Avicenna's Persian father was a member of the Ismā'īlites, a rather rebellious gnostic branch of the Shī'ite movement awaiting the messianic return of Ismā'īl, the son of the sixth imām, as the Mahdī. With the help of a tutor, Avicenna had already by the age of ten learned the whole of the Qur'an by heart. But his father also had Ismā'ilite propagandists instructing Avicenna early on in the sciences (especially medicine) and philosophy. For a year and a half he is said to have been so devoted to his study of philosophy that he "did not sleep completely through a single night or devote himself to anything else by day," reading Aristotle's *Metaphysics,* for example, forty times over in a futile attempt to grasp its meaning.

Also among the philosophical materials he read were the *Letters* of the Ikhwān alafā, who if not a member, was certainly sympathetic to the Ismā'ilites, and the commentaries on Aristotle by al-Fārābī, who, along with Avicenna himself, would become a prime target of al-Ghazālī's *Incoherence of the Philosophers.* In addition to helping him understand Aristotle, the quasi-mystical, neo–Platonic emphasis of Ikhwān and al-Fārābī on the prophetic vision of the hierarchy of being emanating from the One God also helped him see better how he could integrate philosophical wisdom with the teachings of his Islamic religion. For the help he got from reading al-Fārābī he is said to have offered thanks to Allah in the mosque and to have contributed generous alms to the poor.

At the age of twenty-two Avicenna was required by the death of his father to set off in search of a patron. But despite the constant travel this would involve from one rival court to another amidst political strife and warfare that would sometimes land him in prison or put his life in danger, and notwithstanding the rather hedonistic lifestyle he would cultivate along the way, he was able to write the numerous treatises on medicine and philosophy that would make him one of the most renowned intellectual figures of the Middle Ages. He died while on a military expedition under the Emir of Ispahān, but not before emancipating his slaves, giving all his goods away to the poor as a pious act of repentance for his sins, and reciting the whole of the Qur'an.

AVICENNA ON RELIGION. Since there can be no infinite series of causes, the contingent existence of all things in our universe points to a First Cause, a Necessary Being who cannot not be. Being eternally in a state of perfect knowledge, power, and goodness, this Necessary Being is God. Given the eternity of the world, its dependence upon God's creative activity is ontic, rather than temporal. Like rays of the sun, the hierarchy of creatures (separate Intelligences, celestial Souls, celestial bodies, and sublunary bodies) emanates eternally and necessarily out of the limitless intellection by God of His own divine essence and His loving desire to actualize all that is potential as a manifestation of His Divine Wisdom.

At the lower end of the nine heavens emanating from God and governed by their respective, angelic Intelligences, is the single and separated Agent Intellect. Although God is ultimately the Prime Mover of all motion, it is this Agent Intellect that immediately creates the sublunar material universe and individual human souls. In the minds of the latter it triggers the process of abstraction by which the universal essences of particular objects come to be known in science and philosophy. But such illumination is only the initial step of the gnostic journey whereby the human soul seeks its salvation by abandoning the sensible world altogether and losing itself in the realm of the Intelligible, the Orient of pure light.

Among the elite achieving this goal are the prophets, the divine intelligence of whose imaginations enables them to reveal the truth to the masses under the guise of metaphorical language. Participation in the religious rites and prayers resulting therefrom, along with obedience of the religiously inspired moral law, can quicken this return of the soul to its spiritual home. Whether the body will share in this glory is a matter of faith. But the immortality of the soul is beyond doubt, giving rise to the possibility of basking forever in the beatific vision of the divine order of reality emanating from the Pure Being of God.

Sources

Avicenna. *Avicenna on Theology*. Translated by A.J. Arberry. London: John Murray, 1952.
_____. *Avicenna's De Anima*. Edited by F. Rahman. London: Oxford University Press, 1959.
_____. *Avicenna's Psychology*. Translated by F. Rahman. Westport, CT: Hyperion Press, Inc., 1981.
Boer, T.J. de. "Ibn Sīnā." *First Encyclopaedia of Islam*. Vol. 3. Edited by M. Th. Houtsma et al. Leiden: E.J. Brill, 1987. 419–20.

Burrell, David B. *Knowing the Unknowable God: Ibn-Sīnā, Maimonides, Aquinas*. Notre Dame: University of Notre Dame Press, 1986.
Gardet, Louis. "Avicenna." *New Catholic Encyclopedia*. Vol. 1. Edited by W.J. McDonald. New York: McGraw-Hill, 1967. 1131–32.
_____. *La Pensée Religieuse D'Avicenne*. Paris: Librairie Philosophique J. Vrin, 1951.
Gilson, Etienne. *History of Christian Philosophy in the Middle Ages*. New York: Random House, 1954. 187–216.
Glassé, Cyril. "Ibn Sīnā." *The Concise Encyclopedia of Islam*. San Francisco: Harper and Row, Publishers, Inc., 1989. 175–76.
Goichon, A.M. "The Philosopher of Being [Ibn Sīnā]." *Avicenna Commemoration Volume*. Calcutta: Iran Society, 1956. 107–17.
Goodman, L.E. *Avicenna*. London and New York: Routledge, 1992.
Heath, Peter. *Allegory and Philosophy in Avicenna*. Philadelphia: University of Pennsylvania Press, 1992. 19–28.
Houben, J. "Avicenna and Mysticism." In *Avicenna Commemoration Volume*. Calcutta: Iran Society, 1956. 205–21.
Jolivet, Jean. "Avicenna." In *Medieval Philosophy*. Edited by John Marenbon. London: Routledge, 1998. 29–47.
Nasr, Seyyed Hossein. *An Introduction to Islamic Cosmological Doctrines*. Albany: State University of New York Press, 1993. 175–281.
Riordan, Joseph D. "God, Intellect, and Avicenna." In *God Knowable and Unknowable*. Edited by Robert J. Roth, S.J. New York: Fordham University Press, 1973. 23–41.
Stumpf, Samuel Enoch. *Socrates to Sartre. A History of Philosophy*. New York: McGraw-Hill Book Company, 1982. 163–64.
Wisnovsky, Robert. *Avicenna's Metaphysics in Context*. Ithaca, NY: Cornell University Press, 2003.

Ayer, A.J. (1910–1989)

On his father's side, Ayer descended from Swiss Calvinists and on his mother's side, from Dutch Jews. He was baptized and confirmed in the Christian religion. The church-run prep school to which he was sent at the age of seven had a routine that included daily chapel and, on Sundays, two services and a scripture class. When his prayers failed to get him on the school's cricket team, he began doubting their efficacy. After entering Eton (whose headmaster was a Christian, but exceptionally tolerant, minister) his doubts soon broadened. Although still keenly interested in religion, he began doubting whether the Christian religion was intellectually tenable, and suspected that it was more plausible to think that a devil, rather than God, had created the world. To avoid such a conclusion, he ascribed the world's existence to chance. The headmaster required his attendance at chapel, but also gave him free rein to study critical appraisals of traditional theodicy, Church history, the Gospels, and moral philosophy (like Lecky's quite skeptical *History of Morals*). In a debate on religion he expressed the hope that humans would outgrow their need for belief in a deity as a sanction for morality. He read Russell's *Skeptical Essays* and Moore's *Principia Ethica*, and identified with their rejection of mysticism (including Wittgenstein's) and wholehearted commitment to a scientific worldview.

At Oxford, his vigorous defense of atheism earned him (from traditionalists) the label of being the "most dangerous man" on campus. His first wife was a freethinking Catholic, and he went through a religious marriage ceremony with her, but, like the religious funeral service of a later wife, considered it superstitious and a ridiculous farce. Notwithstanding his first and subsequent marriages, he had no compunction about engaging in multiple extramarital affairs, not a few with women half his age.

He served as president of the British Humanist Association, an emphatically atheistic organization. His Gifford lecture was used to disprove the existence of God. His report of a near-death, quasi-mystical experience inclined some to think he had come to believe in an afterlife, but he later denied any change in his beliefs, and adhered to his atheism till the day he died. Among the only two philosophers attending his burial service was his longtime friend and historian, Father Frederick Copleston.

AYER ON RELIGION. To be meaningful, a proposition must express either a tautology or an empirically testable hypothesis. Metaphysical, religious utterances about the existence and nature of God do neither, and to that extent are nonsensical. Implying existen-

tial import as it does, the assertion that "God exists" is more than a description of the divine name, and as such is not analytic. But neither is it genuinely synthetic. Not only is there no possibility of demonstrating the existence of a god, there is also no way of proving that it is even probable. For unless assertions about God's existence say nothing more than that there is regularity in nature, there is no way of verifying their truth or falsehood. If nature had to have an order of one sort or another, there is simply no way of proving that any particular order is or is not indicative of divine orchestration. So too with arguments based upon causality. Serving equally well for anything that could conceivably happen, they are useless and vacuous as explanations.

No less fallacious are arguments from religious experience, since the latter are beyond empirical verification. This view is not to be confused, therefore, with atheism (whose assertion that there is no god is equally nonsensical) or with agnosticism (which assumes that the question whether a transcendent god exists is genuine). Used in reference to a transcendent object, the word god symbolizes nothing. As theists and mystics themselves are accustomed to saying, such a term is either unintelligible or inexplicable. The same may be said about belief in an afterlife. Remembrance of past lives might conceivably verify the possibility of reincarnation. But belief in a substantial soul that goes on living after death has no more factual content than the assertion that there is a transcendent god. And far from enjoying or needing any transcendent, absolute foundation of a religious sort, moral judgments are the mere expression of emotion. By encouraging humans to control their own destiny, science and humanism shut off the ultimate source of religious feeling.

Sources

Ayer, Alfred Jules. *Language, Truth and Logic.* New York: Dover Publications, Inc., n.d.
_____. *The Meaning of Life.* New York: Charles Scribner's Sons, 1990.
Rogers, Ben. *A.J. Ayer: A Life.* London: Chatto and Windus, 1999.

Bacon, Francis (1561–1626)

Although the sympathies of Bacon's father, Keeper of the Great Seal to Elizabeth I, lay with the established Church of England, Bacon's intelligent and strong-willed mother was a zealous Puritan who enthusiastically supported the extensive reform of religion and church government being advocated by the Nonconformist ministers. She kept a close eye on her son's spiritual and moral development lest, like his brother (with whom he resided during his three years of study at Cambridge's Trinity College, and whom she suspected of becoming a "traitor to God"), he might abandon his Protestant faith and turn to Catholicism. She sometimes accused him of neglecting his religious duties, of hanging around with "instruments of Satan," and (hinting at Bacon's reputed homosexualism) of keeping a male "bed companion."

Although he never openly challenged his mother's religious views, he didn't either necessarily conform to her demands. The attitude he himself adopted was more reasonable and tolerant, like that of his father. In a "Letter of Advice to Queen Elizabeth," for example, he would later advocate milder treatment of both Puritans and Catholics by replacement of the oath of supremacy with one that merely required the bearing of arms, if need be, against papal or other enemies of England.

Some scholars suggest that, after the death of his father and launching a political career that would eventually carry him into the office of Lord Chancellor, Bacon no longer really took religion seriously, and only pretended to believe. But the evidence does not seem to support such a view. For, although his grand project (the *Instauratio Magna*) of restoring man's dominion over nature rested upon a distinction of faith and reason, the separation of religion and science, and the giving of priority to the advancement of inductive scientific studies, there is no reason to question the sincerity of the frequent expressions of Calvinistic piety that are to be found in some of his writings, like the *Religious Meditations* and the 1603 *Confession of Faith*. It was to the

Christian religion that he continued to look for the meaning of his life. Faced with death, not many years after being accused of bribery and driven from his high political office, he wrote his last will "bequeathing his soul to God above" and adding a prayer in which he confessed his sins and pleaded with his Lord to remember how he had loved the Christian community, mourned its divisions, cared for the poor and oppressed, and sought God not only in the Scriptures but in all of nature.

FRANCIS BACON ON RELIGION. Natural philosophy is dedicated to the study of the works and creatures of God, so that the divinely hidden knowledge of causes and the secret motions of things might be discovered and put to use in enhancing mankind's God-given dominion over nature and effecting of all things possible, like the prolongation of life. A little of such knowledge may at first incline humans toward atheism. As it is deepened and broadened, however, it brings men's minds back again to religion and provides at least a "broken knowledge" or wonder at the glory of God. Atheism, in fact, is nothing but an exercise in wishful thinking, whose adherents, "not being well satisfied in [their] own mind," are constantly striving to have it confirmed by the assent of others.

By contrast, certainty of belief is the very soul of genuine religion, setting it apart also from heathen religions that have the external trappings of religious worship but either lack any faith in the doctrine of God's nature, attributes and works, or, like the religion of Mohammed, eschew all rational argumentation. But even if there is no enmity between God's word and his works and reason can be used not to prove what is accepted on the basis of divine authority but at least to better understand the revealed mysteries of God and their doctrinal implications, like the immortality of the human soul, it would be wrong to pretend that the truth of all natural philosophy can be found in the Scriptures. For it was never the intention of God's spirit to express matters of nature in the Scriptures. It was a big mistake, therefore, for Plato, Paracelsus, and others to have intermingled their philosophy with theology in such wise as to imply that any philosophy of nature lacking a theological or Scriptural base could be dismissed as being heathenish and profane. Mixing theology and philosophy can only result in either an "heretical religion" or an "imaginary and fabulous philosophy."

Sources

Bacon, Sir Francis. *Advancement of Learning; Novum Organum; New Atlantis. Great Books of the Western World.* Vol. 30. Edited by R.M. Hutchins. Chicago: Encyclopædia Britannica, Inc., 1952.
_____. *The Works of Francis Bacon.* Siebter Band. Stuttgart-Bad Cannstatt: Friedrich Frommann Verlag, 1992.
Copleston, Frederick, S.J. *A History of Philosophy.* Vol. 3, pt. 2. Garden City, NY: Doubleday and Company, Inc., 1962–77. 103–22.
Maistre, Joseph de. *An Examination of the Philosophy of Bacon.* Translated and edited by Richard A. Lebrun. Montreal and Kingston: McGill-Queen's University Press, 1998.
Peltonen, Markku, ed. *The Cambridge Companion to Bacon.* Cambridge: Cambridge University Press, 1996. 172–99.
Spedding, James. *An Account of the Life and Times of Francis Bacon.* Boston: Houghton, Mifflin, 1880.
Sturt, Mary. *Francis Bacon.* London: Kegan Paul, Trench, Trubner and Co., Ltd., 1932.
Zagorin, Perez. *Francis Bacon.* Princeton: Princeton University Press, 1998. See esp. 11–15; 44–51; 224.

Bacon, Roger (c. 1212–1292)

Bacon was born into a wealthy English family that was left in relative poverty by its embroilment on the side of King Henry III against the barons. After receiving some elementary education at home, he went on to Oxford (where he may have studied under the future bishops, saintly Edmund Rich and Robert Grosseteste, and the Franciscan theologian, Adam de Marisco), and then to the University of Paris, from which he received a degree in arts in 1237. There is no evidence of his ever having earned a doctorate of theology or of his having been ordained to the priesthood.

He remained in Paris for another decade, reading Aristotelian philosophy to his students and earning a reputation for a rather anti-authoritarian and exceptionally critical disposition. Inspired especially by the reclusive, mysterious Peter of Maricourt, he devoted so much time and energy to experimental science during the next ten years, first at Oxford and then again at Paris, that his health eventually broke down. In 1257, he followed the example of Adam de Marisco and Alexander of Hales (whom, along with William of Auvergne, he probably encountered in Paris) and joined the Franciscans. But because of his critical attitude and preoccupation with science, the Order, under the leadership of Bonaventure, so restricted his freedom to write and lecture that, as he would later describe his plight, he was "unheard by anyone and as it were buried in oblivion."

He came close to despairing of ever achieving his main goal, which was to integrate secular and Christian learning. Rumors of his brilliance did, however, catch the attention of Guido Foulques, the Archbishop of Narbonne. After the latter's election to the papacy as Clement IV in 1265, he invited Bacon to send him a written version of his reform ideas. Bacon promptly composed and forwarded his *Opus majus, minus,* and *tertium.* Though less than satisfied with what he read, the pope did use his authority to help arrange for Bacon's return to Oxford. Upon the death of Clement, however, Bacon's enemies within the Order (now under the autocratic rule of Jerome d'Ascoli, the future Pope Nicholas IV) again accused him of "some suspicious novelties." His writings were condemned and he was imprisoned for at least two years. Before dying in 1292, however, and being buried in the Franciscan church at Oxford, he managed to publish a *Compendium of Theological Studies,* in which, in addition to expressing again his unitarian vision of philosophical and revealed knowledge, he severely criticized the decline of Christendom in general and theology in particular.

ROGER BACON ON RELIGION. There are six major religious sects in the world: the Pagans, the Idolators, the Tartars, the Jews, the Saracens, and the Christians. In order to gain greater credence, all of these religions claim to possess divine revelation. But divine wisdom, which provides a perception of those things that guide man toward eternal salvation, cannot be plural. There can be only one perfect religion. The others will be either erroneous or superfluous.

That the Christian religion alone contains the truth can best be proven to unbelievers by philosophical reasoning with which they are most familiar. For although Christian faith relies chiefly on Scripture and the Church, it is useful for Christians to have effective reasons for those things which they believe. They should be prepared first to demonstrate what is the fundamental principle of religion, namely, that there is one eternal, infinitely majestic, powerful, wise and good God, who is the First Cause of all causes, the Creator and Ruler of all things. That done, they next need to show why humans, if they want their immortal souls to find happiness in the next life, must obey God and pay Him due reverence.

With such arguments, it can easily be shown that the polytheistic, hedonistic religions of the Pagans, Idolators, and Tartars should be eliminated. It can also be argued that the Christian religion is to be preferred over the religions of Moses and Mohammed. For not only did the latter lack the support Christ received from wise and saintly prophets, the miracles they worked and the laws they proclaimed also bear no comparison to those performed and delivered by Christ. Furthermore, in contrast to the promises of eternal and spiritual blessings made by the perfect religion of Christ, both the legalistic Jewish religion, with its rejection of Christ as the messiah, and the religion of Mohammed, with its amoral justification of adultery, irrationally promise only temporal and physical blessings. And finally, both lack the sacramental share in divine life, which (along with the study of experimental science) will help Christians withstand the coming of the Antichrist.

Sources

Bacon, Roger. *The Opus Majus*. Vol. 2. Translated by Robert Belle Burke. Philadelphia: The University of Pennsylvania Press; London: Oxford University Press, 1928.

Bridges, John Henry. *The Life and Work of Roger Bacon*. London: Williams and Norgate, 1914.

Copleston, Frederick, S.J. *A History of Philosophy*. Vol. 2, pt. 2. Garden City, NY: Doubleday and Company, Inc., 1962–77. 164–71.

Gilson, Etienne. *History of Christian Philosophy in the Middle Ages*. New York: Random House, 1954. 294–312.

Little, A.G., ed. *Roger Bacon Essays*. Oxford: At the Clarendon Press, 1914.

Wesiheipl, J.A. "Roger Bacon." *New Catholic Encyclopedia*. Vol. 12. Edited by W.J. McDonald. New York: McGraw-Hill, 1967. 552–53.

Westacott, E. *Roger Bacon in Life and Legend*. London: Rockliff's, n.d.

Bataille, Georges (1897–1962)

Bataille was born into a French family of peasant stock. His father, a civil servant blinded, paralyzed, and eventually driven mad by syphilis, had become extremely hostile toward the Catholic religion. The mother, too, was rather indifferent to Catholicism, with the result that Bataille was raised without any religious instruction. By the age of fourteen the love he had earlier felt while attending to the disabilities of his father had turned to a hatred. This hatred would later be mingled with feelings of guilt as he and his mother fled the bombed city of Rheims in 1914 and left the father behind. When the father died a year or so later, the mother went temporarily insane and contemplated suicide.

Having converted to Catholicism and been baptized the summer before, Bataille himself fell into a pattern of pious living over the next six years, weekly confessing his sins, praying daily, often reading edifying literature (much of it contemptuous of the flesh and fixated on horror), meditating on a regular basis, and contemplating the possibility of devoting the whole of his life to God by becoming either a priest or a monk. Toward that end he spent a year (1917–1918) in the seminary of Saint-Fleur. After leaving the seminary, he moved to Paris with his mother, began studying library science at the *École des Charles,* and contemplated marriage to a childhood friend. As evidenced by his short but happy stay at Quarr Abbey during a trip to England in 1920, he had not yet dismissed the possibility of withdrawing from the world. But a negative reaction to Bergson's book on laughter, the experience of a famous bullfighter's horrendous death in Spain, the sensuous enticements of a certain "absolutely monstrous and beautiful woman," and his reading of Nietzsche and Chestov, gradually ate away at his Catholic faith and lead him into the most dissolute of lifestyles.

While serving as librarian at the Bibliothèque Nationale for the next two decades, marrying twice, and engaging himself with intellectuals in various artistic (Surrealist), sociological (Durkheimian), and philosophical (Hegelian à la Kojève) circles, he would write multiple novels and books trying to describe his newly concocted, atheological conception of religion. At one point, in 1937, he and some colleagues founded a secret society (the Acéphale) for the sake of performing mysterious rituals that would dramatize union with the universe through departure. Suffering from tuberculosis and living off the charity of famous artist friends, he died while still working on the mystical implications of eroticism and death.

BATAILLE ON RELIGION. Hegel's audacity in claiming that he had satisfied his every desire by reducing Infinite Being to the Finite Thought of his own perfect self-consciousness can be seen as paradigmatic of modern man's smug satisfaction in defining autonomy in terms of conscious efforts at individualistic labor, language, and thought. By limiting knowledge to that which is rational, practical, and productive (i.e., project oriented), however, scientific humanism has only succeeded in excluding what is most essential to self-consciousness, namely, the sacred dimension of existence, or, in other words, the feeling of intimacy, the inner experience of "not-knowing immediacy," that characterized primitive religion. For humans can become genuinely conscious of themselves only to the extent that

they acknowledge the existence of something that escapes their conscious knowledge. By positing the existence of a transcendent God as some Being into which the human soul can be reabsorbed at death, traditional theistic religions failed to make such an acknowledgment and thereby sapped the experience of life and death of its immediacy. To that extent they were actually antireligious.

Nietzsche's atheological declaration of the death of God, on the other hand, left a terrible emptiness in the face of which human death becomes an instantaneous ecstasy of nonknowledge, an utterly incomprehensible, dizzying and laughable transgression beyond the limits of selfhood to nothing. Eroticism is like that, too, in that, unlike goal-oriented work, it is "purely squandering, an expenditure of energy for itself" leading to nothing but the rapturous annihilation of self. Religious rituals, like the sacrifice of humans or animals that takes the slave or oxen out of their profane utilitarian environment and returns them to their natural "not-knowing immediacy," can dramatize the search for intimacy and, like some kinds of mysticism (e.g., Buddhist), facilitate the rapturous experience of a "Sunday of the Negative."

Sources

Bataille, Georges. *Essential Writings.* Edited by Michael Richardson. London: Sage Publications, 2000.

_____. *Inner Experience.* Albany: State University of New York Press, 1988.

_____. *Theory of Religion.* New York: Zone Books, 1989.

Bankston, Carl L., III. "Georges Bataille." In *World Philosophers and Their Works.* Vol. 1. Edited by John K. Roth. Pasadena, CA, and Hackensack, NJ: Salem Press, Inc., 2000. 192–98.

Boldt-Irons, Leslie Anne, ed. *On Bataille: Critical Essays.* Albany: State University of New York Press, 1995.

Gemerchak, Christopher M. *The Sunday of the Negative: Reading Bataille Reading Hegel.* Albany: State University of New York Press, 2003. See esp. 1–21.

Land, Nick. *The Thirst for Annihilation: Georges Bataille and Virulent Nihilism.* London and New York: Routledge, 1992.

Richman, Michele H. *Reading Georges Bataille: Beyond the Gift*. Baltimore and London: The Johns Hopkins University Press, 1982.

Surya, Michel. *Georges Bataille: An Intellectual Biography*. Translated by Krzysztof Fijalkowski and Michael Richardson. London and New York: Verso, 2002.

Bayle, Pierre (1647–1706)

Bayle was the son of a Huguenot minister. The Calvinist Reformed Church to which the family belonged in their hometown of Carla represented a distinct, persecuted minority in seventeenth-century Catholic France. At the age of twenty-one, after attending the local elementary school and extensive reading at home in his father's library, Bayle was given the chance to study philosophy in the Protestant school at Puylaurens. Within only three months he left that school to enroll at the Jesuit academy of Toulouse. Convinced by his Jesuit teachers' arguments for an authoritative ecclesiastical magisterium, he converted to Catholicism and tried convincing his brother to do the same. But upon completion of his philosophy program with financial assistance from the bishop of Rieux, he objected to what he perceived to be the idolatry associated with the Catholic doctrine of transubstantiation, and reconverted to Calvinism.

Branded a relapsed heretic, he became subject to especially severe punishment, and was forced to flee to Geneva. There he studied under Calvinist theologians and in frequent letters to his family gave evidence of his renewed Protestant faith. But contrary to persistent goading from family members, he decided against becoming a pastor. Secretly returning to France, he eventually obtained professorial appointments at the Protestant academy at Sedan and the *Ecole Illustre* in Rotterdam and while foregoing a chance to marry, committed himself wholeheartedly to the writing and publication of works critical of Catholic "superstitions" and in defense of Calvinism.

At both places he was in contact with Pierre Jurieu, a fanatical Protestant theologian prophesying the demise of Catholicism. Jurieu later opposed the kind of religious toleration Bayle was beginning to champion in publications like his 1686 *Commentaire Philosophique,* accused Bayle of being a crypto-atheist and enemy of religion, and eventually succeeded in having him dismissed from his teaching position. This gave Bayle the opportunity to work full-time at the completion of his *Dictionnaire,* whose myriad articles trumpeting the impossibility of reconciling reason with faith invited attacks from all religious parties and exploitation by the atheistic *philosophes*. The death of his father and brothers due to religious persecution inclined him to fight all the harder for toleration of all religions — Catholic, Muslim, Jewish, and Socinian, as well as his own Protestantism. He himself remained a faithful, albeit skeptical, communicant of the Reformed Church till the day he died.

BAYLE ON RELIGION. The essence of religion consists of an inward disposition, a certain persuasion of the soul or intellectual judgment with regard to God, that manifests itself outwardly by humble, willful feelings of respect, fear, and love deserved by the majesty of the Supreme Being. All external acts of religion are pleasing to God, therefore, only inasmuch as they are accompanied by such inward acts of the soul. If the disposition of the soul is contradictory (as happens when, because of the intolerance of one religion for another, people are forced to convert to a particular religion only out of fear of their persecutors or to retain their property), the external religious acts are mere exercises in hypocrisy and bad faith.

God Himself has shed upon the souls of all humans the natural light of reason by which to test the truth of religion. All religious questions, therefore, require the use of reason, and any religious teaching (especially when it involves morality), whether it is said to be based on Scripture or Tradition, is false when refuted by the clear and distinct ideas of this natural light. But reason alone cannot be the rule of faith. Given the obscurity of human knowledge about the problem of evil and other matters, it is impossible for us to know with certainty that any of the abstract dogmas of religion are the absolute truth. Nor does God expect such certitude. All that God requires is that individuals seek the truth as carefully as they can, and, believing they have found it, to love it and take it for their guide for virtuous behavior. The ultimate standard of judgment on religious questions, therefore, is not in the understanding but in the conscience that is formed by the faith the Holy Spirit instills in us as we listen to the Word of God revealed in Scripture. At some point, our understanding must bow to faith. But just as knowledge of God does not check the passionate, temperamental, and habitual inclinations of humans toward evil, so a lack of such knowledge in a society of atheists need not result in a corruption of morals.

Sources

Bayle, Pierre. *The Great Contest of Faith and Reason: Selections from the Writings of Pierre Bayle*. Translated and edited by Karl C. Sandberg. New York: Frederick Ungar Publishing Co., 1963.

_____. *Historical and Critical Dictionary. Selections*. Translated by Richard H. Popkin. Indianapolis, New York, Kansas City: The Bobbs-Merrill Company, Inc., 1965.

Brush, Craig B. *Montaigne and Bayle: Variations on the Theme of Skepticism*. The Hague: Martinus Nijhoff, 1966.

Lennon, Thomas M. *Reading Bayle*. Toronto: University of Toronto Press, 1999.

Mason, H.T. *Pierre Bayle and Voltaire*. London: Oxford University Press, 1963.

Popkin, Richard H. "Pierre Bayle's Place in 17th Century Scepticism." In Paul Dibon, ed. *Pierre Bayle: Le Philosophe De Rotterdam*. Amsterdam: Elsevier Publishing Company, 1959. See esp. 1–19.

Rex, Walter. *Essays on Pierre Bayle and Religious Controversy*. The Hague: Martinus Nijhoff, 1965.

Sandberg, Karl C. *At the Crossroads of Faith and Reason: An Essay on Pierre Bayle*. Tucson: The University of Arizona Press, 1966.

Bentham, Jeremy (1748–1832)

Bentham's father belonged to the Church of England and sincerely believed in its teaching and practice. He hoped to raise his precocious son as a faithful communicant of the same church. Toward that end he denied him any access to frivolous or irreverent reading, and exposed him instead to histories, chronicles, and a variety of moral and religious books that were often illustrated with horrific scenes of martyrs being tortured to death and the damned burning in hell. Far from edifying him, it left him with the impression that he might have been better never to have been born, and made him think of religion as something terrifying and repulsive. He was especially turned off by the kind of moralistic, religiously inspired, melancholic asceticism found in the writings of Dr. Samuel Johnson.

Bentham's reading of Richardson's *An Apology for the Conduct of Mrs. T.C. Phillips* (memoirs of a prostitute whose legal troubles were exacerbated by ecclesiastical contrivance) convinced him further that the Church was not only gloomily moralistic, but also tyrannical, creating its own martyrs. At Westminster school he would memorize the whole of the Anglican catechism. But his hostility toward religion continued to rankle. It reached an early climax when, at the age of twelve, his father enrolled him at Oxford, and he was forced to sign the Thirty-nine Articles. Upon expressing his doubt that some of the Articles could be reconciled with either Reason or Scripture, he was told by his religious tutor not to question authority and to sign the articles anyway.

The impression of the Church's hypocrisy never left him. For all practical purposes, he abandoned institutional religion. In 1818 he published a sweeping attack on the Anglican establishment and its evils of clericalism, arguing that any attempt to impose its catechism as part of the educational program would be to force children into lying. He claimed, however, to be attacking religion not as it ought to be or as it might be but only as it has been. And although he would fight relentlessly for the separation of Church and State (opposing all oaths, religious tests for public office, etc.) till the day he died, he also championed total freedom of religious belief, including that of

Roman Catholics (like his friend, Dan O'Connell) against which he had a natural aversion.

BENTHAM ON RELIGION. Like the theological appetite for absurd mysteries, metaphysical speculation about entities that supposedly transcend the physical world must be rejected as a useless exercise in abstraction when the language it uses cannot be empirically verified or properly defined. Thus, although the word soul can be a useful fiction in referring to the whole of the human psyche, Platonic talk about it as a separate substance apart from the body has no foundation in fact, and yields no support to the notion of immortality.

Propositions about the existence of God make even less sense. Historically, natural religion (whose beliefs differ from those of revealed religions only to the extent of lacking any written and acknowledged declaration about God) has assumed the existence of "an almighty Being, by whom pains and pleasures will be dispensed to mankind, during an infinite and future state of existence." But this deity is said to be an "unknown and incomprehensible agency," and with good reason, for teleological and other arguments prove nothing about its existence. Imaginative descriptions of God as invisible, omnipresent, infinite, eternal, and the like, are mere abstractions that may tell us something about those who utter them, but have no basis in experience. There also being no evidence that Jesus was divine, we are left with the conclusion that the term God refers to a nonentity, in whom people are duped into believing only out of fear of its purported limitless power, and which they then try to appease through the practice of asceticism on the assumption that by denying themselves pleasures and suffering pain they will merit eternal bliss. Far from being of any social utility, such religious beliefs blind humans to what experience alone can teach, and disengage them from the moral pursuit of the greatest good for the greatest number. All religious views should be tolerated, but atheism holds out the best promise of a perfect utilitarian society.

Sources

Bentham, Jeremy. *Works*. Edited by John Bowring. 11 vols. New York: Russell and Russell, Inc., 1962.

Atkinson, Charles Milner. *Jeremy Bentham: His Life and Work*. London: Methuen and Co., 1905.

Crimmins, James E. *Secular Utilitarianism. Social Science and the Critique of Religion in the Thought of Jeremy Bentham*. Oxford: Clarendon Press, 1990.

_____, ed. *Utilitarians and Religion*. Bristol, England: Thoemmes Press, 1998.

Mack, Mary P. *Jeremy Bentham: An Odyssey of Ideas*. London: Heinemann, 1962.

Stephen, Leslie, Sir. *The English Utilitarians*. Vol. 1. New York: Augustus M. Kelley, 1968. 169–326.

Berdyaev, Nicolai (1874–1948)

Born into an aristocratic family, with a Tolstoyian, freethinking father and a mother of French Catholic persuasion, Berdyaev was baptized as an infant into the Russian Orthodox church. He grew up, however, with little exposure to traditional, Orthodox doctrine and ritual, with the result that he could later claim never to have known authority in his family, his school, his philosophical studies, and "particularly not in religious life." After a sudden inner transformation during his early teen years, he decided to devote his life to philosophy, promptly started reading Hegel, Schopenhauer, Mill, Kant, and other major philosophers, and, after entering the University of Kiev, became fascinated with the revolutionary writings of Mikhailovsky and Marx.

Although he joined the Marxist movement and got himself arrested and exiled, upon returning to Kiev three years later and getting married, he began challenging the party's materialism and positivism from an Idealistic perspective. Eventually, following moves to St. Petersburg and Moscow where he befriended Serge Bulgakov and other thinkers interested in religious philosophy and bringing Russia's intelligentsia back to religion, he himself returned to Orthodox Christianity. Under the influence of Dostoevsky, he would continue writing critically of the Russian hierarchy's reactionary subservience to the dictatorial powers of the Czarist and Communist regimes. He also challenged the traditionally authoritarian and negative asceticism of historic Christianity in general and the "un-ecumenical, parochial, almost sectarian" attitude of Russian Orthodoxy in particular. At one point he was actually charged by church officials with blasphemy. But his rediscovery of the mysterious beauty of the Orthodox liturgy, his reading of the Church Fathers, and his periodic pilgrimages to ancient monasteries had stirred his faith in religion as the best sanctuary of personal freedom and creativity, and notwithstanding his prophetic criticism he would remain true to the Orthodox religion for the rest of his life.

Not long after the Revolution he was officially banished from Russia, along with others of his intellectual friends, as being hopelessly inconvertible to communism. During the remaining years of his exile, first in Berlin, and then in Paris, his many writings and lectures gave expression to his great zeal for ecumenism. Protestants, Catholics, and Orthodox all joined together at his funeral service in praising his prophetic challenge to materialism and his tireless efforts to unite Christians, not only among themselves, but with non–Christians as well.

BERDYAEV ON RELIGION. Originating in the desire to escape existential isolation, religion can be defined as an experience of intimacy and kinship with the Divine Being. But being is action, not substance; movement, not immobility; life, not thing. Abstract metaphysics has been wrong, then, to conceive of God categorically as a substance, a thing, or a nature. Described more accurately by the great mystics, the living God is spirit, active liberty. The interior life of the Divine is one of free, creative love emerging from the undifferentiated, mysterious abyss (the *Ungrund*). As one who loves, God feels a need for His other self, the beloved. This love is realized in the Trinity and the mystery of creation. The basic and original phenomenon of religious life, therefore, is the movement of God towards man and of man towards God.

Although every religion reveals the divine, Christianity is the most concrete and fullest, albeit mythological, expression of this drama of personal love and freedom between God and man. The religious life does not originate, however, solely in the will of God. While the birth of God in the human soul is the movement of God towards man, the birth of man in God is equally the work of man and his freedom. The Kingdom of God, or the creation of an ideal, truly theocratic society as the goal of human history, can be realized, therefore, only through man's free cooperation and the participation of creation itself. The first step in that direction must be the inner, spiritual enlightenment and transfiguration of man and the world. Having deprived culture of its soul by exploiting humans as means to their respective ends, neither bourgeois capitalism nor collectivistic socialism has helped. And given, in fact, the anti–Christian, egoistical actualization in this fallen world of the possibility of evil latent in the *Ungrund,* the only chance of ever realizing the Kingdom of God and eschatological resurrection of the dead lies in the dynamic, existential still-point of inward time that transcends the historical realm of objectification.

Sources

Berdyaev, Nicolai. *The Beginning and the End.* Translated by R.M. French. London, 1952.

———. *Christian Existentialism.* A Berdyaev synthesis selected and translated by Donald A. Lowrie. New York: Harper and Row, 1965.

———. *The Divine and the Human.* Translated by R.M. French. London: The Macmillan Company, 1949.

———. *Dream and Reality.* Translated by K. Lampert. London: Bles, 1950.

———. *Freedom and the Spirit.* New York: Charles Scribner's Sons, 1935.

Calian, Carnegie Samuel. *The Significance of Eschatology in the Thought of Nicolas Berdyaev.* Leiden: E.J. Brill, 1965.

Copleston, Frederick C., S.J. *Philosophy in Russia: From Herzen to Lenin and Berdyaev.* Notre Dame: University of Notre Dame Press, 1986.

———. *Russian Religious Philosophy: Selected Aspects.* Tunbridge Wells, Kent, UK: Search Press Ltd.; Notre Dame: University of Notre Dame Press, 1988.

Lowrie, Donald A. *Rebellious Prophet: A Life of Nicholai Berdyaev*. New York: Harper, 1960.

Spinka, Matthew. *Nicolas Berdyaev: Captive of Freedom*. Philadelphia: The Westminster Press, 1949.

Bergson, Henri (1859–1941)

Born of Anglo-Polish Jewish parents, Bergson grew up in Paris without much interest in religion. While studying at the École Normale Supérieure he was so enthusiastic in his embrace of Herbert Spencer's naturalistic materialism that fellow students dubbed him "the atheist." Long walks through the countryside surrounding Clermont-Ferrand (where he began teaching philosophy) left him, however, with a sense of the wholeness of nature that seemed to lie beyond scientific, empirical observation. He remained committed to the theory of evolution, but, influenced by his reading of Maine de Biran's antidualistic insistence upon the significance of inward experience, he began interpreting the evolving universe in a less analytical, more intuitive way to take into better account its nonmechanical, organic dimensions (e.g., life, freedom) by focusing on duration and the "vital thrust" (*élan vital*) of the evolutionary process.

Although Bergson's supposedly anti-intellectual emphasis upon cognitive feeling (i.e., intuition) and the groundless suspicion of his having pantheistically identified God with the *élan vital* were deemed by some in the Vatican's Holy Office inimical to Catholic thought, his 1907 publication of *Creative Evolution* was clearly religious in tone (and on that account, all the more attractive to the likes of William James). This would become even more so the case twenty-five years later when, under the influence of Plotinian mysticism, he wrote and published *The Two Sources of Morality and Religion* in which the closed, "survivalist" morality of static, retrogressive religions is contrasted with the open, "saintly" morality of dynamic, more catholic (universal) and progressive religions inspired by a transcendent God of love.

His lectures at the Collège de France had greatly impressed leading figures (e.g., Maritain, Marcel) in the revival of French-Catholic thought in the early twentieth century, and in his last will Bergson himself acknowledged that his reflections had led him "closer and closer to Catholicism." He saw Catholicism, he said, as "the complete fulfillment of Judaism," and "would have become a convert" except for a determination to stand by his fellow Jews in their time of Nazi persecution (which he did by rising from his sickbed and queuing up for several hours in cold conditions to register as a Jew). He claimed, however, to have "moral adherence to Catholicism," and asked the Cardinal Archbishop of Paris to authorize a priest to say prayers at his funeral. The request was granted.

BERGSON ON RELIGION. Unlike analysis, which breaks the evolving universe down into separate, inert parts, emotive intuition catches a direct glimpse of the process from the inside out, capturing the enduring essence of the universe as an organic whole, whose parts, under the influence of an *élan vital*, are dynamically interrelated like the mutually constitutive notes of a melody. Tracked downwardly, this intuition of duration takes us into the realm of dispersed matter. Following its upward course, we make contact with an increasingly intensive concretion of all duration, at the peak of which we encounter God as "the living and consequently still moving Eternity," the "Principle of Creation," from whose center emanate the waves of organizing energy that bring matter alive. But it is only in dynamic religion, generated by the rare intuitive experience of the mystics, that such contact reaches its climax.

In its more external and static primitive stage, religion functions, mythologically and ritualistically, merely as a defensive reaction: first, against egoistic proclivities of human intelligence by encouraging a closed morality that forbids any self-seeking divergence from societal custom; second, against the frustrating thought of the inevitability of death by fostering belief in the survival of separated souls and the efficacy, if not of prayer and sacrifice, possibly of magical incantation. Inspired by proto-mystics (Isaiah, Plotinus, etc.) and especially by the great Christian mystics (Paul, Teresa, etc.), there occurred sudden shifts from this static religion, with its animistic, polytheistic, and henotheistic, historical variations, toward a monotheistic experience of a transcendent God of love who prompts individuals to pursue a morality that is open to a love of all mankind. Whether this experience of universal love ultimately involves personal immortality (union with God, perhaps, of the sort experienced by the mystics) is impossible to say, but it is not unlikely, given the soul's apparent independence and the anthropocentric thrust of evolution.

Sources

Bergson, Henri. *Creative Evolution*. Translated by Arthur Mitchell. Westport, CT: Greenwood Press, 1975.

_____. "Introduction to Metaphysics." In *The Creative Mind*. Edited by Mabelle L. Andison. New York: Philosophical Library, 1946. 187–237.

_____. *Matter and Memory*. Translated by Nancy Margaret Paul and W. Scott Palmer. London: Swann, Sonnenschein and Co.; New York: The Macmillan Co., 1911.

_____. *The Two Sources of Morality and Religion*. Translated by R. Ashley Audra and Cloudesley Brereton. New York: Henry Holt and Company, 1935.

Bilsker, Richard. *On Bergson*. Belmont, CA: Wadsworth/Thomson Learning, 2002. 61–71.

Collinson, Diané. "Henri Bergson." Collinson, Diané. *Fifty Major Philosophers*. London, New York, and Sidney: Croom Helm, 1987 130–34.

Gallagher, I.J. "Bergson, Henri Louis." *New Catholic Encyclopedia*. Vol. 2. Edited by W.J. McDonald. New York: McGraw-Hill, 1967. 323–25.

Goudge, T.A. "Bergson, Henri." *Encyclopedia of Philosophy*. Vol. 1. Edited by Paul Edwards. New York: Macmillan and Co. and The Free Press, 1967. 287–95.

Kolakowski, Leszek. *Bergson*. Oxford and New York: Oxford University Press, 1985. 72–87.

Lacey, A.R. *Bergson*. London and New York: Routledge, 1993. 215–19.

Maritain, Jacques. *Bergsonian Philosophy and Thomism*. Translated by Mabelle L. Andison. New York: Philosophical Library, 1955.

Miller, Lucius Hopkins. *Bergson and Religion*. New York: Henry Holt and Company, 1916.

Ryan, John K., ed. "Henri Bergson: Heraclitus Redivivus." *Twentieth-Century Thinkers*. Staten Island, NY: Alba House, 1967. 13–35.

Stumpf, Samuel Enoch. *Socrates to Sartre. A History of Philosophy*. New York: McGraw-Hill Book Company, 1982. 368–75.

Thomas, H., and D.L. Thomas. "Bergson." *Living Biographies of Great Philosophers*. New York: Garden City Publishing Co., Inc., 1941. 310–22.

Berkeley, George (1685–1753)

Berkeley's father had come from England before settling in Ireland. He and his wife raised Berkeley with strong Protestant convictions in the predominantly Roman Catholic southeastern part of the country. After four years at Kilkenny College and another seven working toward B.A. and M.A. degrees at Trinity College in Dublin, Berkeley was awarded a fellowship at the latter school. While holding such a fellowship he was prohibited from marrying and was obliged to take Holy Orders. He showed no hesitation in meeting this obligation. Later he would claim to have been somewhat skeptical already at the age of eight. But it was not his faith that he was doubting. His belief in the Protestant version of Christianity was strong and sincere.

In 1708 he was already preaching as a layman in the college chapel, using the "Pascalian Wager" to support his belief in immortality. Within two years he was ordained a deacon and priest of the Church of England. All the while, prompted by his reading of Locke and Malebranche, he had been developing the theory of immaterialism he would expound in publications over the next three years in an attempt to reverse what he perceived to be the waning influence of religion caused by a rising tide of skepticism, materialism, and atheism. His subsequent writings would be motivated mainly by a desire to challenge freethinking deists and others who he thought contradicted their own teaching by rejecting freedom of thought and action.

After being appointed dean of Kerry in 1724, resigning his fellowship, and marrying shortly thereafter, Berkeley set sail for America in hopes of implementing the "Bermuda Project" he had concocted, with the idea of founding a college that would have the double aim of converting the Indians and preparing the sons of the colonists for the ministry. Denied the funds he had been promised, the project failed, and he returned several years later to become the highly respected bishop of Cloyne. Having inherited a strong prejudice against Roman Catholics from his father, he consistently argued against the Roman system. But he was also a tolerant man, and even while thanking God for having been educated in the Church of England, his prayer was "not that I shall live and die in this church, but in the true Church," which he considered to be invisible. He died while his wife was reading to him the Pauline passage about Christ's victory over death.

BERKELEY ON RELIGION. All the impious schemes of atheism and irreligion — among which must also be counted skepticism, pantheism, materialism, fatalism, and even certain pretensions to deism and natural religion which, despite all their talk of cosmic harmony and natural decorum, have no real sense of a God, and, therefore, admit of no ultimate principle of good actions, no fear or hope of an afterlife, no final judgment, and no eternal reward or punishment — rest upon two interrelated, false doctrines: (1) the existence of unperceived matter, and (2) the reality of abstract ideas. The notion of a material substance as a substratum of the primary qualities is a mere abstraction that has no concrete reality. The extension, size, shape, and location of an object are no less subjective than its color, sound, or taste. Unlike spiritual substances whose existence consists of perceiving, material objects exist, therefore, only to the extent that they are perceived, or in other words, only as ideational groupings of sense data.

That such ideas exist as something more than mere products of the human imagination, and yet have no causal foundation in any matter independent of mind, implies the existence of an infinite mind or God who creates sense data and the minds to perceive it, and who keeps things in existence even when humans no longer have them in mind. Although it is futile to try to prove the existence of God from any idea of his perfection, the regularity with which sense data are imprinted upon the human mind can make God's existence even more evident than that of any other human spirit. Nature, in fact, can be described as a language by which, along with his revealed word, its Author provides humans with at least an analogical knowledge of his own perfection. Such a sense of the divine presence cannot but fill the human heart with the strongest incentive to virtue, and in turn afford the human soul, which because of its indissolubility is immortal, its best chance of salvation.

Sources

Berkeley, George. *Philosophical Works*. Introduction and notes by M.R. Ayers. Totowa, NJ: Rowman and Littlefield, 1975.

Berman, David. *George Berkeley: Idealism and the Man*. Oxford: Clarendon Press, 1994.

Copleston, Frederick, S.J. *A History of Philosophy*. Vol. 5, pt. 2. Garden City, NY: Doubleday and Company, Inc., 1962–77. 9–62.

Luce, A.A. *The Dialectic of Immaterialism*. London: Hodder and Stoughton, 1963. 182–93.

_____. *The Life of George Berkeley: Bishop of Cloyne*. London: Thomas Nelson and Sons Ltd., 1949.

Tipton, I.C. *Berkeley: The Philosophy of Immaterialism*. London: Methuen and Co. Ltd., 1974. 297–350.

Blanshard, Brand (1892–1987)

With a grandfather who was a minister of Wesleyan Methodism (with its emphasis upon the need for personal conversion), and a saintly, albeit theologically liberal, father who, during and after study at Oberlin Seminary, accepted pastorates of Congregational churches in Ohio, Michigan, and Montana, Blanshard was raised within the ancient structure of Christian theism. As a result of the early deaths of both his parents, he came under the influence of his grandmother's loving but very puritanical standards, being regularly sent to church and Sunday school and held to a biblically-based code of conduct. Though he could not accept her fundamentalism, it did not cause him to reject religion outright.

Listening to his father preaching on

many occasions had stirred in him an early and lasting interest in sermons, and he claims that had he "kept away from philosophy," he might himself have become a "more or less successful popular preacher." And in fact, not only did he continue to harbor throughout his undergraduate studies at Michigan and Oxford the thought of entering the ministry and often made a point of visiting churches for the sake of hearing preachers of note, he also actually engaged in some preaching during a stint in the YMCA during World War I, and then later at Swathmore, as an active member (until World War II and its challenge to pacifism) of the noncreedal Society of Friends. But although the impression he had gotten from his earliest readings in college that philosophical inquiry could actually help in the defense of religion was reinforced by his encounter with F.H. Bradley and others at Oxford, and though he would persist in maintaining against analytical thinkers (like Bertrand Russell) the cognitive value of mystical experiences (which he himself never claimed to have had) and the value of religion and the moral law, the rationalistic proclivities triggered by his philosophical studies under the likes of Dewey and Hocking at Columbia and Harvard eventually inclined him to abandon both the traditional concept of a transcendent God and the "anthropomorphic concept of his goodness."

His 1952–1953 Gifford and Carus Lectures and their later publication (*Reason and Goodness*; *Reason and Belief*) were, by his own account, an attempt to bring both ethics and theology back within the realm of rational reflection. By the time of his retirement in 1961 from years of teaching philosophy at the universities of Michigan, Swathmore, and Yale, the "service of reason" had clearly become his personal religion.

BLANSHARD ON RELIGION. Religion is an attempt to adjust one's nature as a whole (thought, feeling, and will) to what is held to be ultimately true and good. At the beginning, when religion was chiefly a matter of impulsive feeling, and image and truth were barely distinguished, the ultimate reality was conceived mythologically along animistic lines. Little by little, the personified powers governing nature were moralized and fused into the concept of one God, a process that reached its acme in Christian theism. In both Catholicism and Protestantism, however, reason remained subservient to faith, and theism took the form of a supernaturalistic conception of the Ultimate as totally transcendent and beyond rational comprehension. Its underlying, two-tiered cosmology and anthropology devastated human morality by subjecting man's intellect and conscience to the conflicting claims of two radically distinct realms. Despite inconsistencies within themselves and scientific truths, its creeds and dogmas were presented as revealed certainties, obedient acceptance of which was deemed essential to salvation. But such blind faith in revelation is now rightly being replaced by respect for reasonableness, or the disposition to guide one's beliefs and conduct by rational appraisal of relevant facts and involved values.

From such a perspective the world is seen as one intelligible whole, all the facts and events of which are bound together by causal and logical necessity. To use the term "God" to identify this world's ideal end might be unwarranted. But devotion to the theoretical and practical use of reason to embrace the revelation of this ideal in nature as the ultimate goal of man's practical and moral life certainly can be called religious; along with the reverence and humility that comes with recognizing man as a minute part of the infinite whole, such devotion constitutes one variation of what is the only true religion, namely, the religion that sees things as they are. So conceived, religion deserves to be taken seriously, and will last as long as man does.

Sources

Blanshard, Brand. "Autobiography" and "Replies to My Critics." In *The Philosophy of Brand Blanshard*. Edited by Paul Arthur Schilpp. LaSalle, IL: Open Court Press, 1980. 3–185; 930–43; 977–93; 1002–14; 1040–55; 1083–99.
_____. *Reason and Belief*. London: George Allen and Unwin Ltd., 1974.

Dupré, Louis. "Faith and Reason." In Schilpp, *Blanshard*. 994–1001.

Ferré, Frederick. "Brand Blanshard on Reason and Religious Belief." In Schilpp, *Blanshard*. 908–29.

Irish, Jerry A. "The Rationalist and the Reformer: A Critique of Blanshard's Views of Protestantism." In Schilpp, *Blanshard*. 1056–84.

Owens, Joseph A. "An Appreciation of Blanshard's Views on Catholicism." In Schilpp, *Blanshard*. 1015–39.

Thomas, George F. "Blanshard's View on Christian Ethics." In Schilpp, *Blanshard*, 944–76.

Blondel, Maurice (1861–1949)

Blondel was born into a wealthy, middle-class Burgundian family. An aunt encouraged him early on in his youth to meditate on the life of Jesus and introduced him to a range of ideas expounded by the Apostle Paul. His diary repeatedly refers to the "grace-filled moments" he experienced at the age of thirteen on the day of his First Communion. After completing preliminary studies and obtaining lower degrees in literature, science and law, he enrolled in 1881 at the École Normale Supérieur of Paris and began studying the history of philosophy and contemporary philosophical issues. Grappling with the latter triggered a desire on his part to find a modern way of thinking that might serve as a foundation for the convictions of his religious faith, or in other words, a Christian philosophy that could show in secular France how reasonable is the practice of Catholic faith. He decided to write his doctoral dissertation on action in hopes of capturing a transcendental orientation of the human will that would eliminate the imbalance between the real and the ideal.

For the next ten years, while also teaching at a number of secondary schools, he worked and reworked the thesis before finally defending it against a hostile committee at the Sorbonne, winning its approval for publication, and earning his doctorate. The following year he was married, but given the suspicions his book had aroused from both secular philosophers and Christian theologians he was denied a professorship at the Sorbonne, and only through the help of a former instructor did he finally land a professorial position at the University of Aix-Marseille. He stayed there until 1929, when blindness forced him into early retirement.

The ten volumes of work he produced in the remaining twenty years of his life had to be dictated. Conservative, neo-Scholastic theologians continued accusing him of being a Modernist (giving rise to Martin Heidegger's claim that while he was in the Jesuit Noviate he had to read Blondel's *L'Action* in secret). But despite Blondel's criticism of the prevailing brand of Thomism, there was no doubt about his ongoing devotion to the Catholic faith on the part of at least four popes — Leo XIII, Pius X, Pius XII, and Paul VI — all of whom praised his work. His personal papers reveal that despite the frustration of his youthful desire to fulfill his manhood by becoming a priest, he remained a deeply spiritual man who spent hours praying and meditating before the Blessed Sacrament, attended Mass and communed daily his whole life long, and went out of his way to serve the poor.

BLONDEL ON RELIGION. Religion is a legitimate concern of philosophy. For any philosophical investigation of human existence readily uncovers an inadequation between the sense of being humans have and the reality they actually experience, between the concrete perceptions humans have and their universal conceptualization, between the phenomenal object humans explicitly will and the primitive *élan* of their implicit willing. In other words, no matter what human activity (science, art, politics, love, etc.) is undertaken, it is inevitably frustrated by suffering, weakness, and finally death. But far from justifying a nihilistic conclusion that human life has no meaning, the consciousness of such failure is possible only on the assumption that there is something unique and necessary, something transcendent and godlike, in human willing, thinking, and being, that inevitably inclines them beyond the phenomenal order.

There is nothing in such a critical experience that proves the existence of God. But it does give rise to the idea of God as the omniscient, absolute Being in relation to which human life might possibly find its ultimate meaning — the realization, that is, of its implicit will. So, instead of succumbing to the temptation of egoistically trying to make gods of themselves that would only turn the *élan* of their wills against itself and take them back to where they started, humans would be wise to remain open to the possibility of God himself drawing the human will toward its inherently transcendent goal through the influx of divine grace. While philosophy cannot prove the possibility of ever satisfying man's needs through such supernatural means, neither can it prove its impossibility. And if, in fact, the historic dogmas and rites of the Christian religion resonate to the transcendental orientation of human thinking, being, and action, it would behoove nonbelievers to take the Christian message seriously, recognizing all the while that any choice on their part to embrace it or any other religious message would remain a matter of faith.

Sources

Blondel, Maurice. *Action (1893): Essay on a Critique of Life and a Science of Practice.* Translated and introduced by Oliva Blanchette. Notre Dame: University of Notre Dame Press, 1984.
_____. *The Letter of Apologetics and History of Dogma.* Translated by Alexander Dru and Illtyd Trethowan. New York, Chicago, San Francisco: Holt, Rinehart, and Winston, 1964.
Bonasea, Bernardine M. "Maurice Blondel: The Method of Immanence as an Approach to God." In John K. Ryan, ed. *Twentieth-Century Thinkers.* Staten Island, NY: Alba House, 1967. 37–58.
Bouillard, Henri, S.J. "The Thought of Maurice Blondel: A Synoptic Vision." *International Philosophical Quarterly* 3 (1968): 392–402.
Macquarrie, John. "Blondel, Maurice." *Encyclopedia of Philosophy.* Vol. 1. Edited by Paul Edwards. New York: Macmillan and Co. and The Free Press, 1967. 323–24.
Redmond, R.X. "Immanence Apologetics." *New Catholic Encyclopedia.* Vol. 7. Edited by W.J. McDonald. New York: McGraw-Hill, 1967. 387–88.
Schaber, Johannes. "Blondel, Maurice." In *Biographisch-Bibliographisches Kirchenlexikon.* Vol. 15. Verlag Traugott Bautz, 1999. http://www.bautz.de/bbkl/. 196–236.
Somerville, J.M. "Blondel, Maurice." *New Catholic Encyclopedia.* Vol. 2. Edited by W.J. McDonald. New York: McGraw-Hill, 1967. 617–18.
_____. "Blondel, Maurice (1861–1949)." *Thought* 36 (1961): 371–410.

Boethius (c. 480–c. 524)

Boethius was born into an aristocratic family whose fourth century ancestors had converted to Christianity and counted among its members many civil and church leaders (including a pope). He was raised in the home of the future Roman consul, Q. A. Memmius Symmachus, who had a great love for philosophy and the Christian religion. Under his influence, Boethius dedicated himself early on to translating and reconciling all the writings of Plato and Aristotle, and did in fact translate many of the latter's works on Logic, along with Porphyry's introduction to the same. The project was cut short, however, by his political involvement and eventual execution (on trumped-up charges of treason) by the Ostrogothic, Arian king, Theodoric the Great.

Not long after his death Boethius came to be venerated as a Christian martyr (under the name St. Severinus). The cult became especially popular in the thirteenth century, and in the nineteenth was officially approved by church officials for the diocese of Pavia, in whose neighborhood Boethius had been imprisoned. More recently, however, questions have been raised about whether Boethius really was a Christian, and if he was, about the quality of his Christian faith. The questions have been prompted by the fact that although the book which he wrote while in prison awaiting the summons to execution (the *Consolation of Philosophy*) contains profoundly religious, philosophical arguments for the existence of God and Divine Providence, there is no reference in it to any doctrine that is specifically and unmistakably Christian. But even if his final work is, at best, rather neutral in its assimilation of pagan reason with Christian faith, other of his writings — the *Theological Tractates* (*Opuscula sacra*) written during the latter years of his life — clearly indicate his acceptance of Christian beliefs about the Blessed Trinity and the Incarnation.

Based as they were on his study of Augustine, his writings established him throughout the Middle Ages as a major theological authority on such matters. One of them (the *De Fide Catholica*), whose authenticity most but not all historians acknowledge, specifically rejects the Arian, Sabellian, and Manichaean heresies and celebrates the Scriptural, universal, and local authority of the Catholic Church's teaching. Combined with the fact that it is highly improbable that he could ever have been appointed to the consulship in the sixth century had he been an overt pagan, these writings have convinced most scholars that Boethius was indeed a Christian, and in all likelihood one of strong personal convictions.

BOETHIUS ON RELIGION. If philosophy is the love of wisdom, then, in the final analysis, philosophy is the love of God. For wisdom is more than an intellectual virtue; it is a divine reality, existing in itself as the living thought and cause of all that is. At its highest, speculative level, therefore, philosophy goes beyond the investigation of physical bodies and their forms to study God as the immaterial Supreme Form to which all that is owes its being and direction. Transcendent and ineffable, God evades all logical categories. Still, philosophy can lend rational support to what the Catholic faith reveals about the triune personal relationships within God, the distinct reality of Christ's two natures, and the history of mankind from Creation to the Last Judgment. But even without the aid of revelation, reason can tell us much about God and our own selves.

On the assumption that God is that than which nothing better can be conceived, it is reasonable to conclude that God exists, since it is obvious that there are imperfect beings whose existence presupposes the existence of the perfect. Being perfect, God is Goodness Itself, uniting within Itself all that is good. As such, God is identical with happiness. Humans become happy, therefore, by participating in the goodness of God and becoming godlike. This occurs when, recalling its preexistent vision of the Good, the soul aligns its will with God's will, reverses its descent into the dark, earthly realm made evil by its distance from God, frees itself from the ever-changing web of Fate, and ascends back to the inner circle of the divine presence from which it came, there to find eternal rest in the still point of God's immutable, simple mind. If, in the meantime, good individuals suffer while the bad seem to prosper, this is all part of the providential plan by which God, with the eternal immediacy of universal foreknowledge, lovingly governs the world (including Fate), even while respecting human freedom. In the end justice will prevail. So hope in, and prayers to, God are not in vain.

Sources

Boethius. *The Consolation of Philosophy*. Translated by V.E. Watts. Harmondsworth, UK: Penguin Books, 1980.

———. *The Theological Tractates*. Translated by H.F. Stewart and E.K. Rand. London: William Heinemann, Ltd.; Cambridge, MA: Harvard University Press, 1936.

Barrett, Helen M. *Boethius: Some Aspects of His Times and Work*. Cambridge: At the University Press, 1940.

Copleston, Frederick, S.J. *A History of Philosophy*. Vol. 2, pt. 1. Garden City, NY: Doubleday and Company, Inc., 1962–77. 116–20.

Gersh, Stephen. *Middle Platonism and Neoplatonism: The Latin Tradition*. Vol. 2. Notre Dame: University of Notre Dame Press, 1986.

Gilson, Etienne. *History of Christian Philosophy in the Middle Ages*. New York: Random House, 1954. 97–106.

Haring, N.M. "Boethius." *New Catholic Encyclopedia*. Vol. 2. Edited by W.J. McDonald. New York: McGraw-Hill, 1967. 631–33.

Marenbon, John. *Boethius*. Oxford: Oxford University Press. 2003.

Reiss, Edmund. *Boethius*. Boston: Twayne Publishers, 1982.

Bradley, Francis Herbert (1846–1924)

Like many another mid–nineteenth-century philosopher, Bradley was raised in a deeply, albeit rather narrowly, religious environment. He was one of twenty-two children fathered and raised (rather tyrannically, it is said) by the Rev. Charles Bradley, an Evangelical preacher whose finely honed sermons were very popular. Upon completion of his elementary studies at Cheltenham and Marlborough, he went to University College, Oxford. There he read broadly, but showed little taste for the kind of moralizing treatises being turned out by Tolstoy, or for literal readings of the Bible and its account of the historical Jesus, or for functional interpretations of religion that would reduce the latter to its satisfaction of human needs.

Notwithstanding his initial achievement of only second-class honors in the *literae humaniores,* he was eventually awarded a Fellowship at Oxford's Merton College, and, except for occasional winters on the Riviera to alleviate his suffering from ongoing health problems, remained there for the rest of his life. As was required of Fellows, he forewent the joys of marriage (even to the adorable "E.R." he met while traveling in France), and, despite a basically social disposition, remained something of a recluse. Early on in his scholarly endeavors he developed an interest in the kind of theological questions raised earlier at Tübingen by F.C. Baur's attempt to explain the evolution of Christianity in dialectical terms of Hegel's philosophy of history.

His subsequent, anti-empiricist writings in the fields of ethics and logic, as well as his later metaphysical publications, clearly evidenced an Hegelian influence. But he was also an original thinker. Unlike Hegel (or Spinoza), he did not identify the Absolute, the Perfect Whole, of his metaphysical ruminations with the God of religious faith. Because of its personal relations, the God of religion, he thought, was necessarily other than the sum reality of the universe, and to that extent limited and less than perfect. His metaphysics, therefore, was never merely an apology for traditional religious beliefs. Nor did he appreciate any attempt to use religion to justify egalitarian, pacifist, and other humanitarian sentiments being expressed by contemporary,

liberal-minded utilitarians. But he also never had in mind to undermine religion as such, or to espouse atheism. Throughout his life he remained respectful of the faith he had inherited as a boy, and saw in religion, despite its many contradictions, the best chance of bringing people together through their relations with God. He is buried in Oxford's Holywell Churchyard.

BRADLEY ON RELIGION. Religion arises when individuals encounter an object, in comparison to which they feel themselves powerless and worthless. Rooted, therefore, not so much in wonder as in fear and admiration, religion may be defined in general as a reflective, fixed and supreme feeling of fear and admiration toward an object of whatever sort, be it other worldly or not, many (as in polytheism) or one (as in monotheism), or — as in the highest sense of religion — the one perfect object which is utterly good. The God of religion is not to be confused, however, with the Absolute. By the Absolute is meant the world as a whole, not as an aggregate of the isolated particulars conceived by science or common sense, but as the unitary, systematic totality of all that is, an eternally conscious experience that is both immanent and transcendent to all its parts, reconciling all their diverse conceptualizations within itself. Experiencing everything as a part of itself, the Absolute cannot be in any kind of relational opposition to the world, and to that extent cannot be a person by striking up a practical relation between its own and the finite will.

But religion is nothing if it is not practical. However inconsistent it may be with the recognition by the higher religions of God's perfection as the All in All (indwelling Life and Mind), therefore, or however much it might imply the finiteness of God, it may well be necessary to identify the God of religion as personal, a God who can say to himself "I" as against "you" or "me," and relate (differentiating, while at the same time uniting) his own Good Will to that of ours. By thus acknowledging the reality of the Ideal Good, religion goes beyond the conflicting moral claims of self-assertion and self-sacrifice, affording believers confidence in the ultimate triumph of the Good over evil, and (although this is not essential to religion) some hope of themselves conquering death and possibly finding immortality. To take the personality of God as the last word about the Universe, however, would be to fall into serious error.

Sources

Bradley, F.H. *Appearance and Reality*. London: Swan Sonnenschein and Co.; New York: The Macmillan Company, 1897.
_____. *Collected Essays*. Oxford: At the Clarendon Press, 1935.
_____. *Essays on Truth and Reality*. Oxford: At the Clarendon Press, 1914.
_____. *Ethical Studies*. Oxford: At the Clarendon Press. 1876.
Eslick, L.J. "Bradley, Francis Herbert." In *New Catholic Encyclopedia*. Vol. 2. Edited by W.J. McDonald. New York: McGraw-Hill, 1967. 744.
Ferm, Vergilius, ed. *An Encyclopedia of Religion*. Paterson, NJ: Littlefield, Adams and Co., 1964. 86–7.
Gardiner, Patrick L., ed. *Nineteenth Century Philosophy*. New York: The Free Press, 1969. 401–42.
Lofthouse, W.F. *F.H. Bradley*. London: The Epworth Press, 1949.
Sprigge, T.L.S. "Bradley's Doctrine of the Absolute." In *Appearance versus Reality: New Essays on Bradley's Metaphysics*. Edited by Guy Stock. Oxford: Clarendon Press, 1998. 193–217.
Wollheim, Richard. *F.H. Bradley*. Harmondsworth, UK: Penguin Books, 1969.

Braithwaite, Richard B. (1900–1990)

Braithwaite grew up in a Quaker environment. His father was a Banbury, Oxfordshire, banker who was also an historian of Quakerism. As a young boy of eleven, Braithwaite was sent to Sidcot, a Quaker boarding school that put great emphasis upon the pastoral care of its individual students and included in its religious programming weekly, mandatory Meetings for worship. Upon graduating from Sidcot he enrolled in another Quaker boarding school, Bootham in York, and remained there for most of the next four years. There too, given its Quaker atmosphere, Braithwaite would have been expected to participate in the regular Sunday, non-sacramental Meetings, during which the Friends meditated in silence until one or another individual would be illuminated by the inner light to address some particular issue. With the bloody First World War in full swing during the years of his stay at the school, among the issues he no doubt heard raised in these Meetings was the evil of all war and violence, a traditional Quaker position. Not surprisingly, when he himself was old enough to fight in that war, he chose instead to become a conscientious objector and served only for a short time in the Friends' Ambulance Unit.

In the years following the war he continued his education at Cambridge, excelling in mathematics and the moral science, and after being elected to what would become a lifelong fellowship at King's College and marrying a second time following the death of his first wife, began lecturing at Cambridge, mainly on ethics and the philosophy of science. While spending the rest of his life teaching there and elsewhere around the world (e.g., Johns Hopkins, Western Ontario, City University of New York) and developing a reputation for being an exceptionally inspiring professor, he was also active in university politics (e.g., supporting admission of women to Cambridge) and in providing leadership to his profession (e.g., as president of the Aristotelian Society, the British Society for the Philosophy of Science). All the while, he also retained his concern with religion, as evidenced especially by publication of his 1955 Eddington lecture (*An Empiricist's View of the Nature of Religious Belief*). By that time, however, his own practice of religion had changed. Reports of Nazi horrors and personal experiences during the Second World War had inclined him to reject the pacifism he had inherited from his Quaker upbringing, and he soon thereafter left the Quaker religion and joined the Church of England. He was baptized and confirmed in King's College chapel in 1948. After his death at the age of ninety, his ashes were interred in the same Cambridge chapel.

BRAITHWAITE ON RELIGION. Logical Positivists originally argued that the key question regarding religious statements was not whether they are true or false, but how they could be known either to be true or to be false. If such statements had any meaning, the Positivists said, it had to be discovered by their method of verification. But since religious statements are unverifiable by any of the standard methods used to verify statements about empirical facts, scientific hypotheses, or logically necessary statements, they were rightly said to lack cognitive meaning. Contrary to what the Positivists themselves thought, however, that need not have led to the conclusion that religious statements are altogether meaningless. For like similarly noncognitive, conative moral statements that transcend feelings and declare intentions to pursue particular policies of action (say, a Utilitarian one), noncognitive religious statements can also go beyond the mere expression of emotion and declare commitment to a particular way of life. A Christian's assertion that God is love can be read, for example, as a declaration of one's intention to follow an agapeistic way of life. True religion, therefore, is essentially allegiance to a set of moral principles.

In contrast to purely moral systems, religions (or at least the higher ones) preach not only a conversion of the will (external behavior), but also of the heart (internal behavior). It is conceivable, of course, that any two religions might have the same ethical policy (e.g., love of one's fellow human beings). What sets them apart — more than any ritualistic peculiarities — is the unique matrix of mythology or storytelling within which each religion embeds its moral principles. Such stories will have empirical propositional elements. But whether they are true or false is not decisive. What matters is whether they function psychologically to cause individuals to act in accordance with the behavioral policy being preached by the particular religion telling the stories. As Matthew Arnold noted, poetic imagination, no less than emotion, plays a major part in religion by guiding conduct.

Sources

Braithwaite, R.B. *An Empiricist's View of the Nature of Religious Belief.* Cambridge: At the University Press, 1955.
Diamond, Malcolm L., and Thomas V. Litzenburg, Jr., eds. *The Logic of God: Theology and Verification.* Indianapolis: The Bobbs-Merrill Company, Inc., 1975. 121–26.
Hick, John. *Philosophy of Religion.* 3rd ed. Englewood Cliffs, NJ: Prentice-Hall, Inc., 1983. 87–90.
Mellor, D.H. "Braithwaite, Richard Bevan." *Oxford Dictionary of National Biography: From the earliest times to the year 2000.* Vol. 7. Edited by H.C.G. Matthew and Brian Harrison. In association with The British Academy. 2004. 302.
_____, ed. *Science, Belief, and Behavior: Essays in Honour of R.B. Braithwaite.* Cambridge and New York: Cambridge University Press, 1980.

Brightman, Edgar Sheffield (1884–1953)

Brightman was the son and grandson of Protestant ministers. As was typical of children born in nineteenth century Methodist parsonages, he grew up moving frequently from one town to another. His faith in his childhood religion, however, would not change. He remained a devout and active Methodist throughout his life. While pursuing B.A. and M.A. degrees at Brown University he volunteered to instruct his Kappa Sigma fraternity brothers for two hours every Saturday evening in their study of the Bible, played an active role in the Y.M.C.A., helped his seriously ill father manage the church to which he had been assigned in Middletown, Rhode Island, and did some preaching at another church nearby. In 1908 he started studying theology and philosophy at Boston University and, after acquiring an S.T.B. two years later, was admitted as a Methodist minister to the New England Southern Conference. He spent the next year and a half at the University of Marburg studying biblical theology, church history, and philosophy, before being called back to teach philosophy, psychology, and courses on the Bible at Nebraska Wesleyan University.

After getting his Ph.D. at Boston University and marrying in 1912, he accepted a position at Wesleyan University in Middletown, where, in addition to teaching ethics and religion, he preached at local churches and wrote his first book, a work on the Bible that evoked harsh criticism from conservative opponents of "higher criticism," with one reviewer calling him "an infidel, a Hun, and moral leper." He spent the last thirty-four years of his life teaching philosophy at Boston University. Many students have attested to the help he gave them in reinterpreting the religious faith with which they had grown up and against which they were rebelling.

His notion of a personal but finite God struggling within Himself to overcome the nonrational Given of His divine being, was not, however, very well received by some of his fellow Christians. Nor did they all appreciate his tolerant attitude toward non–Christian religions (like the Hinduism of his good friend, Swami Akhilananda) or the support he gave to the struggle for social justice and peace as a member of the Methodist Federation for Social Action, the Civil Liberties Union, and the Committee on Peace through Justice. Misgivings about World War I had turned him into a pacifist supporter of conscientious objectors, and he would later remark that had he not been raised a Methodist, he might have become a Quaker. By most accounts he died a humble and devout Christian, leaving behind a second wife (the first had died), three children, fourteen books and more than two hundred scholarly articles.

BRIGHTMAN ON RELIGION. All human knowledge begins, continues, and ends in experience. Our experience consists, however, of our entire conscious life, not just sensations and perceptions. Included in our consciousness is awareness of the rationality of the universe, the emergence of novelties (e.g., life and intelligence), the existence of personality (the quality of being a person, or self, that is potentially self-conscious, rational, and ideal), and the existence of values (love, truth, goodness, beauty, holiness, etc.). All of these facts need to be interpreted in terms of their relation to each other and to their totality. Their most

coherent interpretation is provided by a theistic hypothesis of a Supreme Person whose Mind and Will are the best explanation for whatever rational order, creative advance, personality, and value are to be found in this world.

But there is also something in the universe, a Given within the divine personality, that is not created by God and is not the result of voluntary divine self-limitation, which God finds as either obstacle or instrument of his will. The apparent futility, waste, and absurdity running through the process of evolution is concrete evidence of the same. If we are to avoid making God evil and hope to give a coherent account of all the facts, therefore, the hypothesis of God as the Source and Conserver of Values will also have to include finiteness, not in the sense that God began or will end, but in the sense that his absolutely good and loving Will is limited by the Given. It is the worshipful attitude and reverent devotion toward such a God, as expressed in symbolic rites and other conduct, that constitute the essence of religion and differentiate it from other social, value-oriented phenomena. That the Will of God is recognized as being finite can inspire humans to cooperate with the unshakable purposes of the Eternal Person. This elevates human life to its loftiest ideal plane, and affords man his best chance of immortality. For a good God who conserves values must also be a conserver of persons.

Sources

Brightman, Edgar Sheffield. *The Finding of God.* New York: The Abingdon Press, 1931.

_____. *Personality and Religion.* Nashville: The Abingdon Press, 1933.

_____. *A Philosophy of Religion.* Westport, CT: Greenwood Press, 1969.

_____. *The Problem of God.* New York: The Abingdon Press, 1930.

_____. *Religious Values.* New York: The Abingdon Press, 1927.

Bertocci, Peter A., and M. Alicia Corea. "Edgar Sheffield Brightman Through His Students' Eyes." *The Philosophical Forum* XII (1954): 53–67.

Callahan, Daniel. "Human Experience and God:

Brightman's Personalistic Theism." In *American Philosophy and the Future*. Edited by Michael Novak. New York: Charles Scribner's Sons, 1968. 219–46.

Howie, John. "Brightman, Edgar Sheffield." In *American National Biography*. Vol. 3. Edited by John A. Garraty and Mark C. Carnes. New York and Oxford: Oxford University Press, 1999. 552–53.

Newhall, Jannette E. "Edgar Sheffield Brightman: A Biographical Sketch." *The Philosophical Forum* XII (1954): 9–21.

Broad, Charlie Dunbar (1887–1971)

Broad's paternal grandparents converted from rather lukewarm membership in the Church of England to an enthusiastic embrace of Methodism. With a deep interest in natural science, his father's thinking was influenced considerably by the debate over evolution and higher criticism of the Bible, and he would later share these views with C.D. The father held to his theistic beliefs and its moral implications, but dissociated himself from any particular Christian sect or church, and was especially hostile toward the ritualism and clericalism of Roman Catholicism and High Anglicanism (an attitude that would later influence C.D.'s own distrust of corporate, ecclesiastical institutions and his preference for the Quaker type of religious person). He admitted that he would have been unfit for the Church, and claimed the same about his son, C.D., when someone offered to have him appointed for pastoral service in the Anglican Church.

By his own account, Broad was raised in a home and school atmosphere in which the truth of liberal Protestant Christianity was simply taken for granted, but without much sectarian bias or biblical fundamentalism. His youthful study of Mill, Kant, and Schopenhauer had convinced him of the truth of subjective idealism, if for no other reason than that it did seem to do justice to the religious facts of the world. But a few years of exposure at Cambridge to the writings of G.E. Moore and Bertrand Russell quickly disillusioned him

in that regard and turned him into a skeptic. Reading T.H. Huxley, Haeckel, Renan, and other skeptical scholars also helped him overcome a native fear of hellfire and damnation and inclined him to reject Christianity in favor of a "rather crude and self-conscious rationalism" based on natural science.

A devout Roman Catholic classmate at Cambridge inclined him to think that were he ever to return to Christianity, it would be to Roman Catholicism. If he never made such a move and denied his Master, it was due, he confessed, not to greed (as in the case of Judas) but to a lack of moral courage (as in the case of St. Peter, the biblical account of whose denial fascinated him). Although he acknowledged to the end being "wholly devoid of religious or mystical experience," he considered them of great interest and extreme importance to any theoretical interpretation of the world. Any Speculative Philosophy ignoring the mystical and religious experience of that aspect of Reality lying beyond ordinary sense perception, he concluded, would be extremely one-sided.

BROAD ON RELIGION. Beliefs of even the most perfect religions are mixed up with a great deal of positive error and sheer nonsense. Not to mention the unverifiable, polytheistic implications of the popular sense of the word God or misleading philosophical applications of the term to the Absolute or the Universe as a whole, the theological sense of a personal God who is omniscient, omnipotent, unique, and morally perfect is especially difficult to support.

Traditional arguments for the existence of such a personal God are all fallacious; the ontological, because it employs a meaningless concept of a most perfect being and illogically draws an instantial conclusion from purely conditional premises; the cosmological, because, even if the human intellect could be satisfied by presupposing an intrinsically necessary existential proposition, it would not prove the uniqueness of that which is necessary, and would imply that there are no really contingent facts; the teleological, because, even if a hypothesis of design based upon superficial observation would enable the prediction of further phenomena, it would prove only that a designing mind had existed in the past, not that it does exist now, or that it is creative or morally perfect. Nor is there any reason to conclude that the aspect of Reality supposedly experienced by mystics is anything personal. And it would be irrational to believe in the existence of a personal God simply on the authority of others. Attempts to prove the possibility of miracles (upon which rest so many Christian doctrines) or of personal immortality (a *sine qua non* of any religious view of the world) have also found little support from science (notwithstanding recent psychical research). It would be ridiculous, therefore, for any religion to claim to have the last word on any of these matters. But it would be almost as farfetched to assume that the whole religious experience of mankind is a gigantic system of pure delusion. Outgrowing its current literalism, religion could purify its doctrines and come closer to the truth.

Sources

Broad, C.D. "Autobiography." In *The Philosophy of C. D. Broad*. Edited by Paul Arthur Schilpp. New York: Tudor Publishing Co., 1959. 3–68.
_____. *Religion, Philosophy and Psychical Research*. New York: Humanities Press, 1969.
_____. "Replies to W.T. Stace." In Schilpp, *The Philosophy of C.D. Broad*. 718–25.
Muirhead, J.H., ed. *Contemporary British Philosophy: Personal Statements (First Series)*. London: G. Allen and Unwin, 1927. 77–100.
Stace, W.T. "Broad's View on Religion." In Schilpp, *The Philosophy of C.D. Broad*. 171–95.

Bruno, Giordano (1548–1600)

Born of Roman Catholic parents and baptized "Filipe," Bruno was sent at the age of fifteen to the Monastery of St. Domenico to prepare for the priesthood. He initially took to the monastery as a place where his natural intelligence and religiosity could best be nurtured. But shortly after ordination as a Dominican priest, the voicing of his sympathy for past heretics, doubts about Christ's divinity and the doctrine of the Trinity, and dabbling in the writings of mystics and alchemists incurred the wrath of his monastic superiors. Threatened with the punishment of excommunication or worse, he changed his name, abandoned his cowl, and fled the monastery, first to Rome, Genoa, and other Italian cities, and then, after being excommunicated *in absentia,* wandered over the next fifteen years to Switzerland, Germany, France, and England.

In Geneva, the Calvinist stronghold, Bruno often attended Protestant services to listen to sermons and theological disputations, but never partook of the sacrament. He was not impressed by what he heard, and his anti–Aristotelianism and challenge of traditional doctrines aroused the hostility of Geneva's Calvinist authorities. Lutheran authorities in Germany would also later excommunicate him during his stay in that country. And any attempt to reconcile with the Roman Church, he was told, would require papal absolution and his return to the monastery.

Lured into returning to Venice in 1592, he was betrayed by his deceitful host and handed over to the Venetian and Roman Inquisition on charges of having defamed the Catholic faith, denied its traditional doctrines concerning the Trinity, the Incarnation, Transubstantiation, and the Virgin birth, misrepresented the facts of Jesus' life and death, and condoned sexual promiscuity. While admitting during his trial that he had always insisted upon the freedom of philosophy to pursue its own rational course, he claimed still to love the Catholic faith and, despite occasional bouts of skepticism, never to have taught anything directly opposed to the Catholic religion. Contrary to suspicions of being a pantheist, he specifically professed his belief that God is not only "in all," but also "above all." Unsatisfied, and unable on several occasions to get Bruno, despite some initial wavering, to recant, the Roman Inquisitors eventually condemned him as an inveterate heretic and ordered that he be burned alive at the stake, after having been stripped naked and his tongue tied to prevent any last-minute heretical outbursts. The execution was brutally carried out

on February 17, 1600, in Rome's Campo de"
Fiori.

BRUNO ON RELIGION. By the light of reason alone it is clear that the only religion beyond all controversy and worth observing is
one that lifts humans up from the savage condition of life common to brutes and the unciv-
ilized, and teaches them to love not only
neighbors and friends, but also strangers and
enemies. As any rational interpretation of the
New Testament would reveal, this was also the
heart of the gospel preached by that good and
just man, Jesus. Its law of mutual love was
meant to expel the bestial vices from the human
heart and to bring all human souls into union
with the infinite God who, as the cosmic soul
of our infinite universe, is at once in all things
(especially humans) emanating from him, and
yet transcendent to them. But this simple message was lost through the excessive asceticism
of the Christian religion, its canonization of
fanatics, its superstitious proclivities, and,
above all, its intolerance of any ideas other
than assertions by church authorities about
the triune nature, the special providence, the
punitive wrathfulness, and so forth, of God–
dogmas which might, at best, be accepted in
faith and only when interpreted allegorically.

Such distortion of the true religion had its
roots in Judaism — that most barbaric of religions — and carried over into the religion of
the Mohammedans. These historical religions
had lost sight of that natural religion by which
the Egyptians of old had given symbolic expression to their belief in the presence of God
in all things when they worshiped the gods in
the form of the sun, animals, and other natural phenomena. Still, adherence by the weak
and ignorant masses to the rites and ceremonies instituted by Christianity and other
positive religions can be helpful in the maintenance of peace and harmony in any society.
And while the wise minority might prefer a
more philosophical, or rational, form of religion, even they should conform, at least outwardly, to traditional religious practices, lest
by their disobedience they contribute to public disorder by setting a bad example for the
foolish majority.

Sources

Bruno, Giordano. *Cause, Principle and Unity: Five
    Dialogues.* Translated by Jack Lindsay. New
    York: International Publishers, 1964.
_____. *The Expulsion of the Triumphant Beast.* Trans-
    lated by Arthur D. Imerti. New Brunswick,
    NJ: Rutgers University Press, 1964.
_____. *The Heroic Frenzies.* Translated by Paul Eu-
    gene Memmo, Jr. New York: Garret Publishing
    Co., 1966.
Copleston, Frederick, S.J. *A History of Philosophy.*
    Vol. 3, pt. 2. Garden City, NY: Doubleday and
    Company, Inc., 1962–77. 65–71.
Finocchiaro, Maurice A. "Philosophy versus Reli-
    gion and Science versus Religion: The Trials of
    Bruno and Galileo." In Hilary Gatti, ed. *Gior-
    dano Bruno: Philosopher of the Renaissance.*
    Aldershot, Hants, England, and Burlington,
    VT: Ashgate, 2002. 51–96.
Greenburg, Sidney Thomas. *The Infinite in Gior-
    dano Bruno, with a Translation of His Dialogue:
    Concerning the Cause, Principle, and One.* New
    York: Octagon Books, 1978.
Grunewald, Heidemarie. *Die Religionsphilosophie des
    Nikolaus Cusanus und die Konzeption einer Re-
    ligionsphilosophie bei Giordano Bruno.* Hildes-
    heim: Gerstenberg Verlag, 1977. See esp. 135–
    202.
McIntyre, J. Lewis. *Giordano Bruno.* London:
    Macmillan and Co., Limited; New York: The
    Macmillan Company, 1903. See esp. 180–96;
    294–322.
White, Michael. *The Pope and the Heretic.* New York:
    HarperCollins Publishers, 2002.
Wright, William Kelley. *A History of Modern Philos-
    ophy.* New York: The Macmillan Company,
    1941. 27–36.

Buber, Martin (1878–1965)

After the disappearance of his mother
and the remarriage of his father, Buber, at the
age of three, was put in the care of his grandparents. Solomon, the grandfather, was highly
esteemed around the world as a scholar of the
Haskalah (the Jewish Enlightenment).
Notwithstanding his enlightenment, he often
took his grandson with him to worship among
Sadagora's *Hasidim* (followers of the eighteenth-century Polish mystic, Baal-Shem Tov).
Later, while spending summers with his father, Buber was exposed to the latter's more
liberal form of Judaism, but to little effect.
Tormented by his inability to comprehend the

infinity of time and space, the young Buber lost much of his religious fervor and sought consolation in his reading of Kant and Nietzsche.

During the period of his doctoral work on Nicholas of Cusa and Jakob Boehme, he regained his interest in Judaism and became involved in the Zionist movement and the Jewish Renaissance. But feeling a need to get to know Judaism at a much deeper level, he eventually turned to an intensive study of Hasidism, and in subsequent years (while teaching Jewish religious philosophy at the University of Frankfurt and also developing biblical themes) devoted much of his time and energy to the translation and interpretation of the writings of Hasidic and other mystical traditions. Under the influence of his reading of Hasidic text and its recognition of the mysterious presence of the divine in all things human (especially in the human community), he became increasingly disillusioned with what he considered to be the static, institutionalized forms of religion and its demarcation of everyday, profane life from the realm of the sacred.

This did not endear him to Orthodox Jewish leaders and resulted in him being forbidden to teach religion at the Hebrew University of Jerusalem. He was careful not to offend Conservative Jews following the *Halakhah* (Jewish Law), but he did not himself feel bound to observe its many ritualistic prescriptions. He seldom frequented the synagogue, but prayed often as an expression of the interhuman/divine dialogue that he considered to be the essence of true religion. While acknowledging the special role Judaism has played historically in actualizing such dialogue, he had great respect for other religions (including Islam), and worked tirelessly for their reconciliation. His death, memorialized by a traditional Jewish funeral, was declared by Ben-Gurion to be "a great loss to Israel's spiritual life."

BUBER ON RELIGION. Religion should be distinguished from religiosity. By religiosity is meant the dynamic and ever-creative sense of wonder, trust and responsibility one feels upon catching a glimpse of God, the eternal Thou, in one's encounter with every particular Thou, be it another person, a tree, a cat, or a poem by Rilke. The latter reveal the presence of God in such a meeting because, by recognizing the other as distant, independent and equal, the I remains fully open to the presence of the other's being, in the light of which the whole of the universe shines forth, manifesting the ultimate mystery of reality. God appears as the wholly Other, the dreadful, transcendent *Mysterium Tremendum,* but also as the wholly Same, the wholly Present, who is nearer to oneself than one's own I. As such, the person of God can be addressed, but never expressed, in joyful communal worship.

This incomprehensibility of God's personal presence was acknowledged by ancient Judaism's reluctance to name or image God. Hasidism, Taoism and Zen Buddhism showed similar appreciation for the ultimately mysterious dimension of particular reality, and along with all other religions, must be respected for the uniqueness of their message. But religion in general has consisted of various peoples trying to use their respective customs and teachings to express and shape their religiosity. As a result, religion has often lapsed into one or another form of gnostic solipsism, reducing God to an It that could be exploited to explain the riddle of life or to provide security, success or aesthetic refreshment in a world of holocausts and other brutal events. But a God so conceived as the author of nature, the lord of history, or the innermost self, was rightly declared dead by Nietzsche, forcing the faithful simply to endure the apparent eclipse of God in the modern world, and to learn anew that any encounter with the living God will inevitably send them back into the world to seek, at whatever cost to their own lives, peace and justice for all.

Sources

Buber, Martin. *Between Man and Man.* Translated by Ronald Gregor Smith. New York: The Macmillan Company, 1966.

_____. *Eclipse of God.* Translated by Maurice Friedman et al. New York: Harper Torchbooks, 1957.

_____. *I and Thou.* Translated by Ronald Gregor Smith. New York: Charles Scribner's Sons, 1958.

_____. *Meetings: Autobiographical Fragments.* London and New York: Routledge, 2002.

_____. *Religion als Gegenwart.* In Rivka Horwitz, *Buber's Way To I and Thou.* Heidelberg: Verlag Lambert Schneider, 1978. 43–55.

_____. *Two Types of Faith.* Translated by Norman P. Goldhawk. New York: Harper Torchbooks, 1961.

Brague, Rémi. "How to Be in the World: Gnosis, Religion, Philosophy." In *Martin Buber: A Contemporary Perspective.* Edited by Paul Mendes-Flohr. n.p.: Syracuse University Press, 2002. 133–47.

Friedman, Maurice. *Encounter on the Narrow Ridge: A Life of Martin Buber.* New York: Paragon House, 1991.

_____. *Martin Buber and the Eternal.* New York: Human Sciences Press, Inc., 1986.

Gordon, Haim, and Jochanan Bloch, eds. *Martin Buber: A Centenary Volume.* n.p.: KTAV Publishing House, Inc., 1984.

Moore, Donald J. *Martin Buber: Prophet of Religious Secularism.* 2nd ed. New York: Fordham University Press, 1996.

Silberstein, Laurence J. "Buber, Martin." In *Encyclopedia of Religion.* Vol. 2. Edited by Mircea Eliade. New York: Macmillan and Co., 1987. 316–18.

Stroumsa, Guy G. "Presence, Not Gnosis: Buber as a Historian of Religion." In *Martin Buber: A Contemporary Perspective.* Edited by Paul Mendes-Flohr. n.p.: Syracuse University Press, 2002. 25–47.

Carnap, Rudolf (1891–1970)

Carnap acknowledged that as he was growing up in the German towns of Ronsdorf and Barmen he experienced what a positive effect a living religion was having in the lives of his parents and in his own life. That any man embraces some traditional or other form of religion, therefore, in no way diminishes, Carnap said, the respect he has for that man's character. But as for himself, even before initiating his study of philosophy (especially Kant), physics and mathematics (under Frege) at the universities of Jena and Freiburg, he was beginning to have doubts about the religious doctrines regarding the world, man, and God.

As a university student his skepticism be-

came more deliberate and definite. Conversations with fellow students and the reading of works by Haeckel and other freethinkers propounding the scientistic view that empirical observation was the only source of knowledge, he soon came to the conclusion that a literal interpretation of religious doctrines could not be reconciled with the theory of evolution, determinism, and other results of modern science. One by one he gradually abandoned all the supernatural features of religious doctrine, dismissing the divinity of Christ, rejecting both theistic and pantheistic ideas of God, and rejecting any notion of personal immortality. Reading Freud and anthropologists helped him explain the historical fact of widespread religious belief as a mere phenomenon of cultural evolution.

Three years at the front in World War I left him disillusioned about his earlier convictions of continuous progress, but life in the trenches did not trigger any revival of religious beliefs. He would remain convinced for the rest of his life, as he went about laying the foundations of logical positivism with publications like *The Logical Structure of the World* and *Pseudoproblems in Philosophy*, that traditional theological dogmas, if interpreted literally, are refuted by modern science, and, if interpreted metaphysically, are both irrelevant and devoid of cognitive content. He also insisted to the end, however, that his abandonment of religious convictions "led at no time to a nihilistic attitude" such as might undermine the moral responsibility of every individual to cooperate in the development of a social community in which every individual can realize his or her potential as a human being.

CARNAP ON RELIGION. Freud discovered the origin of the conception of God as a substitute for the father, and anthropologists have traced the historical evolution of religious conceptions. Still, many people continue to rely on the symbols and images of religious mythology. It would be wrong to deprive them of the support they get from religion, let alone to ridicule them. But theology, understood as a system of religious doctrines in distinction from a system of valuations and prescriptions for life, is a different matter altogether. The scientific method is the only way to acquire well-founded, systematically coherent knowledge. Traditional religious doctrines about the world, man, and God or alleged beings of a supernatural order must be examined, therefore, according to the same rigorous standards as any other claim to knowledge.

But if taken in a direct and literal sense, based on a literal interpretation of statements in the Bible or other holy scriptures, most such religious doctrines are incompatible with the results of modern science. A literal interpretation of the biblical account of creation, for example, has been refuted by the theory of organic evolution. Similarly, the notion of a personal God interfering in the course of nature and history in order to reward or punish the free choice of individuals cannot be reconciled with the physicists' theory of determinism. And a belief in immortality as the survival of a personal, conscious soul after disintegration of the body and its brain is incompatible with the strong impression of continuity in the scientific view of the world, according to which the evolution of the human species from lower organisms occurred without any sudden changes. Refined reformulations of such crude literal interpretations of religious doctrines by contemporary theologians in such a way as to defy empirical verification are best dismissed as irrelevant to science and devoid of any cognitive content. Far from resulting in nihilism, this rejection of literal or metaphysical interpretation of religious doctrines helps achieve the humanist goal of using reason to improve the life of mankind.

Sources

Carnap, Rudolf. "Autobiography." In Schilpp, *The Philosophy of Rudolf Carnap*. 6–9.
_____. "Replies and Expositions." In Schilpp, *The Philosophy of Rudolf Carnap*. 875.
"Rudolf Carnap (1891–1970)." *The Internet Encyclopedia of Philosophy*. http://www.iep.utm.edu/c/carnap.htm. 1–12.
Schilpp, Paul Arthur. *The Philosophy of Rudolf Car-
nap*. LaSalle, IL: Open Court Press; London: Cambridge University Press, 1963.
Stumpf, Samuel Enoch. "Rudolf Carnap." *Socrates to Sartre. A History of Philosophy*. New York: Mc-Graw-Hill Book Company, 1982. 424–28.

Cassirer, Ernst (1874–1945)

Cassirer was born to a wealthy Jewish family in Breslau, Poland. Visits to his grandfather as a teenager awakened his interest in reading and intelligent conversation. After graduating from the Gymnasium with highest honors, he enrolled at the University of Berlin and began studying Kantian thought under the Jewish social philosopher, Georg Simmel. Simmel's concern about the relation of the rational individual to the whole of society influenced Cassirer's lifelong commitment to the preservation of the individual's spiritual autonomy. It was also Simmel who directed Cassirer to Hermann Cohen, the first Jew to hold a full professorship in Germany (at the University of Marburg), and who during the latter third of the nineteenth century helped initiate a Kantian-inspired Idealist reaction against the wave of mysticism that had swept over German culture earlier in the century. After allaying suspicions that he was among the converted Jews despised by Cohen, Cassirer impressed the latter with his grasp of philosophical issues and became his lifelong colleague and friend.

Having completed a dissertation on Leibniz to qualify for his doctorate, Cassirer returned to Berlin, married, fathered a child, and was soon at work on a history of epistemology. The success of the latter encouraged him to follow Cohen's advice to pursue an academic career, first, with a recommendation from Wilhelm Dilthey, as a *Privatdocent* at the University of Berlin, then as a professor and rector (the first Jew ever) at the University of Hamburg, and finally, after Hitler's rise to power made it impossible for him as a Jew to continue working in Germany, at a variety of universities in England, Sweden, and the United States. His subsequent writings on the relation of mythology and religious consciousness show broad familiarity with all the world's religions, but it was especially to the prophetic books of the Jewish Old Testament that he looked for examples of the individual moral responsibility that he associated with the origin of religion.

Unlike other German scholars who, to save their necks and careers in times of anti–Semitic persecution, severed ties with their Jewish origin, Cassirer never abandoned his Jewish identity. Although he considered most religious creeds and rituals all too divisive, he remained, according to the testimony of those who knew him best, a deeply religious man morally motivated by the sympathy of the Whole which, in his view, constituted the heart of any genuine religion.

CASSIRER ON RELIGION. Like language, art, science and other areas of human culture, religion is a symbolic way human consciousness has of expressing its experience of reality. Religious consciousness, however, is inextricably interwoven with mythic consciousness. Underlying both is a substratum, not of thought, but of a certain cognitive feeling. At the primitive level of mythic consciousness, it consists of what might be called a sympathy of the Whole, or the feeling of the indestructible unity of life (hence the fear of death as one of the original constitutive factors of myth and religion). It is not that primitive man lacks the ability to appreciate empirically the differences of things, but all such differences are obliterated by a stronger feeling: the deep conviction of a fundamental and indelible solidarity of life that bridges over the multiplicity and variety of single forms. As a result, the symbol and that to which it refers are experienced in mythic consciousness as being one and the same (e.g., the dancer assuming the nature of the god whose mask he wears).

Although still influenced by the mythic sympathy of the Whole, religious consciousness gives scope to a new feeling of individuality. Unlike mythic consciousness, which altogether lacked the category of the ideal, religious consciousness now separates the ideal from the real (e.g., "time" from particular days or seasons), thereby recognizing sensuous im-

ages as pointing beyond themselves to a meaning which they never exhaust, to "something other and transcendent." Every religion has its own way of breaking loose from its mythical foundations, thereby revealing its historical, spiritual, and moral particularity (e.g., the pure inwardness of prophetic Judaism's spiritual/ethical relation between the I and the Thou). But overall, there is a dynamic evolution in human consciousness from the mythic awareness of impersonal natural forces to religious recognition of functional gods and, ultimately, to the mystical experience of the nameless Self that is Pure Being.

Sources

Cassirer, Ernst. *An Essay on Man*. New Haven: Yale University Press, 1956.

_____. *Language and Myth*. New York: Dover Publications, Inc., 1946.

_____. *The Philosophy of Symbolic Forms*. Vol. 2: *Mythic Thought*. New Haven and London: Yale University Press, 1955.

Gawronsky, Dimitry. "Ernst Cassirer: His Life and Work." In Schilpp, *The Philosophy of Ernst Cassirer*. 3–37.

Itzkoff, Seymour W. *Ernst Cassirer: Philosophy of Culture*. Boston: Twayne Publishers, 1977.

Lipton, David R. *Ernst Cassirer: The Dilemma of a Liberal Intellectual in Germany 1914–33*. Toronto: University of Toronto Press, 1978.

Schilpp, Paul Arthur, ed. *The Philosophy of Ernst Cassirer*. New York: Tudor Publishing Co., 1958. 845–53.

Verene, Donald Phillip. "Ernst Cassirer." In *Encyclopedia of Religion*. Vol. 3. Edited by Mircea Eliade. New York: Macmillan and Co., 1987. 107–9.

Verkamp, Bernard J. *The Sense of Religious Wonder: Epistemological Variations*. Scranton, PA: University of Scranton Press, 2002. 40–41.

Chrysippus (c. 280–205 B.C.)

Chrysippus was born at Soli in Cilicia, but his father was from neighboring Tarsus, and it is possible that as a youth Chrysippus may have been exposed to the intellectual life of the latter city. His father apparently left him a considerable amount of wealth, but he was somehow deprived of it, and would remain poor throughout his life, relying on the patronage of friends and student fees to support himself. Stripped of his inheritance, he ventured on to Athens. There, after rejecting the skepticism of Academic philosophy on grounds that certain knowledge is attainable and being disillusioned by Aristo's crowd-pleasing, ethically-spineless and cynical rhetoric, he turned to Stoicism, possibly listening to a lecture or two by Zeno himself, before finally settling in for the remainder of his long life as a loyal, albeit argumentative, disciple of the latter's gentle, hardworking successor, Cleanthes.

Though he added little that was new in the thinking of that school, and seemed to have a penchant for playing the devil's advocate for its opponents, he generally used what Diogenes Laertius described as his godlike dialectical skills to great effect in defending Stoic views against Academic and Epicurean critics. "Give me doctrines," he once barked impatiently to his plodding master, "and I will find arguments to support them!" Eschewing an Aristotelian life of contemplative solitude, he worked incessantly, compiling over seven hundred books which, despite their solecistic style, were responsible, according to Diogenes, for rescuing Stoicism from extinction.

Details about his personal practice of religion are no more known with certainty than are other biographical aspects of his life. It is safe to assume, however, that he shared the view ascribed to the Stoics by Stobaeus, to the effect, namely, that "the wise man is the only true priest," the only one with sufficient piety to know how to serve the gods and to divine the signs they send to humans in dreams, in the flight of birds, or in sacrificial rituals. Chrysippus no doubt considered himself among the wisest of men, and he certainly believed in divination. It is also probable that, like other Stoics, he was loathe to break with the sacrificial rites and other traditions of popular religion. In any event, among the stories reported by Diogenes about his death is one that tells of his dying from the wine he drank several nights earlier at a sacrificial feast to which he had been invited by his pupils. Presumably,

such a feast would have been to some extent a religious event.

CHRYSIPPUS ON RELIGION. If there are no gods, nothing in the universe is more excellent than man. But any man who denies that there is anything greater than man is unspeakably arrogant. For man cannot create the things which we see in the universe. The being that actually creates such things transcends man. Since only God transcends man, God can be said to exist. Popular religions have come up with various imaginative names and myths to describe the deity, often representing it rather childishly in painting and sculpture as human in form. Being loving, prescient, and powerful, these gods are rightly thought to provide ominous signs in dreams and oracles that make it possible for priests (i.e., wise men) to divine the future. But many of these popular gods can be assimilated to inanimate things (e.g., Rhea to the earth or Poseidon to the sea) or to the immortal souls of heroic human beings. And, to be sure, the sun, the moon, the stars, or the cosmos as a whole can all be rightly called gods. But having a beginning and an end, all such gods will eventually perish. Only Zeus, conceived as the eternal Fire of Reason or the Cosmic Soul, is imperishable.

So conceived, God is the Lord and Cause of all that is good (antithetical evil caused by man merely subserving the perfection of the whole), providently sowing in Passive Matter the divine seeds of potential form and setting everything in a continuous, orderly motion (Fate). The Divine Fire keeps growing, absorbing all Matter into itself until, in the next cosmic conflagration, Reason becomes coincident with Itself before once again solidifying into another cosmos in which all that has already happened will occur again (the same individuals, the same experiences, etc.). In the meantime, as parts of the divine nature of the universe, humans should strive to live in accordance with their own rational nature and that of the universe, virtuously choosing to align their divine spirit (daimon) with Right Reason (the universal law of God's fateful will). Only the souls of the wise that have thereby risen above their passions will survive after death till the next conflagration.

Sources

Bevan, Edwyn. *Later Greek Religion*. London and Toronto: J.M. Dent and Sons, Ltd.; New York: E.P. Dutton and Co., 1827. 15–34.

Cicero, Marcus Tullius. *Brutus; On the Nature of the Gods; On Divination; On Duties*. Translated by Hubert M. Poteat. Chicago: The University of Chicago Press, 1950. See esp. 193; 240; 299; 302; 375; 453.

Copleston, Frederick, S.J. *A History of Philosophy*. Vol. 1, pt. 2. Garden City, NY: Doubleday and Company, Inc., 1962–77. 129–44.

Cotton, George E.L. "Chrysippus." In *A Dictionary of Greek and Roman Biography and Mythology*. Vol. 1. Edited by William Smith. New York: AMS Press, Inc., 1967. 700–1.

Diogenes Laertius. "Chrysippus." *Lives of Eminent Philosophers*. Vol. 2, no. 7. Translated by R.D. Hicks. Cambridge, MA: Harvard University Press, 1972. 287–319.

Gould, Josiah B. *The Philosophy of Chrysippus*. Leiden: E.J. Brill, 1970.

Long, A.A. Epictetus: *A Stoic and Socratic Guide to Life*. Oxford: Clarendon Press, 2002. See esp. 32; 163–66.

Saunders, Jason L. *Greek and Roman Philosophy after Aristotle*. New York: The Free Press; London: Collier-Macmillan Limited, 1966. 59–132.

Cicero, Marcus Tullius (106–43 B.C.)

Cicero was born into a conservative Roman family at a time when, even though traditional religious beliefs may have been weakened by an influx of Greek, Epicurean and Stoic philosophy, the majority of Rome's population was still of a pious, somewhat superstitious mindset. It is likely, therefore, notwithstanding Cicero's own reticence about his early boyhood, that as he was growing up he would have participated in his family's regular worship of the *Lar Familiaris* and other spirits of the field and pantry on the Calends, Nones, and Ides of every month. At the age of sixteen, on that year's feast day of Liber (the god of growth), he went through a special rite of passage to receive his *toga virilis*, and at

about the same time was committed by his father to the care of Q. Mucius Scaevola, the Chief Pontiff of the state religion who lived next door to the Vestal Virgins and among his many tasks had the responsibility of organizing the periodic religious sacrifices of animals and vegetables for the sake of appeasing Jupiter (Zeus) and other of the Roman gods.

Given the amount of time that Cicero spent with the Pontiff, he no doubt had ample opportunity to frequent the sacred temples, witness the sacrificial rites, and familiarize himself with the many religious festivals. How much of this traditional Roman religion he ever interiorized, however, is debatable. The fascination he soon developed thereafter with Greek philosophy may well have inclined him, as it had many of Rome's more educated citizens, to conclude that, apart from the useful purpose it serves in protecting the state by suppressing popular sedition, the traditional religion was of no vital concern to his own personal life. It is hard to say, for more often than not he would refrain from drawing any explicit assertions about his own religious beliefs or practices.

In many of the speeches he made during subsequent years of precarious political involvement he rejected the Epicurean notion of divine indifference in favor of a more Stoical view and pointed to the traditional belief of the Roman people in the sovereign providence of their gods as the major factor in Rome's domination of the world. In 53 B.C. he became a member of the college of augurs (whose priestly function it was to observe and interpret omens for guidance in public affairs), but in his book about divination expressed serious doubts about its authenticity. After the death of his daughter Tullia he speculated hopefully about the possibility of an afterlife, but came to no definite conclusion. The many letters he wrote before finally being executed by Marc Antony reveal next to nothing about his personal practice of religion as a mature adult.

CICERO ON RELIGION. No race or nation has ever been so wild or effete, nor any human so brutish, as not to have had some notion of the existence of the gods. Humans have a natural instinct to believe that there are gods. They are born with the notion that a benevolent, divine power is influencing their lives and relationships. Reflection upon the order of nature reinforces this innate belief in divine providence, for it is no more reasonable to assume that the radiant beauty of the universe has resulted from the blind, chance play of atoms, than to think that innumerable letters of the alphabet being tossed onto the ground might form themselves into an intelligible book. The deity can only be understood, therefore, as "intelligence unhampered, free, dissociated from mortal matter, perceiving all things, moving all things and itself with the property of continual motion."

Existence of the gods does not, however, automatically validate attempts to divine the future. Whatever political value it might once have had, divination has no foundation in reality, and like any other form of superstition must be clearly distinguished from true religion and annihilated. Care must be taken, however, lest in trying to wipe out superstition, religion be overthrown. For, as philosophy has trained us to think, it is both judicious and wise to adhere to the traditional religious rites and ceremonies by which our ancestors rendered to the divine Being the veneration and reverence it deserved, and on which account Rome has excelled over all other nations. Religion, however, must go hand in hand with morality. Reason (the most godlike human faculty) being the essential basis for communion between man and God, it is virtue, or right reason, that especially joins humans to God, inclining them to obey the eternal law written on all their hearts at birth by living with each other as brothers. Innately sensitive to the divine spark within them, peoples of all nations have wisely believed also that the human soul can endure death to experience everlasting happiness.

Sources

Cicero, Marcus Tullius. *The Basic Works of Cicero* (including the *Tusculan Disputations*, Book 1). New York: The Modern Library, 1951.

_____. *Brutus; On the Nature of the Gods; On Divination; On Duties*. Translated by Hubert M. Poteat. Chicago: The University of Chicago Press, 1950.

_____. *Selected Works*. Translated by Michael Grant. Baltimore, MD: Penguin USA, 1960.

_____. *Selected Works of Cicero* (including *On the Laws*, Book 1). New York: Walter J. Black for The Classics Club, 1948.

Barnes, Jonathan, and Miriam Griffin, eds. *Philosophia Togata I: Essays on Philosophy and Roman Society*. Oxford: Clarendon Press, 1997. See esp. 174–98.

Clark, A.C. "Cicero." *Encyclopædia Britannica*. Vol. 5. Chicago, London, and Toronto: Encyclopædia Britannica, Inc., William Benton Publisher, 1959, 2002, 2005. 692–98.

Copleston, Frederick, S.J. *A History of Philosophy*. Vol. 1, pt. 2. Garden City, NY: Doubleday and Company, Inc., 1962–77. 162–64.

Everitt, Anthony. *Cicero: The Life and Times of Rome's Greatest Politician*. New York: Random House, 2002.

Jones, William Thomas. *The Classical Mind*. New York: Harcourt, Brace and World, Inc., 1969. 333–37.

Lacey, W.K. *Cicero and the End of the Roman Republic*. London: Hodder and Stoughton, 1978.

MacKendrick, Paul. *The Philosophical Books of Cicero*. New York: St. Martin's Press, 1989.

McKeon, Richard. "Introduction." In Cicero, *Brutus; On the Nature of the Gods; On Divination; On Duties*. 1–65.

Rawson, Elizabeth. *Cicero: A Portrait*. London: Bristol Classical Press, 1998.

Cleanthes of Assos (331/0–232/1 B.C.)

Born in Assos in the Troad, Cleanthes is said by Diogenes Laertius to have originally been a pugilist. Apparently, it was on that account that he traveled to Athens with only a few drachmas in his purse. After meeting up with Crates and Zeno of Citium, however, he turned to the study of philosophy, working by night watering gardens to earn a living and spending most of the daylight hours engaged in philosophical debate. He remained a devoted disciple of Zeno for the next nineteen years, and although his classmates considered him slow and stupid (nicknaming him "the ass"), he would eventually succeed Zeno and for the rest of his long life direct the school of

Stoic thought Zeno had established in the "painted colonnade" of an Athenian temple.

Although little more is known for sure about the details of his life and only fragments of the fifty works he is said to have written survive, the best of the latter, his famous *Hymn to Zeus*, does give us an indication of the religious zeal with which he was devoted to the preservation of Zeno's philosophy, as well as some idea of his own personal faith and religious practice. For the *Hymn* is itself an exercise in worship, being not only a song of praise to the Eternal Reason by which the author of nature guides the universe but also a prayer for wisdom through deliverance from shameful ignorance, a creed expressing basic Stoic articles of faith, and a moralistic sermon, all wrapped into one beautiful piece of poetry. The poem exudes a religious sense of wonder, suggesting that Cleanthes had personally actualized what Zeno had claimed was every man's potential to experience the fiery presence of God in the world around him.

That he also practiced what he preached and was altogether indifferent to the experience of pleasure or pain is illustrated by the story Diogenes Laertius tells of Cleanthes' last days. When his physician told him one day that he could resume his usual diet after the medicine prescribed earlier had succeeded in curing his gum disease, the eighty-year-old philosopher declined to do so, and declaring that he had already gone too far down the road to turn back, continued fasting until finally dying from starvation. Such equanimity in the face of death, along with the virtuous manner in which he is said to have instructed his students, gave Chrysippus, the best of his students and his eventual successor as director of the school, good reason to hold him in high reverence.

CLEANTHES ON RELIGION. The birth and development of conceptions of deity in the human mind can be assigned to four different causes. First, the ability to divine the future has inclined humans to admit the existence of gods who provide omens of things to come. Second, countless blessings humans have enjoyed (good climate, fertile soil, etc.) have

shaped their conception of a provident God. The third factor is fear. Terror in the face of storms, earthquakes, comets and other ominous celestial phenomena have caused mortals to feel that there must be some divine being who dwells in the heavens above and rules over all things. The weightiest reason for belief in the existence of deity, however, has been contemplation of the regular and beautiful movements of the heavenly bodies, the mere sight of which is sufficient to prove that here is no handiwork of chance but of a divine, creative Intelligence.

The existence of God can also be demonstrated from the fact that if there is a difference in value between one nature and another, there must be some nature which is the best of all. Pitiable, evil-prone creature that he is, man hardly deserves such a title. The perfect and supreme Living Being, therefore, must be something better than man, a Being who possesses all virtues complete, immune from any kind of evil. Such a Being is God. Many are the names of this God: Sun, Fire, Aether, Mind, Spirit, Soul, Cosmos, Fate, Zeus, and so on. But all refer to the Active Principle that fashions particular things out of the passive substance of matter, even turning to a fair design the disorder caused by the reckless deeds of ignorant, sinful men.

As rational creatures, humans alone are godlike, ensouled, one and all, by the flame of Reason. Instead of seeking sensual delights and lawless gains, men and women alike ought, therefore, to cultivate lives of virtue. Aligning their own reason with the universal Law of Nature, they should forever be singing hymns of praise to the mighty works of Zeus, and prayerfully following Fate wherever it might lead them, in death and beyond, until the next universal conflagration.

Sources

Adam, James. *The Vitality of Platonism and Other Essays* (On *The Hymn of Cleanthes*). Cambridge: At the University Press, 1911. 113–89.

Bevan, Edwyn. *Later Greek Religion*. London and Toronto: J.M. Dent and Sons, Ltd.; New York:

E.P. Dutton and Co., 1827. 9–15. (Fragments and the *Hymn to Zeus* and *Prayer* of Cleanthes).

Cicero. *On the Nature of the Gods.* (Fragments)

Cotton, George E.L. "Cleanthes." In *A Dictionary of Greek and Roman Biography and Mythology.* Vol. 1. Edited by William Smith. New York: AMS Press, Inc., 1967. 779–80.

Diogenes Laertius. *Lives of Eminent Philosophers.* Vol. 2, no. 7. Translated by R.D. Hicks. Cambridge, MA: Harvard University Press, 1972. 272–85.

Saunders, Jason L. *Greek and Roman Philosophy after Aristotle.* New York: The Free Press; London: Collier-Macmillan Limited, 1966. 59–132 (Fragments), 149–50 (*Hymn to Zeus*).

Clifford, William Kingdon (1845–1879)

After graduating from King's College, London, Clifford went on to Trinity College, Cambridge, where he demonstrated exceptional interest and talent in mathematics and natural science. His oratory and argumentative skills won him election to Cambridge's notorious debating club, the so-called "Apostles." At the time — a time when the evangelical tradition prevailed at Cambridge — Clifford was reputed to have been an ardent High Churchman, or someone, in other words, who respected the ritual, doctrine, and authority of the Anglican Church. By hindsight this seems rather surprising in view of the fact that not long thereafter Clifford would claim that "there is one thing in the world more wicked than the desire to command, and that is the will to obey." According to his lifelong friend, Frederick Pollock, however, such an assertion could be reconciled with insistence upon the need to follow one's conscience that was central to the Catholic doctrine with which Clifford was apparently very familiar, and which, à la his reading of Thomas Aquinas, he was using to "maintain the Catholic position on most points with extreme ingenuity." He seemed to have had little taste, however, for the usual Protestant version of Natural Theology, and when, while reading the likes of Darwin and Spencer, difficulties in juxtaposing science and dogma proved increasingly insurmountable, he gradually abandoned the posi-

tion of quasi-scientific Catholicism as untenable, severed whatever attachment he had had to the High Church of England, and became openly hostile toward what he supposed was the obscurantism of all ecclesiastical institutions and their priestly ministers.

In 1866 he refused to sign (as was expected of scholars) the Church of England's Thirty-nine Articles, but not long thereafter also dismissed rumors of his pending conversion to Roman Catholicism on grounds that he had not yet taken leave of his senses. While respecting the Christian convictions of the young woman (Lucy) he married in 1873, he himself remained an agnostic. The shock of parting with his and others' old beliefs could be broken, he claimed, by the joy which the "sons of God shall have cause to shout" when their empirical analysis "strips from nature the gilding that we prized" and reveals a "new and ever more glorious picture." After dying of tuberculosis at the age of thirty-four, he was buried in Highgate cemetery, Middlesex. Moncure Conway, an old freethinking friend of his who had himself abandoned Methodism to head up an Institute for Advanced Religious Thought, arranged and presided over a memorial service.

CLIFFORD ON RELIGION. Whether traditional religion is defined as a body of doctrines, or as a cult with an influential, well-organized priesthood and a machinery of sacred things and places, or as a mixed body of moral and ceremonial precepts, or, finally, as morality touched by emotion, its value is highly questionable. In the first place, it is always and everywhere wrong for anyone to believe anything upon insufficient evidence. Even if such a belief turned out to be true or proved to be of little harm in terms of the actions it prompted, it would still do serious damage to Mankind by increasing the latter's credulity, undermining the scientific habit humans have developed of testing things and inquiring into them and increasing their reliance on authorities who, even though they are of good, honest character and the highest motivation (like Mohammed or the Buddha), have no way of knowing as human beings what they are talking about when they say either that God is one or that there is no God.

It is, of course, in the very nature of belief to go beyond experience, but we are justified in doing so only when there is evidence that what we do not know is like what we do know. Religious beliefs in a supernatural deity obviously lack any evidence of such uniformity of nature with the evolving universe we know, and to that extent it is wrong to hold them. Secondly, all the evidence suggests that the very structure of a sacerdotal religion has been and continues to be the greatest threat to the moral autonomy of Mankind. Finally, all the evidence also indicates that not only are the moral codes prescribed by traditional religion of a purely secular origin, but also that adherence to them would not decline were they stripped of the emotional consolation or pleasure religion has traditionally afforded such obedience. Indeed, with the fading away of belief in a superhuman deity, a yet nobler figure comes into view, that of Him who made all Gods and shall unmake them, namely Man, who alone generates and respects the voice of man's conscience.

Sources

Clifford, W.K. *The Ethics of Belief and Other Essays* (*The Ethics of Religion, The Influence upon Morality of a Decline in Religious Belief*, etc.). Amherst, NY: Prometheus, 1999.

_____. *Lectures and Essays*. Edited by Leslie Stephen and Frederick Pollock and introduced by F. Pollock. London: Macmillan and Co., 1879.

Chisholm, Monty. *Such Silver Currents: The Story of William and Lucy Clifford, 1845–1929*. Cambridge, UK: The Lutterworth Press, 2002.

Hollinger, David A. "James, Clifford, and the Scientific Conscience." In the *Cambridge Companion to William James*, edited by Ruth Anna Putnam. New York: Cambridge University Press, 1997. 69–83.

Lewis, Albert C. "Clifford, William Kingdon." *Oxford Dictionary of National Biography: From the earliest times to the year 2000*. Vol. 12. Edited by H.C.G. Matthew and Brian Harrison. In association with The British Academy. 2004. 121–24.

Madigan, Timothy J. "Ethics and Evidentialism: W.K. Clifford and 'The Ethics of Belief.'" *The Journal for the Critical Study of Religion, Ethics, and Society* 2.1 (Spring/Summer 1997): 9–18.

Pollock, Frederick. "Biographical Introduction." In Clifford, *Lectures and Essays*. 1–43.

Cohen, Hermann (1842–1918)

Born in Coswig/Anhalt, Germany, Cohen was the son of a cantor, the Jewish religious official responsible for singing the liturgy in the synagogue. The father was also a teacher in the small Jewish community's synagogue and saw to it that his son received a traditional Jewish upbringing and education during his childhood and youth, and then in 1857, apparently with the thought of preparing him for a career as a rabbi, enrolled him in the Rabbinical Seminary in Breslau. Four years later, while still in the seminary, Cohen began studying philosophy at the University of Breslau. His interest in Plato and Aristotle inclined him to forego the rabbinate in favor of a career in philosophy, and over the next twenty years he would devote himself almost exclusively to that discipline, achieving the doctoral degree from the University of Halle in 1865 and, after further study at the University of Berlin, becoming at Marburg University the first Jew ever to hold a professorship in Germany (thanks to a recommendation from the very Protestant Friedrich Lange).

He stayed there until 1912, initiating a neo–Kantian revival with a variety of publications on Kant and his own version of Idealism. The latter found expression in the three volumes of his *System of Philosophy* and attracted outstanding students like Ernst Cassirer from Germany and elsewhere. But already in 1880 he had returned (as he himself put it, in the Jewish religious sense of *teshubah* or conversion) to Judaic matters, writing a book-length response, *A Profession of Faith on the Jewish Question*, to an accusation by the historian Treitschke that German Jewish writers were antinational and anti–Christian. And the older he grew, the more fervently and extensively did he address specifically Jewish questions.

After retiring from the University of

Marburg in 1912, he and the wife he had married in 1878 (the daughter of Louis Lewandowsky, the renowned composer and director of music for the synagogue in Berlin) moved back to Berlin, where he did some lecturing at that city's liberal rabbinical seminary, published a work on the concept of religion in the system of philosophy, and worked on the book, *Religion of Reason: Out of the Sources of Judaism*, that would be published only after his death in 1918 and which he apparently had in mind initially to publish under the subtitle, "A Jewish Philosophy of Religion and a Jewish Ethics." According to his friends, he died with his faith in the provident, personal God proclaimed by the Jewish psalmist and prophets fully intact.

COHEN ON RELIGION. Without confidence in the eventual triumph of morality human existence is intolerable. But only the idea of God can support such confidence. It was helpful of Kant, therefore, to posit the existence of God as the guarantor of morality. His conclusions, like all philosophy, can be viewed as an integral part of the divine revelation that goes on through man's use of the reason with which he has been endowed by the Creator. The Judaic religion anticipated Kant's moral idea of God by referring to its one and only God as the Supreme Lawgiver and Archetype of right conduct. But it also went beyond ethics by presenting God as something more than an abstract postulate of morality, revealing Him instead as a personal and living God whom one might approach with prayerful adoration — the real, only, and unique Being, who has created nature, grounds its becoming, and correlates it to himself.

In contrast to the ethical preoccupation with mankind as a whole, the individual human was recognized as an I, who, fully aware of his own suffering and guilt, stands in direct and loving relation with God as his only source of solace and forgiveness. Although nothing was learned from such divine action about the actual being of God, it did reveal God's will regarding the holiness humans would have to show each other if the prophetic messianic ideal of a united mankind were ever to be

achieved. Genuine repentance for the sins causing poverty, war and social strife would have to be accompanied by love and justice toward all, especially the widow, the orphan, and the stranger. Or, even if one is as innocent as Job, it might mean being asked, as a member of a chosen people, to suffer for others. By drawing them nearer to God, such holiness becomes the immortality of all good people, extending their lives into eternity. While, therefore, it is natural to have a special love for one's own particular religion, every genuine religion ought to be loved as a manifestation of the everlasting divine spirit of mankind.

Sources

Cohen, Hermann. *Reason and Hope: Selections from the Jewish Writings of Hermann Cohen.* Translated by Eva Jospe. New York: W.W. Norton and Company, Inc., 1971.

_____. *Religion of Reason Out of the Sources of Judaism.* Translated and introduced by Simon Kaplan. Introduced also by Leo Strauss. New York: Frederick Ungar Publishing Co., 1972.

Ebbinghaus, Julius. "Cohen, Hermann." *Encyclopedia of Philosophy.* Vol. 2. Edited by Paul Edwards. New York: Macmillan and Co. and The Free Press, 1967. 125–28.

Kaplan, Simon. "Translator's Introduction." In Hermann Cohen, *Religion of Reason: Out of the Sources of Judaism.* New York: Frederick Ungar Publishing Co., 1972. xi–xxii.

Melber, Jehuda. *Hermann Cohen's Philosophy of Judaism.* New York: Jonathan David Publishers, 1968.

Moses, Stéphane, and Hartwig Wiedebach, eds. *Hermann Cohen's Philosophy of Religion.* Hildesheim, Zürich, New York: George Olms Verlag, 1997.

Schwarzschild, Steven S. "Cohen, Hermann." In *Encyclopedia of Religion.* Vol. 3. Edited by Mircea Eliade. New York: Macmillan and Co., 1987. 559–61.

Seeskin, Kenneth. *Searching for a Distant God: The Legacy of Maimonides.* New York and Oxford: Oxford University Press, 2000. 107–09; 124–28; 155–57.

Coleridge, Samuel Taylor (1772–1834)

Christened after his godfather, Coleridge was the son of the Reverend John Coleridge, a first-rate Christian and Ottery's "perfect parson" in the Church of England (by his son's later account). After some nine years of study at London's conservative and severe Under Grammar School of Christ's Hospital, Coleridge spent a year (1792) at Cambridge, another in the military, and over several more — while getting married, lecturing on religion and other matters, and trying to launch a career in poetry and journalism — concocted with his newfound friend, Robert Southey, "pan-socratic" plans for an ideal, brotherly community in America. Due to lack of funding and Southey's abrupt withdrawal, the scheme was dropped, and Coleridge, who at Cambridge had left the Church of England to join the Unitarians, began delivering sermons to their congregations and considered making a career of ministering to their spiritual needs.

An annuity in 1798 from Josiah Wedgwood and his brother allowed him instead to devote himself entirely to his love for poetry, philosophy, and theology. Publication of "The Ancient Mariner," "Kubla Khan" and other major poems (some in collaboration with William Wordsworth) soon followed, and despite ongoing marital/extramarital problems and the development of an addiction to opium, Coleridge would continue throughout the rest of his turbulent life producing poetic fragments and writing on a variety of issues that included, more often than not, religion. Abandoning his earlier Unitarianism and the pantheistic inclinations inspired by his reading of Spinoza and Schelling and impressed on a trip to Germany by Kant's philosophy and German higher criticism of the Bible, he returned to the Church of England, sincerely professing his reverence for its doctrine and liturgy and in many of his subsequent writings (e.g., *Aids to Reflection, On the Constitution of the Church and State, Confessions of an Inquiring Spirit, Lay Sermon*) reflecting, along lines of the traditional Anglican Trinitarian theology, on the nature of religious faith and language, the relation of faith and reason, the role of symbol in religious experience, the nature of the church, and Christian duties to the poor. Before dying in 1834, the still quite lucid Coleridge repeated on his deathbed the Trinitarian formula that had been used to baptize him as a child.

COLERIDGE ON RELIGION. Reverence of the Invisible, substantiated by the feeling of love, is the essence and proper definition of religion. Unlike the Understanding (sense knowledge), Reason, as the divine intelligence working within man, can arrive, without the aid of any special revelation, at some awareness of this Invisible Being as an impersonal divine force immanent in Nature, but also, contrary to atheistic Pantheism, transcendent to it. When rendered by the Imagination into symbolic and mythical images of sense, such knowledge, along with other eternal verities revealed by Reason alone (the freedom of the will, the immortality of the soul), constitutes the essence of that religion which might have been natural to man had Adam retained his perfection. But given the mysterious corruption of the human will (as represented but not caused by Adam), the actual existence of the one God, who as Absolute Will and Personeity is the cause of its own being and internal triune relations (Unity and Distinction), cannot be known without special revelation.

Attempts to prove rationally the existence of God do more harm than good; like the mechanistic, absentee God of lifeless Deism, the deity whose existence is demonstrated does not at all correspond to the biblical God of Love man needs as a moral and responsible being. More than mere intellectual assent, faith is an act of practical reason by which, with divine grace, one freely chooses to align the whole of one's moral being to the Absolute Will. Without such "religation" there is no religion. The mystical linking of one's own "I am" with the eternal self-affirmation of God simultaneously expresses one's faith in immortality. While (Lutheran/Anglican) Christianity is the superior religion (rooted as it is in Judaic monotheism, from which the Persians, Hindus, and Chinese have learned nothing), all religions should be tolerated for the sake of expediency. But not every hideous doctrine asserted in the name of religion has a right to toleration. Every religion must submit to the Truth.

Sources

Coleridge, Samuel Taylor. *Coleridge's Writings.* Vol. 4: *On Religion and Psychology.* Edited by John Beer. Houndmills, UK: Palgrave Press, 2002.

_____. *The Collected Works of Samuel Taylor Coleridge.* Edited by Kathleen Coburn and Bart Winer. 16 vols. Bollinger Series 75. Princeton: Princeton University Press, 1969.

_____. *Confessions of an Inquiring Spirit.* Edited by H. St J. Hart. Stanford, CA: Stanford University Press, 1957.

_____. *Notebooks of Samuel Taylor Coleridge.* Edited by Kathleen Coburn. 4 vols. Bollinger Series 50. Princeton: Princeton University Press, 1957.

Barth, J. Robert, S.J. *Coleridge and Christian Doctrine.* Cambridge, MA: Harvard University Press, 1969.

_____. "Coleridge, Samuel Taylor." In *Encyclopedia of Religion.* Vol. 3. Edited by Mircea Eliade. New York: Macmillan and Co., 1987. 561–62.

Boulger, J.D. *Coleridge as Religious Thinker.* New Haven: Yale University Press, 1961.

Gillman, James. *The Life of Samuel Taylor Coleridge.* London: William Pickering, 1838.

Holmes, Richard. *Coleridge: Darker Reflections, 1804–1834.* New York: Pantheon Books, 1998.

_____. *Coleridge: Early Visions.* New York: Viking Penguin, 1990.

Jasper, David. *Coleridge as Poet and Religious Thinker.* London: Macmillan Press, Ltd., 1985.

McFarland, Thomas. *Coleridge and the Pantheist Tradition.* Oxford: Clarendon Press, 1969.

Perkins, Mary Ann. "Religious Thinker." In *The Cambridge Companion to Coleridge.* Cambridge: Cambridge University Press, 2002. 187–99.

Perry, Seamus. *Samuel Taylor Coleridge.* New York: Oxford University Press, 2003.

Pym, David. *The Religious Thought of Samuel Taylor Coleridge.* New York: Harper and Row Publishers, Inc., 1978.

Robertson, John Mackinnon. "Coleridge, Samuel Taylor." *Encyclopædia Britannica.* Vol. 6. Chicago, London, and Toronto: Encyclopædia Britannica, Inc., William Benton Publisher, 1959, 2002, 2005. 9–11.

Wendling, Ronald C. *Coleridge's Progress to Christianity.* Lewisburg: Bucknell University Press; London: Associated University Presses, 1995.

Comte, Auguste (1798–1857)

Comte was the son of parents who were deeply committed to their Roman Catholic faith at a postrevolutionary time when, because of its close links to the monarchy, Catholicism was under attack for supposedly being antipatriotic. The baptism, during which he was given the additional names of the Virgin Mary (Marie) and several saints (Isodore and Francis Xavier), had to be performed in relative secrecy, since the churches of Montpellier had been closed by the revolutionary government. At the lycée he began attending at the age of nine, Comte proved to be an outstanding student, but was constantly rebelling against authority, including that of religion. As he would later remind his father, he had on his own accord already stopped going to church at the age of thirteen, and, consistent with the freethinking, irreligious environment of the school, had ceased to believe in God. He claimed that attempts by Napoleon to introduce more Catholic practices into the school would only serve to make the new generation of students more stupid than his own.

During a year of home-schooling he was profoundly influenced by his teacher, Daniel Encontre, a leading Protestant thinker who had in mind to reorganize the church and reconcile religion with science by playing up its universal dimensions. And he would subsequently ridicule the Catholic marriage ceremony his mother arranged to have him go through during a period of severe mental disbalance that included an attempted suicide. But he never cut himself off completely from his Catholic roots, and in fact would later "congratulate [him]self on being born in Catholicism" because it had kept him from succumbing to what he always considered the dangers inherent in Protestantism and Deism.

When, therefore, he ultimately came up with his own version of a universal religion along secular, humanistic lines (the so-called Religion of Humanity), its external form was very similar to that of the Catholic Church, what with its *Catechisme* of Positivist doctrines, its calendrical commemoration of Positivist saints and his deceased, "divine" wife (Clotilde), its rites of passage, and its setting up of himself as an authoritarian spiritual leader. His ideal became, as Thomas Huxley once noted, "Catholic organization without Catholic doctrine, or Catholicism minus Christianity."

COMTE ON RELIGION. Human intelligence has developed historically through three stages: the Theological, or fictitious; the Metaphysical, or abstract; and the Scientific, or positive. In the Theological stage, the human mind, seeking Absolute knowledge (essences and causes of all effects), supposes that all phenomena are created by the immediate action of supernatural beings. This method of philosophizing began with fetishism, developed into polytheism as the spirits animating all entities evolved into the many gods of nature, and then climaxed in monotheism when it substituted the providential action of a single Being for the varied operations of the numerous divinities.

While each of these religious forms contributed something to the progress of humanity in one or another historical environment, they were all lacking a foundation in the facts. To that extent, the affections they expressed or the stories they told had no real or intelligible sense, and along with an equally unintelligible metaphysics, must now — if the current threat of anarchy is to be met — be replaced by the positive religion of Humanity. Instead of worshiping some remote supernatural being for whose existence or providence science provides no evidence, the object of religious veneration should be Humanity itself, the *Grand-Être,* whose supreme being is in a constant state of becoming by way of inspiring, morally directing, and incarnating the past, present, and future instinctively altruistic activity of its individual members.

With love (best represented by maternal affection) as its universal principle, such a relative religion will provide a new, dynamic intellectual orientation to family life, language, and other static elements of society, regulating and unifying individuals in a way not unlike that of the priestly, papal, and sacramental Catholic community of the Middle Ages. After transitory, objective lives of service, saintly humans will be incorporated into the body of Humanity and live forever as motivating forces in the collective memory of all mankind.

Sources

Comte, Auguste. *The Catechism of Positive Religion.* Translated by Richard Congreve. London: John Chapman, 1858.
_____. *The Positive Philosophy.* Freely translated and condensed by Marriet Martineau. New York: Calvin Blanchard, 1855.
_____. *System of Positive Polity.* 4 vols. Translated by J. H. Bridges, Frederic Harrison, et al. London: Longmans, Green, and Co., 1875–77.
Copleston, Frederick, S.J. *A History of Philosophy.* Vol. 9, pt. 1. Garden City, NY: Doubleday and Company, Inc., 1962–77. 74–77; 93–117.
Pickering, Mary. *Auguste Comte: An Intellectual Biography.* 2 vols. Cambridge: Cambridge University Press, 1993.
Standley, Arline Reilein. *Auguste Comte.* Boston: Twayne Publishers, 1981.
Stumpf, Samuel Enoch. *Socrates to Sartre. A History of Philosophy.* New York: McGraw-Hill Book Company, 1982. 326–34.
Wernick, Andrew. *Auguste Comte and the Religion of Humanity: The Post-Theistic Program of French Social Theory.* Cambridge: Cambridge University Press, 2001.

Condorcet, Antoine-Nicholas de (1743–1794)

His military father having died when Antoine was only three, Condorcet was raised in the Catholic faith by an especially devout and overly protective mother. While receiving his earliest formal education from the Jesuits in Reims and at the Collège de Navarre in Paris he showed exceptional talent in the study of mathematics. His work in this area resulted in his induction into the Academy of Sciences in 1769. At about the same time he had occasion to accompany D'Alembert on a pilgrimage of sorts to Verney for the sake of visiting Voltaire. As evidenced by his subsequent biography of Voltaire and participation in preparation of the *Encyclopédie,* the encounter deeply impressed the twenty-six-year-old thinker and no doubt reinforced his incipient hostility toward what he had come to think of as the superstitious beliefs and practices of "revealed religions."

But in contrast to Voltaire's defense of a tolerant union of church and state conducive to social order, Condorcet insisted that as soon as public opinion would allow for it, the state should become totally secular. As an enthusiastic (more Girondist than Jacobin) supporter of the Revolution, he worked for reform of the educational system by calling for the prohibition of religious instruction in the public schools, pushed for civil marriage and divorce, objected to state subsidizing of any faith, opposed monastic life as a form of slavery, defended confiscation of monastic lands (even while supporting pensions for the monks and nuns displaced), and championed complete religious freedom (as opposed to mere toleration).

Although he considered Protestantism, with its limited degree of free inquiry, slightly better than Roman Catholicism, he had little taste for either branch of Christianity, claiming that both were nothing more than a conglomeration of superstitious prejudices confounding and oppressing the masses. The only religion he found somewhat compatible with his own deistic views was that of Mohammedanism. Its dogmas, he said, were the most simple; its practices, the least absurd; its principles, the most tolerant; and its founder, a composite figure of political, poetic, and military talent. Given the hostility toward his own independent way of thinking, Condorcet eventually felt compelled to go into hiding. On the day following his capture and imprisonment, he was found to have died, either from exhaustion or by an act of suicide.

CONDORCET ON RELIGION. Religion originated when, already in the first stage of the progress of the human mind, there occurred a separation of the human race into a quasi-priestly class of charlatans and sorcerers who arrogantly held themselves above reason and a class of credulous dupes who humbly renounced their own reason and believed everything they were taught. Primitive man may have entertained a purely deistic religion of sorts, but if he did, it was soon thereafter converted into a vile mass of absurd superstitions. There developed a vast, duplicitous system of hypocrisy whose supposed mysteries were known in their entirety only to a few adepts.

When, in ancient Greek times, philosophers encouraged people to think for themselves or to live lives of natural virtue, they were accused by the priests of impiety toward the gods, for fear that the masses would learn that the existence of the gods was a priestly invention, or that morality was altogether independent of religious dogma. The nationalistic religions of the Roman empire, with their incomprehensible rituals and mythologies, were eventually swallowed up, along with numerous Egyptian and Jewish sects, by the religion of Jesus.

Fearing the kind of confidence in one's own reason and human perfectibility that is the bane of all religious beliefs, Christianity signaled the complete decadence of philosophy and science, initiating a medieval dark age whose only achievements (except for contributions from the superior, less dogmatic, and more tolerant religion of Mohammed), were theological daydreaming, superstitious imposture, and religious intolerance. The invention of printing helped Protestantism champion freedom, but only for Christians. And so it was not until later centuries that the spirit of liberty and free inquiry really took hold for all mankind, challenging forevermore the ignorance of science off of which all religions and priestcraft have fed, and giving rise to the possibility of a complete separation of state and whatever little is left of religion in the future.

Sources

Condorcet, Antoine-Nicolas de. *Sketch for a Historical Picture of the Progress of the Human Mind.* Translated by June Barrclough. London: Weidenfeld and Nicolson, 1955.

Acton, Harry Burrows. "Condorcet, Marie Jean Antoine Nicolas Caritat." *Encyclopædia Britannica.* Vol. 6. Chicago, London, and Toronto: Encyclopædia Britannica, Inc., William Benton Publisher, 1959, 2002, 2005. 224–25.

Copleston, Frederick, S.J. *A History of Philosophy.* Vol. 6, pt. 1. Garden City, NY: Doubleday and Company, Inc., 1962–77. 195–97.

Morley, John Viscount. *Biographical Studies.* London: Macmillan and Co., Limited, 1923. 93–163.

Schapiro, J. Salwyn. *Condorcet and the Rise of Liberalism*. New York: Octagon Books, Inc., 1963. See esp. 178–86.

Coomaraswamy, Ananda Kentish (1877–1947)

Coomaraswamy's family had religious connections with a Hindu temple in the north India city of Allahabad alongside the banks of the Ganges River, but had relocated for several generations in Northern Ceylon (Sri Lanka). As members of the Velella caste, they situated themselves socially somewhere between the priestly Brahmins and the warrior class of Kshatriyas. The father, Sir Mutu, who was the first Hindu admitted to the English bar, became a member of the British parliament, and married Lady Elizabeth Bibi, before finally returning to Ceylon and fathering Ananda. When Sir Mutu died shortly thereafter, the mother brought the three-year-old Coomaraswamy back to England. She soon became involved in various spiritualistic practices that were then in vogue. Her religious idiosyncrasies had little affect on her son, however, since it was the custom of upperclass English families at the time not to exert much influence on the upbringing of their children.

She sent him off to a private boarding school (Wycliff College) while he was still in his early teens. There, in pursuit of a secondary education, he had the option of studying religion, but showed a special interest in mastering a number of classical and modern languages and cultivating his understanding of geology. After graduating with a science degree from London University, he returned to Ceylon at the age of twenty-two and within a few years became director of a Mineralogical Survey being conducted on that island. His reports and discovery of several new minerals contributed a few years later to his reception of a Doctorate in Science from London University. The travel involved exposed him also to what he perceived to be the negative impact of western education and industrialism on his native culture, and he would spend much of his time and energy in future years trying to revive an appreciation of Oriental painting and culture.

For such work in India he received the *jajnopavite* or "sacred thread" that symbolized his formal affiliation with the Hindu tradition. After returning to England and being exiled for refusing to join the British Army during World War I, he moved to America and accepted a position at the Boston Museum of Fine Arts. The multiple books he would write in subsequent years about the universal values underlying various religious and artistic traditions only served to make him a better Hindu. Plans to return to India to become a *sannyasin* were cut short by his death. *Shraddha* ceremonies accompanied the return of his ashes to both India and Ceylon.

COOMARASWAMY ON RELIGION. In view of the fact that God is known only according to the mode of the knower, it is inevitable that there are many religions with a variety of religious beliefs that divide humans against each other. But only the most profound ignorance and despair could have given rise to the dictum that East and West shall never meet. For underlying all the religions is a common metaphysical basis, a purely intellectual wisdom that remains one and the same for all humans at all times. Underlying the respective religious expressions about the duality of good and evil, for example, is the common metaphysical conviction that evil is a mere privation. Or underlying the various religious views about how the human soul is immortal is the common metaphysical notion that to be immortal is to enjoy a liberated consciousness, or, in other words, a converted consciousness that has escaped time and is buried forever in the eternal present of the Godhead through a total and uncompromising denial of self.

It is the goal of the comparative study of religion, therefore, to show that diverse cultures represent dialects of a common spiritual and intellectual language, and that, as such, they are fundamentally related to one another. But this should not be taken to mean, as the theosophists seem to have in mind, that an eclectic version of some new religion can be fashioned out of all existing religions. Such eclecticism would only result in confusion and caricature. What it does suggest is that instead of claiming that their own religion is absolutely the best, adherents of one or another religion should only assert that it is the best for them. Instead of trying to convert other people to one's own religious views, therefore, one should help them discover through a deeper appreciation of their own beliefs what they have in common with others. On the assumption that the various dogmatic formulations setting religions apart are no more than paraphrases of the basic metaphysical principles they all share, they can agree to disagree.

Sources

Coomaraswamy, Ananda K. *The Dance of Shiva: Fourteen Indian Essays*. New York: The Noonday Press, 1957.

_____. *The Essential Ananda K. Coomaraswamy*. Edited by Rama P. Coomaraswamy. Bloomington, IN: World Wisdom, Inc., 2004. See esp. 67–96.

_____. *Hinduism and Buddhism*. New Delhi: Munshiram Manoharlal Publishers, Pvt., Ltd., 1996.

_____. *Time and Eternity*. Ascona, Switzerland: Artibus Asiae Publishers, 1947.

_____. *What is Civilization? And Other Essays*. Delhi, Bombay, Calcutta, Madras: Oxford University Press, 1989. See esp. 13–41.

Coomaraswamy, L. "Coomaraswamy, Ananda Kentish." *New Catholic Encyclopedia*. Vol. 4. Edited by W.J. McDonald. New York: McGraw-Hill, 1967. 296–97.

Pontynen, Arthur. "Ananda Kentish Coomaraswamy." In *World Philosophers and Their Works*. Vol. 1. Edited by John K. Roth. Pasadena, CA, and Hackensack, NJ: Salem Press, Inc., 2000. 404–10.

Sastri, P.S. *Ananda K. Coomaraswamy*. New Delhi: Arnold-Heinemann Publishers, 1974. See esp. 43–55.

Croce, Benedetto (1866–1952)

Croce was born in Pescasseroli, a remote mountain village in the Abruzzi region of southern Italy. Being rigorously Catholic, the parents sent Croce at the age of nine to a boarding school in Naples run by Catholic priests for the sake of providing children of the nobility and gentry with a moral and religious education. Croce became a fervent believer. But four years later, while attending secondary school and pursuing further the passion for literature and art that his mother had instilled in him as a child, he experienced a religious crisis. By his own account, it was not so much that he doubted some of the doctrinal claims being made by the priest instructing him in the philosophy of religion, as it was the inability to bring himself, despite repeated resolutions, to love a God whose actions traditional mythology had made to seem so capricious and arbitrary.

He soon lost his interest, however, in whether he was a believer or not. By force of habit and conformity, he continued for a while to engage in some religious practices, but eventually dropped them also, and one day came to see that he was, in fact, "altogether quit of religious beliefs." Subsequent schooling at the Liceo Genovese in Naples and that city's university pricked his interest in De Santis' works on literary criticism and the lectures of an ex-priest uncle (Bertrando Spaventa) on neo–Hegelian philosophy, but he had yet to find a new vision to compensate for the loss of his religious faith. The depression he was feeling was further exacerbated when, after losing both his parents and a sister during an earthquake (in whose debris he was himself buried for twelve hours), he was sent at the age of seventeen to live with another uncle (Silvio Spaventa) in Rome. Cut off from the friends of his youth, and alienated by the pessimistic political atmosphere in the Spaventa household, he would probably have committed suicide during the next three years had he not found some minimal consolation in his study of philosophy at the University of Rome.

Finally taking advantage of his rich inheritance, he returned in 1886 to Naples and, without ever acquiring a university degree or position, devoted the rest of his life to scholarship, founding the review *La Critica* and writing in its pages and elsewhere on history, art, economics, ethics, politics and religion.

Although he was highly critical of the Catholic Church's defensive reaction against modern thought, and had some of his own writings placed on the Church's Index of Forbidden Books, he was still claiming to the end that his "philosophy of the Spirit" was in no sense outside the limits of Christianity, but by demythologizing it was instead helping it grow anew.

CROCE ON RELIGION. Humans have a nostalgia for transcendence. But there is nothing mysterious or transcendent about reality. Religion of old may have been more than a mere exercise in superstition, and Christianity in particular may have played a revolutionary role in moving human consciousness beyond a conception of the deity as an undifferentiated unity to one of a more personal God with whom humans might engage. But all the subsequent mythological and metaphysical talk about the existence or nature of the deity is no longer relevant since modern philosophy has shown that the word "God" refers simply to man's own nonascetical spirit of self-overcoming and has no external point of reference to any Supreme Being or Nature.

But how are individuals to cope in a demythologized world that is without a personal God and transcendent values? A positivistic approach to science, with its exclusive, superficial reliance upon reason and empirical observation, is certainly not the answer. What is needed instead is a "new religion of liberty and history" that cultivates a faith in the coherence of history as the ultimate reality toward which humans might freely aspire. With such faith individuals will come to understand what possibilities for effective action their own place in time leaves them, and resign themselves to acting as best they can within the limitations of their specialized vocations. In the process they will find salvation or eternal life through a sense of personal wholeness, not because they have embodied all possibilities of reality here and now or merited everlasting bliss for their souls in some afterlife, but because what they have produced in their respective fields of endeavor will contribute to the ever-growing totality of human history. If, therefore, there is

anything at all that is mysterious and worthy of reverence, it is only the future of human history — that which has not yet happened, but which will become real through human action within this world.

Sources

Croce, Benedetto. *The Conduct of Life*. Translated by Arthur Livingston. New York: Harcourt, Brace, 1924.

_____. *History as the Story of Liberty*. Translated by Sylvia Sprigge. New York: W.W. Norton, 1941.

_____. *History of Europe in the Nineteenth Century*. Translated by Henry Furst. New York: Harcourt, Brace and World, Harbinger Books, 1963.

_____. *My Philosophy, and Other Essays on the Moral and Political Problems of Our Time*. Selected by R. Klibansky. Translated by E.F. Carritt. London: George Allen and Unwin, 1949. (Includes essays from *Filosofia e storiografia*).

_____. *Philosophy, Poetry, History: An Anthology of Essays*. Translated and introduced by Cecil Sprigge. London: Oxford University Press, 1966.

Carr, Herbert Wildon. *The Philosophy of Benedetto Croce*. London: Macmillan and Co., Limited, 1927. See esp. 173–88.

Casale, Giuseppe. *Benedetto Croce between Naples and Europe*. New York: Peter Lang, 1994.

Moss, M.E. *Benedetto Croce Reconsidered*. Hanover and London: University Press of New England, 1987.

Roberts, David D. *Benedetto Croce and the Uses of Historicism*. Berkeley, Los Angeles, and London: University of California, 1987. See esp. 168–209.

Sprigge, Cecil. *Benedetto Croce: Man and Thinker*. New Haven: Yale University Press, 1952. See esp. 34–47.

Daly, Mary (1929–)

Born into an Irish-Catholic family in Schenectady, New York, Daly received her elementary, secondary, and undergraduate education at Catholic schools. With a few exceptions, Daly found the nuns and priests teaching her less than inspiring, and the atmosphere of these schools extremely oppressive of women. The desire to study Catholic philosophy, which she had felt already during her high school years, received little impetus from the "incompetent" priests who taught philosophy at the college and seemed openly contemptuous of women's intellects. Several years of study at the Catholic University of America for an M.A. in English, and a few more at St. Mary's College (Notre Dame) in successful pursuit of a Ph.D. in religion, proved somewhat better, and through exposure to the writings of Thomas Aquinas, helped cultivate a "philosophical *habitus*." But when, after a short stint of teaching theology and philosophy at Cardinal Cushing College in Boston, she applied to Catholic University for the sake of pursuing a "better" doctorate in theology, she was ignored, and had to look abroad.

She was admitted to the University of Fribourg (Switzerland), where after six wonderful years of study, teaching, and travel, she achieved doctorates in both theology and philosophy, writing her dissertation in the latter field on Jacques Maritain's ideas about the "Natural Knowledge of God." An unofficial visit to Rome during the Second Vatican Council and experiencing an exhilarating sense of hope despite all the "cardinalate pomposity" and patriarchal posturing accelerated her work on the book a British publisher had earlier invited her to write on women and the church. Its eventual publication (entitled: *The Church and the Second Sex*) triggered a long battle with the Jesuit-run Boston College where she had been employed to teach theology upon her return from Europe.

Threats of termination and denial of promotion and tenure met with nationwide protests in her support. But subsequent publications (e.g., *Beyond God the Father* and *Pure Lust*) and lectures at various universities (not to mention her openly Lesbian admissions) hardened the opposition of academic and ecclesiastical administrators and inclined her to take an indefinite leave of absence from formal teaching, to abandon all hope of purging the institutional church of its "degrading and vampiric" treatment of women, and to devote her time and energy to spinning a "postchristian feminist" web of memories and prophecies.

DALY ON RELIGION. Since all being is derived from participation in ultimate reality, the ongoing struggle of women toward self-transcendence must also involve the pursuit of ultimate transcendence. Toward that end, the patriarchal idolization of God as the Father who explains everything, dictates all morality, and judges everyone in the end, will have to be destroyed. A demonic front for the projection of male superiority, it obstructs not only women, but all humans, from realizing their potential as images of a God whom they perceive from the shock of their own nonbeing and self-affirmation — not as a mere Noun that passively receives the contents of the lost self but as dynamic Being, an intransitive Verb of Verbs, so to speak, that eternally confronts nonbeing by recreating Itself and all things ever anew.

To live, move and have their own being in a God so perceived, women and others will also have to reinterpret the myth of the fall of Adam and Eve. In its original, patriarchal context this story was used to justify a sexual caste system, stereotyping women as the source of evil. It should be read rather as a veiled prophecy of the fall of liberated women into a new kind of adulthood. There is also a need to move beyond Christolatry, with its masculine symbolism for the divine incarnation, toward an increased awareness of the power of Being in all persons. Myths about Mary, the Virgin Mother of God, that revive an earlier belief in the Great Goddess, might actually help in that regard. By emphasizing Mary's freedom from male domination they obliquely point to the Second Coming of women and the New Being of the Antichrist. In the meantime, women will need to break the submissive silence imposed upon them by traditional morality, join together in an antichurchly Cosmic Covenant, and work courageously toward transforming a culture of rapism into one of reciprocity between the Earth, all her creatures, and the Eternal Thou, who, as the Final Cause, causes not by conflict but by the attraction of Being personal.

Sources

Daly, Mary. *Beyond God the Father: Toward a Philosophy of Women's Liberation.* Boston: Beacon Press, 1973.

_____. *The Church and the Second Sex.* Boston: Beacon Press, 1985.

_____. "God is a Verb." *Ms.* (December 1974): 58–62; 96–98.

_____. *Outercourse: The Be-Dazzling Voyage.* San Francisco: HarperCollins Publishers, 1992.

_____. "Radical Feminism, Radical Religion." In *Women and Religion.* Edited by Elizabeth Clark and Herbert Richardson. New York: Harper and Row, 1977. 259–71.

Moore, Brooke Noel, and Kenneth Bruder. Philosophy: *The Power of Ideas.* 5th ed. Boston: McGraw Hill, 2001. 372–75.

Derrida, Jacques (1930–2004)

Born in Algeria, the son of Sephardic Jewish parents who, notwithstanding assimilation to a secularized, French-dominated culture, observed Jewish tradition, Derrida had frequent occasion while growing up to observe Jewish ceremonies and to experience the anti–Semitism unleashed in Algeria by the Vichy regime in the early 1940s. After stripping the Algerian Jews of their French citizenship, the Nazi sympathizers next moved to reduce the percentage of Jews admitted to educational institutions, and Derrida himself, at the tender age of twelve, was expelled from the secondary school in which his parents had enrolled him. The bigotry carried over into Algeria's postwar racial laws, scarring his soul still more, and along with the family's eventual move to France, spawning a lifelong ambivalent relation to identity.

While pursuing a higher education (before and after five years of military service), he developed an interest in French Existentialism and closely studied what phenomenological and structuralist thinkers were saying about a philosophy of language. During subsequent years of teaching at the Sorbonne and the École Normale Supérieure, however, he soon became disillusioned with what he perceived to be the "logocentrism" or lust for absolute meaning of traditional schools of thought and launched against it a program of deconstruction. Along the way he became increasingly ambivalent about his own Jewish and religious identity. When asked by his mother whether he believed in God, he replied that if he did believe in God it was only in a secret God who could not be revealed or named, implying, as he would later state explicitly, that he would "rightly pass for an atheist" in the sense of rejecting all idolatrous, ontotheological attempts to conceive of God as existing, absolute being. Such a radical atheism, he added, is essential to any authentic belief in God. So, he would not confess to being either an atheist or a believer in any traditional sense of those terms. So too with his Jewish identity.

Although he would rebel against exterior Judaism (its public prayers, ritual, and signs of heteronomy, like circumcision) and become "a kind of Marrano of French Catholic culture" or in a more positive sense, a Christian Protestant, he would insist upon still being an interior Jew, albeit perhaps, "like Jesus, the last Jew" — typical Derridean statements that invite conflicting interpretations, but which seem to suggest that the dialectical negation of Judaism by Christianity has resulted, at least in his own consciousness, in the sublation of both onto a higher level of synthesis and the need for constant dialogue.

DERRIDA ON RELIGION. If, as Saussure pointed out, the signifier (audio-image/word) and the signified (idea/concept) of any sign (mark/trace) are entirely relative through their negative relation to other entities within their own or other linguistic systems, no meaning (truth or disclosure of Being) is ever fully present, but is infinitely deferred. There is always a non-coincidence (a *différance*) of Being and meaning. In this coded play of differences is the space (*khôra*) whence originates the construction and deconstruction of all inscriptions (texts), including those of religion. Not only is *différance* the condition for thinking God, it is also that which calls into question all talk about, or naming of, God, deconstructing the beliefs, dogmas, and institutions of Judaism, Christianity, Islam, and other religions by challenging especially the metaphysics of presence underlying both ontotheology (with its rationalistic conception of God in terms of Absolute Being) and negative theology (with its silent, but still hyper-essentialistic appropriation of the eminent Godhead).

In the process, deconstruction becomes itself something like a religion without a religion. Without embracing the determinate content of any specific religion, and to that extent remaining quasi-atheistic, it adopts many religious structures, like faith, messianicity, the other, the gift, justice, hospitality, and so on, all of which, in one way or the other, have to do with the pursuit of that which (like God, for example) is wholly other, unnameable, and impossible. Whether these structures, being universal in nature, are the ground of religion, or come to light only through religion, is hard to say. But be that as it may, when applied to religion itself they work to its advantage from within by challenging it to constantly reread its ancient texts in ever new ways, so as to avoid conceiving of faith, the other, justice, and so on in terms of any determinate set of beliefs, historical figures (e.g., Messiahs), or legal systems.

Sources

Derrida, Jacques. "Circumfession: Fifty-nine Periods and Peri-phrases." In Geoffrey Bennington and Jacques Derrida, *Jacques Derrida*. Chicago: The University of Chicago Press, 1993.

_____. "Faith and Knowledge: the Two Sources of 'Religion' at the Limits of Reason Alone." In Jacques Derrida and Gianni Vattimo. *Religion*. Stanford, CA: Stanford University Press, 1996. 1–78.

_____. "How to Avoid Speaking." In Howard Coward and Toby Foshay, eds., *Derrida and Negative Theology*. Albany: SUNY Press, 1992. 73–142.

_____. "Khôra." In Thomas Dutoit, ed., *On the Name*. Stanford, CA: Stanford University Press, 1995.

_____. *Memoirs of the Blind: The Self-Portrait and Other Ruins*. Translated by Pascale-Anne Brault and Michael Nooas. Chicago: Chicago University Press, 1993.

_____. *Of Grammatology*. Translated by Gayatri Spivak. Baltimore: Johns Hopkins University Press, 1974.

Caputo, John D. *Deconstruction in a Nutshell: A Con-versation with Jacques Derrida*. New York: Fordham University Press, 1997.

_____. *The Prayers and Tears of Jacques Derrida: Religion without Religion*. Bloomington and Indianapolis: Indiana University Press, 1997.

_____, and Michael J. Scanlon, eds., *God, the Gift, and Postmodernism*. Bloomington and Indianapolis: Indiana University Press, 1999.

Gasché, Rodolphe. *Inventions of Difference: On Jacques Derrida*. Cambridge, MA: Harvard University Press, 1994.

Hart, Kevin. "Jacques Derrida (b.1930): Introduction." In Graham Ward, ed., *The Postmodern God*. Oxford: Blackwell Publishers, 1997. 159–67.

Ofrat, Gideon. *The Jewish Derrida*. Translated from the Hebrew by Peretz Kidron. Syracuse, NY: Syracuse University Press, 2001.

Sherwood, Yvonne, and Kevin Hart. *Derrida and Religion: Other Testaments*. New York and London: Routledge, 2005.

Descartes, Rene (1596–1650)

His family's normal parish church of Notre Dame having been abandoned to the Protestants, Descartes was baptized into the Catholic faith at La Haye's Saint-Georges Church. At the age of eleven he was sent by his father to the Jesuit-run College of La Flèche. His eight years there were capped by formal courses in philosophy and possibly some self-study of theological texts. Despite his later criticism of some of the pedagogical methodologies then in use and his disillusionment with the lack of clarity and certainty in almost every field except mathematics, he held his Jesuit instructors, and especially Father Dinet, in high regard.

While reflecting a few years later (during a stint of military service in Bavaria) on how to find a better foundation for philosophy, he experienced the three dreams which left him with the conviction that his vocation was to seek the truth by reason. However the dreams might be interpreted, they in fact began on a note of enthusiasm and ended with Descartes vowing to make a pilgrimage to Loreto, Italy, where angels were believed to have brought the original House of the Blessed Virgin. It was symbolic of his lifelong fidelity, notwithstanding his rationalism, to the religion of his childhood. The sincerity of his religious convictions has sometimes been called into question, but without much evidence other than speculation about his motives for delaying publication of his *Traité du monde* in the face of a real threat of ecclesiastical censorship. He was first and foremost a philosopher, not a theologian. He no doubt considered reason the final arbiter of philosophical truth. But he did not think that reason on its own, apart from revelation and faith, could explain all the mysteries of reality.

During twenty-some years in Holland he would face restrictions upon the public display of his Catholic faith, but still managed to practice it by staying with families that had a private priest or moving to regions where it would be tolerated. Though often accused of being an atheist, and suspected by Sweden's Queen Christina of being less credulous than becomes a pious man, Descartes thought it part of his mission to use reason to challenge atheism. After his death in Sweden, it was discovered that he had carried with him an extract of his baptismal register. This may have been simply a way of documenting the time of his birth, were such documentation needed. But most scholars have interpreted it as a personal witness to the faith of his childhood.

DESCARTES ON RELIGION. Among the innate ideas that can be grasped through intellectual intuition are the ideas of God and immortality of the soul (mind). Infidels and others whose religion and morality depend solely on their fear of God and expectation of another life can be convinced of these ideas, not by revelation, but by reason alone. That God does exist can be rationally demonstrated: first, on grounds that the idea of a perfect being could only have been produced in me by God and, secondly, because the very concept of God as a perfect being implies existence. From the idea of divine perfection, it can also be deduced that God is the omnipotent, immutable Creator who freely set and keeps matter in motion, and that God's infinite truthfulness precludes the possibility of any deception that might undermine the certainty of clear and distinct ideas, like the awareness of myself as a thinking thing that is independent of, but intimately interactive with, my body.

Knowledge of the soul's distinction from and independence of the body proves, in turn, the soul's immortality. For it implies that as a pure, simple substance the soul escapes the degeneration to which the body is subject by virtue of its accidental configurations. Unless God chooses to deny the soul his concurrence, therefore, it is naturally incorruptible. Whether God might ever freely will to destroy a human soul is one of those questions that cannot be settled "by the power of human reason." But God has "revealed to us that this won't happen." And although we should reject all ideas that are not rationally clear and distinct as "suspect of error and dangerous," this should not keep us from believing what the Catholic religion teaches has been divinely revealed about the soul or the inner nature of God, since such belief, "as all faith in obscure matters," is an act, not of our intelligence, "but of our will."

Sources

Descartes. *The Philosophical Works of Descartes.* Translated by Elizabeth S. Haldane and G.R.T. Ross. Cambridge: Cambridge University Press, 1983.

Copleston, Frederick, S.J. *A History of Philosophy.* Vol. 4. Garden City, NY: Doubleday and Company, Inc., 1962–77. 74–160.

Gilson, Etienne. *God and Philosophy.* New Haven: Yale University Press, 1960. 74–98.

Gouhier, H. *La pensee religieuse de Descartes.* Paris: J. Vrin, 1924.

Küng, Hans. *Does God Exist?* Garden City, NY: Doubleday and Co., Inc., 1980. 3–41.

Verkamp, Bernard J. *The Sense of Religious Wonder: Epistemological Variations.* Scranton, PA: University of Scranton Press, 2002. 21–24.

Dewey, John (1859–1952)

The lakeside town of Burlington, Vermont, where Dewey was born and grew up, had many different churches. The largest single denomination, and the one to which Dewey's own family belonged, was that of the socially idealistic Congregationalists. He had a good relation with his well-read, religiously conservative father, but because of the latter's six-year military service during the Civil War, it was his mother, Lucina, who had the greatest influence upon his boyhood years, trying constantly to instill in him her own pious devotion to Jesus as the supernatural Lord and Savior. While attending Burlington's University of Vermont he was formally admitted to membership in the Congregational church, taught Sunday school classes, and actively participated in religious groups. As a professor of philosophy at the University of Michigan between 1884 and 1894, he remained a member of the Congregational church, regularly attended Sunday morning worship services, and frequently gave addresses to Christian campus organizations on biblical and church history topics.

Despite growing doubts about the possibility of reconciling his religious faith with reason, he preserved his faith in God as the organic unity of the ideal and the real in the person of Christ. But in the mid–1890s his interest in church matters rapidly declined. After accepting chairmanship of the Philosophy Department at the newly founded University of Chicago in 1894, he terminated his membership in the Ann Arbor Congregational Church, and generally disengaged himself over the next ten years from church-related groups. He later opposed attempts to offer special programs of religious education in the public schools, and objected to financial support of parochial schools.

While abandoning institutional religion and its belief in the supernatural, however, he continued throughout the rest of his years to enjoy a profoundly meaningful religious life, tirelessly witnessing through his pursuit of a democratic humanism and ethical naturalism to what he himself called the "religious meaning of democracy" and the "ultimate religious value" of everyday life. In 1933, he signed "A Humanist Manifesto" calling upon Americans to put their trust in a new religion of shared liberal social values, and thought that the institutional churches could be of some help in implementing such a program. He strongly supported toleration of all religious traditions.

His funeral in 1952 was held at the Community Church in New York, a church that shared his commitment to a natural piety.

DEWEY ON RELIGION. Religions traditionally have been based upon a belief in the supernatural, the symbols of which have imposed themselves as cults, dogmas and myths to the point of obscuring the community of life and favoring an intolerable and divisive superiority of the few. But the existence of God as a particular transcendent being who causes and directs the universe, although logically possible, lacks empirical evidence. Extreme opponents of traditional religions argue that with this discrediting of the supernatural by modern science, everything religious must go. But there is a major difference between religion, *a* religion, and the religious. There is no such thing as religion in the singular. There is only a multitude of religions. The culturally based differences of supernaturalistic beliefs and practices among them are so great that no meaningful common element can be extracted from them. Relieved, however, of all these historical encumbrances, a genuinely religious element — a common faith — that is well worth preserving can be emancipated.

This religious element consists of any attitude — a natural piety that imagines the actualization of the ideal potential of human nature as a cooperating part of a larger, organic whole (i.e., Nature) through an intelligent (i.e., scientific), democratic search for the truth — that lends deep and enduring support to the processes of living. Such an attitude does not exist by itself apart from aesthetic, scientific, moral, political, or social experiences, but may qualify all of the latter as being religious to the extent of providing the self with a lasting adjustment to nature, a liberating sense of community, and profound feelings of security, peace, and ultimate meaning. To avoid further alienating people of traditional religious beliefs and leaving them in despair, the unity of ideal ends that gives rise to this common faith might still be symbolized by continued use of the term "God," but only so long as it is clear that no supernatural being is intended thereby.

Sources

Dewey, John. *The Collected Works*. Edited by Anne S. Sharpe. Carbondale, IL: Southern Illinois University Press, 1991.

_____. *A Common Faith*. New Haven: Yale University Press, 1934.

_____. *Experience and Nature*. Chicago: Open Court, 1925.

_____. "A God or The God?" *Christian Century* I (February 8, 1933): 193–96.

_____. *Human Nature and Conduct*. New York: Henry Holt, 1922.

_____. *The Quest for Certainty*. New York: Minton, Balch, 1929.

_____. "Religion and Our Schools." *Hibbert Journal* 7 (July 1909): 827–43.

Cockerham, David. *Toward a Common Democratic Faith; Political Ethics of John Dewey and Jacques Maritain*. Unpublished Doctoral Dissertation. Indiana University, 2006.

Hartshorne, Charles. "Dewey's Philosophy of Religion." In *Beyond Humanism: Essays in the Philosophy of Nature*. Gloucester, MA: Peter Smith, 1975. 101–14.

Rockefeller, Steven C. *John Dewey: Religious Faith and Democratic Humanism*. New York: Columbia University Press, 1991.

Roth, Robert J., S.J. "John Dewey and Religious Experience." In Robert J. Roth, ed., *American Religious Philosophy*. New York: Harcourt, Brace and World, 1967. 85–108.

Schaub, Edward L. "Dewey's Interpretation of Religion." In Paul Schilpp, ed., *The Philosophy of John Dewey*. Evanston: Northwestern University Press, 1939. 3–45.

Dilthey, Wilhelm (1833–1911)

Born in the village of Biebrich am Rhein, Dilthey was the son of a liberal-minded, Calvinist clergyman and court preacher to the Duke of Nassau. His mother was the daughter of a renowned musician who instilled in her young son such a love for listening to music that he came to regard it as a religious act. It was the wish of his parents that he follow in his father's footsteps and become a clergyman. Thus, after completing his secondary education at the *Gymnasium* in Wiesbaden, and despite his own preference for law, he was encouraged to take up the study of theology, first at Heidelberg, then at Berlin. His major instructors at both schools were historians of

philosophy whose rather pantheistic leanings, combined with the lingering influence of his childhood exposure to the Pietistic emphasis of his parents upon the inward experience of God, awakened in him the possibility of devoting the rest of his life to uncovering the "history of the Christian *Weltanschauung* of the West." While, therefore, he would go on to pass some qualifying examinations in the field of theology for the sake of satisfying parental expectations, and would even preach a trial sermon or two in his hometown, his real interest had shifted from theology as such to its history and the evolution of philosophy, science, and world history in general.

Like many other of his European contemporaries whose ties with traditional Christian beliefs had been loosened by the postrevolutionary, scientific spirit of the age, he had lost much of his faith in traditional Christianity, replacing its other-worldly attitude with the this-worldly enthusiasm of Romantic humanism. He would remain interested throughout the rest of his life in the scientific and historical study of religion, but he no longer felt qualified to serve in the ministry. He instead threw himself into scholarly work, and in hopes of retrieving what he still suspected was the genuinely religious-philosophical *Weltanschauung* lying buried under the wreckage of traditional theology and metaphysics, he dedicated much of his time and energy to the study of great thinkers like Bruno, Goethe, Schleiermacher, and Hegel, whose panentheistic interpretation of religion he found most appealing. But unlike Comte, he never conceived it to be his vocation in life to serve as the prophet of some new religion. After professorships at Basle, Kiel, Breslau and Berlin, he retired from teaching in 1905 and devoted himself exclusively to his scholarly research and writing. He died in 1911, without ever having completed his *Life of Schleiermacher* or any other of his major projects.

DILTHEY ON RELIGION. Given the dynamic interplay between the conceptualization of any cultural system as a whole and selection of its relevant parts (ideas, persons, actions, artifacts, etc.), any concept of religion is problematic. As a working definition, however, religion may be described as that cultural system whereby humans seek supreme happiness in terms of their relation to that which is invisible, either in the sense of unseen supernatural powers activating the regular processes and chance events of nature (as in primitive religion), or, under the influence of religious geniuses (prophets and mystics) trying to blend the tragic dimensions of life, in the sense of some strange and unfamiliar personal force emanating from the depths of life with which the lonely ascetic might commune, or finally, when traditional mythology is reinterpreted in a more rational and comprehensive way, in the sense of an unseen supernatural order, in the context of which everything takes its value and meaning.

Among the objective expressions of such religiosity are the various religious worldviews (*Weltanschauungen*): a theistic defense of the freedom of both man and God; a panentheistic affirmation of divine immanence in the world; or even a revolt against otherworldliness. For most people today the possibility of experiencing such religious states of mind in their own personal existence is sharply circumscribed. By encountering an historically religious phenomenon like Luther, however, one can imaginatively relive ways of life that are beyond one's existential capacity. The experience of the other can become one's own lived experience *(Erlebnis)*, which in turn can become the key for understanding *(Verstehen)* the historical reality of the other. As an exercise in wringing from every experience its content, this will not only alert one to the relativity of every sort of belief (including one's own), but also increase knowledge of oneself, and renew one's appreciation for the continuity of the creative force operating at the heart of human history.

Sources

Dilthey, Wilhelm. *Selected Works.* Vol. I. *Introduction to the Human Sciences.* Princeton: Princeton University Press, 1989.
_____. *Selected Works.* Vol. III. *The Formation of the Historical World in the Human Sciences.* Princeton: Princeton University Press, 2002.
Collingwood, R.G. *The Idea of History.* Oxford: Oxford University Press, 1956. 172–75.
Copleston, Frederick, S.J. *A History of Philosophy.* Vol. 7, pt. 2. Garden City, NY: Doubleday and Company, Inc., 1962–77. 142–46.
Ermarth, Michael. *Wilhelm Dilthey: The Critique of Historical Reason.* Chicago and London: The University of Chicago Press, 1978.
Hodges, H.A. *The Philosophy of Wilhelm Dilthey.* London: Routledge and Kegan Paul, Ltd., 1952.
_____. *Wilhelm Dilthey: An Introduction.* London: Kegan Paul, 1944. See esp. 93–101.
Makkreel, Rudolf A. *Dilthey: philosopher of the human studies.* Princeton: Princeton University Press, 1992.
Misch, G. *"Vorbericht"* to Band V of Dilthey's *Gesammelte Schriften,* vii–cxvii. Leipzig and Berlin: Verlag von B.G. Teubner, 1924.
Oakes, Guy. "Dilthey, Wilhelm." In *Encyclopedia of Religion.* Vol. 4. Edited by Mircea Eliade. New York: Macmillan and Co., 1987. 353–55.
Plantinga, Theodore. *Historical Understanding in the Thought of Wilhelm Dilthey.* Toronto: University of Toronto Press, 1980.
Rickman, H.P. *Wilhelm Dilthey: Pioneer of the Human Studies.* London: Paul Elek, 1979.

Duns Scotus, John (c. 1266–1308)

Born into a family that had been among the early benefactors of the Franciscan Order in Scotland, Duns Scotus was himself, because of his exceptional talent and piety, considered a likely candidate for the religious life. Thanks to the interest in him shown by a paternal uncle, who had joined the Scottish Franciscans himself and been appointed their Vicar General, Duns Scotus was sent to the friary of Dumfries at the age of twelve to prepare for reception into the Order. Three years later he became a novice, and after another ten years of spiritual training and study of philosophy and theology (possibly for brief periods at Oxford and Paris) he was ordained a priest in 1291.

After continuing his studies (possibly at Paris) under the Fransciscan theologian Gonsalvo of Balboa, he returned to Oxford (and probably Cambridge) to lecture for a few years (1297–1301) on Lombard's *Sentences.* It was especially the many written versions of these and future commentaries on Lombard that would eventually earn him the title of *Doctor subtilis* and a reputation for being one of the more original of Scholastic thinkers. Soon thereafter, upon a recommendation from Gonsalvo, he was accepted as a candidate for a master's chair at the University of Paris. But because he refused on conscientious grounds to side with France's king, Philip the Fair, in the latter's ongoing struggle with Pope Boniface VIII over the question of lay investitures, he was forced to interrupt his studies and return to Oxford for a year.

He returned to Paris after the death of Pope Boniface, and finally received the advanced degree in 1305. For the next two years he lectured in Paris on a variety of philosophical and theological matters, including, against fierce opposition from other theologians at the University of Paris, a defense of the immaculate conception of Jesus' mother, Mary. Being faced on that account with accusations of heresy at a time when France's king was again challenging the pope and demanding loyalty to himself, Duns Scotus and his superiors once again deemed it best for him to leave Paris. He was sent to Cologne to help reorganize that city's house of studies. He lectured there until his premature death a year later, leaving many of his writings unfinished and himself open to many faulty attributions. His body was interred in Cologne's Franciscan church. Known already during his life for his deep spirituality, he came to be venerated by the Franciscans and others in subsequent centuries as belonging among the blessed.

DUNS SCOTUS ON RELIGION. The primary object of the human intellect and the starting point for any knowledge of God is a univocal concept of Being. From the notion that, logically speaking, being can be predicated univocally of everything that exists, metaphysics proceeds to demonstrate the existence of God by proving the possibility and actual existence of an infinite being. If there is a perfect, first efficient and final cause of all finite beings, there is the possibility of an infinite being called God. Given the impossibil-

ity of explaining the essentially intrinsic possibility of all finite beings from themselves or nothing, there must be some first efficient and final cause of all being. Therefore, the existence of an infinite being called God is not only possible but necessary, since it is itself uncaused. Being infinite, the divine essence is imitable in an infinite number of ways, giving rise to infinite ideas in the divine intellect. But it is the divine will which chooses which ideas will be the paradigms of God's creative activity.

To appreciate this and other of the divine attributes, however, one must go beyond philosophy and turn to the Sacred Scriptures, none of which, incidentally, are accepted by the Manichaeans, only part of which are accepted by the Jews, and much of which has been adulterated by the followers of Mohammed (e.g., with promises of an eternal happiness of sensuality that is only fit for pigs). Only the Apostolic Tradition of the Christian and Catholic religion has preserved the Bible's credibility. What the Bible tells us is that it was love of his own essence, and a perfectly free choice to communicate this love that prompted the creation of finite creatures — a natural order of things that reached its climax in the Incarnation through the graceful cooperation of Jesus' mother, Mary. In response to such infinite love, humans are expected to use their freedom to obey the absolutely free, but essentially rational dictates of the divine will. Those who, with the help of divine grace, do, can expect to rise bodily to eternal, beatific love in the next life.

Sources

Duns Scotus. *De Primo Prinicipio.* Edited and translated by Allan B. Wolter. Chicago: Franciscan Herald Press, 1982.

_____. *God and Creatures: The Quodlibetal Questions.* Edited and translated by Felix Alluntis and Allan Wolter. Princeton and London: Princeton University Press, 1975.

_____. *Philosophical Writings.* A selection edited and translated by Allan Wolter, O.F.M. Edinburgh and London: Nelson, 1962.

Adams, Marilyn McCord. "Duns Scotus on the

Goodness of God." *Faith and Philosophy* 4.4 (October 1987): 486–505.

Balić, C. "Duns Scotus, John." *New Catholic Encyclopedia*. Vol. 4. Edited by W.J. McDonald. New York: McGraw-Hill, 1967. 1102–6.

Bettoni, Efrem. *Duns Scotus: The Basic Principles of His Philosophy*. Translated by Bernardine Bonansea. Washington, D.C.: The Catholic University of America Press, 1961.

Bonansea. B.M., O.F.M. *Man and His Approach to God in John Duns Scotus*. Lanham, NY, and London: University Press of America, 1983.

Copleston, Frederick, S.J. *A History of Philosophy*. Vol. 2, pt. 2. Garden City, NY: Doubleday and Company, Inc., 1962–77. 199–274.

Cross, Richard. *Duns Scotus*. New York and Oxford: Oxford University Press, 1999.

Gilson. Etienne. *History of Christian Philosophy in the Middle Ages*. New York: Random House, 1954. 454–64.

Minges, P. Parthenius, O.F.M. *Joannis Duns Scoti: Doctrina Philosophica and Theologica: Proposita et Exposita*. Buffalo, NY: Ex Typographia Collegii S. Bonaventurae, 1930.

Wolter, Allan, O.F.M. *The Philosophical Theology of John Duns Scotus*. Ithaca and London: Cornell University Press, 1990.

Emerson, Ralph Waldo (1803–1882)

Emerson's father, who was the liberal-minded (deistic) minister of the Unitarian First Church in Boston, died when his son was only eight. Emerson's interest in religion was influenced, therefore, far more by his mother and his father's sister, Mary Moody Emerson. The mother was a very devout Protestant who every day would read books by a variety of Christian authors offering spiritual counsel about immediate religious experience. The self-educated aunt preferred Calvinism to Unitarianism, but described herself as a "deistic pietist," and poured her thoughts into volumes of unpublished manuscripts to which Emerson would frequently turn for inspiration. She encouraged Emerson to become a minister.

After graduating from Harvard and spending close to ten years teaching school, traveling, and reading prodigiously (e.g., de Staël, Plato, Sampson Reed, Montaigne) he followed her advice and took up the study of divinity, largely under the guidance of William Ellery Channing, a cofounder of American Unitarianism. In 1829 he was appointed pastor of the Second Church of Boston. Within several years, however — not long after the death of his beloved first wife, Ellen — Emerson was having serious misgivings, not only about Calvinism (for whose emphasis upon human depravity he had a particular distaste) or for the Unitarian practice of Communion, but for historical Christianity in general and its "absolutely incredible scheme of redemption."

Although he still thought of himself as a "disciple of Christ," and would continue preaching in liberal Quaker circles, he soon resigned his pastoral position and in most of his future writings would look for the essence of the religious impulse in the self-reliant life of the individual and the fundamental identity of all things (as he had read in the *Bhagavad Gita*). He had come to believe that every man makes his own religion, his own God. Upon later sharing such views with students at Harvard's Divinity School in 1838, Emerson was accused of impiety, blasphemy, and the foulest atheism. He would remain a deeply religious man for the rest of his life, propounding his transcendentalist convictions about the reality of "spirit" in Nature, and wrestling with moral issues like slavery, war, fate, and so on. But it was his final showdown with organized religion.

EMERSON ON RELIGION. The essence of all religion lies in the intuitive sentiment of virtue inscribed on the soul that unites man with the great Over-Soul, the impersonal Universal Being permeating the whole of Nature. Already current in ancient times, this religious sentiment found its purest expression in Palestine, and especially in the unique example set by Jesus, the only soul in history who appreciated the worth of man. Preferring the eternal revelation in the human heart to that of Moses, he saw that the law in man's soul is supreme, and in obedience to himself, discovered his own divine identity.

Paul, Augustine, and others who shared

Christ's faith in the mysterious infinitude of the human soul, fulfilled the office of a true teacher by showing Christians that God is, not was; that he speaketh, not spake; and that the gleams that flash across their minds are God's own. The religious sentiment they ignited in the various national churches helped humanize the people. But now, as its religious form becomes ever more fixed and stationary, true Christianity, with its initial faith in the closeness of God and man, is lost. By personalizing Jesus as a demigod like Osiris or Apollo, proclaiming the age of inspiration past, and authoritatively imposing traditional dogma and ritual, the churches have discouraged members from thinking for themselves, and enslaved them to the example and secondary knowledge of past models.

In the end, however, the human mind suffers no religion but its own, and sooner or later will rediscover God within the creative wills of a few delicate spirits. Such religious self-consciousness inclines man to strive confidently here and now toward moral perfection, notwithstanding the intransigence of the real world. And because love and justice never die, it can leave the impression that at least some good souls might find immortality. But it also can degenerate into extreme subjectivism, and as such leave man feeling terribly alone as the God within is experienced as an Abyss of nothingness.

Sources

Emerson, Ralph Waldo. *Emerson: A Modern Anthology*. Edited by Alfred Kazin and Daniel Aaron. Boston: Houghton Mifflin Company; Cambridge: The Riverside Press, 1958.
_____. *Essays and Journals*. n.p.: Nelson Doubleday, Inc., 1968.
Doherty, Joseph F. "Emerson and the Loneliness of the Gods." In Robert E. Burkholder and Joel Myerson, *Critical Essays on Ralph Waldo Emerson*. Boston: G.K. Hall and Co., 1983. 424–33.
Geldard, Richard G. *God in Concord: Ralph Waldo Emerson's Awakening to the Infinite*. Burdett, NY: Larson Publications, 1999.
Huggard, William A. *The Religious Teachings of Ralph Waldo Emerson*. New York: Vantage Press, 1972.
Makarushka, Irena S.M. *Religious Imagination and Language in Emerson and Nietzsche*. New York: St. Martin's Press, 1994.
Moran, Michael. "Emerson, Ralph Waldo." *Encyclopedia of Philosophy*. Vol. 3. Edited by Paul Edwards. New York: Macmillan and Co. and The Free Press, 1967. 477–79.
Richardson, Robert D., Jr. *Emerson: The Mind on Fire*. Berkeley: University of California Press, 1995.
Sassian, David. "Emerson, Ralph Waldo." In *Encyclopedia of Religion*. Vol. 5. Edited by Mircea Eliade. New York: Macmillan and Co., 1987. 100–1.

Empedocles (c. 495–435 B.C.)

The son of a wealthy and influential citizen of Akragas (Sicily), Empedocles himself grew up to become a formidable player in the social and political affairs of his hometown, championing democracy, serving as a physician, and carrying on a number of public works at his own expense. The near-miraculous cures (e.g., reviving a woman who had been thought to be dead) he supposedly worked inclined some to think that he possessed magical powers. These and his other civic activities made him so popular that he was once invited by the people to become their king. But he turned them down to devote more of his time and energy to the pursuit of an interest in philosophy and religion he had developed while studying as a youth under Parmenides.

Later he would convert to the Pythagorean doctrine of the transmigration of souls and seek to combine its implications about the process of becoming in a theory of his own with what his teacher had taught him about the oneness and permanency of being. Most of his teaching was concentrated on one individual, a physician and friend, named Pausanias. As a result, he left no school. But as long as he lived he was highly revered, partly because of his aforementioned political savvy and medical expertise, but also because of his reputed wisdom. According to one story, the people gathered on a certain occasion at a banquet all rose from their chairs upon his entrance to the room and prostrated themselves before him as before a god. He apparently found their behavior to have been quite appropriate. For although he would sometimes describe himself as "a sinner and fugitive from the gods," in the opening lines of his *Purifications* he acknowledged that he no longer wandered among his fellow citizens as a mere mortal, but "like a god immortal, honored by all, fittingly crowned with sacred fillets," and revered by the thousands of men and women who followed him around in search of prophecies, cures, or advice about how to be saved.

Pausanias added to the popular impression of his teacher's apotheosis. For after the sixty-year-old Empedocles disappeared late one evening following a banquet, and the subsequent search turned up only one of his famous bronze-studded sandals at the edge of the crater atop Mt. Aetna, Pausanias suggested that no further search should be conducted, because what had happened was that, in line with his own teaching about how the purified will "sprout up again as gods immortal," Empedocles had experienced a divine rapture of sorts. On that account, he added, his teacher ought to be worshiped as the god he had become.

EMPEDOCLES ON RELIGION. Fools suppose that what did not exist before comes into being or that something may die and perish entirely. But from what does not exist nothing can come into being, and for what exists to be destroyed is impossible and unaccomplishable. What does really exist are four material elements of fire, air, earth, and water (respectively symbolized in popular religion by bright Zeus [or a nonanthropomorphic Apollo], life-bringing Hera, Aidoneus, and Nestis), along with two quasi-material substances of love (*Philia*, symbolized by the goddess Aphrodite or Cypris), which governed the divine sphere (the One) within which the four elements, at the start of the current cycle, were commingled in perfect unity, and strife *(Neikos)*, that inclined some of the godlike souls (*daemons*) toward murder and perjury, causing the sphere to tremble and its elements to fall apart into the chaotic mess that we now call our world.

In accordance with the ancient decree of the gods, these erring, immortal souls were exiled from the company of the blessed gods and made to migrate across thousands of seasons from one bodily form to another. All of us, including myself, are such miserable fugitives, having once been bushes, birds, fishes, or young boys and girls. Lest we end up killing and consuming animals that may in fact be the reincarnation of our own parents, we would be wise, therefore, to emulate our earliest ancestors who refrained from drenching their altars with the blood of bulls and venerated their goddess of Love with nothing more than holy images, perfumes, and libations of golden honey. To purify ourselves we must instead pursue wisdom by going beyond our sense perceptions, thinking clearly (i.e., holistically), and letting Love regain control of our lives. Those who do will become gods again, escaping the misery of human existence in this world and reentering as discrete, but not necessarily personal, individuals the harmonious dwelling-place of the gods from which the human *daimon* had been banished for some primordial crime in the first place.

Sources

Empedocles. *The Extant Fragments*. Edited with commentary by M.R. Wright. New Haven and London: Yale University Press, 1981.

Barnes, Jonathan. *Early Greek Philosophy*. Harmondsworth, UK: Penguin Books, 1987. 161–202.

Brandis, Christian A. "Empedocles." In *A Dictionary of Greek and Roman Biography and Mythology*. Vol. 2. Edited by William Smith. New York: AMS Press, Inc., 1967. 13–14.

Diogenes Laertius, "Empedocles." *Lives of Eminent Philosophers*. Vol. 2, no. 8. Translated by R.D. Hicks. Cambridge, MA: Harvard University Press, 1972. 366–91.

Jaeger, Werner. *The Theology of the Early Greek Philosophers*. Oxford: At the Clarendon Press, 1948. 128–54.

Kahn, Charles H. "Empedocles." *Encyclopedia of Philosophy*. Vol. 2. Edited by Paul Edwards. New York: Macmillan and Co. and The Free Press, 1967. 496–99.

——. "Religion and Natural Philosophy in Empedocles' Doctrine of the Soul." *Archiv für Geschichte der Philosophie* 42.1 (1960): 3–35.

Lambridis, Helle. *Empedocles*. University, AL: The

University of Alabama Press, 1977. See esp. 7–21.

Long, Herbert S. "The Unity of Empedocles' Thought." *American Journal of Philology* LXX (1949): 142–58.

Millerd, Clara Elizabeth. *On the Interpretation of Empedocles.* New York and London: Garland Publishing, Inc., 1980.

Trépanier, Simon. *Empedocles: An Interpretation.* New York and London: Routledge, 2004.

Epictetus (c. A.D. 55–135)

Born of a slave woman in the Phrygian city of Hierapolis, Epictetus was still a slave of Nero's very wealthy secretary (a former slave himself), Epaphroditus, observing all the stormy vicissitudes of daily sycophantic life in the imperial court around him, when he had the good fortune of encountering the Stoic philosopher, Musonius Rufus. From the latter he learned, among other things, that by using the divine fragment of Reason within him he could come to understand what was or was not under his own control and be freed of any concern about external things, like his own lameness, poverty, or enslavement, which in and of themselves did not really matter. Manumitted by his master, he began teaching the (Cynic-tainted) Stoic philosophy in Rome, only to be banished from Italy soon thereafter, along with all other philosophers, by the Emperor Domitian.

Moving on to Nicopolis, Greece, he set up a school of his own, and for the rest of his life made it his mission to share with the mostly wealthy young men who frequented his classes (like Arrian, his future intellectual biographer) the wisdom he had picked up from his mentor. He wrote nothing, and although what fragments remain of Arrian's recordings give us few details of his personal life, they are enough to leave the impression of a man who was deeply religious. On the assumption that he would not have encouraged others to do what he himself did not practice, it is likely that he occasionally consulted the oracles and participated in the sacrificial rites, the worshipful singing of hymns, and prayer.

But if he was pious in his daily life, it was primarily in the sense of living in an awareness of God's provident care of the world and conceiving of his own profession of teaching as a divine calling to preach, not some new academic theory, but the good news of inner freedom. His message and the religious tone and intensity with which he delivered it, was accompanied by such a virtuous display of simplicity, humility and charity that not a few Christian thinkers would later conclude that he must have been under the influence of Jesus or the Apostle Paul. But while he may have heard of the latter's preaching in the region and time of his birth, and although his *Discourses* indicate that he knew of the Galileans, there is no evidence that he was actually influenced by Jesus or the early Christians.

EPICTETUS ON RELIGION. The most important factor in religion is to have the right opinion about the deity (Zeus and all the subordinate gods he has fathered). First, we must believe that the deity exists, for otherwise it would make no sense to say, as we do, that the goal of life is to follow the gods. That the deity does exist is evident to anyone who studies the nature of man and the world, for God is omnipresent in Nature as Universal Mind. Secondly, we must believe that the existent deity takes an active interest in earthly and human affairs, and not only in general, but in individual human lives. That God oversees everything and directs it into a dramatic, unified structure is evident from the regularity and interconnectedness of all natural phenomena.

This is especially the case with humans, who by being endowed with a rational capacity to understand the divine order, are connected and attached to God as fragments of His own being. God perceives their every movement as something belonging to Himself and sharing in His own nature. As their maker, He provides for their every need. Knowing that God is within them, humans should never feel alone, nor ever forget that as sons of the one, same Father, they are all brothers, fellow citizens of the world, each with a role of their own to play. They should constantly sing to God hymns of praise and thanksgiving, periodically offering the traditionally religious libations, sacrifices and first fruits. And instead of worrying (or consulting ornithomancers) about matters that make no difference or over which humans have no control anyway, they should rely on the diviner within themselves to see what alone is up to them, namely, the cultivation of an interior disposition that will allow them freely to accept the hand that fate has dealt them, and to ride out the storm of daily vicissitudes with a degree of godlike indifference. Those who by the exertion of their own wills can thus align their reason with the Universal Mind governing Nature will themselves become divine, even while remaining in their "little bodies." The rest will just stay as they are.

Sources

Epictetus. *The Discourses of Epictetus.* Translated by Robin Hard. London: J.M. Dent; Vermont: Charles E. Tuttle, 1995.

_____. *The Handbook and Fragments.* In Epictetus, *The Discourses.* 287–317.

Bonhöffer, Adolf Friedrich. *The Ethics of the Stoic Epictetus.* Translated by William O. Stephens. New York: Peter Lang, 1996.

Brandis, Christian A. "Epictetus." In *A Dictionary of Greek and Roman Biography and Mythology.* Vol. 2. Edited by William Smith. New York: AMS Press, Inc., 1967. 31–33.

Copleston, Frederick, S.J. *A History of Philosophy.* Vol. 1, pt. 2. Garden City, NY: Doubleday and Company, Inc., 1962–77. 175–79.

Long, A.A. *Epictetus: A Stoic and Socratic Guide to Life.* Oxford: Clarendon Press, 2002.

More, Paul Elmer. *Hellenistic Philosophies.* Princeton: Princeton University Press, 1923. See esp. 94–100.

Seddon, Keith H. "Epictetus." *The Internet Encyclopedia of Philosophy.* http://www.iep.utm.edu/e/epictetu.htm. 1–24.

Stadter, Philip A. *Arrian of Nicomedia.* Chapel Hill: University of North Carolina Press, 1980. See esp. 19–25.

Epicurus (341–271 B.C.)

Ancient rumor had it that while helping to prepare the ink for the use of pupils in the elementary school his father had started on the island of Samos, he was also expected to help his mother prepare the magical rites she was supposedly performing as a sorceress at a conventicle of displaced individuals who felt excluded from the more public forms of worship. If there is any truth to the story, it may help to explain the hatred he would later express for all forms of superstition. There is some evidence to suggest that while growing up he received some instruction from Nausiphanes, a philosopher with leanings toward both Democritean atomism and Pyrrhonist skepticism. Epicurus himself claimed to have been self-taught.

In any event, after leaving Samos at the age of eighteen and wandering to Athens, Colophon, Mytilene, Lampsacus, and then back to Athens in the year 306, he felt sufficiently learned to set up in his house and garden his own school of philosophy for a small group of male and female followers. While gently presiding over this school for the remaining thirty-six years of his life, and writing hundreds of works without (he claimed) ever quoting another author, he lived a quiet, unostentatious life, purposely disengaged from Athens' then turbulent political affairs, and devoted entirely to the kind of philosophic fellowship in which "each by turns [is] guide to each" and finds "unspeakable pleasure" as "thought leaps out to wed with thought." Unlike Socrates, however, he was never accused of atheism or infidelity to the national religion. As he encouraged others to do, he himself worshiped the city's gods, participated in its traditional religious services and popular festivals, and performed whatever other religious duties the laws prescribed.

Plutarch would later accuse Epicurus of hypocrisy in this regard, claiming that he conformed outwardly to the religious traditions only out of fear of having his real beliefs exposed to the multitudes, and to that extent was no different from the latter whom he was always criticizing for praying and sacrificing only out of a superstitious fear of losing the favor of the gods and being punished. But convinced as he was about the indifference of the gods toward human affairs, and as self-confident and autonomous as he always seemed to be, it is unlikely that his adherence to traditional religious practices was motivated by fear either of the gods or of his fellow humans. If he worshiped, it was probably because he found it such a delight to contemplate the excellent, dialogical tranquility of the gods as an ideal of human virtue.

EPICURUS ON RELIGION. Religions of old would have us acknowledge the gods as the fierce lords of nature to whom prayers and sacrifices must be made to avert divine wrath both in this life and in the next. And, as every race of men has grasped proleptically, the gods do exist, appearing to humans in their sleep as anthropomorphic images with ethereal bodies composed of the finest atoms. But they are not such as the many believe them to be. They are not creators. As Democritus argued, our world results simply from atoms falling eternally through space and periodically swerving into each other to form accidental configurations. Nor do the gods care about this world. What happens to humans now, in this life, is of no concern to them. And as for human life after death, there is none, for at the moment of death the atoms simply disengage from each other, terminating the existence of the individual. There is no reason, then, to fear either death or the gods.

Trying to avert eternal punishment by appeasing the gods with ritualistic prayers and sacrifices not only has nothing to do with genuine religion, but might actually block the peace of mind that is essential to it. True religion consists rather in right thought and the contemplation of the gods as they really are, namely, as beings that are happy and immortal precisely because they are totally indifferent, without any needs, invulnerable to harm, and, therefore, perfectly at rest. By freely choosing to emulate this ataraxic disposition of the gods, humans can stop worrying and get on with their own lives. Neither wallowing in sensual pleasures that can never satisfy anyway, nor cowering before unavoidable pain (like that of kidney stones), prudent individuals will withdraw from society and all its bothersome entanglements, minimize their needs, and seek their personal happiness by

engaging themselves in the intellectually exciting company of their friends. In the process, they will find communion with the gods, for the gods always welcome men who are like themselves.

Sources

Epicurus. *The Epicurus Reader. Selected Writings and Testimonia*. Translated by Brad Inwood and L.P. Gerson. Indianapolis and Cambridge: Hackett Publishing Company, Inc., 1994.
Armstrong, A.H. "The Gods in Plato, Plotinus, Epicurus." *The Classical Quarterly* 32 (1938): 190–96.
Bevan, Edwyn. *Later Greek Religion*. London: J.M. Dent and Sons, 1927. 38–46.
Copleston, Frederick, S.J. *A History of Philosophy*. Vol. 1, pt. 2. Garden City, NY: Doubleday and Company, Inc., 1962–77. 145–56.
Dunham, James H. *The Religion of Philosophers*. Philadelphia: University of Pennsylvania Press, 1947. 72–94.
Lucretius. *On the Nature of Things*. Translated by H.A.J. Munro. Great Books of the Western World. Vol. 12. Edited by R.M. Hutchins. Chicago: Encyclopædia Britannica, Inc., 1952. 1–97.
Melchert, Norman. *The Great Conversation*. Boston: McGraw-Hill, 2002. 201–06.
Obink, Dirk. "'All Gods are True' in Epicurus." In Dorothea Frede, and Andre Laks, eds. *Traditions of Theology: Studies in Hellenistic Theology, Its Background and Aftermath*. Leiden and Boston: Brill, 2002. 183–222.
Strodach, George K. *The Philosophy of Epicurus*. Evanston: Northwestern University Press, 1963.
Stumpf, Samuel Enoch. *Socrates to Sartre. A History of Philosophy*. New York: McGraw-Hill Book Company, 1982. 106–10.
Wallace, William. *Epicureanism*. London: SPCK, 1880. 24–47.

Eriugena, John Scottus *see* John Scottus Eriugena

Fackenheim, Emil (1916–2003)

Fackenheim's grandparents were conservative Jews who kept kosher. His mother was descended from a long line of rabbis and was very pious in the practice of her religion. So too was his father, who balanced his work as a lawyer with the daily recitation of traditional Jewish prayers in Hebrew. The family adhered to a rather liberal, albeit not a strictly reformed, branch of Judaism. They sincerely believed in the possibility of being an upright Jew and a German at the same time, and did not favor the Zionist movement. They regularly attended synagogue services on Friday evenings.

At the age of nineteen, having completed his studies at the Gymnasium, Fackenheim enrolled at the Hochschule für die Wissenschaft des Judentums in Berlin. It was a Rabbinical seminary, but his primary intention was simply to learn as much as he could about Jewish tradition. His Midrash teacher there (Leo Baeck) provided him with many a *midrashim* and, like Martin Buber, encouraged him to think for himself about their implications.

Three years later, however, a day or so after *Krystallnacht*, he was taken by the Nazis to the concentration camp of Sachsenhausen and held there for three months, underfed and forced to do terribly hard labor in frigid weather. Shortly after his release he was ordained a rabbi, and with some help from Harvard, soon thereafter obtained a scholarship to the University of Aberdeen in Scotland. Fears of Nazi invasion of England resulted in his being interred over the next two years, first in Scotland, then (like prisoners of war) in Canada. Finally released, he pursued advanced studies in philosophy at the University of Toronto, while at the same time (1943–1948) serving as rabbi at Temple Anshe Sholom in Hamilton, Ontario.

For the next thirty-six years he taught philosophy at the University of Toronto and published multiple essays and books on metaphysics, Hegelian and Kantian philosophy and the fate of Judaism in the modern world. But deeply disturbed by the world's indifference to Arab attempts in 1967 to destroy the nation of Israel, he became all the more pro–Zionist and committed to supporting the cause of Jewish survival. Toward that end,

after a number of trips with his wife to Israel, he eventually made *aliyah* himself and accepted a fellowship at the Hebrew University's Institute of Contemporary Jewry in Jerusalem. The memoirs written during his final years testify to his lasting commitment as a philosopher to his Jewish faith.

FACKENHEIM ON RELIGION. Just as modern science and philosophy have expelled God from nature (either on grounds that the ability of science to explain everything renders the "God-hypothesis' otiose, or on methodological grounds that it is illegitimate to infer absolute and transcendent causes from relative and empirical effects), so a variety of modern thinkers have been inclined by their concern about human freedom and the problem of evil to expel God from history, ultimately replacing even an "externally superintending, divine providence" with a humanistic belief in progress, and reducing religious faith in God's presence in history to a merely subjective, emotional experience.

With the Holocaust debunking any notion of progress, some philosophers (including a few Jewish thinkers) have agreed that "God is dead" and that the ancient Midrashic affirmation of God's presence in history is absurd. But Midrash storytelling challenges philosophy's reliance upon discursive language. The God it talks about is infinite, and therefore beyond rational comprehension. It makes no logical truth-claims about the existence or nature of God, but gives expression rather to the wonder authentic Jews experience when, even in the darkest moments of despair, their religious faith gives them a glimpse of God as the incomprehensible, sole Power at work in the epochal events of Jewish history (the Exodus, Sinai, destruction of the temples, Auschwitz and rebirth of the State of Israel). It bespeaks a view of history that is neither progressive nor catastrophic, recognizing as it does that God alone can save man from the unspeakable horror of the Holocaust, but also that God will do so only through the acting of man within history. The divine presence it witnesses to, therefore, is a commanding one, challenging Jews, secular and religious alike, "to survive as

Jews," and never "to hand Hitler yet another, posthumous victory" by despairing either of God or of this world.

Sources

Fackenheim, Emil. *An Epitaph for German Judaism: From Halle to Jerusalem.* Introduction by Michael Morgan. Madison: University of Wisconsin, 2003.

_____. *God's Presence in History: Jewish Affirmations and Philosophical Reflections.* New York: New York University Press; London: University of London Press, Ltd., 1970.

_____. *The Jewish Return into History.* New York: Schocken Books, 1978. See esp. 19–24; 25–32; 261–72.

_____. *To Mend the World.* New York: Schocken Books, 1982. See esp. 317–31.

Morgan, Michael L., ed. *The Jewish Thought of Emil Fackenheim: A Reader.* Detroit: Wayne State University Press, 1987.

Samuelson, Norbert M. *An Introduction to Modern Jewish Philosophy.* Albany: State University of New York Press, 1989. 288–306.

Simon, Julius J. "Emil L. Fackenheim." In *World Philosophers and Their Works.* Vol. 1. Edited by John K. Roth. Pasadena, CA, and Hackensack, NJ: Salem Press, Inc., 2000. 629–34.

Feuerbach, Ludwig (1804–1872)

Among Feuerbach's ancestors was a line of well-known church elders and seventeenth-century Protestant theologians. His father, a hot-tempered, impulsive, socially progressive, liberal-minded jurist, was the first Protestant appointed to a chair at a Bavarian University (in Landshut) in an attempt by the Crown Prince Max Joseph to introduce the Enlightenment to Catholic Bavaria. While still in his mid-teens, Feuerbach was showing a keen interest in religion, as evidenced, for example, by his taking instruction in Hebrew from the son of a local rabbi. At the age of eighteen he began studying theology at Heidelberg under the church historian and exegete, H.E.G. Paulus, and the dogmatic theologian, Karl Daub. The latter's taste for Hegelian and Schleiermachian ideas prompted Feuerbach to go to Berlin to hear Hegel and Schleiermacher for himself.

After clearing himself of suspicions about his supposed involvement in secret and subversive political organizations, he was finally admitted to Berlin's school of theology in 1824 and afforded the opportunity to attend the lectures of both Schleiermacher and Hegel. After hearing Hegel, however, he found what he later described as the "theological mishmash of freedom and dependence" being propounded by Schleiermacher "repulsive to my soul," and in the following year transferred to the school of philosophy, first at Berlin and then at Erlangen, where he got his degree in 1828 and in the following year became a *Privatdocent.* He still subscribed to Hegel's idealism, but used it to contrast the unifying spirit of reason to the egoistic individualism of a religion like Christianity.

The eventual discovery of his authorship of the anonymously published *Thoughts on Death and Immortality* (which called into question the immortality of the human soul) virtually terminated his future prospects for any advanced professorial appointments and forced him to rely on his wife's wealth as he pursued the life of an independent philosopher. Subsequent publications, and especially those of the *Essence of Christianity* and *Lectures on the Essence of Religion*, made him famous, but also marked a complete break with Hegelianism and brought upon him the charge of atheism. He claimed till the day he died in 1872 that his intention was not to destroy religion, but to retrieve its moral and cultural content.

FEUERBACH ON RELIGION. Religion was originally based upon a feeling of dependency on Nature. Natural forces fired the imagination of primitive man, inducing a sense of wonder as well as dread of his own contingency and mortality. Impelled by a desire to live forever in a more hospitable world, he began treating lifeless things as living spirits that might be controlled by magic, or eventually — when religion became polytheistic — as transcendent, anthropomorphic figures whose assistance could be won through prayer and sacrifice. In the more monotheistic religions, however, what came to be projected outward into the transcendental realm shifted from that which set individuals and cultures apart to those attributes which all humans have in common. The primary basis of a spiritual, albeit not necessarily superior, religion like Christianity, therefore, is the self-consciousness that man, in contrast to the brutes, has of his own nature as a member of the human species.

Fascinated by the infinitude of the latter, but all the more aware on that account of his own limitations as a finite individual, he dreams of sharing in the perfection of the species, the abstraction of which he transforms by projecting his own specifically human attributes (Reason, Will, and Affection) into an image of God as a spiritual being of infinite knowledge, freedom, and love. Traditional Christian doctrines about the triune and incarnate nature of God are actually theological reflections on the essentially social and loving nature of man. But by emphasizing the total otherness of their God, religions like Christianity also alienate man from himself; having projected the best of himself onto the image of God, man is left with next to nothing for himself. If, therefore, he is ever to come of age, man will have to dethrone God and become a god unto himself. Atheism, in fact, is the mysterious truth underlying the Christian doctrine of divine *kenosis*: Just as God has renounced himself out of love, so man, out of love, should renounce God.

Sources

Feuerbach, Ludwig. *The Essence of Christianity*. Translated by George Eliot. Evanston, London, and New York: Harper and Row, 1957.
_____. *The Essence of Faith According to Luther*. Translated by Melvin Cherno. New York: Harper and Row, 1967.
_____. *The Essence of Religion*. Translated by Alexander Loos. New York: A.K. Butts and Co., 1873.
_____. *Lectures on the Essence of Religion*. Translated by Ralph Manheim. New York: Harper and Row, 1967.
Copleston, Frederick, S.J. *A History of Philosophy*. Vol. 7, pt. 2. Garden City, NY: Doubleday and Company, Inc., 1962–77. 60–70.
Dupré, L. "Feuerbach, Ludwig Andreas." *New Catholic Encyclopedia*. Vol. 5. Edited by W.J. McDonald. New York: McGraw-Hill, 1967. 904–5.
Fiorenza, Francis Schuessler. "Feuerbach's Interpretation of Religion and Christianity." *The Philosophical Forum* 11.2 (1979–1980): 161–81.
Harvey, Van A. *Feuerbach and the Interpretation of Religion*. Cambridge: Cambridge University Press, 1995.
Kamenka, Eugene. *The Philosophy of Ludwig Feuerbach*. London: Routledge and Kegan Paul, 1970. See esp. 18–32, 35–68.
Wartofsky, Marx W. *Feuerbach*. Cambridge: Cambridge University Press, 1977.

Fichte, Johann Gottlieb (1762–1814)

Fichte was baptized into the Lutheran faith. Already as a young child he had mastered the Bible and Catechism and sometimes led his family in their morning and evening prayers. His mother, a wealthy merchant's daughter who had married a peasant, wanted her gifted son to enhance his social status by becoming a clergyman. His uncanny ability to repeat verbatim the sermon he had heard earlier in the morning church service so impressed the visiting Freiherr von Miltitz that the latter had him put in the care of a Lutheran pastor and for a number of years paid for all the young boy's educational expenses. The next six years of Fichte's life were spent at the quasi-monastic seminary at Pforta. Its repressive regimen inclined him on one occasion to run away, until in a moment of prayer he remembered the grief it would cause his parents, and returned.

In 1780 he became a student of theology at the University of Jena and was soon, along with his study of Spinoza's *Ethics,* wrestling with the difficulty of reconciling human freedom with divine sovereignty, reason and faith, and other such issues. No longer enjoying the patronage of the deceased Miltitz, he had to engage in tutorial work to support himself, but his intention was still to become a village pastor. During a happy two-year period in Zurich Fichte did some preaching and, to his future wife whom he met there, wrote that he was proud not to be numbered among the "contemptible, empty-headed Pietists."

From Leipzic where he next went in search of employment he wrote that he belonged neither to the Lutheran nor to the Reformed Church, but to the Christian community, or that variety of it where "there is most freedom of thought and charity of life." By this time he had given up any thought of a full-time clerical career. Pursuant to a request to explain to a pupil Kant's *Critique of Pure Reason*, he became enamored of the latter's thought and spent much of the remainder of his life trying to supplement what he perceived to be its deficiencies (e.g., initially, regarding the role of revelation). After landing a professorship at the University of Jena, scheduling his lectures on Sunday close to the traditional hour of divine service, and seeming to identify God with the moral order of the universe, he was accused of atheism and forced to resign. His last writings from Erlangen and Berlin were largely of a practical nature, but also included some that were deeply religious, describing knowledge and love of the Absolute (God) as the blessed goal of life.

FICHTE ON RELIGION. To speak of God as substance or as personal would make no sense, since personality implies finitude and substance suggests extension in time and space, or materiality. But Kant was right. Although it can be proven neither from the point of view of empirical science, nor from the innatist perspective of dogmatic rationalism, the existence of God (along with human freedom and immortality) can be postulated as a theological corollary of the moral coincidence of virtue and happiness. To be effective, however, such rational faith must, more often than not, be supplemented by the religious experience of God as the cause, not of the content of the moral law, nor of its authority, but of its existence in the human self.

Given their betimes overwhelming natural impulses and proclivity toward evil, some humans can remain faithful to the rational dictates of morality only if God identifies himself to them through some special revelation

in the realm of the sensuous world as the holy and just legislator of the moral law. The few who have achieved moral perfection through a completely free and autonomous commitment to obedience of the moral law, and feel no need for such supplementary, religious incentive, might still sense the reality of God in their experience of the super-sensible moral order of the universe itself as being divine (the *ordo ordinans*). At the heart of that cosmic order is the Absolute Ego which, contrary to Kant's critical theory of the "thing in itself," becomes self-conscious through positing of the non–self-objective Nature as a field of moral action. This transcendent, ordering force can be identified with neither the finite knowing subject, nor with any notion of a personal, substantial divine being. One might, however, think of it as the eternal and infinite Will or Creative Life Force to which it is our vocation, as rational human beings, to devote ourselves in life, and to abandon ourselves in death.

Sources

Fichte, Johann Gottlieb. *Attempt at a critique of all revelation*. Translated by Garrett Green. Cambridge and New York: Cambridge University Press, 1978.
_____. *The Popular Works of Johann Gottlieb Fichte*. Translated by William Smith, with a memoir of Fichte's life. Bristol: Thoemmes, 1999.
_____. *Science of Knowledge*. Edited and translated by Peter Heath and John Lachs. Cambridge: Cambridge University Press, 1982.
_____. *The Vocation of Man*. LaSalle, IL: Open Court, 1965.
Adamson, Robert. *Fichte*. Edinburgh and London: William Blackwood and Sons, 1881.
Copleston, Frederick, S.J. *A History of Philosophy*. Vol. 7, pt. 1. Garden City, NY: Doubleday and Company, Inc., 1962–77. 50–120.
Döring, Woldemar Oskar. *Fichte: Der Mann Und Sein Werk*. Hamburg: Hansischer Gildenverlag, 1947.

Ficino, Marsilio (1433–1499)

Even Giovanni Corsi, who wrote his "Life of Marsilio Ficino" within a decade of the latter's death, admitted that "little is known of Ficino's early childhood." But there is no reason to doubt that he was baptized a Catholic, since Catholicism was no less the main religion in the city of his birth (Florence) than in any other part of fifteenth-century, pre–Reformation Western Europe. His father, who was a doctor to Cosimo de Medici, wanted his son to pursue a medical career. And Ficino not only did study medicine as a young man, but considered the practice of it an essential part of his future, priestly vocation. But his early studies also included Latin, philosophy, and theology. Concerned about what he perceived to be the antireligious implications of the Aristotelian scholasticism to which he was exposed, he early on was prompted by his reading of Augustine and Plotinus to champion Platonic philosophy (rooted as he thought it was in the primeval tradition initiated by Zoroaster, Hermes Trismegristus, Orpheus, *et alia*) as the "true sister" of the "true religion" (i.e., Christianity, but not to the total exclusion of other faiths).

After being encouraged by Cosimo (who himself was enthusiastic about Plato) to learn Greek, Ficino proceeded to use the Villa Careggi provided him by his rich and powerful patron to establish a Platonic Academy. There he would edit the complete works of Plato, translate a number of them, and devote himself to editing and translating the writings of Plotinus, Proclus and other Neoplatonists. It was also to the ideas of Plato that he would often turn in several of his own works, like the *Theologia platonica* and the *De christiana religione*, when trying to explain the Christian religion, its notion of charity, its belief in personal immortality, and so forth. At the rather advanced age of forty, following a rather lengthy bout of melancholy, he was finally ordained to the priesthood.

Some years later he was installed as a canon at the cathedral in Florence. He took his priestly vocation very seriously, seeing the good priest as a healer of both body and soul, "an angel of God standing in God's place, performing His work among men." He preached regularly to large and appreciative crowds at the cathedral, and was constantly engaged in pastoral and clerical activities (like the writing of multiple letters to religious and secular leaders to urge reform). After the Medici were expelled from Florence in 1494, Ficino — thanks to the generosity of his friend, the Bishop of Arezzo — retired to a peaceful life in the countryside. He is buried in the Florentine Church of the Santa Reparata.

FICINO ON RELIGION. In the light of God's own being, the human mind is led to worship the one and infinite God from whom all things emanate and in whom they find their ultimate unity. Religion or divine worship, therefore, is as natural and common to all men as is neighing to the horse. But it is also religion that sets men apart from and makes them happier than the other animals which, while possessing some artistic talent, rudimentary languages, and certain traces of reason, show no sign of religion. It is not to be expected, however, that philosophically minded individuals can be lured into acknowledging this natural religion without being given philosophical food for thought. But when they are so fed with rational arguments (as Divine Providence saw fit to do through Zoroaster, Trismegistus, Pythagoras, and especially the divine Plato), they will readily recognize religion in general, and eventually be convinced to accept the best and truest species of religion contained in the genus.

Although in making sure that no region would be without religion, God permitted a beautiful variety of religious rites to be observed in different places and times, it was in the kind of worship of God through good actions, truthful speech, clear thinking, and charity as taught by Christ that religion achieved its highest expression. So conceived, religion is in perfect harmony with philosophy. The pure contemplation of God both provide affords the human soul a foretaste of the beatific vision it can expect to experience at the end of its ascent. That the human soul is immortal is certain, not only because of its affinity with the eternal objects of its thought, but also and especially because it is inconceivable that the natural desire to know God expressed in religion, but never perfectly satisfied in this life, would go forever unfulfilled. Were such to be the case, man's plight, given his constant frustrations and futile sacrifices, would be worse than that of animals — something a wise and loving God would never allow to happen.

Sources

Ficino, Marsilio. *Letters*. Translated by the Language Department of the School of Economic Science, London. London: Shepheard-Walwyn, 1978–1994. See esp. Vol. 1: 68–69, 110; Vol. 2: 36–37; Vol. 3: "Corsi's Life of Marsilio Ficino," 133–53; Vol. 5: 41–42.
_____. *Opera omnia*. 2 vols. Turin: Bottego d'Erasmo, 1959.
_____. *Platonic Theology*. Translated by Michael J.B. Allen and John Warden. Cambridge, MA: Harvard University Press, 2001.
Allen, Michael J.B., Valery Rees, and Martin Davies, eds. *Marsilio Ficino: His Theology, His Philosophy, His Legacy*. Leiden and Boston: Köln, 2002.
Collins, Ardis B. *The Secular Is Sacred: Platonism and Thomism in Marsilio Ficino's Platonic Theology*. The Hague: Martinus Nijhoff, 1974.
Kristeller, Paul Oskar. *The Philosophy of Marsilio Ficino*. New York: Columbia University Press, 1943. See esp. 289–350.
Schmitt, C.B. "Ficino, Marsilio." *New Catholic Encyclopedia*. Vol. 5. Edited by W.J. McDonald. New York: McGraw-Hill, 1967. 907–8.
Spitz, Lewis W. "Ficino, Marsilio." In *Encyclopedia of Religion*. Vol. 5. Edited by Mircea Eliade. New York: Macmillan and Co., 1987. 320.

Flew, Antony (1923–)

His father being a Methodist minister of religion and tutor in New Testament studies at what would become the Methodist theological college in Cambridge, Flew identified himself as "a son of the manse." The father was also active in interchurch, Christian ecumenical organizations, and Flew often accompanied him to their conferences. At the age of thirteen, Flew was enrolled at Kingswood, a school founded by John Wesley for the education of the sons of Methodist ministers. But already the conscientious commitment to Christianity that he had earlier felt was beginning to wane. He found it a weary duty having to worship, pray, sing hymns, or participate in other religious practices in chapel. By the time of his fifteenth birthday he had begun questioning whether belief in the existence of God could be reconciled with the prevalence of evil in this world. Occasional participation in prewar meetings of the Socratic Club founded at Oxford by C.S. Lewis did little to change his mind.

To keep peace at home, he tried initially to conceal his "irreligious conversion," but at least by the time he had returned from military service in 1945 and resumed his pursuit of academic degrees at Oxford, the truth of his atheistic and "mortalist" views, tinged by the Communist sympathies he had developed already at Kingswood, was outed. Close association as a student and then as a lecturer at Oxford with Gilbert Ryle reinforced the skeptical appraisal of religious belief that would find expression in his famous paper, "Theology and Falsification" and works like *God and Philosophy*, *The Presumption of Atheism*, or *Atheistic Humanism* that he would publish in future years while professing philosophy at the Universities of Aberdeen, Keele, Reading, and other cities around the world.

More recently, however, the atheistic views on which Flew had earlier thought there would be no going back began to crack as he paid closer attention to the latest developments in DNA research. While still rejecting any notion of a personal God who is actively involved in human lives, and denying any hope for or belief in personal immortality, in the introduction to the latest edition of his *God and Philosophy* and multiple discussions with John Haldane and others, the eighty-some-year-old Flew has expressed greater respect for belief in the existence of God as an Aristotelian, deistic type of powerful Intelligent Mind. In his Socratic desire to "follow the evidence wherever it leads," he is now inclined to suspect that it may be the only way that the enormous complexity of DNA material can be adequately explained.

FLEW ON RELIGION. Traditional theism

would seem to have failed not only to provide a meaningful concept of God, but also to respect the principle that it is always wrong to believe anything on insufficient evidence. In the first place, its arguments for the existence of God seemed less than convincing, falsely assuming either an essential link between existence and the idea of perfection, an analogy between the universe and artifacts, the identification of an architect with a creator, and that the existence of the universe as a brute fact requires explanation, or that (as Pascal and Tolstoy put it) we have only two options to consider. Secondly, it either downplayed the problem of evil, or, ignoring the compatibility of free will and determinism, overlooked the possibility that an omnipotent God could have created free creatures who always make right choices. Thirdly, it was too quick to give greater credence to subjective testimonial reports of miracles (e.g., the resurrection of Jesus) than to evidence of the natural laws they contradict. Finally, it also seemed to defy the principle of falsifiability by constantly altering its claims about the existence of God and other matters with a thousand different qualifications, and making no allowance for any evidence that might count against its putative assertions. To that extent it seemed that theistic claims could be dismissed as nonsense.

These objections to traditional theism may need to be reconsidered, however, in the light of new scientific conclusions about the origin and integrated complexity of the universe and living organisms. The cosmological, ontological, and moral arguments for God's existence remain less than convincing. But the so-called "fine-tuning argument" for an "Intelligent Orderer," or Swinburne's claim that the religious hypothesis "explains everything that a secular natural science has to leave as an inexplicable brute fact," could add very strong confirmation to previously held theistic views, albeit without the traditional Christian or Islamic concept of God and personal immortality.

Sources

Flew, Antony. *Atheistic Humanism*. Buffalo, NY: Prometheus Books, 1993.

_____. *God and Philosophy*. New York: Dell Publishing Co., Inc., 1966.

_____. *God and Philosophy*. Buffalo: Prometheus Press, 2005.

_____. *New Essays in Philosophical Theology*. London: SCM Press, Ltd., 1955.

_____. *The Presumption of Atheism*. London: Elek Books, Ltd., 1976.

Habermas, Gary. "Interview with Antony Flew." http://www.biola.edu/antonyflew/. See also *Philosophia Christi* (Winter 2004): http://www.biola.edu/philchristi/.

Hick, John. *Philosophy of Religion*. 3rd ed. Englewood Cliffs, NJ: Prentice-Hall, Inc., 1983. 42; 97–99.

Ostling, Richard N. "Famous Atheist Now Believes in God." *Netscape News*, December 26, 2004. http://cnn.netscape.cnn.

Peterson, Michael, et al. *Reason and Religious Belief*. New York and Oxford: Oxford University Press, 2003. 131; 177–79; 186–88; 226–28; 311.

Foucault, Michel (1926–1984)

Foucault was born into a nominally Catholic family that adhered to traditional rites of baptism, first communion, marriage and burial, but as was typical of their French *bourgeoise* class, harbored a bit of anti-clericalism and agnosticism. Along with his mother (and/or grandmother) and his two siblings, the young Foucault attended Mass every Sunday at Poitiers' Church of Saint-Porchaire, served as an acolyte, and briefly sang in the choir. After performance as a student at the Lycée Henri-IV less than satisfactory to his mother, he was enrolled at the Collège Saint-Stanislas, a not very highly regarded religious secondary school run by the Christian Brothers. Except for its rather eccentric, but learned history professor, a Benedictine monk (Father de Montsabert) from nearby Ligugé Abbey, the school's influence on Foucault was mostly negative, leaving him, by his own account, with much outrage and hostility toward the school's general atmosphere, and a dislike of the brothers and the religion they were teaching.

There is no evidence, however, of his having experienced any sudden loss of faith either at Saint Stanislas, or later at the École Normale Supérieure and the Sorbonne, where much to the disappointment of his physician-father, he forewent the study of medicine to pursue his interest in history and philosophy. Instead, while retaining a lifelong fascination with the Catholic Church as a "superb instrument of power" and making some interesting studies on the respective ways Christianity and Zen Buddhism have of discovering the truth and personal identity, he simply let his childhood religion fade away into the background of his scholarly (and homosexual) lifestyle as a professor at various foreign and French universities.

When he died, his mother, with whom he had maintained close ties throughout his life, insisted that a religious service be held at the burial of his body in the cemetery at Vendeuvre. Michel Albaric, a Dominican monk and librarian who had befriended Foucault and respected his agnostic (as opposed to atheistic) sentiments, was recruited to perform the service. Instead of offering the usual Requiem Mass (which might have left a false impression of Foucault's return to the Roman Catholic faith), Father Albaric presided over a simple service of prayer, silence, meditation, and poetic reading.

FOUCAULT ON RELIGION. Marx rightly prefaced his statement about religion being "the opiate of the masses" with the assertion that religion is also "the spirit of a world without spirit." As was evidenced by the 1978 Islamic revolution in Iran, religion can serve as the voice (the vocabulary, the ceremonial, the timeless drama) whereby a people frames its historical struggle against the repressive powers that be. Intermingling imaginary, erotic, and sensual elements, a religious institution like the church can become for people a superb instrument for finding something that can radically change their subjectivity and renew their entire existence. Among the repressive forces against which people must now struggle is the arrogant, but futile, attempt by modern thinkers to apotheosize humanity and spell out exactly what it means to be human in the absence of the God declared dead by Feuerbach and Nietzsche.

No doubt, religion, and especially Christianity (with its pastoral use of confession and examination of conscience to constitute a hermeneutical, self-denying, blindly obedient subject) can be dangerous, and has itself contributed to the self-diagnosing technologies whereby modern science tries to get individuals to admit to the "truth" of their madness, criminality, homosexuality, or whatever other identification scientists concoct for the sake of ordering and controlling human life. But religion can also help people escape such linguistic prisons. Zen meditation, for example, can afford one the experience of a totally other kind of relationship between the body, mind, and external world than that spelled out by psychology, biology, or any other science. And despite its historically ascetical pole, the Christian version of Cynic *parrhesia* (personal frankness) can lead one, perhaps, into a "night of truth" wherein one discovers that one does not know who one is, and on that account, becomes all the more open to the ultimate mystery of love and the possible experience of something more than egocentric, raw sexuality (e.g., friendship).

Sources

Foucault, Michel. *The Archaeology of Knowledge.* Translated by A.M. Sheridan Smith. New York: Harper and Row, 1972.

_____. *The Care of the Self: The History of Sexuality.* Vol. 3. London: Penguin, 1990.

_____. *The History of Sexuality.* Vol. 1. New York: Pantheon, 1978.

_____. *The Order of Things: An Archaeology of the Human Sciences.* New York: Random House, 1970.

_____. *Politics, Philosophy, Culture: Interviews and Other Writings: 1977–1984.* Translated by Alan Sheridan and others. Edited by Lawrence D. Kritzman. New York and London: Routledge, 1988.

_____. *Religion and Culture.* Selected and edited by Jeremy R. Carrette. New York: Routledge, 1999.

_____. *The Use of Pleasure: The History of Sexuality.* Vol. 2. London: Penguin, 1992.

Bernauer, James. "The Sounds of Silence." *Commonweal* (January 17, 1986): 17–20.

_____, and Jeremy Carrette, eds. *Michel Foucault and Theology: The Politics of Religious Experience.* Hampshire, England, and Burlington, VT: Ashgate, 2004. See esp. 77–98; 117–42.

Burke, Peter, ed. *Critical Essays on Michel Foucault.* Aldershot, Hants, England: Scolar Press; Brookfield, VT: Ashgate, 1992.

Carrette, Jeremy R. *Foucault and Religion: Spiritual Corporality and Political Spirituality.* London and New York: Routledge, 1999.

Eribon, Didier. *Michel Foucault.* Translated by Betsy Wing. Cambridge, MA: Harvard University Press, 1991.

Gutting, Gary, ed. *The Cambridge Companion to Foucault.* Cambridge: Cambridge University Press, 1994.

Macey, David. *The Lives of Michel Foucault.* London: Hutchinson, 1993.

Gadamer, Hans-Georg (1900–2002)

Gadamer's paternal grandfather had been a Catholic before marrying a Protestant wife and converting to the Protestant faith of the other grandparents. His father, an authoritarian parent and renowned professor of pharmaceutical chemistry, was an intellectual deist who had little use for the church or for any intellectual endeavor other than natural science. In contrast to her unreligious husband, the mother was quite devout, harboring a rather secretive inclination toward Pietism. Gadamer later observed that his own religious disposition came from her. She had him baptized, and later, along with his older, sanctimoniously religious epileptic brother, confirmed a Protestant. He found the liturgy of the church services he had to attend with his brother aesthetically terrible, and the sermons he heard more conducive to unbelief than belief.

Questions about his faith grew with his first exposure to the Enlightenment's critique of religion while attending the Gymnasium. They were further stimulated (after his graduation and escape from military service in World War I because of poor health) during a year of study at the University of Breslau by his reading of what Kant and Kierkegaard had to say about the limits of reason, and by his subsequent decade-long work at the University of Marburg as a student and assistant of Heidegger (whose phenomenological hermeneutics would greatly influence Gadamer, but whose subliminal, Aristotelian and Catholic search for an infinite God would also strike Gadamer as being in sharp contrast to the Platonic and Kierkegaardian sense of the divine in terms of finitude).

At Marburg Gadamer also worked closely with Rudolf Bultmann, initiating a close association with theologians that would last throughout the following years of his teaching and prolific writing at various German and (after retirement) American universities. But in the interviews he often gave toward the end of his long life he would always insist upon his still being an agnostic. While asserting that the only thesis of which he was sure was that "people cannot live without hope" or that the "whole of existence" is "more than the flicker of light our consciousness traverses," and often thinking how nice it would be to be able to believe in God, he disclaimed any personal belief in God's existence or in personal immortality. Still, he wanted and got a church funeral, without a homily, but with a reading of Psalms, a Mahler *Lied*, and (to the chagrin of the family) a pastoral blessing and recitation of the Lord's Prayer.

GADAMER ON RELIGION. Modern scientific study of religion consists merely of a supposedly objective attempt to explain how human consciousness, in its infantile stage of development, is susceptible to an exclusively subjective, illusory acceptance of truth claims that have no foundation in fact. It is conceivable, however, that science presents only a partial view of reality, and is incapable of understanding religious and other phenomena, like poetry, paintings, music, and so on., that defy conceptual objectification. Genuine understanding, by which, as Heidegger noted, humans come to be in time (*Dasein*), is neither totally objective nor totally subjective. It is, rather, dialogical in nature, involving a fusion of two horizons: that of the phenomenon itself, with all its original historical and psychological contextual implications, and that of past and present interpreters, with all their prejudices, traditions, questions, concerns, and experiences.

However much they differ, religion and art share this hermeneutical structure. To be understood, therefore, religious phenomena must be allowed to manifest themselves, linguistically and otherwise, in a dialectical manner analogous to the playful, festive and ritualistic way that works of art draw prospective interpreters out of any kind of sovereign subjectivity or supposedly objective frame of mind and lure them into playing along with and celebrating one or another temporal event as a community. Even if religious phenomena lie beyond empirical verification and it is futile to try to prove something like God's existence, they might, therefore, still be valuable, especially in the face of death and other boundary situations. The real illusion, then, may be to think that human beings can live without religion. But whatever significance religion has, it can never be exhausted by authoritarian, dogmatic proclamations, since the disclosure of any phenomenon (its "truth") always also involves some concealment. Though rooted in tradition, religious phenomena remain open to ongoing creative reinterpretations.

Sources

Gadamer, Hans-Georg. *A Century of Philosophy. A Conversation with Riccardo Dottori.* Translated by Rod Coltman with Sigrid Koepke. New York and London: Continuum, 2004.
_____. *Gadamer in Conversation. Reflections and Commentary.* Translated by Richard E. Palmer. New Haven and London: Yale University Press, 2001.
_____. *Hermeneutics, Religion, and Ethics.* Translated by Joel Weinsheimer. New Haven and London: Yale University Press, 1999.
_____. *Philosophical Apprenticeships.* Translated by Robert R. Sullivan. Cambridge, MA, and London: The MIT Press, 1985.
_____. *The Relevance of the Beautiful and Other Essays.* Translated by Nicholas Walker. Cambridge: Cambridge University Press, 1986.
_____. "Religion and Religiosity in Socrates." In

Proceedings of the Boston Area Colloquium in Ancient Philosophy, edited by John J. Cleary. Vol. 1. Lanham: University Press of America, 1986. 53–75.
_____. "The Religious Dimension in Heidegger." In *Transcendence and the Sacred*, edited by Alan M. Olson and Leroy S. Rouner. Notre Dame and London: University of Notre Dame Press, 1981. 193–207.
_____. "Religious and Poetical Speaking." In *Myth, Symbol, and Reality*, edited by Alan M. Olson. Notre Dame and London: University of Notre Dame Press, 1980. 86–98.
_____. *Truth and Method.* Translated by W. Glen-Doepel. London: Sheed and Ward, 1975.
Grondin, Jean. *Hans-Georg Gadamer: A Biography.* Translated by Joel Weinsheimer. New Haven and London: Yale University Press, 2003.
_____. *The Philosophy of Gadamer.* Translated by Kathryn Plant. Montreal, Kingston, and Ithaca: McGill-Queen's University Press, 2003.
Malpas, Jeff. "Hans-Georg Gadamer." *Stanford Encyclopedia of Philosophy.* http://plato.stanford.edu/. 18.

Goethe, Johann Wolfgang von (1749–1832)

Goethe grew up reading the Bible, learning the Lutheran catechism, memorizing Sunday sermons, and partaking of the sacraments. He would later claim to have been less than inspired by the cold formalism of these early religious experiences. News of the Lisbon earthquake and the superstitious response of his elders to local thunderstorms, left him also, already at the age of six, with some doubts about divine providence. As a budding teenage poet, however, he was still preoccupied with biblical themes (e.g., Christ's descent into hell). At sixteen he enrolled at the University of Leipzig and stopped attending church altogether. The kindness of some Pietistic friends during a serious illness soon thereafter tempted him for a while to embrace their practical approach to living the Gospel message. But although he would remain fond of the more cultured Zinzendorfian brand of Pietism and shared its criticism of the Christian establishment, he came to despise the world-negating attitude of the Hallean Pietists whom he later encountered while studying law at Strassburg.

Breaking with the Pietists, Goethe wrote several works (*Letter of the Pastor, The Eternal Jew*) and book reviews during the early 1770s in which he pleaded for religious tolerance by suggesting that the dogmatic absolutism of orthodox theologians had so defaced Christianity as to make it unrecognizable to any returning Christ. During the next decade, while in Wetzlar and Weimar, he further detached himself from institutionalized Protestantism, on grounds that he was not hypocritical enough to identify with church people who were Christian in name only. On a trip to Rome in 1786, he came to a similar conclusion about Roman Catholicism, admiring its aesthetic tastes and sacramentality, but deploring its medieval, cultural backwardness and lack of spiritual substance.

Reflecting the turbulence of his own romantic life, his subsequent novels gave expression to a confusing search for security in the personal feeling of love. But this gave way eventually in his later writings to a "world piety," or sense of being in touch with God as a spiritual force realizing itself in the multiple phenomena of nature. To the end, he worshiped Christ as the ultimate revelation of natural law, but identified with Christianity (Protestant and Catholic alike) only to the extent that it afforded him and fellow poets the freedom to share in that revelatory process.

GOETHE ON RELIGION. Religious piety arises from the exciting aspiration felt in the depths of the human heart to surrender freely and gratefully to something higher than ourselves. But the divine reality never permits itself to be known directly; it can be seen only in symbolic reflection. If the Bible is a source of such revelation, so too is Nature in all its evolving variations. Nature mirrors God as the immanent Spirit that drives the ongoing transformation of its myriad plant, animal, and human forms. This divine life of Nature cannot be discerned, however, by the kind of abstract, scientific understanding which conceives of Nature as nothing more than a machine whose every movement can be mathematically calculated. Only a delicate, deep and calm contemplation, in which feeling is

everything, will capture the divine presence reflected in Nature's organic unity.

Although such religious feeling is cognitive, the intuitive knowledge it delivers in no way exhausts the mysteries of Nature or the being of God. Nature retains its veil, and the All-embracing, All-preserving God remains, notwithstanding a hundred different names, unspeakable and incomprehensible. While poets and artists might tend to polytheism, natural scientists to pantheism, and moral philosophers to monotheism, each individual conceives of God in accordance with personal needs and psychological makeup. The reverence that lies at the core of all religion can manifest itself as a reverence for that which is superior, equal, or inferior to ourselves, giving rise respectively to feelings of fear, fellowship, and compassion. In any religion that is true, the three combine to spawn the highest reverence, namely, reverence for oneself as an immortal being striving now and forever to be the best of all that God and Nature have produced. Although apostolic Christianity, prior to its numbing institutionalization, came closest to expressing such reverence, all religions should be tolerated with the love taught by Christ. Genuine religious belief will increase the creative fertility of any epoch.

Sources

Goethe, Johann Wolfgang von. *Conversations of Goethe with Johann Peter Eckermann.* Translated by John Oxenford. New York: Da Capo Press, 1998.
_____. *Faust. Great Books of the Western World.* Vol. 47. Edited by R.M. Hutchins. Chicago: Encyclopædia Britannica, Inc., 1952.
_____. *Selected Works.* New York: A.A. Knopf, 2001.
_____. *Wilhelm Meister's Journeyman Years or The Renunciants.* Translated by Krishna Winston. New York: Suhrkamp Publishers, 1983.
Busch, Ernst. *Goethe's Religion.* Tübingen: Furche-Verlag, 1949.
Loewen, Harry. *Goethe's Response to Protestantism.* Berne and Frankfurt/M: Herbert Lang and Co., Ltd., 1972.
Naumann, Walter. "Goethe's Religion." *Journal of the History of Ideas* 13 (1952): 188–99.
Otto, Rudolf. *Das Gefühl Des Überweltlichen.* München: C.H. Beck'sche Verlagsbuchhandlung, 1932. 327–33.

_____. *Naturalism and Religion*. New York: Williams and Norgate, 1913. 24–28.

Pelikan, Jaroslav. *Faust the Theologian*. New Haven and London: Yale University Press, 1995.

Richards, Robert J. *The Romantic Conception of Life: Science and Philosophy in the Age of Goethe*. Chicago and London: The University of Chicago Press, 2002. 325–508.

Schaum, K. "Goethe, Johann Wolfgang von." *New Catholic Encyclopedia*. Vol. 6. Edited by W.J. McDonald. New York: McGraw-Hill, 1967. 581–86.

Thielicke, Helmut. *Goethe und das Christentum*. München/Zürich: R. Piper and Co. Verlag, 1982.

Verkamp, Bernard J. *The Senses of Mystery: Religious and Non-Religious*. Scranton, PA: Scranton University Press, 1997. 86–93.

Habermas, Jürgen (1929–)

Habermas' grandfather was a Protestant minister and director of the seminary in Gummersbach. But like many German Christians at the time, his father joined the Nazi Party in 1933 when Habermas was only four and remained a supposedly passive member until the fall of Berlin in 1945. Sheltered in the small town from the tyranny of the Nazi regime and the horrors of war, Habermas himself enjoyed what seemed to him at the time a rather normal life, until at the age of fourteen he was recruited into the Hitler Youth and sent to help in the futile attempt to defend the Western front. With Germany's defeat and a chance to listen to the Nuremberg trials and to see documentaries of how the Jews and others had been treated in the concentration camps, his eyes were finally opened to what he described in his 2004 Kyoto Prize acceptance speech as the "mind-dulling enclave of home-fire kitsch, monumentalism, and resentful death cult" he had grown up in. Unable to understand why Germany's cultural Christianity could not have prevented such a criminal system, he developed a lifelong ambivalence toward religion.

Disillusioned by postwar political developments in Germany, and disgusted by the lack of contrition for Nazi collaboration on the part of Heidegger, whose works, along with those of Marx and Sartre, he had been studying at the universities of Göttingen, Bonn, and Zurich, he finished his doctoral dissertation on Schelling in 1954 and went to work with Adorno and Horkheimer at the Institute for Social Research. While teaching in subsequent years at several German Institutes and the universities of Heidelberg and Frankfurt, refereeing student uprisings, lecturing around the world, and publishing multiple articles and books about his theories of rationality and communicative action, Habermas has consistently pursued a "methodological, dialectical" brand of atheism. Eschewing all uncritical and exclusive religious integrations, and foregoing the theistic guarantees of any particular religion, it seeks to "re-express what it learns from religion in a discourse that is independent of revealed truth." Over the years he has devoted much time and effort to the study of past Christian thinkers like Schleiermacher and Kierkegaard and has cultivated close ties with modern theologians like Johann Baptist Metz. He also admits that notwithstanding his lack of any personal commitment to Christian belief and practice, his own atheistic theories have been "nourished from the legacy of Christianity."

HABERMAS ON RELIGION. Modern rationality is not so bad as that "blackest" of books (the *Dialectic of Enlightenment* by Horkheimer and Adorno) made it out to be. There is, to be sure, a type of purposive rationality operative in the world of technology and business that approximates the instrumental reasoning that arises out of individualistic interests. But there is also a communicative form of rationality that arises within a community of interpreters who conceive of themselves not as competitors, but as partners in the pursuit of a consensus on what needs to be done to enhance a universal ethic of respect for the freedom and dignity of all human beings.

With the linguistification of the sacred, the religious authority, which once prescribed such a consensus, has been broken through the differentiation of society into three distinct secular spheres of science, law/morality, and art, each with its own claims to universal truth and value. Freed of all ideological, dogmatic constraints, such claims are now based only upon revisable theories monitored against experience. This would seem, at first blush, to render modern religion, with its abandonment of totalizing mythological and metaphysical worldviews, altogether superfluous, since the secular conscience already contains within itself the this-worldly ideals now supposedly symbolized by the term "God.' But even if religious discourse — tied as it is to culturally specific religious practices and beliefs — cannot fulfill its aspirations to add universally valid, rational claims to those of science, law/morality, and art by appealing to some transcendence from beyond this world, and to that extent is excluded from public life, it might nonetheless carry an indispensable, inspiring content which philosophy will never be able to replace or suppress. For philosophy can never provide the consolation whereby human suffering, injustice, loneliness, death, and so on, are endowed by religion with meaning and a spirit of forbearance in the private realm.

Sources

Habermas, Jürgen. *The Liberating Power of Symbols: Philosophical Essays.* Translated by Peter Dews. Cambridge, MA: The MIT Press, 2001.

_____. "Public space and political public sphere — the biographical roots of two motifs in my thought." Commemorative lecture, Kyoto (November 11, 2004). http://homepage.mac.com/gedavis/jH/kyoto_lecture_Nov_2004.pdf

_____. *Religion and Rationality: Essays on Reason, God, and Modernity.* Edited by Eduardo Mendieta. Cambridge, MA: The MIT Press, 2002.

_____. *The Theory of Communicative Action.* Vol. 2: *Life, World and System: A Critique of Functionalist Reason.* Translated by Thomas McCarthy. Cambridge: Polity Press, 1987. See esp. 43–111.

Browning, Don S., and Francis Schüssler, eds. *Habermas, Modernity, and Public Theology.* New York: Crossroad, 1992.

Guarino, Thomas. "Postmodernity and Five Fundamental Theological Issues." *Theological Studies* 57.4 (December 1996): 654–89.

Lalonde, Marc P. *Critical Theology and the Challenge of Jürgen Habermas: Toward a Critical Theory of Religious Insight.* New York: Peter Lang, 1999.

Matuštík, Martin Beck. *Jürgen Habermas: A Philosophical-Political Profile.* Lanham, Boulder, New York, and Oxford: Rowman and Littlefield Publishers, Inc., 2001.

Mendieta, Eduardo. "Modernity's Religion: Habermas and the Linguistification of the Sacred." In *Perspectives on Habermas,* edited by Lewis Edwin Hahn. Chicago and LaSalle, IL: Open Court, 2000. 123–38.

Meyer, William J. "Private Faith or Public Religion? An Assessment of Habermas' Changing View of Religion." *The Journal of Religion* 75.3 (July 1995): 371–91.

Siebert, Rudolf J. *The Critical Theory of Religion: The Frankfurt School.* Berlin, New York, and Amsterdam: Mouton Publishers, 1985. 164–334.

Hartshorne, Charles (1897–2000)

Thanks to the conversion of his paternal grandmother to the Episcopal Church, Charles Hartshorne moved with his family away from their earlier Quaker affiliation. Although Hartshorne's father had B.A. and M.A. degrees from Quaker-oriented Haverford College, he had become a scholarly, liberal Episcopalian clergyman and married the daughter of another Episcopal priest. Growing up in the sheltered environment of Pennsylvania Quaker country, Hartshorne early on developed a love for nature that climaxed in a lifelong fascination with birding and ornithology. While pursuing his secondary education at a small private boarding school in Pennsylvania, called Yeates, his reading of Emerson's *Essays* and Matthew Arnold's attack on traditional Christianity (*Literature and Dogma*) started him down the road toward a more mature philosophy of religion by inclining him not to accept any religious belief that lacked clear and convincing philosophical reasons.

Upon enrolling at Haverford College he encountered a group of sophisticated agnostics or atheists and tried, with little success, to appreciate the writings of their favorite author, Nietzsche. More to his own taste was his reading of Royce's *The Problem of Christianity,* Coleridge's *Aids to Reflection,* and a novel by H.G. Wells that used William James' empiricist concept of a finite God in an attempt to solve the problem of evil. After graduation from Haverford and spending the next two years in the Army's Medical Corps, he went to Harvard where, independent of his reading of Whitehead and Peirce, he wrote his doctoral dissertation on the unity of all things in God. He then spent two years abroad and had the opportunity to hear lectures by the likes of Husserl and Heidegger. He returned to Harvard in 1925, became an assistant to Whitehead, co-edited the philosophical writings of Peirce, and did some less than satisfactory teaching.

Moving on to the University of Chicago for his first full-time teaching assignment in its philosophy department, but eventually also in the school of divinity (where he had his greatest influence), he developed an interest in Dewey's pragmatism, married the woman who would help edit his writings, and began publishing the first of the twenty books and over five hundred articles he would write in subsequent years at Chicago, Emory, and finally Texas University. In his latter years he frequently attended services of the Unitarian Church, but declined labeling himself a Unitarian on grounds that those he felt closest to were in other churches, synagogues, and temples. He died on Yom Kippur, 2000, convinced as ever that the life he had lived would continue as part of God's own everlasting life.

HARTSHORNE ON RELIGION. Without God as the ultimate Designer and the Immortalizer of all human achievements, it is hard to understand how cosmic order is possible or how the experiences of mortal man can be of any significance. But thanks to Anselm, there is little room for doubting that God does exist. His *Proslogion 2* may fail to prove that God exists, but *Proslogion 3* argues validly that God cannot possibly fail to exist. For if it is true that the divine existence is either a necessity or an impossibility, and that God, as the greatest possible being, possesses necessary existence, then it follows that God's existence is either logically necessary or logically impossible, and since God's existence is not logically impossible, it must be logically necessary.

Still, it is one thing to talk about God's existence, and quite another to talk about the divine actuality — how God exists, or what his attributes are. Traditional theistic theology, under the excessive influence of ancient Greek philosophy, wrongly concluded that if God is perfect and infinite, he must be absolutely immutable, omnipotent, omniscient, eternal, and passive. Not only did such a view undermine the value of human freedom and the play of chance, it also depicted God as a temporally disengaged and unsympathetic tyrant causing evil. It is true, of course, that God cannot change for the worse, and no less true that the external relation of God to the world implies a certain abstract immutability and omniscience. But there is no biblical or other reason why God cannot change for the better in the concrete by relating internally to the world, lovingly enticing all entities into the fullest actualization of their potentiality by the beauty of his own being, and receiving their free, unforeseen achievements into his own everlasting mindfulness. Eschewing the extremes of both humanism and supernaturalism, such a panentheistic approach provides religion with a God who, because of his mutually constitutive relation with the world, is alone worthy of worship.

Sources

Hartshorne, Charles. *Beyond Humanism: Essays in the New Philosophy of Nature*. Chicago and New York: Willett, Clark and Company, 1937.

_____. *The Divine Relativity: A Social Conception of God*. New Haven: Yale University Press, 1948.

_____. *Man's Vision of God and the Logic of Theism*. Chicago and New York: Willett, Clark and Company, 1941.

_____. *Omnipotence and Other Theological Mistakes*. Albany, NY: State University of New York Press, 1984.

_____, and William L. Reese. *Philosophers Speak of God*. Chicago and London: The University of Chicago Press, 1953.

_____. "Replies." In *Philosophers Speak of God*. 567–731.

Dombrowski, Daniel A. *Analytic Theism, Hartshorne, and the Concept of God*. Albany, NY: State University of New York Press, 1996.

Hahn, Lewis Edwin, ed. *The Philosophy of Charles Hartshorne*. LaSalle, IL: Open Court, 1991. See esp. 159–462.

Peterson, Michael, et al. *Reason and Religious Belief*.

New York and Oxford: Oxford University Press, 2003. 82–83.

Yandell, Keith E. "Charles Hartshorne." In *World Philosophers and Their Works*. Vol. 2. Edited by John K. Roth. Pasadena, CA, and Hackensack, NJ: Salem Press, Inc., 2000. 787–93.

Hegel, G.W.F. (1770–1831)

To avoid abandoning their Lutheran faith, Hegel's ancestors had moved from Catholic Austria to the Protestant, rather Pietistic, territory of Württemberg. Devoted as they were to their religion, his parents placed him in a course of study that would include theology and eventually result in a career in the Protestant church. Diary entries during his teenage years at the *Gymnasium Illustre* in his hometown of Stuttgart reveal an early interest in the Enlightenment (e.g., in Lessing's *Nathan the Wise*), but apart from usual Protestant disdain for Catholicism, gave no indication of his being skeptical about religion. Friendship with one of his professors (von Abel) reinforced his belief in a creator God and the reconciliation of faith and reason. But after enrolling at the University of Tübingen (basically a Protestant seminary) at the age of eighteen and befriending Hölderlin and Schelling, he pursued studies of philosophy (especially Kant and Rousseau) and a brand of abstract, rationalistic theology he did not much like, gave up any thought of becoming a pastor (notwithstanding an oath he had to sign to the contrary), and began entertaining some less than orthodox religious ideas.

Although his earliest writings on the philosophy of religion while tutoring for private families in Berne and Frankfurt show no sympathy for the Enlightenment's confusion of subjective religion for superstition, he increasingly doubted whether any positive (i.e., dogmatic and authoritarian) religion could meet the needs of the people in modern life. He seems to have found little consolation in religion during a period of deep depression in midlife while teaching or working in Jena, Bamberg, and Nuremberg. He claimed that the thought of teaching theology outside the

university under the direction of church authorities "made [him] shudder in every nerve."

The woman he married (Marie) was a deeply religious person, who saw to the baptism of their children, and had the impression (at least before reading of his posthumous publications) of her husband being a genuinely religious man, with profound attachment to the Bible. The theologian who delivered Hegel's funeral benediction obviously exaggerated in comparing him to Christ. And Hegel himself seldom gave any public display of whatever piety he had. But few ever doubted his personal embrace of the profound religiosity to which his lectures on religion (being delivered in reaction to Schleiermacher) gave expression during his last fifteen years as a professor in Heidelberg and Berlin.

HEGEL ON RELIGION. Kantian reflective philosophy has "killed" God by reducing the divine reality either to a moral corollary or to a totally unknowable entity. Schleiermachian pietism can help restore the religious faith of the masses. But for the educated, only a genuinely speculative philosophy can bring God back to life by sublating the traditionally rational attempts to prove God's existence and identifying Divine Being with Absolute Spirit or Thought. This Absolute has an inner life of "self-identity, self-othering, and self-return" that can be logically analyzed in terms of being and all its categories, and identified further, therefore, as "Identity-in-difference" of being and nonbeing, infinite and finite, and so on.

But the Absolute is not some transcendent First Cause in the sense of being ontologically prior to and independent of its external manifestation in nature and spirit. It is rather the Total Process whereby Thought completes the dialectical odyssey outside and back into itself in pursuit of its self-containment or freedom. Nature and spirit arise spontaneously and necessarily as essential moments in the Absolute's free self-manifestation. This process can be tracked phenomenologically in art, religion, and philosophy. As religion develops historically and climactically from the nature — Eastern, Greek, Egyptian, Jewish and Roman religions into Christianity (not

Roman Catholicism so much as Protestantism, with its modern appreciation of freedom)—the Absolute awakens to its own existence through ritualistic, symbolic, communal reflection by the masses on the divine dimension of human experience and personal identity. Just as art is sublated by religion without losing its autonomy, so the religious imagination of the faithful (along with the ritual and morality it inspires) will be preserved even as it develops into the nonfigurative, purely conceptual forms of philosophical speculation and living.

Sources

Hegel, G.W.F. *Hegel Selections.* Edited by J. Loewenberg. New York: Charles Scribner's Sons, 1929.
_____. *Lectures on the Philosophy of Religion.* Edited by Peter C. Hodgson. Translated by R.F. Brown, P.C. Hodgson, and J.M. Stewart, with the assistance of H.S. Harris. Berkeley, Los Angeles, and London: University of California, 1988.
_____. *The Phenomenology of Spirit.* Translated by A.V. Miller. Oxford: Clarendon Press, 1977.
_____. *The Philosophy of Right; The Philosophy of History. Great Books of the Western World.* Vol. 46. Edited by R.M. Hutchins. Chicago: Encyclopædia Britannica, Inc., 1952.
Beiser, Frederick C. *The Cambridge Companion to Hegel.* Cambridge: Cambridge University Press, 1993. 301–48.
Copleston, Frederick, S.J. *A History of Philosophy.* Vol. 7, pt. 1. Garden City, NY: Doubleday and Company, Inc., 1962–77.
Inwood, Michael. *A Hegel Dictionary.* Oxford: Blackwell, 1997.
Jaeschke, Walter. *Reason in Religion: The Foundations of Hegel's Philosophy of Religion.* Berkeley: University of California Press, 1990.
Kolb, David, ed. *New Perspectives on Hegel's Philosophy of Religion.* Albany: State University of New York Press, 1992.
Pinkard, Terry. *Hegel: A Biography.* Cambridge: Cambridge University Press, 2000. See esp. 39–44; 216–20; 576–93.
Stern, Robert, ed. *G.W.F. Hegel, Critical Assessments.* London and New York: Routledge, 1993. 461–94.

Heidegger, Martin (1889–1976)

Heidegger was baptized in the makeshift church into which the working-class Catholic community of Messkirch had withdrawn after abandoning the church of St. Martin to the town's wealthier and more liberal Old Catholic faction. Six years later St. Martin's was returned to the Catholic faction, and his father being the church sexton, Martin had frequent occasion to serve at the altar, ring the church bells, and run errands for the pastor. Upon the recommendation of the parish priest and with financial assistance from the church, he was sent at the age of fourteen to the Catholic seminary in Constance to prepare for the priesthood. At the age of twenty he entered the Jesuit novitiate, but after only two weeks was discharged for reasons of health. For another year and a half he continued his study of theology at the University of Freiburg, wrote a few anti-modernist pieces for Catholic publications, but gave up the thought of becoming a priest.

Over the next eight years, while studying and lecturing on both medieval and modern (especially Husserl and Schleiermacher) philosophy, serving in the military, and getting married (in a Catholic service to a Lutheran girl), he came to be thought of as the rising star on the horizon of Catholic philosophy (even while being rejected for Freiburg's Catholic chair). In 1919, however, in a letter to a Catholic priest and fellow professor of theology, he announced his disillusionment with the system of Catholicism. Husserl got the impression that Heidegger had converted to Protestantism. But Heidegger himself would later claim that he had never left Catholic tradition (its rites and values), only its excessive dogmatism.

After his shameful, anti–Semitic flirtation with the Nazi regime during the thirties and early forties, he turned to Catholic authorities (Archbishop Gröber) and friends (Romano Guardini) in a futile attempt to keep his teaching post at Freiburg, and seemed to some to be undergoing another religious conversion. Be that as it may, there is no reason to doubt that Heidegger remained a deeply religious man to the end of his life. Before dying, he requested his friend and professorial compatriot, Father Bernard Welte, to speak at a

Church funeral and burial. Father Welte stated that Heidegger had "sought the divine God and His glory with patient expectation," but "in his own way."

HEIDEGGER ON RELIGION. To the basic question "why there are beings rather than nothing," traditional metaphysics and Judaeo-Christian theology (preferring philosophical "foolishness" over its proper study of faith) have responded with the affirmation of a divine ground for all beings, a *causa sui,* prime mover, or divine creator. But such ontotheologic conceptualization reduces "God" to an object (albeit the highest, still only a being among beings), losing sight of, and blocking the search for, the Being of all that is.

Although Nietzsche rightly announced the death of God so conceived, his "Will to Power" has also contributed to the "forgetfulness of Being" that in our technological, humanistic age has climaxed in the tendency of humans to think of themselves as pure subjects who, through scientific objectification, can master the whole of nature and exploit it to their own advantage. Given this lack of openness to the holy (the truth or disclosure of Being), the gods of old have, as Hölderlin noted, taken flight, reducing the practice of religion to a mere formality and leaving man alienated from his true essence as *Dasein* (temporal *ekstasis* to the Being that is given [*es gibt*]).

By contrast, Heraclitus and other pre–Socratic thinkers still had a sense of wonder and saw in everything a manifestation of the divine, not in any pantheistic way, but in the sense that the world is a dynamic, unified interplay of earth and sky, mortals and gods (the messengers of the Divine). A dreadful experience through authentic encounter with death can re-awaken mankind to the Nothingness of Being and negatively dispose humans for the retrieval of such a mystical element of religiosity. But whether and how God and the gods again present themselves in time cannot be determined by man. Until they do — with the help of the poets, who alone as guardians of the House of Being (i.e., language) can name the holy — it behooves man to wait in silent godless thinking.

Sources

Heidegger, Martin. *Basic Writings.* Edited by David Farrell Krell. New York: Harper and Row, 1977.

_____. *Identity and Difference.* Translated by Joan Stambaugh. New York: Harper and Row, 1974.

_____. *The Piety of Thinking: Essays by Martin Heidegger.* Translated by James G. Hart and John C. Maraldo. Bloomington and London: Indiana University Press, 1976.

Blackham, J.J. *Six Existentialist Thinkers.* New York: Harper and Brothers, 1959. 86–109.

Caputo, John D. *Demythologizing Heidegger.* Bloomington: Indiana University Press, 1993.

_____. *The Mystical Element in Heidegger's Thought.* New York: Fordham University Press, 1986.

Collins, James. *The Existentialists. A Critical Study.* Chicago: Henry Regnery Company, 1952. 150–87.

Gadamer, Hans-Georg. "The Religious Dimension in Heidegger." In *Transcendence and the Sacred.* edited by Alan M. Olson and Leroy S. Rouner. Notre Dame: University of Notre Dame, 1981. 193–207.

Gall, Robert S. *Beyond Theism and Atheism: Heidegger's Significance for Religious Thinking.* Dordrecht: Martinus Nijhoff Publishers, 1987.

Guignon, Charles B., ed. *The Cambridge Companion to Heidegger.* Cambridge: Cambridge University Press, 1993. 70–93; 270–88.

Hanley, Catriona. *Being and God in Aristotle and Heidegger.* Lanham: Rowman and Littlefield, 2000.

Harries, Karsten. "Heidegger's Conception of the Holy." *The Personalist* 47 (1966): 169–84.

Hemming, Laurence Paul. *Heidegger's Atheism.* Notre Dame: University of Notre Dame Press, 2002.

Macquarrie, John. "Being and Giving: Heidegger and the Concept of God." In *God: The Contemporary Discussion,* edited by Frederick Sontag and M. Darrol Bryant. New York: The Rose of Sharon Press, Inc., 1982. 151–68.

Ott, Hugo. *Martin Heidegger: A Political Life.* Translated by Allan Blunden. New York: Basic Books, 1993.

Perotti, James L. *Heidegger on the Divine.* Athens, OH: Ohio University Press, 1974.

Richardson, William J. "Heidegger and God — and Professor Jonas." *Thought* 40 (1965): 13–40.

Sfranski, Rüdiger. *Martin Heidegger: Between Good and Evil.* Translated by Ewald Osers. Cambridge, MA: Harvard University Press, 1998.

Sheehan, Thomas. "Heidegger's 'Introduction to the Phenomenology of Religion,'" *The Personalist* 60 (1979). 312–24.

_____. *Heidegger: The Man and the Thinker.* Chicago: Precedent Publishing, Inc., 1981.

Zimmerman, Michael E. "Heidegger, Martin." In

Encyclopedia of Religion. Vol. 11. Edited by Mircea Eliade. New York: Macmillan and Co., 1987. 248–49.

Heraclitus (c. 545–485 B.C.)

Little is known for certain about Heraclitus' life except that he was born in and grew up in Ephesus, a city devoted to the worship of the goddess Artemis, and one of the most prosperous and splendid in Asia Minor at the time. Later, as an adult, he would claim, according to Diogenes, that he knew everything and that he had learned it all, not by being taught, but simply by inquiring for himself. It is possible, however, that in his younger years he had received instruction in both Eleatic and Pythagorian schools of thought. His father was probably of noble descent. His own attitude certainly seemed to some of his contemporaries to be that of an arrogant aristocrat. At a time when democracy was on the rise, he is alleged to have looked down on the masses, lampooning their religious credulity and disdaining their unenlightened lust for animal pleasures. It was also said that after having traveled much during his youth and returning home, he refused to take any part in the political life of his city, surrendered his right to inherit a high religious office to his brother, and proclaimed to civic leaders that he was better off playing dice with young boys in the temple of Artemis than to be wasting his time, like them, on politics.

His misanthropy finally became so intense, Diogenes reports, that he wandered off into the mountains and lived there on a diet of grass and herbs until the excessive accumulation of serous fluid in his body left him ill with dropsy and forced his return to Ephesus. Seeing as how the local physicians could not solve the riddle he put them about "how to create a drought after heavy rain," he tried in vain to cure himself by having his body buried in cow dung and died soon thereafter, his body being devoured by dogs. But like most of the other details of his biography, the story is by all scholarly estimates entirely fictitious, maliciously concocted by his enemies to parody what they did not like about his attitude or certain of his doctrines, like, for example, his suggestion that for sinners to try purifying themselves ritualistically by washing their hands with the blood of animals would be like someone "who had stepped into filth trying to wash himself with filth."

His cryptic style of writing also alienated many of his contemporaries, earning him the nickname of the "obscure philosopher." But others would say that if he was obscure, it was mainly because his recollection of the divine unity of opposites was so profound that like the Delphic oracle, he could only utter signs that both revealed and concealed the Being he had encountered, and leave to others the task of interpreting their inexhaustible meaning.

HERACLITUS ON RELIGION. When defiled, the unenlightened masses will sometimes try to purify themselves with blood, as though, like pigs that bathe in mud, they could cleanse themselves of contamination from this world by washing themselves in its own filth. Equally crazy and disgusting, except for the honor intended for Dionysius (and/or Hades), is the manner in which some perform phallic processions and hymns to their god of life (and/or death). The same could be said of the superstitious activities of the magicians, bacchantes, and wizards. And as for the mysteries still others participate in, they are but unholy rituals. Those engaging in such practices often pray to images as though they could talk to their houses, for they have no more clue of what the gods really are than did Homer or Hesiod (not to mention the learned Pythagoras and Xenophanes). Given the barbarian character of their souls, their eyes and ears are bad witnesses; though listening, they are like the deaf; they have no understanding; preoccupied with their own private thoughts, hints from Apollo escape their notice.

And what is really divine? It is the One existing in the tension of conflicting opposites (day/night, winter/summer, war/peace, plenty/hunger), the Cosmic Fire in the dance of whose flames everything is held in a perfect balance of coming and going, and is Itself transformed into the myriad variety of constantly changing, cosmic phenomena. The Fire Itself is the divine *Logos*, the one, unique Wisdom permeating all of Nature and bringing its myriad, conflicting forces into dynamic, albeit hidden, harmony. Compared to this God ("Zeus," if you like), the wisest of mankind will appear as an ape. Still, by virtue of having a soul of unfathomable limits, humans share in the *Logos*, and to that extent can and should strive to live in accordance with the eternal Law of Nature, countering soporific, sweaty desire with dry, fully-alert thinking that makes no distinction between right and wrong. Though mortal, they can upon death, escape rebirth, and become immortal *daemones*, wakeful guardians of the living and dead.

Sources

Heraclitus. *Fragments: A Text and Translation* with a commentary by T.M. Robinson. Toronto: University of Toronto Press, 1987.

Burnet, John. *Early Greek Philosophy*. New York: The Meridian Library, 1959. 130–68.

Copleston, Frederick, S.J. *A History of Philosophy*. Vol. 1, pt. 1. Garden City, NY: Doubleday and Company, Inc., 1962–77. 54–63.

Cornford, F.M. *Greek Religious Thought from Homer to the Age of Alexander*. Boston: The Beacon Press, 1950. 78–87.

_____. *From Religion to Philosophy*. New York: Harper and Row, 1957. 184–93.

Fränkel, Hermann. "Heraclitus on God and the Phenomenal World." *Proceedings of the American Philological Association* LXIX (1939): 230–44.

_____. "A Thought Pattern in Heraclitus." *American Journal of Philology* 59 (1938): 309–37.

Geddard, Richard. *Remembering Heraclitus: The Philosopher of Riddles*. Edinburgh: Floris Books, 2000.

Jaeger, Werner. *The Theology of the Early Greek Philosophers*. Oxford: At the Clarendon Press, 1948. 109–27.

Sweet, Dennis. *Heraclitus: Translation and Analysis*. Lanham, New York, and London: University Press of America, 1995.

Wheelwright, Philip. *Heraclitus*. Princeton: Princeton University Press, 1959.

_____, ed. *The Presocratics*. New York: The Odyssey Press, Inc., 1966. 3–89.

Herbert of Cherbury, Edward (1583–1648)

In contrast to his highborn, irascible and more secular-minded father from whom Herbert inherited his own rather vain and reckless choler, Herbert's mother (according to John Donne's eulogizing of her) was a woman of exemplary piety who was thoroughly orthodox in her Anglican beliefs, encouraged her children to praise God for the blessings they had received, and made religion the rule of her life, scripture the rule of her religion, and the church the rule of her biblical interpretations. Despite Herbert's coldness toward her when she remarried following the early death of his father, she may very well have had a significant influence on the respect for religion shown by Herbert throughout his life. It is also clear, however, that the kind of religion he would eventually champion veered considerably from that envisioned by his mother and England's establishment.

After several years of study at Oxford, marrying and fathering five children, he went abroad in 1608 to France, where over the next twenty years he engaged in various military and diplomatic services. While abroad he had occasion to meet the Roman Catholic priest and theologian, Pierre Gassendi, who was propounding an Epicurean version of atomism as a bridge between orthodox Christian faith and modern science, and the liberal-minded, moderate Dutch Calvinist, Hugo Grotius, who was trying to find a way to bring all Christian sects back together in terms of their common, rational appreciation of natural law. Equally disturbed by the ongoing persecution of the Huguenots in France (despite the 1598 Edict of Nantes) and following the lead of Gassendi, Grotius, and Isaac Casaubon, Herbert began advocating a political policy of religious tolerance and reflecting more seriously on how religion might serve to unite, rather than divide, mankind.

Starting with the prayerful publication of his *De Veritate* in 1624 (at about the same time as his diplomatic career was being terminated) and for the remaining quarter-century of his life back in England, he would publish a variety of treatises (in addition to his *Autobiography*) extolling a quasi–Deistic version of natural religion based on a rational appropriation of the innate common notions. Although he would write from within the Judaeo-Christian tradition, there was nothing exclusively Christian about his new religion. On his deathbed, he sent for Archbishop James Ussher. The Primate came, but refused to administer the last sacrament to Herbert when the latter expressed indifference about its reception.

HERBERT ON RELIGION. Without any special revelation, divine providence has provided all humans with a rational ability to choose for themselves between the conflicting truth claims of all the various religions in the form of a Natural Instinct. Such an instinct may be defined as a faculty or potency which, when actualized, becomes a *sensus* or form of awareness that involves immediate apprehension of the deity — not, to be sure, any conception of the divine essence, but an indeterminate premonition of God's presence.

Historically, this instinctual religion has been corrupted by a priestly class to include all kinds of nonessential rites and ceremonies. But originally, it consisted only of what might be called the "common notions concerning religion," namely: that there is a supreme God; that God is to be worshiped; that religious piety is closely linked with virtue; that repentance of sin is necessary; and that after this life there will be reward and punishment. That such notions are innate and not the product of experience is evidenced by the fact that they are common or universal. To say that they are innate means neither that every infant comes into the world with fully fledged ideas about God, nor that they are revealed in every man "whether he will or no." What it does mean is that such notions are at least virtually innate, in the sense that they are implicit in the human mind, and can be discovered upon the attainment of maturity by any man who is normal and not headstrong, foolish, weakminded and imprudent. The knowledge they provide is not only immediate, direct and pre-

conceptual, it is also sometimes beyond the comprehension of human reason, and must simply be accepted as indisputable. It can and should excite in man a desire for self-preservation, or happiness, in the long run, and trigger behavior conducive to the achievement of that end, even though the nature of the latter remains uncertain or obscure. To that extent, it is religion, and not reason, that humanizes mankind.

Sources

Herbert of Cherbury, Edward. *The Ancient Religion of the Gentiles*. London: Printed for John Nutt, 1705.
_____. *The Life of Edward, First Lord Herbert of Cherbury written by himself*. Edited by J.M. Shuttleworth. London: Oxford University Press, 1976.
_____. *De Religione Laici*. New Haven: Yale University Press, 1944.
_____. *De Veritate*. Bristol: University of Bristol, 1937.
Butler, John. *Lord Herbert of Cherbury: An Intellectual Biography*. Lewiston, NY: The Edwin Mellen Press, 1990.
Carre, Meyrick H. Introduction to Herbert, *De Veritate*. 9–66.
Copleston, Frederick, S.J. *A History of Philosophy*. Vol. 5, pt. 1. Garden City, NY: Doubleday and Company, Inc., 1962–77. 60–63.
Harrison, Peter. *"Religion" and the Religions in the English Enlightenment*. Cambridge: Cambridge University Press, 1990. 61–73.
Hutcheson, Harold R. Introduction to Herbert, *De Religione Laici*. 3–79.
Verkamp, Bernard J. *The Evolution of Religion: A Reexamination*. Scranton, PA: University of Scranton Press, 1995. 159–63.
_____. *The Sense of Religious Wonder: Epistemological Variations*. Scranton, PA: University of Scranton Press, 2002. 19–22.

Herder, Johann Gottfried (1744–1803)

Herder's father was the Pietist schoolmaster in Mohrunger, the small East Prussian town where Herder was born. His mother was equally Pietistic in her Lutheran convictions. Consistent with the Pietistic emphasis upon individualism, they encouraged their son, from boyhood on, to rely on his personal, devout interpretation of the Bible. The father also recommended a reading of his own favorite book, Johan Arnd's *True Christianity*. After completing Latin school, spending several years trying to earn his lodging by copying manuscripts for a popular, albeit sentimentally religious, local vicar, and a short unsuccessful stint at medical studies, he was enrolled, at the age of eighteen, as a student of theology at the University of Königberg where he had the opportunity to attend the lectures of a young Immanuel Kant and to meet Johann Georg Hamann. Two years later, upon the latter's recommendation, Herder was ordained a Lutheran minister and appointed teacher and preacher at the *Domschule* of Riga. He left Riga after five years.

During a subsequent year of travel he met and befriended Lessing and Goethe and saw the publication of several of his own works on aesthetics, the non-divine origin of language, and its various stages of development. In 1771 he was invited to Bückeburg to serve as court preacher and pastor. There, possibly under the influence of Karoline Flachsland (whom he would later marry), Herder experienced something of a conversion to a less rationalistic, more imaginative form of religion. His desire to leave Bückeburg to become professor of theology and university preacher at Göttingen was blocked by Lutheran colleagues who found the theological ideas he had published while at Bückeburg about the role of religion in the history of mankind too liberal. He instead moved to Weimar in 1776, and after being appointed head of the Lutheran clergy, remained there for the rest of his life.

In addition to an ongoing attempt to reconcile traditional Judaeo-Christianity with modern life-science by expounding a quasi–Spinozist, Goethean notion of creation striving for divine perfection, he also offered young ministers much advice in many of his subsequent *Christliche Schriften* on how to deal with radical biblical criticism, and on the importance of following the example of Jesus by eschewing dogmatism, keeping their sermons simple, and inculcating in their own lives the

message of love He preached. By all accounts, despite its moments of depression, doubts, and petty jealousies, Herder's life was to the end a constant proof of his sincerity as a Christian.

HERDER ON RELIGION. By implanting in humans the principle of rational self-activity, God made man a deity upon earth. But this godlike character of humanity is more like a disposition that needs to be developed. Notwithstanding its periodic corruption (as in feudal Europe), religion is essential to the achievement of that goal. No group of people on earth, however savage, has ever been completely without religion. It is meaningless to say that the deities were invented by fear, or that primitive religion was nothing more than a superstitious attempt to appease monstrous forces. Religion is rather the highest expression of humanity, to the extent of having inclined humans to use their intellects to discern the invisible cause of natural phenomena.

Having conjectured the existence of powerful gods, humans sought ways of befriending the deities through religious, childlike worship. In a world full of darkness, confusion, and danger, religion became the tutor of humankind (and never better than in the most genuine humanity exemplified by Jesus). Exercising the heart as well as the intellect, true religion also taught humans to eschew the kind of absolute autonomy that could only turn them into the most savage of creatures, encouraging them instead to obey the laws of nature, freely and lovingly, with childlike simplicity. This helped shape human lives on earth into images of the deity. It promises also to lead humans back to their purest destination. For it is hard to believe that there is no other state of being possible for humans (who find it so hard in this life to realize their potential for knowing their eternal Father). Metaphysical proofs of human immortality based on the simplicity or spirituality of the soul may be lacking, but religion (and none better than the Christian religion) can weave an immortal crown for humankind by tying together all human wants and hopes into faith — the heartfelt conviction, namely, that nature's finest disposition (humanity) will not be left behind in the general progress that is every-where observable in nature.

Sources

Herder, Johann Gottfried. *On World History: An Anthology*. Edited by Hans Adler and Ernest A. Mense. Translated by Ernest A. Mense with Michael Palma. London: M.E. Sharpe, Inc., 1996.

_____. *Philosophical Writings*. Translated and edited by Michael N. Forster. Cambridge: Cambridge University Press, 2002.

_____. *Reflections on the Philosophy of the History of Mankind*. Chicago and London: The University of Chicago Press, 1968.

Barnard, F.M. *Herder on Nationality, Humanity, and History*. Montreal and Ithaca: McGill-Queen's University Press, 2003.

Clark, Robert T., Jr. *Herder: His Life and Thought*. Berkeley and Los Angeles: University of California Press, 1955.

Copleston, Frederick, S.J. *A History of Philosophy*. Vol. 6, pt. 1. Garden City, NY: Doubleday and Company, Inc., 1962–77. 160–69; 198–206.

Koepke, Wulf. *Johann Gottfried Herder*. Boston: Twayne Publishers, 1987.

Nisbet, H.B. *Herder and the Philosophy and History of Science*. Cambridge, UK: The Modern Humanities Research Association, 1970.

Hick, John (1922–)

As a child growing up in Scarborough, England, Hick found the services of the local church to which he was often taken "boring and totally off-putting." More interesting were his mother's dabbling in spiritualism and theosophy, the religious explorations of his maternal grandmother, the Quaker atmosphere of the Bootham boarding school he attended in his middle teens, and the reading of Nietzsche, Leibniz, and other philosophers he had started by the age of seventeen — experiences which left him in a religiously questioning and open state, believing in some sort of divine reality, but not the God of Christian orthodoxy.

Encouraged by a scholarly uncle, he continued his studies at the University of Hull, still with the intention at the age of eighteen of pursuing a career in law and studying phi-

losophy on the side. But while riding a bus one day across town, he had a "powerful evangelical conversion" to Jesus, embraced "with great joy and excitement the world of Christian faith," and much to the lifelong chagrin of his father, promptly switched from the study of law to begin training for the Presbyterian ministry at the University of Edinburgh. During his first year there and the three he spent in World War II (again against his father's will) as a conscientious objector working in the Friends Ambulance Unity, he would remain "a wholehearted evangelical fundamentalist."

As he continued work toward advanced philosophy and theology degrees at Edinburgh, Oxford and Cambridge in the postwar years, and accepted a postordination ministerial assignment in the Presbyterian Church and then professorial appointments at Cornell and Princeton universities, his religious beliefs became less fundamentalist, but were still highly orthodox (contrary to the claims of some at Princeton who wanted to strip him of his ministry and professorship).

While teaching and writing at Cambridge, Birmingham, and California over the next four and a half decades, however, his personal faith would gradually become far more universal and inclusive, reflecting on the practical level the theoretical challenge to traditional interpretations of Christian doctrine that, to the dismay and disappointment of some fundamentalists (who succeeded in getting Hick excluded from the Southern California Presbytery), his many publications of this period presented. In line with his Kantian-based, pluralistic interpretation of religion, he would go beyond his regular attendance at the worship services of the United Reformed Church by occasionally frequenting Quaker meetings, engaging in Buddhist meditation, and becoming a leading participant in current ecumenical dialogue between Christians, Jews, and Muslims.

HICK ON RELIGION. Man is a worshiping animal with an ingrained propensity to construe his world religiously, or a tendency to experience the human environment in depth as other and greater than it seems. But the reality experienced by man is not unambiguous. To preserve man's cognitive freedom, God remains for man a *deus absconditus,* or a God, in other words, who hides behind his creation, leaving man the freedom to recognize or fail to recognize His dealing with us. Faith, then, as the actualization of this innate tendency to interpret reality religiously, is not to be described as either a reasoned conclusion or an unreasoned hunch that there is a God. It is simply an apprehension of the divine presence within the believer's human experience, epistemologically comparable to what Wittgenstein called "seeing as"(e.g., the man Jesus "experienced as" God).

Indirect or direct (as in mysticism), the religious experience is a joint product of a transcendent reality and the religious person's own culturally conditioned, interpretive conceptualization: religious phenomena (the divine *personae* and impersonal absolutes found in the different world religions) are not only projections of a divine *noumenon* (either as the Real *an sich* causing the religious sensation, or the "back side" of the sensible phenomenon) into human consciousness, but also projections of the human consciousness itself as it has been formed by particular historical cultures. This explains how the many different religions can all be experiencing one Ultimate Reality while at the same time making seemingly incompatible truth claims about the nature of God, the existence of evil, the afterlife, and so on. Representing different human perceptions of and response to the same infinite divine Reality, they are all equally true and of value to the extent of making a difference by constituting for various peoples of different times and places an effective context for the salvific transformation of human existence from self-centeredness to Reality-centeredness.

Sources

Hick, John. *An Autobiography.* Oxford: Oneworld, 2002.
_____. *Death and Eternal Life.* London: Collins; New York: Harper and Row, 1976.
_____. *Faith and Knowledge.* Ithaca and London: Cornell University Press, 1970.
_____. *An Interpretation of Religion.* New Haven: Yale University Press, 1989.
_____. "The Non-Absoluteness of Christianity." In John Hick and Paul F. Knitter, eds. *The Myth of Christian Uniqueness.* Maryknoll, NY: Orbis Books, 1987. 16–36.
_____. *Philosophy of Religion.* 3rd ed. Englewood Cliffs, NJ: Prentice-Hall, Inc., 1983.
D'Costa, Gavin. "John Hick's Copernican Revolution: Ten Years After." *New Blackfriars* 66 (1985): 127–35.
_____. *John Hick's Theology of Religion.* Lanham: University Press of America, 1987.
Hewitt, Harold, ed. *Problems in the Philosophy of Religion: Critical Studies of the Work of John Hick.* London: Macmillan, 1991.
Sharma, Arvind, ed. *God, Truth and Reality: Essays in Honour of John Hick.* London: Macmillan, 1993.
Verkamp, Bernard J. "Hick's interpretation of religious pluralism." *International Journal for the Philosophy of Religion* 30 (1991): 103–24.
_____. *The Sense of Religious Wonder: Epistemological Variations.* Scranton, PA: The University of Scranton Press, 2002. 70–72.

Hobbes, Thomas (1588–1679)

Hobbes' father was the poorly educated, rather anti-intellectual vicar of Westport who had next to no understanding of the prayers and homilies he read, was disciplined for neglecting his priestly duties, and after being excommunicated and threatened with civil punishment for having slandered and physically abused a neighboring clergyman, eventually abandoned his family. A rich uncle undertook Hobbes' early education (mainly in classical languages) at church and private schools and then sent him, at the age of fourteen, to Magdalen Hall, Oxford. The Aristotelian, scholastic philosophy he was taught there bored him, and it would not be until after graduation, years of tutorial work, and exposure to other schools of thought on several trips abroad that any real interest in philosophy on his part would be revived. At Oxford he had also encountered a strong Puritan tradition that may have influenced his later sympathy for some of Calvin's thinking, but also his distaste for any form of enthusiasm and what he perceived to be the seditious exploitation of university life by Catholics and Puritans alike.

Later in midlife, after circulating several treatises calling for the subjugation of religion to an absolute sovereign, Hobbes felt the need to flee from England to Paris, where over the next ten years (1640–1651), he joined in the intellectual circle being cultivated by the Minims friar and friend of Descartes, Marin Mersenne. Although the latter helped shape Hobbes' theological interests, his half-hearted attempt to convert Hobbes to Roman Catholicism as he lay severely ill in 1647 came to nothing. Hobbes did receive communion shortly thereafter, but in accordance with Anglican, not Roman, tradition.

After the death of Mersenne in 1648 and circulation of several antipapal manuscripts, Hobbes fled France and returned to England in 1651. Publication of his great masterpiece of political philosophy (the *Leviathon*), a controversy with Bishop Bramhall over freedom of the will, and his criticism of the universities as hotbeds of civil disobedience eventually resulted in Hobbes being suspected of atheism and of trying to subvert religion. Although he succeeded in defending himself against such suspicions, they severely inhibited his right thereafter to print his own views on religious matters. Before dying in 1679 and being buried in the church of Hault Hucknall, he is reported to have received communion on several occasions.

HOBBES ON RELIGION. The seed of religion is to be found in the combination of man's innate curiosity about the causes of things and his fear of death and other calamity. Reluctant to admit his ignorance of the real causes of good or evil fortune, man has invented the "powers or invisible agents" and called divine almost everything around him. When this uniquely human curiosity is concerned only with the causes of natural bodies, there arises a belief in the one, eternal, infinite, and omnipotent God, who might also be said to be a simple, pure corporeal spirit. But such talk about the divine attributes is basically meaningless, and at best is only a devout ex-

pression of our inability to comprehend God. For even though our observation of the movement and order of the material universe may give rise to the belief in a "first mover," it tells us nothing about the nature of the latter. We can only know that God is, not what he is.

But some religions, like Judaism and Christianity, are more than human inventions, and rest upon a divine revelation that can enlighten us about God. The faith we put in such revelation, however, is different from knowledge in that our assent to its articles derives not from the propositions themselves but from our trust in the persons (prophets) or institutions (Scripture, Church) propounding them. When genuine, such faith works with reason, not against it. As reason detects the voice of God in the laws of nature that incline humans to strive for personal survival by way of agreeing to live peaceably under the absolute rule of a sovereign lord, faith embraces civic law and policy as being essential to the kingdom of God. As opposed to superstition (e.g., Catholicism or Puritanical individualism), true religion, therefore, rests upon public approbation, and rejects any distinction between the spiritual and temporal realms. The eternal life promised by Jesus will not be realized until the Second Coming. Until then, even Christians have no choice but to obey their sovereign ruler, however tyrannical he or she might prove to be.

Sources

Hobbes, Thomas. *Body, Man, and Citizen*. Selections from Hobbes' writings. Edited and with an introduction by Richard S. Peters. New York: Collier Books, 1962.

_____. *Leviathan*. *Great Books of the Western World*. Vol. 23. Edited by R.M. Hutchins. Chicago: Encyclopædia Britannica, Inc., 1952.

Copleston, Frederick, S.J. *A History of Philosophy*. Vol. 5, pt. 1. Garden City, NY: Doubleday and Company, Inc., 1962–77. 11–60.

Martinich, A.P. *Hobbes: A Biography*. Cambridge: Cambridge University Press, 1999.

Peters, Richard. *Hobbes*. Harmondsworth, UK: Penguin Books, 1956.

Sorell, Tom, ed. *The Cambridge Companion to Hobbes*. Cambridge: Cambridge University Press, 1996. 1–13; 346–80.

Hocking, William Ernest (1873–1966)

Hocking was born into a Cleveland family of strong Methodist piety, and on the mother's side, of Puritan lineage. Every morning, after breakfast, the children would kneel in a circle to pray with their parents and to recite the biblical verses they had been expected to memorize. At the age of twelve, while attending one of the Sunday special meetings regularly sponsored by Joliet's Methodist Church for the sake of providing members a personal experience of the divine presence, Hocking underwent a conversion, a mystical experience of sorts which afforded him a new vision of himself as one of many human beings participating in the great procession of immortal souls. The experience resulted in his stepping forward to be saved and formally joining the Methodist Church.

A year later, however, his reading of Herbert Spencer's *First Principles* left him doubting any need for the "extra-beliefs" propounded by religion to explain everything. The skeptical spell would last for four years until one day after graduation from high school, while working as a surveyor on the railroad, he had a personal experience of the impossibility of himself as a knowing subject trying to "imagine" the "nothingness of non-being" implied by Spencer's evolutionist portrayal of animal death. Combined with his subsequent discovery of William James' *Principles of Psychology* in the library of the school he next attended for a short time (Iowa State), it helped revive his adolescent religious sense of the spiritual immortality and uniqueness of human life.

After four years of teaching in Davenport he was able to afford Harvard, earning his B.A. there in 1901, his M.A. the following year, and his Ph.D. in 1904. His several years of study with James and further study abroad with Husserl and Dilthey (not to mention his marriage in 1905 to a deeply religious, albeit freethinking, Roman Catholic woman) helped stir in him a vision of a new worldwide community that would unite men of all faiths through their common belief in and awareness of God as the underlying unity of Being. It was to such a vision that he tried for the rest of his life to give expression in his Hibbert and Gifford Lectures during the 1930s, in books he published (*The Meaning of God in Human Experience, Living Religions and a World Faith, The Coming World Civilization*) while teaching at California, Yale, Harvard and elsewhere, or, on a more practical level, in his work from 1930–32 as chair of a commission studying the missionary activity of various Protestant denominations in India, Burma, China and Japan.

HOCKING ON RELIGION. Modern thought has prompted some to reduce religion to nothing more than a way of feeling. They are mistaken, however, in not observing that the feeling they are talking about is itself still idea. For in religion, idea and feeling are inseparable. Even if religion did originate in feeling, therefore, it still needed to produce some great idea or system of ideas in order to find satisfaction and greatness. And as a matter of historical fact, no religion has ever taken itself as merely a matter of feeling. At the heart of every religion has been the idea of God — a non-inferential, intuitively certain, cognitive feeling of the mysterious presence of a Being that, although identical with the essence of the human self, is Absolutely Other than Nature and Man, but which, as Absolute Mind, is ever silently at work in the creation of our universe.

Mystics especially, but others too, have been open to the experience of such knowledge, and have used it to put a religious interpretation upon their instinctive experience of reality as a whole. It is by freely alternating this worshipful view of the whole with practical attention to the particulars of everyday life that genuinely religious people maintain that happy, undivided attitude of prophetic consciousness whereby they feel empowered to change the world through creative love and to bring all the religions of the world to share in a global faith by recognizing their unity in difference. This not only generates in religious people a hope for the permanence of human values and immortality for themselves and their beloved, it also allows them, already here and now, faithfully to anticipate the attainment of what in the course of nature is reached only at the end of infinite progression. To that extent, religion is neither an ineffectual abstraction, nor a mere hypothesis; it works, parenting all the sciences and arts. Whether any humanistic endeavor that tries to get along without the idea of God can work as well is highly doubtful. For without God, the vast universe is devoid of meaning or value.

Sources

Hocking, William Ernest. *Living Religions and a World Faith*. New York: Macmillan, 1940.
_____. *The Meaning of God in Human Experience*. New Haven: Yale University Press; London: Henry Frowde; Oxford: Oxford University Press, 1912.
_____. *Science and the Idea of God*. Chapel Hill: The University of North Carolina Press, 1944.
_____. *Types of Philosophy*. New York: Charles Scribner's Sons, 1959.
Furse, Margaret Lewis. *Experience and Certainty: William Ernest Hocking and Philosophical Mysticism*. Atlanta, GA: Scholars Press, 1988. See esp. 41–74.
Luther, A.R. *Existence as Dialectical Tension. A Study of the First Philosophy of W.E. Hocking*. The Hague: Martinus Nijhoff, 1968.
Rouner, Leroy S. "The Making of a Philosopher: Ernest Hocking's Early Years." In *Philosophy, Religion, and the Coming World Civilization*. Essays in Honor of William Ernest Hocking. Edited by Leroy S. Rouner. The Hague: Martinus Nijhoff, 1966. 5–22.
_____. *Within Human Experience: The Philosophy of William Ernest Hocking*. Cambridge, MA: Harvard University Press, 1969.
Wieman, Henry Nelson. "Empiricism in Religious Philosophy." In *Philosophy, Religion, and the Coming World Civilization: Essays in Honor of William Ernest Hocking*. Edited by Leroy S. Rouner. The Hague: Martinus Nijhoff, 1966. 183–97.
_____, and Bernard Eugene Meland. *American Philosophies of Religion*. Chicago and New York: Willett, Clark and Company, 1936. 108–14.

Horkheimer, Max (1895–1973)

Horkheimer's parents belonged to a generation of assimilated German-Jews. Maintaining *kosher* and other religious practices of the Jewish tradition, they provided Horkheimer with a "strictly conservative, but not orthodox, Jewish atmosphere" in which to grow up. Although Horkheimer would later idealize his parents, in the diary he wrote as a young man he accused them of being "malicious and cowardly egotists" in the way they tried to manipulate his personal relations and insisted upon his working in and eventually taking over a family textile business which, in his view, exploited its workers terribly. The rebellious instincts triggered thereby were directed also against his religious upbringing and helped stimulate Marxist sympathies.

Exempted from military service in World War I, he earned a doctorate at the University of Frankfurt in 1925, and soon thereafter began lecturing at that university's Institute for Social Research. Within five years he was appointed its director. His Marxist proclivities soon became apparent as he tried, in his teaching and prolific writing, to spell out the pedagogical implications of his critical theory by wedding Marx's atheistic appeal for radical social reform with an equally atheistic Schopenhauerian sense of pity for the oppressed of this world. The underlying optimism of his thought soon evaporated, however, with the Nazi rise to power.

Although he was able to flee Germany and spend the war years running the institute from New York and California, he never forgot the plight of his fellow Jews. Reports of their brutal persecution not only spawned the new mood of pessimism expressed in *The Dialectic of Enlightenment, The Eclipse of Reason* and other works he would publish before and after returning to Frankfurt in 1948, it also led him, by his own account, to reidentify with victims of the Holocaust, to sharpen his analytical focus on anti–Semitism, and to develop a new appreciation for the unique characteristics of Jewish solidarity. To some critics,

Horkheimer's reconversion seemed nothing more than compensation for his "all-too-facile dismissal of specifically Jewish problems" prior to the war. And when, in multiple publications before and after his retirement in 1959, he revealed in his ongoing critique of both communist and capitalist ideology an ever increasing sympathy for the function of religion in modern society, others accused him of contradicting his earlier materialistic philosophy. He died at the age of seventy-eight, his despair apparently tempered by the hope of finding some transcendence through solidarity with the victims of this harsh world.

HORKHEIMER ON RELIGION. It is not enough to treat religious conceptions as mere error simply because they are no longer consistent with the criterion of science. Religion can deliver a rudimentary form of knowledge that lies beyond scientific verification. Part of its value, in fact, is the help it can give in liberating reason from the limitations imposed by Positivism. Given its dull passivity, Positivism was unable to cope effectively with the authoritarian society against which the bourgeois ideal of using reason to change the world was itself originally directed. By implying that truth consists only in cold calculations that work or that thoughts are mere subjective means to unquestioned ends, it helped cultivate "identity thinking" that undermines difference and particularity in our technocratic, capitalistic, totally managed societies, and has thereby contributed to the erosion of the critical impulse that lay at the heart of the Enlightenment's conception of reason.

With its recognition of the "Wholly Other," religion is our best hope of reversing this trend and keeping alive some semblance of at least a negative utopian *Weltanschauung*. "God" may very well be a projection of man's own ideal qualities, and there may be very little reason to believe that God actually exists independent of human imagination and feeling. But the concept of an infinite God has long served as a depository of the notion that there are norms other than those to which nature and society give expression in their operation, that there is more to our world than

meets the eye, and that there are good reasons, therefore, to be dissatisfied with our earthly destiny. Although some liberal, secularized forms of theology, no less than traditional theisms and most current forms of atheism, have surrendered to the powers that be, at its nondogmatic best (e.g., non–Zionistic, diaspora Judaism), religion can still embody this human yearning for a transcendent justice that prompts solidarity here and now with the victims of injustice, in hopes the murderers will not have the last word.

Sources

Horkheimer, Max. *Between Philosophy and Social Science: Selected Early Writings*. Translated by G. Frederick Hunter, Matthew S. Kramer, and John Torpey. Cambridge, MA, and London: The MIT Press, 1993.

_____. *Critical Theory: Selected Essays*. Translated by Matthew J. O'Connell and others. New York: Continuum Press, 1982.

_____. *Critique of Instrumental Reason*. Translated by Matthew J. O'Connell and others. New York: The Seabury Press, 1974.

_____. *Dialectic of Enlightenment*. London: Allen Lane, 1973.

_____. "Die Sehnsucht nach dem ganz Anderen." In *Gesammelte Schriften* 7. Frankfurt am Main: Fischer, 1895ff. 386–95.

_____. *Eclipse of Reason*. New York: Oxford University Press, 1974.

Benhabib, Seyla, Wolfgang Bonss, and John McCole, eds. *On Max Horkheimer*. Cambridge, MA, and London: The MIT Press, 1993.

Gur-Ze'ev, Ilan. "Walter Benjamin and Max Horkeimer: From utopia to redemption." http://construct.haifa.ac.il/~ilangz/Utopia4.html. 1–23.

Habermas, Jürgen. "Remarks on the Development of Horkheimer's Work." In *On Max Horkheimer: New Perspectives*, edited by Seyla Benhabib, Wolfgang Bonss, and John McCole. Cambridge, MA, and London: The MIT Press, 1993. 49–65.

Küng, Hans. *Does God Exist?* Translated by Edward Quinn. Garden City, NY: Doubleday and Company, Inc., 1980. 323–39; 489–91.

Siebert, Rudolf J. *The Critical Theory of Religion: The Frankfurt School*. Berlin, New York, and Amsterdam: Mouton Publishers, 1985. 128–46.

_____. "Horkheimer's Sociology of Religion." *Telos* 30 (Winter 1976–77): 127–44.

Stirk, Peter M.R. *Max Horkheimer: A New Interpre-*

tation. Lanham, MD: Barnes and Noble Books, 1992.

Wood, Kelsey, "Horkheimer, Max." *The Literary Encyclopedia.* http://www.litencyc.com. 1–7.

Hügel, Friedrich, Baron von *see* Von Hügel, Friedrich, Baron

Hume, David (1711–1776)

Baptized into Presbyterianism, and raised by a deeply religious mother, Hume grew up practicing his religion, observing, for example, the Scottish Sabbath that included early morning family prayers, attendance at several church services and sermons, fasting between services, evening spiritual reading, and, before retirement, the singing of Psalms. He regularly examined his conscience in accordance with the book of popular devotion, *The Whole Duty of Man,* and gave no sign of objecting to the strict Calvinistic doctrines of predestination, and such. After enrolling at the age of twelve at the University of Edinburgh, however, his religious beliefs began to wane, due largely, he himself says, to his reading of Locke and Clarke. This loss of religious conviction was reinforced by his private study of philosophy during the decade following his graduation from the university. A manuscript book he wrote before he was twenty and would later burn contained multiple references to arguments for and against the existence of God he had found in his reading of classical Greek and Latin texts, Descartes' *Meditations,* Pierre Bayle's *Historical and Critical Dictionary,* or writings of other rather skeptical, seventeenth-century French philosophers, and at least in one entry anticipated his later theory about the polytheistic origin of religion.

Certainly, by his mid-twenties he had come to think of religion as a negative influence upon human life and morality. Although he had removed from his first publication (*A Treatise on Human Nature*) some of its more antireligious pages, the book still gained him a reputation for atheism. The antidogmatic, anticlerical, and secularistic tone of many of his subsequent publications on superstition, miracles, morality, and religion, reinforced that popular impression and no doubt contributed to his being rejected for a professorial chair at the University of Edinburgh in 1745 and the failed attempt in 1756 to have him formally excommunicated by the Church of Scotland.

He would later express shock at the dogmatic atheism of the French *philosophes,* but contrary to the wishful thinking of some of his friends, he had not remained a Christian at heart and never admitted to any awareness of having converted to Catholicism in a delirious moment of severe illness. Notwithstanding efforts by a few good friends to get him, on his deathbed, to reconsider his religious skepticism, he declined, chastising institutional religion instead for its bad morality and, with remarkable tranquility of mind, reaffirming his disbelief in personal immortality and claiming to approach death without any anxiety or regret.

HUME ON RELIGION. Unlike self-love and other original instinctive sentiments, religious beliefs have never been absolutely universal or identical in all ages. To that extent they may be said to have originated from only secondary propensities to allegorize the unknown causes of frightful natural events as voluntary agents like ourselves and to heap upon the heroic deeds of the latter such excessive praise as to deify their being. Through the attribution of infinity to the divine, this primordial polytheism eventually gave way to monotheism, thereby increasing superstitious fanaticism, cruelty, and monkish asceticism.

Attempts to establish religion upon reason have generally been futile. *A priori* arguments about God as the ultimate cause of all reality are especially weak: first, because there is nothing to prove that the whole of our universe is without its own ground; second, because it makes no sense to infer the fact of God's existence from our combined ideas of God and his existence; and third, because the constant conjunction between cause and effect required of any causal law can never be experienced in the case of God's relation to the world. The *a posteriori* argument based upon the quasi-instinctive observation of mechanical order in the universe does yield some probability to belief in an intelligent Creator remotely analogous to the human mind. But since there is an infinite difference between a human architect and a designer–God, and since we are never justified in either ascribing to a cause "any qualities, but what are exactly sufficient to produce the effect," or in inferring "other effects from the cause, beyond those by which alone it is known to us," such a purely theoretical conclusion can tell us nothing more about the nature of God or his supposedly provident plans. Nor does it necessarily have any real bearing on morality or religious practice. In the final analysis, religion is an inexplicable mystery, founded on faith, not reason.

Sources

Hume, David. *Dialogues Concerning Natural Religion.* Buffalo, NY: Prometheus Books, 1989.
_____. *Dialogues concerning natural religion and the posthumous essays, Of the immortality of the soul and Of suicide.* Edited by Richard H. Popkin. Indianapolis: Hackett Publishing Co., 1980.
_____. *An Enquiry Concerning Human Understanding. Great Books of the Western World.* Vol. 35. Edited by R.M. Hutchins. Chicago: Encyclopædia Britannica, Inc., 1952.
_____. *The Natural History of Religion.* Edited by James Fieser. New York: Macmillan Publishing Company, 1992.
_____. *A Treatise of Human Nature.* Abridged and edited by John P. Wright et al. London: Everyman/J.M. Dent; North Clarendon, VT: Tuttle Publishers, 2003.
Copleston, Frederick, S.J. *A History of Philosophy.* Vol. 5, pt. 2. Garden City, NY: Doubleday and Company, Inc., 1962–77. 63–196.
Melchert, Norman. *The Great Conversation.* Boston: McGraw-Hill, 2002. 419–23.
Mossner, Ernest Campbell. *The Life of David Hume.* Oxford: At the Clarendon Press, 1980.
Penelhum, Terence. *David Hume: An Introduction to His Philosophical System.* West Lafayette, IN: Purdue University Press, 1992.
Schmidt, Claudia M. *David Hume: Reason in History.* University Park, PA: The Pennsylvania State University Press, 2003. See esp. 339–76.
Yandell, Keith E. *Hume's "Inexplicable Mystery": His Views on Religion.* Philadelphia: Temple University Press, 1990. See Bibliography for extensive secondary sources on Hume's ideas about religion.

Husserl, Edmund (1859–1938)

Husserl was born into a Moravian (Czech) family of German-speaking liberal Jews. During the early years of his education he showed an interest in only mathematics and physics. While pursuing a doctoral degree in mathematics at the universities of Leipzig, Berlin, and Vienna, however, he sensed a need for a more radical grounding of mathematics and became increasingly interested in philosophy. In Leipzig he befriended Thomas Masaryk, who because of his denunciation of anti–Semitism would later be recognized as the "conscience of the Czech nation" and become its first president. Eventually, Masaryk would sever ties with all churches, but at the time was in the process of converting from his native Catholic faith to Protestantism. He was also studying philosophy in Vienna under Franz Brentano, a former Catholic priest who before becoming a professor at the University of Vienna had resigned his clerical status over misgivings about the church's newly proclaimed doctrine of infallibility.

Masaryk influenced Husserl to attend Brentano's lectures and to initiate a close study of the New Testament. By Husserl's own account, it was the "overwhelming religious experiences" he was then having that inclined him to devote the rest of his life to philosophy. Not long thereafter, in 1886, both he and his bride-to-be (also of Jewish descent) converted to and were baptized in the Evangelical Lutheran Church. Picking up especially on Brentano's notion of intentionality, and following Brentano's advice to pursue further study under his former student Karl Stumpf at the University of Halle, Husserl gradually overcame bouts of skepticism and lay the foundation of the mature "transcendental phenomenology" he would be expounding during his latter years to the likes of Heidegger, Levinas, and Marcuse at the University of Freiburg.

Notwithstanding his conversion to Christianity, Husserl — as a born Jew — was humiliated when the Nazis forced him into a leave of absence, and with the shameful collaboration of Heidegger, deprived him of library privileges and excluded him from participation in international philosophical conferences. His final withdrawal to a Benedictine monastery to be near a former student contributed to the dubious claim that before dying there in 1938 he was thinking of converting to Catholicism.

HUSSERL ON RELIGION. To see religion for what it really is one must first suspend all preconceptions, and especially those which assume from a naturalistic point of view that it can be explained exclusively by the physical sciences. So bracketed, religion manifests itself as a spiritual phenomenon that is constituted to be what it is by its existence in the consciousness of the absolute ego. Given the intentionality of human consciousness, the essence of religion — at least at the higher, monotheistic level of mythic culture — can thus be described as an awareness or idea of God, not as a First Cause, but possibly as an ultimate necessary being grounding the cognitive contingency of the world, or as the infinite, ultimate *telos* which, by instituting universal norms, gives meaning to all the striving of mankind toward a perfect world of total, communal inter-subjectivity. Even though this *telos* transcends individual — not to mention animal — consciousness, it may, as the ultimate structure of the human spirit, be nothing more than the immanent ideal of consciousness, and as such something other than the personal, transcendent God acknowledged by most religions.

Questions remain, however, about how such consciousness, with its intrinsic teleology, could ever have surfaced and sustained itself as the ultimate evolutionary impetus without some stimulus from beyond. Reason cannot answer such questions. But religious faith, inspired by an empathetic, intuitive appreciation for the exceeding goodness of individuals like Jesus who experience themselves as the embodiment of divine being, rests upon the conviction that, notwithstanding suffering and death, life is ultimately meaningful because it is under the direction of a transcendent God.

If nothing else, such faith — at least when liberated from dogmatism — can, like the fictionalized poetic accounts of triumphant human striving, help keep humans living as if the universal goal were still a practical possibility.

Sources

Husserl, Edmund. *The Crisis of European Sciences and Transcendental Phenomenology: An Introduction to Phenomenological Philosophy.* Translated by David Carr. Evanston, IL: Northwestern University Press, 1970.

_____. *Husserliana, Gesammelte Werke.* Edited by H.L. Breda. The Hague: M. Nijhoff, 1950.

_____. *Ideas.* Translated by W.R. Boyce Gibson. New York: Collier Macmillan Publishers, 1962.

_____. *Logical Investigations.* 2 vols. Translated by John N. Findlay. New York: Humanities Press, 1970.

Allen, Douglas. "Husserl, Edmund." In *Encyclopedia of Religion.* Vol. 6. Edited by Mircea Eliade. New York: Macmillan and Co., 1987. 538–40.

Dupré, Louis. "Husserl's Thought on God and Faith." *Philosophy and Phenomenological Research* XXIX, no.2 (December 1968): 201–15.

Hart, James G. "The Study of Religion in Husserl's Writings." In *Phenomenology of the Cultural Disciplines*, edited by Mano Daniel and Lester Embree. Dordrecht: Kluwer Academic Publishers, 1994. 265–96.

Ijsseling, S. "I, We, and God." In *Husserl-Ausgabe und Husserl-Forschung, Phenomenologica* 115 (1990): 129–49.

Kockelmans, Joseph J. *Edmund Husserl's Phenomenology.* West Lafayette, IN: Purdue University Press, 1994.

Mall, R.A. "The God of phenomenology in comparative contrast to that of philosophy and theology." *Husserl Studies* 8, no. 1 (1991): 1–15.

Smith, A.D. *Husserl and the Cartesian Meditations.* London and New York: Routledge, 2003.

Strasser, Stephen. "History, Teleology and God in Husserl." In *The Teleologies in Husserlian Phenomenology. Analecta Husserliana* 9, edited by Anna-Teresa Tymieniecka (1979): 317–33.

Iamblichus (c. A.D. 240–c. 325)

Iamblichus was born and grew up in Chalcis at a time when Syria was being overrun by the Persian King Shapur. He was apparently "of illustrious birth, belonging to the well-to-do and fortunate classes," and possibly even "descended from the royal line of priest-kings of Emesa." The family's wealth allowed him to get a good education. After some initial tutoring, he attached himself (probably in Rome) to Porphyry, the leading disciple of Plotinus. In addition to his study of the neo–Platonic works of the latter, however, he also investigated the philosophy of Pythagoras and Egyptian-Chaldean theology. This led to some tension between the student and his teacher, as evidenced especially by Iamblichus' reply in his *De Mysteriis* to a letter written by Porphyry attacking the practice of theurgy.

Returning to Syria, he founded his own school in Apamea, long a base for many another philosopher. Daily he and his students would meet to read, study, and debate the works of Plato, Aristotle, and Pythagoras. According to his biographer, Eunapius, he was a very congenial fellow who often dined with his students and occasionally accompanied them on outings to the hot springs of Gadara and elsewhere in the adjacent countryside. But he also saved time to engage in prayer and other religious exercises. Numerous reports circulated about miraculous feats that he was alleged to have performed. One of them, spread by a slave of his, suggested that once while praying he levitated about ten cubits off the ground and was transfigured into a figure of gold. Intrigued by the rumor, his students pleaded for a demonstration of his seemingly miraculous powers. He reluctantly satisfied them by invoking several water spirits while on a visit to the aforementioned hot springs, but also cautioned them against thinking that he was some kind of magician. It is impious at best, he said, for any humans to be dabbling in miracle-working, adding that the gods alone are capable of working wonders and that he himself was merely a channel (and a diffident one at that) of their supernatural powers.

That he took the theurgic rites seriously and saw his own performance in them as a climax to his philosophical pursuit of wisdom need not be doubted. But it is also clear that in his view no performance of the sacred rites could be effective (i.e., saving) without the practitioner being of a virtuous character. It would be inaccurate, therefore, to conclude that Iamblichus betrayed Platonic philosophy to Chaldean superstition. He knew the difference between magic and religion, and it was to the latter that he tried to wed his philosophy.

IAMBLICHUS ON RELIGION. Religious piety should be practiced. But this can be done only to the extent that he who worships becomes similar to the God that is worshiped. And only philosophy, under the impetus of the daemonic genius with which every man is born, can effect such similitude. It does this primarily by providing insight into the truth that beyond the One, *Nous*, and all the other invisible and visible gods emanating from them, is the Great Father and Supreme Source of all being. To behold the incorporeal Divine Essence for Its own sake, rather than for what humans might benefit thereby, the divine element in man, namely the intellect, must be purified of all vice and contamination resulting from descent of the soul into the body. Few — only the genuine philosophers — ever achieve such purification. This they do by practicing virtue, especially the virtue of temperance which gives them mastery over sensual pleasures. In the process they become more and more like God, who is wholly just.

Philosophical reflection, however, is not, in and of itself, enough to effect final union with the gods. Before the soul can be carried aloft to the gods, its ethereal vehicle must be purified through the philosopher's participation in the kind of simple, spiritualistic theurgic worship of the invisible gods that is suitable to enlightened souls. Such worship is not to be confused with the type of magical rituals that are rightly performed by those still clinging to their bodies, and which, in accordance with the condition of these uninitiated masses, are filled with corporeal things (e.g., animal sacrifices) being offered to the lower gods. It is of a more excellent, soulful sort, consisting of the correct performance of unspeakable, unintelligibly symbolic acts through which the gods themselves can work to save the wise. When they die, those who have been initiated and purified by such philosophical/religious activity will be admitted to the company of the gods, while those who have not will face immediate reincarnation.

Sources

Iamblichus. *The Exhortation to Philosophy. Including the Letters of Iamblichus and Proclus' Commentary on the Chaldean Oracles.* Translated by Thomas Moore Johnson. Edited by Stephen Neuville. Grand Rapids, MI: Phanes Press, 1988.
_____. *De mysteriis.* Translated with an introduction and notes by Emma C. Clarke, John M. Dillon, and Jackson P. Hershbell. Leiden and Boston: Brill, 2004.
_____. *On the Pythagorean Way of Life.* Translated by John Dillon and Jackson Hershbell. Atlanta, GA: Scholars Press, 1990.
_____. *Protrepticus.* Excerpts in Edwyn Bevan, Later Greek Religion. London and Toronto: J.M. Dent and Sons, Ltd.; New York: E.P. Dutton and Co., 1927. 219–32.
Bevan, Edwyn. "Iamblichus." *Later Greek Religion.* London and Toronto: J.M. Dent and Sons, Ltd.; New York: E.P. Dutton and Co., 1827. 218–30.
Copleston, Frederick, S.J. *A History of Philosophy.* Vol. 1, pt. 2. Garden City, NY: Doubleday and Company, Inc., 1962–77. 219–20.
Finamore, John F. *Iamblichus and the Theory of the Vehicle of the Soul.* Chico, CA: Scholars Press, 1985.
Lloyd, A.C. "Iamblichus." *Encyclopedia of Philosophy.* Vol. 4. Edited by Paul Edwards. New York: Macmillan and Co. and The Free Press, 1967. 105.
Proclus. *The Elements of Theology.* Translated with commentary by E.R. Dodds. Oxford: At the Clarendon Press, 1963. xx.
Rist, J.M. *Plotinus: The Road to Reality.* Cambridge: At the University Press, 1967. 36.
Whittaker, Thomas. *The Neo-Platonists: A Study in the History of Hellenism.* Cambridge: Cambridge University Press, 1928. 121–31.

Irigaray, Luce (1932–)

For fear that biographical information will "disrupt people when they read" what she has written, Luce Irigaray (as she prefers to be addressed so as to avoid being identified only by the name of her father) has taken an uncompromising position against revealing any details of her personal life. A few facts, however, are known. She was born in Belgium and spent most of the first three decades of her life there. In 1955 she earned an M.A. from the University of Louvain, and for the next three years taught at a secondary school in Brussels. At the age of thirty she enrolled at the University of Paris and within two years received both an M.A. in psychology and a diploma in psychopathology. Returning to Belgium she worked for three years at the Fondation Nationale de la Recherche Scientifique. She then went back to Paris, first as a research assistant, but eventually as the director of that city's Centre National de Recherche Scientifique. All the while she continued studying at the University of Paris toward doctoral degrees in linguistics (1968) and philosophy (1974), teaching at the university's extension in Vincennes, and taking psychoanalytical training at the Freudian school with Jacques Lacan. Publication of her second dissertation (*Speculum of the Other Woman*), in which the supposedly phallocentric proclivities of Freud and Lacan were challenged, resulted in her being ostracized from the Freudian school, dismissed from Vincennes, and denied other professorial assignments in France.

Since then, while continuing to direct the institute for scientific research in Paris, she has been giving lectures and seminars throughout Europe and writing countless articles and books on feminine subjectivity, sexual difference, intersubjectivity, and a variety of other feminist issues. Among her more recent writings, much to the "shock, outrage, disappointment, and mystification in her readers"(according to Elizabeth Grosz), have been a number of papers emphasizing the importance of the "notions of God and the divine to women's struggles for personal and social autonomy." This is not, Grosz insists, an attempt on Luce Irigaray's part to revive some medieval model of feminine pietistic *jouissance* (e.g., Saint Teresa) à la Lacan, or to resurrect mythic, prehistoric female goddesses, or to establish some sort of female-dominated religion. But while continuing to protest against all historically patriarchal religions (like

Roman Catholicism) as forms of women's oppression, and claiming that Christianity will remain inadequate for women so long as it is modeled on a Father-son genealogy and fails to recognize the divinity of woman in and of herself (apart from motherhood), she also insists that without some concept of God as the incarnate horizon of possibility women will never achieve the perfection of which all humans are capable.

IRIGARAY ON RELIGION. There were times (e.g., the ages of Aphrodite and the cult of Demeter) when women possessed their own religions, times when the divine truth expressing earthly fertility, sexual difference, and the close association of human and the divine, body and mind, and natural and spiritual was given to women and passed on from mother to daughter. But these periods of history were eventually censored by religious phallocratic patriarchies. Pursuant to a "logic of the same" that demands unchanging, total, authoritative definitions of ultimate principles, these patriarchies stripped God of any real otherness, reduced the divine to a projection of the male's own subjective self, and enslaved man himself to the image of God as the absolute Master. In the process, women were denied an identity of their own, made to mirror their male masters, and associated with everything opposed to the male principle (i.e., chaos, darkness, passivity, deviltry).

Christianity was no exception in this regard. The case could be made, perhaps, that for Jesus spiritual becoming and corporeal becoming were no less inseparable than they were in the teachings of the Buddha, and that Jesus himself refuted the notion of himself as the androgynous totality of Mankind. But his followers quickly locked Jesus into its patriarchal, ascetical system of belief in life after death, and like the other monotheistic religions, spoke only of God the Father and God made man, and nothing about God the Mother or God made woman or God as a couple. Whatever its roles in the early church, women were again excluded from any real participation in redemption of the world except in terms of mothering sons. Older religions

offered much better examples of the divinity of woman. To become divine again (i.e., free, autonomous, and sovereign) women today need to emulate that example by imagining God as the ideal Other, or infinite horizon, of their sexually differentiated subjectivity in relation to their bodies, their daughters, and the rest of nature, including emancipated males.

Sources

Irigaray, Luce. "Divine Women." Translated by Stephen Muecke. In *Local Consumption Occasional Papers* 8, Sydney (1986).
_____. "Equal to Whom." Translated by Robert L. Mazzola. *Differences* 1 (1989): 59–76.
_____. *The Irigaray Reader.* Edited with an introduction by Margaret Whitford. London: Basil Blackwell, 1991.
_____. *Sexes and Genealogies.* Translated by Carolyn Burke and Gillian C. Gill. London: Athlone University Press, 1984.
_____. "Sexual Difference." In *French Feminist Thought: A Reader.* Edited by Toril Moi. London: Basil Blackwell, 1987. 118–30.
_____. *Speculum of the Other Woman.* Translated by Gillian C. Gill. Ithaca, NY: Cornell University Press, 1974.
_____. *Thinking the Difference.* Translated by Karin Montin. New York: Routledge, 1994. See esp. 8–14.
_____. *This Sex Which Is Not One.* Translated by Catherine Porter with Carolyn Burke. Ithaca: Cornell University Press, 1985. See esp. 86–105.
_____. *To Be Two.* Translated by Monique M. Rhodes and Morco F. Cocito-Monoc. New York: Routledge, 2001. See esp. 85–93.
Grosz, Elizabeth. "Irigaray and the Divine." In *Transfigurations: Theology and the French Feminists.* Edited by C.W. Maggie Kim, Susan M. St. Ville, and Susan M. Simonaitis. Minneapolis: Fortress Press, 1993. 199–214.
_____. *Sexual Subversions. Three French Feminists.* Sydney, Wellington, London, and Boston: Allen and Unwin, 1989. 140–83.
Jantzen, Grace. *Becoming Divine: Towards a Feminist Philosophy of Religion.* Bloomington and Indianapolis: Indiana University Press, 1999.
Jones, Serene. "This God Which Is Not One." In *Transfigurations: Theology and the French Feminists,* edited by C.W. Maggie Kim et al. 109–42.
Moi, Toril. *Sexual/Textual Politics: Feminist Literary Theory.* London and New York: Methuen, 1985. 127–49.
Sanders, Vicki A. "Luce Irigaray." In *World Philoso-*

phers and Their Works. Vol. 2. Edited by John K. Roth. Pasadena, CA, and Hackensack, NJ: Salem Press, Inc., 2000. 914–19.

Whitmore, Margaret. *Luce Irigaray: Philosophy in the Feminine.* London: Routledge, 1991.

James, William (1842–1910)

William James' father, Henry Sr., was a man of deep but troubled religious faith. Disgusted by the insufferable religious dogmatism he had encountered at Princeton Theological Seminary, the father abandoned any thought of becoming a Presbyterian minister and devoted himself instead, first to publicizing the theologian Robert Sanderman's antiritualistic, antiauthoritarian appeal for a return to a primitive Christian sense of brotherhood, and then, after several bouts of anxiety and depression, to developing a spiritual vision of his own out of Swedenborg's mystical ideas about the rejection of selfhood and communion with God. He thereafter became preoccupied with creating a family environment wherein William and his other children could develop spiritually.

Although William himself never embraced the rather simplistic beliefs of his father, and in fact suffered considerably from trying to satisfy paternal expectations, he did respect their underlying religiosity, and tried mightily throughout his life to reconcile the latter pragmatically with his own commitment to modern science. After wrestling neurotically over career choices (Art, Chemistry, Medicine) for better than a decade and finally getting his M.D. from Harvard, a spiritual breakthrough came with his reading of Renouvier on free-will and making it his "first act of free-will … to believe in free-will." Already in the *Principles of Psychology* (which he had begun writing soon after landing a job teaching physiology and philosophy at Harvard), but especially in his publications, *The Will to Believe* and *The Varieties of Religious Experience* (his Gifford Lectures), he defended the empirical reality and pragmatic truth of religion against reductionist attempts to explain it away along materialistic lines.

Although he had a keen appreciation for religious pluralism and was never a champion of Christian orthodoxy, he became increasingly convinced in his latter years that there is — as all religions suggest and religious people experience — a transcendent world, an "unseen order" or "ideal realm," that is being "cared for by a mind so powerful [albeit finite] as on the whole to control the drift of the Universe." At his funeral service in Harvard's Appleton Chapel, the pastor of Boston's Old South Church (a former student) eulogized him, in accordance with his beloved wife's wishes, as a deeply religious man.

JAMES ON RELIGION. There is no single sentiment or act that can be classified as religious. Religious sentiments and acts are simply man's natural emotions and actions being instinctively directed to a religious object. Ignoring the institutional, clerically organized, ritualistic side of religion, personal religion might be said to consist, therefore, of the feelings, acts, and experiences of individual men in their solitude, so far as they apprehend themselves in relation to whatever they consider divine or godlike, whether it be a concrete deity, an abstract Ideality, or a supreme primal reality — a "something more" — to which they feel impelled to respond with solemnity, seriousness, and a joyful spirit of sacrifice. The radically tough-minded, with their crude reliance on the sensible facts of nature, will claim to need no religion at all. The radically tender-minded, seeking security against the vicissitudes of daily life, will favor one or another — pantheistic or theistic — monistic form of religion that conceives of the unity of the world as an absolute *terminus a quo.* But those who, like me, are neither tough nor tender in any radical sense, may prefer a pragmatistic or pluralistic/melioristic type of theism, according to which the world's perfection is taken only as a possible *terminus ad quem,* and the divine creator is viewed as but one helper — the *primus inter pares* of all the shapers of the great world's fate — to whose *fiat* man must add his own.

Even when empirical evidence is lacking, the will, under the influence of our passional nature, not only lawfully may, but must, decide to believe or not to believe in God, for consisting of possible and desirable alternatives, it is a living option that is both unavoidable and momentous. Not to make it is to risk losing the kind of truth that might be elicited or come about only by way of believing it. Any belief that works to perfect the world and man's place in it is true, whether or not it corresponds to the facts or coheres with whatever else we might know.

Sources

James, William. *Pragmatism, and four essays from The Meaning of Truth*. Cleveland and New York: The World Publishing Company, 1967.

_____. *The Varieties of Religious Experience*. New York: New American Library, 1958.

_____. *The Will to Believe and other essays in popular philosophy; Human Immortality*. New York: Dover Publications, Inc., 1956.

Barzun, Jacques. "James, William." In *Encyclopedia of Religion*. Vol. 7. Edited by Mircea Eliade. New York: Macmillan and Co., 1987. 517–19.

Bowen, David Warren et al. "William James." In *World Philosophers and Their Works*. Vol. 2. Edited by John K. Roth. Pasadena, CA, and Hackensack, NJ: Salem Press, Inc., 2000. 927–43.

Brown, Hunter. *William James on Radical Empiricism and Religion*. Toronto: University of Toronto Press, 2000.

Fontinell, Eugene. *Self, God, and Immortality. A Jamesian Investigation*. Philadelphia: Temple University Press, 1986.

Hartshorne, Charles, and William L. Reese. *Philosophers Speak of God*. Chicago and London: The University of Chicago Press, 1963. 335–52.

Kallen, Horace M. "William James." *Encyclopædia Britannica*. Vol. 12. Chicago, London, and Toronto: Encyclopædia Britannica, Inc., William Benton Publisher, 1959, 2002, 2005. 883–85.

Simon, Linda. *Genuine Reality: A Life of William James*. New York, San Diego, and London: Harcourt Brace and Company, 1998.

_____. *William James Remembered*. Lincoln and London: University of Nebraska, 1996. See esp. 46–49.

Stewart, David. *Exploring the Philosophy of Religion*. Upper Saddle River, NJ: Prentice Hall, 1998. 135–41.

Wainwright, William J. *Philosophy of Religion*. Belmont, CA: Wadsworth Publishing Company, 1988. 148–53.

Wernham, James C.S. *James's Will-to-Believe Doctrine*. Kingston and Montreal: McGill-Queen's University Press, 1987.

Jaspers, Karl (1883–1969)

Born in Oldenburg, Jaspers was raised by parents who generally ignored the ecclesiastical world. His father had serious misgivings about the integrity of institutionalized religion and abandoned it altogether in his latter years. But he also saw religion as one of the regulative forces that forestalls unforeseeable evil, and on that account thought it important to go along with his fellow men and have his son enrolled at a school where he received religious instruction in biblical history, catechism, and church history. Although this instruction planted ideas in Jaspers' mind that he would never forget, it had little momentary effect. He considered his confirmation a mere exercise in societal mores — an occasion to receive worldly presents, but without any religious emphasis — and the instruction prior to it, a mere joke, filled as it was with literalist biblical interpretations and antipapal diatribe. During his last year in the Gymnasium, he felt that to be true to himself he would have to leave the church. His father encouraged him to wait before making such a move until he was closer to death and no longer active in the world.

Already during his teen years he had become fascinated by his reading of Spinoza, but stayed with his study first of law and then medicine. He eventually earned his M.D. at the University of Heidelberg, where also he would later teach psychiatry and chair the department of Philosophy. In 1910 he married Gertrude Mayer and was greatly affected by her Jewish faith and deep respect for everything religious. It was another twenty years, however, before he developed any real interest in theology.

His intense study of Kierkegaard during the First World War had not only spawned his concept of *Existenz*, but also contributed to the realization he would achieve after World

War II through dialogue with Protestant theologians that although philosophical faith, as the primal source of religious meaning, must have its own independent base, genuine philosophizing cannot neglect the factuality of the church and of theology. He also admitted that university life could be enhanced by having separate departments for the teaching of biblical (Catholic, Protestant, and Jewish) and Buddhist forms of faith. But while acknowledging the social and historical significance of various religious traditions, and eschewing the kind of hostility toward religion displayed by some Existentialists like Sartre, he did, like the latter, reject any intrusion of a personal, triune and incarnate God as a threat to human freedom, and to that extent remained quasi-atheistic throughout his life.

JASPERS ON RELIGION. The depersonalization and alienation of the human situation in the modern age has resulted largely from scientist and rationalistic attempts to reduce man to one or another kind of empirical being. But far from being a completely determined psycho-physical phenomenon, man is radically free, and to that extent can best be described as *Existenz,* or as a creature, in other words, whose very being it is to be open to Transcendence, that totality of Being that encompasses every horizon of human experience. Popular religion has named this Transcendence "God,' and so long as it expresses itself in the symbolic language of mythology and leaves individuals free to try deciphering for themselves traces of the hidden God in every word, action, thing, or person around them, it remains true and a helpful stimulus to philosophical reflection.

But when religion claims a special revelation on the basis of some otherworldly, mystical experience, and uses its authority and cultic practice to impose a dogmatic, exclusive conception of God such as would convert Transcendence into a real, objective presence, it must then be opposed as a threat to the philosophical faith from which the religious attitude emerged in the first place. Prompted negatively by the limits of the human situation (e.g., finiteness) and, more positively, by

a precognitive reading of the ciphers that both reveal and conceal the transcendent dimensions of reality, such faith is the fundamental awareness experienced by the individual self as it discovers its own freedom. Resisting nihilistic and mystical temptations to deny the ultimate meaning of its own existence and of the world around it, the self affirms, without any proof or objective knowledge to go by, an existential relationship with Transcendence, surrenders prayerfully to the will of God, and like Jeremiah, Job, or Jesus, actively suffers, without any hope of personal immortality, the human foundering that comes to a climax in the experience of death.

Sources

Jaspers, Karl. *Myth and Christianity*. New York: Noonday Press, 1958.
_____. *The Origin and Goal of History*. Translated by Michael Bullock. New Haven: Yale University Press, 1953.
_____. *The Perennial Scope of Philosophy*. Translated by Ralph Manheim. New York: Philosophical Library, 1949.
_____. *Philosophy*. Translated by E.B. Ashton. Chicago: University of Chicago Press, 1969.
Collins, James. *The Existentialists*. Chicago: Henry Regnery Company, 1952. 80–114.
Kolakowski, Leszek. "Jasper, Karl" In *Encyclopedia of Religion*. Vol. 7. Edited by Mircea Eliade. New York: Macmillan and Co., 1987. 557–58.
Schilpp, Paul Arthur, ed. *The Philosophy of Karl Jaspers*. LaSalle, IL: Open Court, 1981. See esp. 75–81; 611–701.

John Scottus Eriugena (c. 800–877)

As his name "Eriugena" implies, John Scottus was "born of Ireland," possibly received his education in the Latin and Greek languages there, and in all likelihood fled the country in 840 because of Viking raids. He apparently had no clerical status in the church, but might have been a monk. In any event, he sought refuge at the court of Charles the Bald and became a teacher of liberal arts in its palace school. At the king's request he also undertook the translation of the complete Neoplatonic writings of Dionysius the Areopagite, who at the time was wrongly identified with Denys, the apostle of Gaul. This work, along with his translation of other Greek texts by theologians like Maximus the Confessor and Gregory of Nyssa, exposed John Scottus himself and the whole of the Western medieval world to an entirely new vision of reality.

Lured by Archbishop Hincmar into the controversy over predestination stirred up by Gottschalk of Orbais, he attacked the Saxon monk's supposedly Augustinian views about the divine predestination of some souls to salvation and others to damnation, but in the process also upset other theologians, like Prudentius of Troyes and Florus of Lyons, by his own interpretation of the doctrine. It was later condemned at the councils of Valencia and Langres. His attempt to interpret the Eucharist along symbolic lines was also condemned by Hincmar and the Council of Vercelli.

Probably his most original and important work was the *De Divisione Naturae* (the *Periphyseon*), whose five books take a fictional Master and his Pupil on a paradoxical quest for the truth about how all sensible and intelligible things take their origin in and ultimately return to God as the incomprehensible and unspeakable, transcendent abyss of nothingness or nonbeing. But because of its supposed pantheistic implications, it too was condemned by the Council of Paris, ordered by the pope to be burned, and later placed on the Vatican's Index of Forbidden Books.

Although there is considerable confusion about the details of his latter years, the evidence seems to suggest that after the death of his patron, Charles the Bald, John Scottus was invited to teach at England's Abbey of Malmesbury, which had a strong Irish tradition. Its chronicler, William of Malmesbury, claimed that John Scottus' students eventually stabbed him to death with their pens, inclining some in later centuries to canonize him as a martyr and include him temporarily in the Roman Martyrology.

JOHN SCOTTUS ERIUGENA ON RELIGION. It is not unreasonable to demand from Catholics a rational account of their Christian religion. For true philosophy, as the divisional and analytical movement of the human mind that engages the soul in the dialectical process of Nature itself, is no different from true religion. Scripture is the ultimate authority for the truths it (and the Catholic Creed) expresses literally for the edification of the uneducated, but these truths have been imbued by the Holy Spirit with infinite meanings which can be interpreted allegorically, spiritually, and historically from different viewpoints by multiple theories, no one of which is better than another except to the extent of its reasonableness. Biblical statements about the incomprehensibility of God can be interpreted, therefore, to refer to the dimension of Nature's nonbeing, the superessentiality of which transcends all sensual or intellectual (i.e., categorical) perception, and in its infinite formlessness embraces all possibilities. The biblical doctrine of creation can, in turn, be interpreted as an eternal process whereby all that is (archetypical Ideas; angelic intelligences; humans; animals; plants; inanimate objects) emanates as a self-manifestation of the divine goodness, and then, under the influence of Christ's deified humanity, is drawn back into union with God.

For humans, this will mean recovering, with the help of the liberal arts, a vision of their own godlike essence, the perfect, asexual human nature that has eternally existed in God as a possibility, but which — as symbolized by the biblical account of the Fall — was lost when the pre-existing human soul freely succumbed to pride, cloaked itself in illusory flesh, and became preoccupied with the pursuit of carnal pleasure. The resurrected bodies of all humans will be spiritualized; the wicked, to be tortured by the frustration of their carnal desires; the blessed, to blend totally with the perfect Idea of themselves in the divine mind, even while — like iron melting in a fire — retaining their distinctness from the transcendent God.

Sources

John Scottus Eriugena. *De Divina Praedestinatione. Corpus Christianorum Continuatio Mediaevalis (CCCM)* 50 (1978).

_____. *Homily on the Prologue to St. John's Gospel.* In John J. O'Meara, *Eriugena.* 158–76.

_____. *Periphyseon* (Division of Nature). Translated by John O'Meara. Montreal: Éditions Bellarmin; Washington, D.C.: Dumbarton Oaks, 1987.

Bett, Henry. *Johannes Scotus Erigena: A Study in Medieval Philosophy.* New York: Russell and Russell, Inc., 1964.

Carabine, Deirdre. *John Scottus Eriugena.* New York and Oxford: Oxford University Press, 2000.

Copleston, Frederick, S.J. *A History of Philosophy.* Vol. 2, pt. 1. Garden City, NY: Doubleday and Company, Inc., 1962–77. 133–53.

Gilson. Etienne. *History of Christian Philosophy in the Middle Ages.* New York: Random House, 1954. 113–28.

Lynch, L.E. "John Scotus Erigena." *New Catholic Encyclopedia.* Vol. 7. Edited by W.J. McDonald. New York: McGraw-Hill, 1967. 1072–74.

Moran, Dermot. *The Philosophy of John Scottus Eriugena: A Study of Idealism in the Middle Ages.* Cambridge: Cambridge University Press, 1989.

O'Meara, Dominic. "The Problem of Speaking about God in John Scottus Eriugena." In Dominic O'Meara, *The Structure of Being and the Search for the Good.* Aldershot, Brookfield, VT, Singapore, and Sydney: Ashgate, 1998. 151–67.

O'Meara, John J. *Eriugena.* Oxford: Clarendon Press, 1988.

Pelikan, Jaroslav. *The Growth of Medieval Theology* (600–1300). Chicago and London: The University of Chicago Press, 1978.

Stumpf, Samuel Enoch. *Socrates to Sartre. A History of Philosophy.* New York: McGraw-Hill Book Company, 1982. 150–53.

Kant, Immanuel (1724–1804)

Kant was born of parents whose Halle-version of Pietistic emphasis upon bible study, personal conversion, lay priesthood, and practical faith contrasted sharply with the rather formal and dogmatic character of Protestant (Lutheran) orthodoxy. From the age of eight to sixteen, he was enrolled at the Collegium Fridericianum, where his pastor, Franz Schulz, soon thereafter became the director and, notwithstanding a taste for Wolffian rationalism, subjected his students to intensely Pietistic rounds of prayer, hymn-singing, accusatory soul-searching, and Bible-based religious instruction. How much influence this Pietistic education actually had on Kant's intellectual development is debatable. Throughout his life he would remain highly respectful of the inner peace Pietists, like his very devout mother, maintained in the face of every adversity. But by his own account, his experience at the Fridericianum only served to trigger the resistance he would show for the rest of his life to any kind of servile, emotional form of religious practice.

At sixteen, he enrolled in the University of Königsberg's school of theology, but devoted most of his early years there studying science and the quasi-deistic, Wolffian philosophy being propounded by his favorite teacher, Martin Knutzen. When finally he did get around to taking a course in Dogmatics he was invited to enter the ministry, but declined, and thereafter showed little interest in contemporary theological developments. After graduating from the university and spending several decades as a *Privatdozent* and university professor, he gradually abandoned Leibnizian-Wolffian metaphysics, and stimulated by his reading of Rousseau, converted to a more critical philosophy that gave priority to morality over religion and, when published, brought down on him the wrath of Prussian authorities.

Although he would continue to postulate the existence of God and personal immortality as corollaries of the categorical imperative in his writings, there is reason to doubt how much credence he himself any longer put in such religious ideas. The supposedly antirational, ingratiating attitude of organized religion irritated him to no end, and he consistently declined participating in any kind of public prayer or worship service. Confident to the end that he had fulfilled his duty and on that account, could hope, true to the etymological connotations of his first name, that any God who existed would still be with him, he expressed no fear of dying. When finally he did die, and his body was being carried from his home for burial in the university's cathedral, every church bell in Königsberg tolled in his honor.

KANT ON RELIGION. Rationalists are wrong in thinking that reason alone can deliver innate knowledge of God's existence and nature. But dogmatic empiricists are also wrong in claiming that reality consists of nothing more than sensible phenomena. The inability of science to explain the organic, internal purposiveness found in nature suggests at least the possibility of a supersensible, intuitively intelligent (albeit, perhaps, nonmoral) deity. A sense of cosmic mystery is further enhanced by the regulative idea of wholeness that underlies our every thought. It is our innate, moral sense of duty, however, that especially suggests the existence of a "noumenal" realm that escapes both sensible intuition and rational comprehension. For to acknowledge that we are by nature obliged to obey the categorical imperative of acting always as one would want everyone else to act and treating all one's fellow human beings as ends in themselves, is to imply that we are free.

This natural ability of ours to choose to transcend the laws of the physical universe in turn gives rise to the idea of linking virtue, even while it is being pursued for its own sake, with happiness — if not one's own, at least that of others. And since this highest good is not, and cannot, ever be achieved in this life, we have good reason to hope that as humans we are immortal, and that there is a holy, omniscient and just God who will reward those who do their duty and punish those who do not. Given the universal propensity of mankind to evil, this religious reinforcement of human duties as divine commands is necessary. But morality must remain autonomous, and it might be better to look for God in the essentially divine nature of the moral order itself. This was exemplified in the person of Jesus, who transformed the servile, external cult of Judaism into the moral, internal disposition of love, and demonstrated thereby that genuine religion has nothing to do with the performance of prayers, liturgical rituals, or cultic taboos.

Sources

Kant, Immanuel. *Critique of Pure Reason*. Translated by J.M.D. Meiklejohn. London: J.M. Dent and Sons, Ltd.; New York: E.P. Dutton and Co., Inc., 1959.

_____. *Foundations of the Metaphysics of Morals and What is Enlightenment?* Translated by Lewis White Beck. New York: Macmillan Publishing Company; London: Collier Macmillan Publishers, 1990.

_____. *Lectures on Philosophical Theology*. Translated by Allen W. Wood and Gertrude M. Clark. Ithaca, NY: Cornell University, 1978.

_____. *Opus Postumum*. Translated by Eckart Förster and Michael Rosen. New York: Cambridge University Press, 1993.

_____. *Religion Within the Limits of Reason Alone*. Translated by Theodore M. Greene and Hoyt H. Hudson. New York and Evanston: Harper and Row Publishers, 1960.

Cassirer, Ernst. *Kant's Life and Thought*. New Haven and London: Yale University Press, 1981. See esp. 17–18; 377–97.

Caygill, Howard. *A Kant Dictionary*. Oxford: Blackwell, 2000. 192–95; 215–16; 353–54; 389–93.

Copleston, Frederick, S.J. *A History of Philosophy*. Vol. 6, pt. 1. (209–41) and pt. 2 (see esp. 101–70). Garden City, NY: Doubleday and Company, Inc., 1962–77.

Fackenheim, Emil L. *The God Within; Kant, Schelling, and Historicity*. Toronto: University of Toronto Press, 1996.

Greene, Theodore M. "The Historical Context and Religious Significance of Kant's *Religion*." In I. Kant, *Religion Within the Limits of Reason Alone*. New York and Evanston: Harper and Row, 1960. ix–lxxviii.

Kuehn, Manfred. *Kant: A Biography*. Cambridge: Cambridge University Press, 2001.

Palmquist, Stephen R. *Kant's Critical Religion*. Aldershot, Burlington, VT, Singapore, and Sydney: Ashgate Publishers Ltd., 2000. (Includes excellent bibliography of recent works on Kant's thought on religion).

Seung, T.K. "Kant, Immanuel." In *Encyclopedia of Religion*. Vol. 8. Edited by Mircea Eliade. New York: Macmillan and Co., 1987. 247–52.

Kemp Smith, Norman (1872–1958)

Hoping, perhaps, that her son might eventually enter the Presbyterian ministry, Kemp Smith's mother had him baptized "Norman" after the famous nineteenth-century Scottish preacher, Dr. Norman Macleod. The addition of "Kemp" to his surname came much later, only after his marriage at the age of thirty-eight to Miss Amy Kemp. The youngest of six children of a bankrupt Dundee cabinetmaker, he took his elementary and secondary education at the local public schools. Matriculating at St. Andrews University in 1888, he began his study of philosophy and eventually took his degree with highest honors under the professorial supervision of Andrew Seth (Pringle-Pattison), Henry Jones, and William Knight. During the next three years, while intermittently launching his teaching career as an assistant to Henry Jones, he studied French and German philosophies and languages abroad at the Universities of Jena, Zürich, Berlin and Paris.

Upon returning to Glasgow in 1896, he became an assistant to, and was greatly influenced by, the Kantian scholar, Robert Adamson. The publication of his *Studies in the Cartesian Philosophy* four years later won him the doctor's degree from St. Andrews, and in 1906 a professorial appointment in Princeton University's Philosophy Department. With the outbreak of World War I in 1916 he returned to Britain and served in the Army's Intelligence and Information Departments. While in London he had occasion to hear and befriend Baron Friedrich von Hügel, the renowned German Catholic philosopher of religion then living in Kensington. The latter's writings on the mystical element in religion would have a profound affect upon the development of Kemp Smith's own idealistic thoughts about the role of spiritual values in the ordering of the universe.

In the summer of 1918 Kemp Smith published his *Commentary to Kant's Critique of Pure Reason*. Its warm reception helped him get selected the next year to succeed Pringle-Pattison to the Edinburgh Chair of Logic and Metaphysics. Despite heavy teaching and administrative work until his retirement twenty-six years later, he continued publishing a number of books and articles on Kant, Hume, Descartes, and his own Idealist/Realist philosophy. Von Hügel had encouraged him to seek membership in some historical church as a way of honing his religious sense of "creatureliness." But despite his sympathy for the Presbyterian religion of his youth and native country, he consistently refrained from forming any definite Church connections. After his peaceful death in 1958 a cremation service was conducted by two of his Edinburgh pupils.

KEMP SMITH ON RELIGION. Belief in Divine Existence might be easy if the Design Argument were valid. But the phenomena of Nature and historical events are not only worthless as evidence of design, but are also (contrary to Hume's and Kant's inconsistent assertions) insufficient for producing an impression of design. Nor, if one distinguishes properly between that which is artificial (e.g., a watch) and that which is natural, can one arrive at the existence of God analogically by magnifying human attributes of foresight or purpose in such wise as to identify an omnipotent, omniscient, omnipresent and eternal Creator with a Divine Artificer. Short of disclaiming belief in God's existence, therefore, the one remaining alternative is to assume with Old Testament (OT) writers that humans "experience the Divine in a direct and immediate manner," albeit always also as mysterious and never in total isolation from what is other than the Divine.

The initial experience in which religion took its rise was through and in connection with the cosmic setting of our human life, spawning through a dread and fascination of natural phenomena a primordial sense of the Divine as "that upon which all things rest." And although the indefinite, ambiguous conception and practical bearings of the divine during this first stage of religion would later, through the influence of human institutions and traditions, find a more sophisticated theological, liturgical, and social expression in the higher forms of religion, the experience of the "non-creatureliness" of God "in connection with the inexhaustibly varied, infinitely vast, and profoundly mysterious natural order" by which we are upheld, would remain the primary basis for religious credibility. Only in conjunction with this belief in Divine Existence and the orderliness of our Universe is an afterlife for human beings credible. Believing that our present lives are divinely conditioned, it is natural to believe in immortality, not as a way of escaping the present life, but to find its deeper meaning.

Sources

Kemp Smith, Norman. *The Credibility of Divine Existence. The Collected Papers of Norman Kemp Smith*. Edited by A.J.D. Porteous, R.D. MacLennan, and G.E. Davie. London, Melbourne, and Toronto: Macmillan; New York: St. Martin's Press, 1967. See esp. 3–60; 363–438.

Barmann, Lawrence F., ed. *The Letters of Baron Friedrich von Hügel and Professor Norman Kemp Smith*. New York: Fordham University Press, 1981. See esp. 1–14; 37; 40; 48–53; 98–100; 152–53; 306–11.

Kierkegaard, Søren (1813–1855)

As a young boy, Kierkegaard was confirmed in the Lutheran faith by his former pastor, Bishop Jakob Mynster, Primate of the Church of Denmark and a close friend of Kierkegaard's father. The latter harbored Pietistic feelings of profound guilt and fear for having once, in a moment of youthful rebellion against his impoverished condition, cursed God and for later, before the death of his first wife, having seduced the servant who would eventually become the mother of the last of his seven children, his favorite son, Søren. In hopes of preparing him for the ministry, the father subjected his son to a very stern religious upbringing. But after experiencing while still a teenager the death of his mother and five of his siblings and discovering the cause of his father's brooding melancholy, Kierkegaard himself fell into despair, turned bitterly against his father and the religion of his upbringing. Abandoning any thought of a ministerial vocation, he took up the study of literature and philosophy and adopted the hedonistic lifestyle of his aesthete companions at the University of Copenhagen.

In 1838, however, the father, before dying, made a heartfelt confession of his sins to Kierkegaard, filling the son with "indescrib-able joy" at discovering anew what a father's love can be, and thereby also how loving God, our Father, can be. He resumed his study of theology, completing the equivalent of doctoral work with his thesis on the concept of irony, and with the money left him by his father launched his career as an independent writer. Soon thereafter he broke an engagement with his beloved Regina Oslen, and over the next decade and a half published a steady stream of psychological, philosophical and theological writings.

A nasty battle with local scandal-mongers subjected him to much personal abuse and public ridicule. But his relentless attack against the Hegelian rationalization of Christian thought and against what he perceived to be the hypocritical distortion of the religion of Jesus by the established Church of Denmark created an even greater public furor. Convinced that it was his mission to save the masses from losing their individuality in the herd and to dispel Europe of its illusion of being Christian, he stood his ground to the end, refusing on his deathbed to receive communion from the King's official, and declining an invitation from a visiting, friendly pastor to retract anything he had written. After a funeral service in the Cathedral Church of Our Lady, he was buried in the cemetery beside his father, with his nephew protesting all the while about the dishonesty of the Church in affording a religious burial to one of its sharpest critics.

KIERKEGAARD ON RELIGION. Essentially, it is the God-relationship that makes a man a man. But there is an infinite gulf between man and God that neither empirical observation nor rational speculation can bridge. Nature can be contemplated in hopes of finding God, but despite the discovery of evidentiary bits of divine wisdom, the result is always objective uncertainty about the existence of God. So too, while dialectical thinking can conjure up an objective idea of Absolute Mind, it only serves to blur the distinction between the infinite and finite, and to that extent can never present a God who is "totally other," an Absolute Thou to whom man might relate existentially.

Such a transcendent God can be discovered only through religious faith. Faith, however, neither arises from, nor climaxes in thought. It is rather an embrace of objective uncertainty with all the passion of the infinite. It is an act of the will, a choice to leap beyond the abyss of absurdity resulting from the paradoxical nature of the Absolute Other, even as it has revealed itself in the God-Man, Jesus Christ. Having despaired of ever finding satisfaction in the aesthetic approach to life along lines of unreflective, sensual immediacy or the seductive exploration of unlimited possibilities, and having given up also on ever seriously meeting on one's own the demands of marriage or any other ethical state of life that requires continuous and permanent self-commitment, one becomes keenly aware of one's own insufficiency as an individual, finite creature, and like Abraham, surrenders one's will to the absolute demands of God. Such infinite resignation is one's best and only chance of finding within this world the inward joy of authentic existence. It is also one's best hope for the next life. Eschewing any Platonic attempt at recollecting oneself back to eternity, it stakes one's life unreservedly on the if of human immortality by striving constantly to become oneself through one's relation to God.

Sources

Kierkegaard, Søren. *Eighteen Upbuilding Discourses.* Edited and translated by Howard V. Hong and Edna H. Hong. Princeton: Princeton University Press, 1990.

_____. *Either/Or.* 2 vols. Translated by David F. Swenson and Lillian Marvin Swenson. Princeton: Princeton University Press, 1959.

_____. *Fear and Trembling; The Sickness Unto Death.* Translated by Walter Lowrie. Garden City, NY: Doubleday and Company, Inc., 1954.

_____. *The Journals of Kierkegaard.* Edited and introduced by Alexander Dru. New York and Evanston: Harper and Row, Publishers, 1959.

_____. *Philosophical Fragments/Johannes Climacus.* Edited and translated by Howard V. Hong and Edna H. Hong. Princeton: Princeton University Press, 1985.

_____. *Practice in Christianity.* Edited and translated by Howard V. Hong and Edna H. Hong. Princeton: Princeton University Press, 1991.

_____. *Stages on Life's Way.* Edited and translated by Howard V. Hong and Edna H. Hong. Princeton: Princeton University Press, 1988.

_____. *Works of Love.* Translated by Howard Hong and Edna Hong. New York: Harper and Row, 1962.

Collins, James. *The Mind of Kierkegaard.* Chicago: Henry Regnery Company, 1965.

Copleston, Frederick, S.J. *A History of Philosophy.* Vol. 7, pt. 2. Garden City, NY: Doubleday and Company, Inc., 1962–77. 105–22.

Diem, H. *Kierkegaard's Dialectic of Existence.* Edinburgh and London: Oliver and Boyd, 1959.

Dupré, L.K. *Kierkegaard as Theologian.* New York: Sheed and Ward, 1963.

_____. "Kierkegaard, Søren Aabye." *New Catholic Encyclopedia.* Vol. 8. Edited by W.J. McDonald. New York: McGraw-Hill, 1967. 174–76.

Melchert, Norman. *The Great Conversation.* Boston: McGraw-Hill, 2002. 497–515.

Taylor, Mark C. "Kierkegaard, Søren." In *Encyclopedia of Religion.* Vol. 8. Edited by Mircea Eliade. New York: Macmillan and Co., 1987. 298–301.

Leibniz, Gottfried Wilhelm (1646–1716)

Leibniz was born in the Protestant city of Leipzig. Both his father (a professor of moral philosophy) and his mother (raised in the home of a theology professor) were pious Lutherans, and promptly had their newborn son baptized in Leipzig's St. Nicolai Church. The mother's example of trying patiently to live with all in peace and harmony is said to have been especially responsible, after the father's early death, for sowing in the young Leibniz the seeds of his lifelong respect for religion. He proved to be a very precocious lad, and by his own account, was already, at the age of thirteen, studying not only Greek and Scholastic philosophy, but also works of church fathers and theologians that supposedly convinced him of the truth of the Augsburg Confession. Notwithstanding his increased interest in mathematics, law and philosophy during his college years at the universities of Leipzig and Jena, he retained a keen interest in religious matters and appended to one of his earliest writings a Euclidean rendition of the cosmological argument for the existence of God.

After the University of Altdorf awarded him the doctorate in law he had been denied at Leipzig because of his youth, he spent the next year supporting the Archbishop of Mainz's effort to rebuild a Germany ravaged by the Thirty Years War. During his extensive, diplomatic travels in subsequent years, he had occasion to meet with Malebranche, Arnauld, Spinoza and other great religious thinkers, with the result that in addition to all his other works, he produced a steady stream of writings on religion (including that of China). Contrary to the claims of the French *philosophes*, he insisted that faith (Catholic or Protestant) and reason are not incompatible. He became especially interested in trying to find a way to reunite Catholics and Protestants, or at least Lutherans and Calvinists. This brought him into frequent contact with Catholic leaders, some of whom tried to convert him to the Roman Catholic Church.

Suspicions arose about whether he had changed his religious affiliation, or perhaps had lost his faith altogether. But notwithstanding the supposedly Catholic perspective of his *System of Theology* and *The Catholic Demonstrations*, he remained a Lutheran throughout his life. Because of his growing preference for natural (non-ritualistic) religion, however, he seldom took communion and even declined summoning a clergyman to his deathbed. The royal court and citizens of Hannover paid little attention to his death, but he was buried with Christian services in that city's Neustädter Church.

LEIBNIZ ON RELIGION. Given the conformity of reason with faith, there is a philosophical system that can be used not only to foster the principles of true religion (love of God and neighbor), but also to demonstrate common ground between all religions, be they revealed or natural. At its core is the understanding of substance as a monad or unit of being that is capable of, and inclined toward, action. The ultimate monad, therefore, will be that being whose very essence it is to act — namely, God. Like other eternal truths, the idea of God is virtually innate. Connoting supreme perfection, it necessarily implies the existence of God.

Further proof of God's existence can be deduced from the observation of cosmic contingency and harmony. Given their potential nonbeing (prime matter), the monadic aggregations of a corporeal sort — ranging from inanimate objects to fully conscious human beings — that fill our universe can have the fact of their existence explained sufficiently only by a God who cannot not be. And although it is in their nature to mirror the whole of the universe through their respective and individuating degrees of perceptive power, the same monadic aggregations are "windowless," and to that extent must rely upon divine orchestration for the harmonious arrangement their monads enjoy within and outside themselves. God freely chose to create the world that had the greatest amount of perfection within any system of "compossibles." But even "the best of all possible worlds" must necessarily involve some metaphysical, physical, and moral evil to the extent of being imperfect, full of suffering, and disorderly. The latter moral disorder results from a lack of perception of what it really means to be human, and will only be corrected when pious souls come to see, already here and now, their union with each other in the "city of God," and finally, as immortal spirits, enjoy the beatific vision of universal harmony.

Sources

Leibniz, Gottfried Wilhelm. *Discourse on Metaphysics; Correspondence with Arnauld, Monadology*. Introduction by Paul Janet; translated by George Montgomery. LaSalle, IL: Open Court Publishing Company, 1988.

_____. *Discourse on the Natural Theology of the Chinese*. Translated with an introduction, notes and commentary by Henry Rosemont, Jr. and Daniel J. Cook. Society for Asian and Comparative Philosophy. [Honolulu]: The University of Hawaii Press, 1977.

_____. *Philosophical Papers and Letters*. Translated and edited, with an introduction by Leroy E. Loemker. Chicago: The University of Chicago Press, 1956.

_____. *Theodicy*. Edited with an introduction by Austin Farrer; translated by E.M. Huggard. LaSalle, IL: Open Court, 1985.

Adams, Robert Merrihew. "Leibniz's Examination

of *The Christian Religion.*" *Faith and Philosophy* 11, no. 4 (October 1994): 517–45.

Aiton, E.J. *Leibniz: A Biography.* Bristol and Boston: Adam Hilger, Ltd., 1985.

Copleston, Frederick, S.J. *A History of Philosophy.* Vol. 4. Garden City, NY: Doubleday and Company, Inc., 1962–77. 270–336.

Coudert, Allison, P., Richard H. Popkin, and Gordon M. Weiner, eds. *Leibniz, Mysticism and Religion.* Dordrecht: Kluwer Academic Publishers, 1998.

Ross, G. MacDonald. *Leibniz.* Oxford: Oxford University Press, 1984.

Saw, Ruth Lydia. *Leibniz.* Harmondsworth, UK: Penguin Books, 1954.

Sleigh, R.C., Jr. "Leibniz, Gottfried Wilhelm." In *Encyclopedia of Religion.* Vol. 8. Edited by Mircea Eliade. New York: Macmillan and Co., 1987. 510–12.

Stumpf, Samuel Enoch. *Socrates to Sartre. A History of Philosophy.* New York: McGraw-Hill Book Company, 1982. 245–53.

Lessing, Gotthold Ephraim (1729–1781)

Lessing was the eldest son of a learned theologian who had given up a professorial career to become the pastor of Kamenz. His grandfather had written a doctoral dissertation on a subject that would later become dear to Lessing himself, namely, the toleration of not only different Christian sects, but of all religions. Notwithstanding his pastoral duties, the father, embodying the ideal of a Protestant clergyman, had continued his studies of church history and especially of the Reformation period. From him and his mother (the daughter of the previous pastor of Kamenz), Lessing was early on taught to pray and given instruction in the Bible and Catechism. Both parents entertained hopes that their son would eventually enter the ministry and become a pastor and preacher.

After removing their son from a local public school because of its dalliance in the theatrical arts, they enrolled him at the school of St. Afra in Meissen whose primary goal was to educate theologians and divines and required twenty-five hours of the week for public worship, prayer meeting, and Bible class. This did not, however, keep Lessing from pursuing an interest in Greek and Roman drama or from writing a comedic play of his own, *The Young Scholar.* At the age of seventeen, Lessing matriculated at the University of Leipzig and had occasion to initiate a lifelong friendship with, and influence upon, a fellow student, Johann Wolfgang Goethe. The school's poor theology program did little to sustain Lessing's interest in that field, and prompted by a free-thinking friend, Christlieb Mylius, he was soon preoccupied, much to the chagrin of his parents, with poetry and the theater.

Abandoning the universities at the age of twenty, he moved to Berlin in search of an independent life of creative writing that would eventually climax in the 1779 publication of his last great drama (*Nathan the Wise*), in which he would raise questions about whether any one religion has a corner on the truth. Although he discarded the Christian religion of his parents, and because of his supposedly quasi-pantheistic, evolutionary views and his non-literalist approach to the Bible, had an ongoing battle with "intolerant" Lutheran theologians for the rest of his life, he remained deeply committed to the religion of Christ as an "affair of the heart" that, like other religions, can be rationally confirmed, but must be evaluated ultimately only by the fruit it bears in the form of charitable deeds.

LESSING ON RELIGION. What education is for the individual, revelation is for the whole human race. Revelation provides nothing which the unaided human reason would not eventually come upon by itself. But given the differences in each man's natural religion, concern for community life required the construction of positive religions. For even if primal man had come up with the notion of a single God, such a belief could not possibly have endured in its integrity, and it would have taken millions of years to have combated subsequent polytheistic errors had God not chosen to give reason a new impetus through a special revelation of his unitary being to ancient Israel.

Meanwhile, other nations, like Persia and Egypt, made their way according to the light of reason, illuminating Judaic revelation, and inclining at least some postexilic Jews to believe in the immortality of the human soul. Christ, however, was the first truly practical teacher of the latter doctrine, conditioning eternal reward as he did, not on external civic conduct, but on inner purity of heart. Reliance on this and other New Testament doctrines (e.g., Trinity) will be outgrown as revealed truths develop into truths of reason. The time of a new, eternal gospel will come, motivating humans, if not the first time around, perhaps in a second reincarnation, to do good because it is good, rather than for any promise of reward. In the meantime, all positive religions are to be tolerated. Those who fear the comparison of one religion to another betray a weak trust in the everlasting truth of God, for all positive religions are equally true, to the extent of accommodating natural religion to community needs of various times and places. But all are also equally false, to the extent of distracting from what is essential, as has happened, for example, in the Christian religion (which is not to be confused with the religion practiced by Christ himself) when, on the basis of its claim that Christ was more than a man, it has introduced many uncertain and ambiguous beliefs and cultic practices.

Sources

Lessing, Gotthold Ephraim. *Lessing's Education of the Human Race*. John Dearling Haney. New York: Teachers College, Columbia University, 1908.

_____. *Lessing's Theological Writings*. Selections in translation with an introductory essay by Henry Chadwick. Stanford, CA: Stanford University Press, 1957.

Brown, F. Andrew. *Gotthold Ephraim Lessing*. New York: Twayne Publishers, Inc., 1971.

Chadwick, Henry. "Introductory Essay." In *Lessing's Theological Writings*. 9–29.

Copleston, Frederick, S.J. *A History of Philosophy*. Vol. 6, pt. 1. Garden City, NY: Doubleday and Company, Inc., 1962–77. 147–52; 198.

Garland, H.B. *Lessing: The Founder of Modern German Literature*. London: Macmillan and Co., Ltd., 1962.

Starr, Adolf. *Gotthold Ephraim Lessing*. Translated by E.P. Evans. Boston: William V. Spencer, 1866.

Levinas, Emmanuel (1906–1995)

Levinas was born to Jewish parents in Kaunas, Lithuania, where Jews were ostracized by both the Lithuanian Christians and the Russian oppressors. Growing up in the Russian-dominated, small-town, Jewish environment, he gained an early familiarity with the Hebrew Bible and Russian novelists. During the revolutionary war–years the family was forced to resettle in the Ukraine. There Levinas was one of only very few Jews who passed the test for admission to a Russian grammar school. After graduating from the *Gymnasium* back in Kaunas, he decided in 1923 to avoid the already virulent anti–Semitism in Germany by pursuing his higher education in Strasbourg, France. While studying the usual canon of Western philosophers, he developed an especial taste for Bergson's concept of time. He did, however, spend two years (1928–1929) in Germany studying under Husserl and Heidegger.

During the next decade, while living as an Orthodox Jew in Paris with his wife and daughter, he would devote much of his time translating the two German philosophers into French and introducing them to French scholars like Sartre, Merleau-Ponty, and Derrida. But terrible experiences of personal imprisonment as a French soldier and the loss of some family members in the Holocaust under the Heidegger-supported Nazi regime disillusioned Levinas of Heidegger's charm altogether and raised serious misgivings about Christianity's failure to thwart its members (Protestant and Catholic alike) from compromising the Gospel message and becoming the chief perpetrators at Auschwitz.

The wartime experiences did, however, also deepen his Jewish faith in a God, who though long dead in a Nietzschean sense, lives on, kenotically, in the unknowable otherness of the suffering poor, hungry and persecuted. Although he would eventually pick up on his philosophical career, teaching at Poitiers, Paris-Nanterre and the Sorbonne after writing and publishing his highly regarded doctoral thesis (*Totality and Infinity*) and the equally original *Otherwise than Being*, he also spent many of the postwar years at the École Normale Israélite Orientale in Paris, lecturing and publishing exegetical books on the Talmud. In addition to ongoing collaboration with philosophical colleagues (e.g., Derrida) before and throughout his retirement, Levinas remained in frequent dialogue with Christian theologians also, trying to get beyond the negative impressions of Christianity the Holocaust and his youthful reading of the history of the Inquisition and the Crusades had left him with. But all the while he never compromised an inch on his Jewish identity and faith.

LEVINAS ON RELIGION. Consistent with Descartes' discovery in the third of his *Meditations*, and contrary to Husserl's phenomenological analysis of the constitutive power of human intentionality, the infinite is always transcendent, something more and other than the object intended by the knowing subject. It is otherwise than either the horrific, meaningless, and anonymous being in general (Heidegger's *"es gibt"* or Sartre's *"il y a"*) or the egocentric, ontological totality imagined by the likes of Hegel (including Heidegger and Nietzsche, with their "resolute will" and "will to power"). Like the Platonic Good, it is beyond Being. It is the Other in the ethical sense of the completely independent Alien (a defenseless stranger, a widow, an orphan, or whoever) who, from the unassailable height of alterity and the disarming proximity of facial encounter, calls or breaks the knowing subject out of any narcissistic, categorical view of reality and leaves him/her passively and asymetrically disposed, prior to any sort of existentialist decision-making, to become available ("Here I am!") for addressing, even to the point of kenotic sacrifice, whatever needs the other might have.

In this prehistorical discovery of the infinite as the Other lies a "spirituality of the soul," or a "religiosity of the self," that can, on philosophical (i.e., ethical) grounds alone and apart from any revelation or so-called religious experience, survive the "death" of the god of traditional metaphysics and ontotheology.

Unable to comprehend the Infinite, the knowing subject remains atheistic. The face of the Other does not reveal a God in whose personal existence one might believe or to whom one might sacrifice. It is at best a trace of the God who, as an anonymous third party (the He [*Il*] in the depth of the Other), is forever absent. But it is this very distance or transcendence of God that inclines the Ego to offer itself to the Other and witness thereby to what an eternal "religion of love" like Judaism has always championed, namely a profound humanism.

Sources

Levinas, Emmanuel. *Collected Philosophical Papers.* Translated by Alphonso Lingis. The Hague: Martinus Nijhoff Publishers, 1986.

_____. "God and Philosophy," Translated by Richard Cohen. *Philosophy Today* 22 (1978): 127–33.

_____. *Is It Righteous To Be?: Interviews with Emmanuel Levinas.* Edited by Jill Robbins. Stanford, CA: Stanford University Press, 2001.

_____. *Otherwise Than Being: Or Beyond Essence.* Translated by Alphonso Lingis. Pittsburgh, PA: Duquesne University Press, 1998.

_____. *Totality and Infinity.* Translated by Alphonso Lingis. Pittsburg, PA: Duquesne University Press, 1969.

Ajzenstat, Oona. *Driven Back to the Text: The Premodern Sources of Levinas's Postmodernism.* Pittsburgh, PA: Duquesne University Press, 2001.

Kosky, Jeffrey L. "After the Death of God: Emmanuel Levinas and the Ethical Possibility of God." *Journal of Religious Ethics* 24 (Fall 1996): 235–59.

Miething, Frank. "Levinas, Emmanuel." In *Biographisch-Bibliographisches Kirchenlexikon.* Vol. 19. Verlag Traugott Bautz, 1999. http://www.bautz.de/bbkl/. 900–32.

Putnam, Hilary. "Levinas and Judaism." In *The Cambridge Companion to Levinas,* edited by Simon Critchley and Robert Bernasconi. Cambridge: Cambridge University Press, 2002. 33–62.

Robbins, Jill, ed. *Is It Righteous To Be?: Interviews with Emmanuel Levinas.* Stanford, CA: Stanford University Press, 2001. See esp. 255–86.

Sugarman, Richard. "Emmanuel Levinas: The Ethics of 'Face to Face'/The Religious Turn." In *Phenomenology World-Wide,* edited by Anna-Teresa Tymieniecka. Dordrecht: Kluwer Academic Publishers, 2002. 409–30.

Strasser, Stephan. "Emmanuel Levinas (born 1906):

Phenomenological Philosophy." In Herbert Spiegelberg, *The Phenomenological Movement.* The Hague: Martinus Nijhoff Publishers, 1982. 610–49.

Wyschogrod, Edith. "God and 'Being's Move' in the Philosophy of Emmanuel Levinas." *The Journal of Religion* 62 (1982). 145–55.

Locke, John (1632–1704)

Locke's father was a lawyer with Calvinistic persuasions no less strong than his appreciation for political freedom. His mother was equally pious, with the result that he was baptized by a Puritan minister and, after the family's move from Wrington to Beluton, brought up in accordance with the strict discipline of a Puritan home that emphasized simplicity, sobriety, and hard work. His Puritan convictions were challenged somewhat when, at the age of fourteen, he enrolled at a school (Westminster) whose director had High Church sentiments. Upon entering Christ Church, Oxford, in 1652, however, he again became subject to the discipline of Puritan authorities running the university and was expected regularly to attend sermons and to engage in discussions of religious matters with his tutor. Retention of the fellowship to teach moral philosophy he was subsequently granted at Oxford was contingent upon his remaining unmarried and eventually receiving Holy Orders. Some of his friends encouraged him to make the latter move.

Locke himself felt he had no such vocation, trained instead for the profession of medicine, and finally turned to diplomatic work. At the same time, disgusted by the dry Aristotelianism he had been fed at Oxford, he was developing a taste for Descartes and the "new (empirical) philosophy" being propounded by the likes of Robert Boyle. Having grown disdainful of religious enthusiasm, Locke at this time was still defending the right of civil authorities to enforce its rulings regarding religious matters of indifference. His position in this regard changed only after he became personal secretary and advisor to the Earl of Shaftesbury, an anti-papal, vigorous opponent of any form of absolutist government. Thereafter, Locke was of the opinion that only atheism was beyond toleration.

After Shaftesbury's death, Locke fled to Holland, and over the next six years — during which he was threatened with arrest and lost his fellowship at Oxford — he showed some interest in Socinian literature. Upon returning to England in 1689, he also familiarized himself with Deism. But although he shared some common ground with both schools of thought, he was neither a Socinian nor a Deist. Most of his remaining years were spent developing a critically rational approach to the study of the Bible which he had always considered the bedrock of his personal religion within the ambit of the Church of England. As he lay dying, he asked for the prayers of his friends. He was buried next to the parish church of High Laver.

LOCKE ON RELIGION. It is religion that should most distinguish humans from beasts. But to conserve their own power, priests everywhere have, through their emphasis upon doctrinal absurdities and nonessential rites and ceremonies, excluded reason from having anything to do with religion. As a result, natural religion degenerated into polytheism and amorality, and often became that wherein men appeared more senseless than beasts themselves. Relying on reason alone, pagan philosophers also failed to secure monotheism and the practice of virtue. Only the clear revelation brought by Jesus Christ made the one invisible God and his divine law known to the world.

There is nothing irrational about Christian revelation. Those delivering it proved their divine authority by the performance of multiple miracles. And because the Word of God cannot be doubted, it is safe to assume that Scripture teaches nothing that is contrary to reason. Much of its message can in fact be shown to be quite reasonable. Our complex idea of the eternal existence of an almighty and omniscient God, for example, can be rationally deduced from the intuition of one's own temporally finite, but powerful and intelligent being, since that which has a beginning cannot have produced itself or come from nothing or a being void of knowledge and power. So, too, from our ideas of reflection we are able to frame the complex idea of an immaterial spirit or soul. But as to the immortality of the latter, that, like much of the rest of the biblical message, is above reason. On all such matters of faith various interpretations are likely to arise. And so long as belief in Jesus as the Messiah and the concomitant articles of his resurrection, rule, and Second Coming are recognized as necessary to salvation, differing religious views and practices should be tolerated as much as is possible, short of allowing for atheism or religions which are themselves intolerant of other religions or subversive of civil authority because of their foreign allegiances.

Sources

Locke, John. *A Letter Concerning Toleration; An Essay Concerning Human Understanding. Great Books of the Western World.* Vol. 35. Edited by R.M. Hutchins. Chicago: Encyclopædia Britannica, Inc., 1952.
_____. *On the reasonableness of Christianity.* Chicago: Henry Regnery Company, 1965.
Aaron, Richard I. *John Locke.* London: Oxford at the Clarendon Press, 1965. 292–301.
Chappell, Vere, ed. *The Cambridge Companion to Locke.* Cambridge: Cambridge University Press, 1994. See esp. 172–98.
Copleston, Frederick, S.J. *A History of Philosophy.* Vol. 5, pt. 1. Garden City, NY: Doubleday and Company, Inc., 1962–77. 76–152.
Cranston, Maurice. *John Locke: A Biography.* London: Longmans, Green and Co., 1957.
Marshall, John. *John Locke: Resistance, Religion and Responsibility.* Cambridge: Cambridge University Press, 1994.
Spellman, W.M. *John Locke.* New York: St. Martin's Press, 1997.

Lucretius (c. 99–55 B.C.)

Born, if not in Rome itself, certainly in Italy, Lucretius was a Roman citizen by birth. The friendly tone of equality with which he later addresses his famous poem ("De Rerum Natura") to C. Memmius, a senator and governor of Bithynia, suggests that Lucretius either belonged to the aristocracy himself, or was at least assimilated to it. His beautifully crafted poem also leaves the impression of a writer who was well educated in Greek and Latin literature, who had traveled throughout Italy, Sicily, Greece and the Near East, and who was quite familiar with the cultural and political life of Rome. The Rome he experienced while growing up was not an especially happy place to be, what with the Social and Mithridatic Wars raging all about, the bloody dictatorship of Sulla, the uprising by Spartacus and other gladiators that ended with six thousand of them being crucified along the Appian Way, and incessant political assassinations.

Small wonder that he would develop a taste for what Empedocles had to say about the reconciliation of cosmic forces of love and strife, or that he would find attractive an Epicurean philosophy that encouraged mankind to rise above the daily vicissitudes of life by putting aside all fear of death or eternal punishment and emulating the unruffled quietude of the gods through enjoyment of friendship and other this-worldly pleasures. He clearly did convert to Epicureanism and conceived of it as his mission to share with Memmius and others the mystical experience of being initiated into its religious brotherhood. Rather than suggesting (as did Jerome's *Chronica Eusebii*) that Lucretius composed his poem only in lucid moments between presuicidal bouts of insanity brought on by a love potion, the enthusiasm and passion he displays in the poem is more likely indicative of a state of ecstatic rapture, not unlike that of the priestesses of Apollo (to whom he compares himself) delivering their divinations in the temple of Delphi.

His celebration of Epicurus as the great liberator of mankind from its enslavement to superstition should not be seen as implying any hostility toward religion as such. He certainly was not an atheist, for his poem speaks of the gods with great conviction and reverence, as evidenced best perhaps by its opening, prayerful hymn of praise to the goddess Venus as the divine embodiment of Love. He died at about the age of forty, leaving publication of his unfinished poem in the hands of others.

LUCRETIUS ON RELIGION. It is not hard to explain why belief in the gods has spread around the world and generated solemn religious rites in all the great cities, or why even now it implants in mortals a dreadful awe that on festive occasions attracts flocks of people to the new shrines springing up everywhere. One reason for such belief and worship was a false interpretation of the orderly movement of the heavenly bodies and the regular succession of the seasons. Unable to explain these and other natural phenomena (thunderbolts, raging winds, earthquakes, etc.), people were terror-stricken and conceived of stupendously powerful gods who wrathfully govern all things and purposely arrange the world for the sake of human beings. It was, of course, preposterous to think that way, since there is no evidence that our atomistic universe, marked as it is by so many serious flaws, was created for us by any divine agency. But it was precisely such thinking that spawned so much of the superstition that in the past has crushed human life by perpetrating wicked and irreligious deeds (like the pitiful sacrifice of Iphianassa) and filled mankind with dread of divine judgment both now and in the afterlife.

Thanks to Epicurus, superstition has now been trampled underfoot, and the main reason for religious belief and practice — namely, the visions of beautiful, immortal, and blissful divine figures experienced by humans in their sleep or waking hours — can resurface. Given their exceptionally fine, barely perceptible, atomistic bodies, and dwelling far outside our world, these gods are by their very nature free from all distress and are fully self-sufficient. As such, they have no need of, and are not influenced by, our worship. True piety, therefore, is that which is practiced for our own sake. It consists in contemplating all things with the kind of tranquil mind revealed to us by the images emanating from the gods. This will not protect us from all evils (like the plague) in this life, but it will incline us to emulate the blissful indifference of the gods, and free us to enjoy what great pleasures this world does have to offer.

Sources

Lucretius. *On the Nature of Things.* Translated with introduction and notes by Martin Ferguson Smith. Indianapolis/Cambridge: Hackett Publishing Company, Inc., 2001.

Johnson, W.R. *Lucretius and the Modern World.* London: Duckworth, 2000.

Kennedy, Duncan F. *Rethinking Reality: Lucretius and the Textualization of Nature.* Ann Arbor, MI: University of Michigan Press, 2002. See esp. 93–105.

Mair, Alexander W. "Lucretius." *Encyclopædia Britannica.* Vol. 14. Chicago, London, and Toronto: Encyclopædia Britannica, Inc., William Benton Publisher, 1959, 2002, 2005. 466–67.

Morford, Mark. *The Roman Philosophers: From the Time of Cato the Censor to the Death of Marcus Aurelius.* London: Routledge, 2002. 98–130.

O'Neill, W.H. "Lucretius." *New Catholic Encyclopedia.* Vol. 8. Edited by W.J. McDonald. New York: McGraw-Hill, 1967. 1061–62.

Ramsay, William. "Lucretius." In *A Dictionary of Greek and Roman Biography and Mythology.* Vol. 2. Edited by William Smith. New York: AMS Press, Inc., 1967. 828–30.

Sikes, E.E. *Lucretius: Poet and Philosopher.* Cambridge: At the University Press, 1936. 80–90.

Wormell, D.E.W. "The Personal World of Lucretius." In D.R. Dudley et al., *Lucretius.* New York: Basic Books, 1965. 35–63.

MacIntyre, Alasdair (1929–)

MacIntyre's parents were both doctors, with degrees from Glasgow University. Their religious affiliation was with the Scottish Presbyterian Church. His early education, including religious studies, was taken at Epsom College, with some thought of preparing himself to become a Presbyterian minister. At the age of eighteen he enrolled as a classics major at London University's Queen Mary College. Upon graduation he pursued further study in philosophy and theology at Manchester University, using his acquired linguistic skills to study relevant texts in their original Greek and Latin. In 1951, he was appointed lecturer in the philosophy of religion at Manchester, and several years later published his first book, an interpretation of the Marxist ideology that he had come to embrace as a socioeconomic complement to his Christian faith to the extent of its being a "revelation of Christian eschatology" in modern dress.

During the next fifteen years, while teaching at Manchester, Leeds, Oxford and Essex universities, he would devote much of his time to writing about the difficulties in Christian belief, the logical status of religious belief, the seeming impossibility of skeptics and believers sharing a common understanding of religious concepts, the vacuity of then current theologies, and so on. By the late sixties, however, he had abandoned both Marxism and Christianity (on grounds that both lacked scientific support, were corrupted by power, and had put too much emphasis upon doctrinal orthodoxy) and turned to the study of the historical and cultural origins of ethics.

Since 1970 he has been teaching at various universities in the United States (Brandeis, Boston, Wellesley, Vanderbilt, and finally Notre Dame) and publishing multiple books and essays in criticism of the "cultural desert" supposedly created in recent centuries by the individualistic, antinomian, and nontraditional proclivities of the liberal establishment. Unconvinced by his own earlier arguments about the possibility of justifying morality apart from religious faith, he has increasingly sided with the Roman Catholic Church's official embrace of the Thomist tradition of faithful, metaphysical reasoning as the best way still for grounding morality in the modern world. On a more personal level, he began, at least from the late eighties on, referring to himself as an "Augustinian Christian," reflecting his appreciation for the way Thomas Aquinas had used Aristotle to give new life to traditional Augustinian thought.

MACINTYRE ON RELIGION. It once seemed that any attempt to present religious belief as an explanatory hypothesis was futile and would not only overlook the rootedness of religious beliefs in the passionate, unconditional attitude of worship, but would also result in the highly misleading conception of God as some kind of "super-object." On that

account, it seemed reasonable to assume that every religion is a form of life that has its own criteria (e.g., the authority of the Bible or of the pope) by means of which is determined what is and what is not included in that religion, and that its beliefs are to that extent beyond refutation by those using inappropriate (i.e., scientific) criteria.

This view is no longer acceptable, however, since it now seems obvious that religions do make some factual claims (e.g., about the problem of evil and belief in a good God), and because it seems to buy irrefutableness at the expense of a belief becoming no less vacuous in practice than all those attempts by the likes of Bultman, Tillich, Bonhoeffer, William Hamilton, or John Robinson, who (not unlike the demythologizers of Marxism) have no more to say about the content of the moral life than anyone else, and only use traditionally Christian, religious language to mask a secular-humanistic, atheistic vacuum. What is needed to counter the current confusion resulting from the prevailing varieties of Humean/Nietzschean subjective emotivism is a return to the kind of rational religious ethics envisioned by Maimonides, Averröes and Thomas Aquinas when, for the sake of sustaining the rules, standards of excellence, and goods internal to the practice of their respective communities, they embedded Aristotle's virtue ethics, with its teleological scheme of man-as-he-is in potency to man-as-he-should-be, within the framework of their respective traditional theistic beliefs. Especially to be appreciated, if humans are ever to achieve moral autonomy, are the community-based virtues acquired through acknowledgment of their vulnerability and dependence upon others.

Sources

MacIntyre, Alasdair. *After Virtue: A Study in Moral Theory.* London: Duckworth, 1981.

_____. *Against the Self-Images of the Age: Essays on Ideology and Philosophy.* New York: Schocken Books, 1971.

_____. "Is Understanding Religion Compatible with Believing?" In *Faith and the Philosophers,* edited by John Hick. New York: St. Martin's Press, Inc., 1964. 115–33.

_____. "The Logical Status of Religious Belief." In *Metaphysical Beliefs*. London: SCM Press, Ltd., 1979.

_____. *Marxism and Christianity*. New York: Schocken Books, 1968.

_____. *Three Rival Versions of Moral Enquiry: Encyclopaedia, Genealogy, and Tradition*. Notre Dame: University of Notre Dame, 1990.

_____. *Whose Justice? Which Rationality?* Notre Dame: University of Notre Dame Press, 1988.

_____, and Paul Ricoeur. *The Religious Significance of Atheism*. New York and London: Columbia University Press, 1969.

Barrett, David. "Alasdair MacIntyre." In *World Philosophers and Their Works*. Vol. 2. Edited by John K. Roth. Pasadena, CA, and Hackensack, NJ: Salem Press, Inc., 2000. 1155–62.

Knight, Kelvin, ed. *The MacIntyre Reader*. Notre Dame: University of Notre Dame Press, 1998.

McMylor, Peter. *Alasdair MacIntyre: Critic of Modernity*. London and New York: Routledge, 1994.

Meilander, Gilbert. "Review Essay: *Dependent Rational Animals: Why Human Beings Need the Virtues*." *First Things* 96 (October 1999): 47–55.

Oakes, Edward T. "The Achievement of Alasdair MacIntyre." *First Things* 65 (August/September 1996): 22–26.

Maimonides, Moses (1135–1204)

The father from whom Maimonides received his initial religious instruction, was a rabbinic scholar and judge who would later (c. 1159) author the famous letter encouraging persecuted North African Jews to adhere to the Mosaic Law, their traditional prayers, and their belief in an unbreakable Covenant between God and Israel. While Maimonides was still only eleven years of age, a fanatical Almohad movement, driven by the preaching of its leader (Ibn Tumart) to preserve the integrity of Islam by wiping out any Jewish or Christian deviation from its traditional monotheism, gained control of the western section of Muslim Spain, including Cordova, Maimonides' birthplace. Whether that city's Jews were forced to choose between conversion to Islam and death or exile, however, is a matter of considerable debate, and the claim by al-

Qifti that Maimonides himself apostatized is unreliable. In fact, it was while he and his family were still living under the Almohads that he had begun writing in Arabic his *Commentary on the Mishna*, to which were attached the quasi-creedal, thirteen "principles and foundations of our Law." But there certainly was harassment, and it may well have contributed to the family's decision to move east, across Northern Africa, to Palestine, and finally to Egypt (1167).

To provide for himself, his wife and son, and the wife and daughter of his deceased brother, Maimonides took up the practice and teaching of medicine, even while studying philosophy and continuing his work of reforming the religious code (the *Misheh Torah*) by trying to summarize the Talmud's spiritual content into one well-organized and readable whole. He gained the reputation of being a rabbinical authority, and notwithstanding some opposition from within the Jewish community, was constantly called upon to serve as a judge on matters of Jewish law. Whether he was ever the head of the entire Egyptian Jewish community, however, is questionable. His attempt to reconcile Jewish doctrine with reason in his major philosophical work (*Guide to the Perplexed*) also met with opposition from Orthodox Jews, and he would later even be accused of being an atheist or an agnostic. But neither the book's content, nor the last years of his life that he spent striving to "become similar to God in his actions," lend much support to such charges.

MAIMONIDES ON RELIGION. Although other religions, like Christianity and Islam, are to be tolerated to the extent that they prepare the way for the coming of the Messiah, they differ from Judaism as a wood carving differs from the living man it images. As the only true religion revealed by God, Judaism was meant to correct the idolatrous and superstitious worshiping of intermediaries between God and the universe that had corrupted mankind's original religion. Abraham encouraged the Israelites to be faithful to their God. But they relapsed into their Egyptian captors' paganism, prompting God to commission Moses to teach them the Commandments, the first two of which, by insisting upon the Unity of God and condemning idolatry, constitute the essence of true religion.

Traditional Judaism, with its anthropomorphic talk about a personal God, its emphasis upon reward and punishment of obedience of the Law, and its preoccupation with prayerful, sacrificial ritual, remains truly religious, but only so long as it leads people beyond literal interpretations and blind obedience to a deeper contemplation of God as the Totally Other who has absolutely no likeness to anything created. Toward that end, all Jews must continually acknowledge the thirteen essential articles of their faith pertaining to God's existence, uniqueness, incorporeality, eternity, revelation, justice, and so on. Those perplexed on how to reconcile such religious faith with their study of the philosophical sciences need to be shown (carefully, lest the masses be scandalized) that although faith and reason are essentially harmonious and mutually corrective, apart from the demonstration of the existence and unity of God, all theology is at best negative and dialectical, with many questions (about the divine attributes, creation, etc.) remaining unanswerable or open to a variety of answers. However humbling, such a rational appreciation of monotheistic faith is the epitome of holiness, and offers the human soul (or at least the active intellect) its best chance of immortality.

Sources

Maimonides, Moses. *The Book of Divine Commandments*. Translated by Charles B. Chavel. London: Soncino Press, 1940.

_____. *Guide of the Perplexed*. Translated by Shlomo Pines. Introduced by Leo Strauss. Chicago: University of Chicago Press, 1963.

_____. *A Maimonides Reader*. Edited by Isadore Twersky. New York: Behrman House, 1972.

Benor, Ehud. *Worship of the Heart: A Study in Maimonides' Philosophy of Religion*. Albany: State University of New York Press, 1995.

Burrell, David B., C.S.C. *Knowing the Unknowable God: Ibn-Sīnā, Maimonides, Aquinas*. Notre Dame: University of Notre Dame Press, 1986.

Cohen, Rev. A. *The Teachings of Maimonides*. Prolegomenon by Marvin Fox. New York: KTAV Publishing House, Inc., 1968.

Davidson, Herbert A. *Moses Maimonides: The Man and His Works*. Oxford: University Press, 2005.

Guttmann, Julius, et al. "Maimonides." *The Universal Jewish Encyclopedia*. Vol. 7. New York: The Universal Jewish Encyclopedia, Inc., 1942. 287–96.

Heschel, Abraham Joshua. *Maimonides: A Biography*. New York: Farrar, Straus, and Giroux, 1982.

Pines, Shlomo. "Maimonides." *Encyclopedia of Philosophy*. Vol. 5. Edited by Paul Edwards. New York: Macmillan and Co. and The Free Press, 1967. 129–34.

Seeskin, Kenneth. *Searching for a Distant God: The Legacy of Maimonides*. New York and Oxford: Oxford University Press, 2000.

Twersky, Isadore. "Maimonides, Moses." In *Encyclopedia of Religion*. Vol. 9. Edited by Mircea Eliade. New York: Macmillan and Co., 1987. 131–36.

Malebranche, Nicolas (1638–1715)

Although Malebranche was born with a painful malformation of the spine that seriously threatened to shorten his life, he also had, according to his biographer, Yves Marie André, "a spirit stronger and more beautiful than the earth had ever seen." It was surely the latter, and not (as André himself and others have suggested) the mere feebleness of his body and the world-weariness resulting therefrom, that turned his attention to matters of eternal concern and made him so fit for the simple, intellectual life he would subsequently lead. Educated at home for the first sixteen years, he developed a style of writing that, as Condillac would later observe, was "so seductive that he appears clear even in those passages where he was unintelligible." The two following years in pursuit of a master's degree at the Collége de la Marche pricked his interest in mathematics, physics, and anatomy, leaving him more impressed "by his observation of the ways of an insect than by the whole history of Greece and Rome," and laying the foundation for his later induction into the Académie des Sciences. He had also studied philosophy at the college, but found it less than satisfactory, based as it was, not on reason, but merely on the "authority of Aristotle."

At the age of eighteen, with the intention of becoming a secular priest, he enrolled at the Sorbonne to study theology, expecting it to be based on the authority of the Bible, but finding it "only a confused mass of human opinions, frivolous discussions and hairsplitting subtleties." Four years later, after turning down the offer of a Notre Dame canonry that would have committed him to a quasi-monastic life of routinely celebrating the sacred rites, he entered the Oratory in Paris. There he started out studying Church history, Hebrew and Biblical criticism, but at about the same time as he was ordained to the priesthood in 1664 he came across Descartes' *Traité de l'Homme*, and was inspired, notwithstanding the Order's distaste for philosophical speculation, and much to the initial chagrin of his superiors, to devote the rest of his life using Cartesian metaphysics and epistemology to render Catholic dogma more intelligible to his contemporaries.

Multiple editions of his first work, *De la Recherche de la Vérité*, and subsequent writings brought him great renown, but also much criticism from the likes of Antoine Arnauld and Jacques Bossuet who had misgivings about Malebranche's mixture of reason and faith, or his views on the efficacy of divine grace and other matters. Despite the ongoing polemic, he remained a faithful Catholic and regular recipient of the Church's sacraments up to the end of his unexpectedly long life of seventy-seven years.

MALEBRANCHE ON RELIGION. Religion is the true philosophy — not the philosophy of the pagans, nor of those who speak to others before the Truth has spoken to them, but the philosophy of infallible, immutable, incorruptible Reason, the second person of the Trinity, the Word, the idea of God in which He knows Himself. Faith in Jesus Christ, therefore, is the true religion. But faith is not opposed to Reason, and in fact is founded on Reason, for while faith will pass away, understanding will endure eternally. Relying on Reason, the Catholic religion, compared to the religion of the Jews or the Mohammedans, comes much closer to knowing and proclaiming the existence, attributes, and activity of God as the one and only true cause of all that happens. As Anselm and Descartes have demonstrated, the very idea of an infinite God implies not only His existence, but also His perfection (omnipotence, immutability, freedom, etc.).

Yet no religion provides a direct vision of the divine essence. In order to have produced them, God must have had in Himself the ideas of all the things which He has created. Our ideas of the eternal truths, moral laws, and the extension of matter are occasioned, therefore, by the attention we freely pay to their intelligibility, or in other words, by our vision of them within the matrix of the divine archetypes. But such seeing of all things in God is not the same as seeing God Himself. It is only after death, in the immortal soul's Beatific Vision, that we will see God in all His infinite perfection. And in seeing the perfection of God, we will also finally discover what we ourselves are in relation to God and the Order He has established through his Power and Love. But that will happen only if during this life we have freely chosen to live in accordance with the divine orientation God Himself has instilled in us for the sake of revealing His own glory. We do this, as Jesus has taught us, by loving our fellow human beings, and especially those who are least able to take care of themselves.

Sources

Malebranche, Nicolas. *Dialogues on Metaphysics*. Translation and introduction by Willis Doney. New York: Abaris Books, 1980.

_____. *Dialogues on Metaphysics and on Religion*. Translated and introduced by Morris Ginsberg, with a preface by G. Dawes Hicks. London: George Allen and Unwin, Ltd., n.d.

_____. *Treatise on Ethics*. Translation with introduction by Craig Walton. Dordrecht: Kluwer Academic Publishers, 1992.

André, Yves Marie. *La Vie Du R.P. Malebranche*. Genève: Slatkine Reprints, 1970.

Church, Ralph Withington. *A Study in the Philosophy of Malebranche*. London: George Allen and Unwin Ltd., 1931.

Copleston, Frederick, S.J. *A History of Philosophy*. Vol. 4. Garden City, NY: Doubleday and Company, Inc., 1962–77. 187–210.
Pyle, Andrew. *Malebranche*. London and New York: Routledge, 2003.
Rodis-Lewis, G. "Malebranche, Nicolas." *New Catholic Encyclopedia*. Vol. 9. Edited by W.J. McDonald. New York: McGraw-Hill, 1967. 110–12.

Marcel, Gabriel (1889–1973)

His mother having died when he was only four, Marcel was raised by a father who had abandoned his Catholicism to become an agnostic along the lines of a Kierkegaardian aesthete. Marcel's stepmother (the sister of his deceased mother) felt that only Christianity could make sense of life and had a keen sense of morality, but could not bring herself, intellectually, to join the believers, and so remained something of an agnostic also. Notwithstanding this skeptical home environment, and despite — or perhaps because of — the loss of his mother and other tragic, dehumanizing experiences as a student and a Red Cross official during World War I, Marcel developed an early interest in the theoretical foundations of religion. As a budding philosopher given to reflection he felt that were he ever to become a Christian it would have to be in one or another form of Protestantism.

His marriage at the age of twenty-nine into a rather open-minded Protestant family spawned some sympathy for the Reformed Church. But prompted by François Mauriac, Marcel would later convert to Catholicism because Protestantism seemed "all too divided among a variety of sects that were not at all in agreement on the essentials." What he perceived to be the superstitious and legalistic proclivities of some Catholics and the "essentially Thomist dogmatism" he encountered in others disturbed him, but he felt that the Catholic Church had "the richest and most global vision." The memory of his baptism and first communion always filled him, he said, with expansive joy. (His Protestant wife offered no objection to his conversion, and in fact, after developing a love of the Catholic liturgy and its Gregorian chant, converted to Catholicism herself a few years prior to her death).

Despite occasional skirmishes with some "rigidly orthodox Catholics," "certain liberal Protestants," or a few "more or less fanatic Jews" regarding certain of his plays or philosophical works, he felt no inhibition as a man of religious convictions to express himself freely. Although reluctant to identify himself as a "Christian" Existentialist, he went to his grave convinced that "in its purity and its integrity" the "testimony of the Christian" alone added a dimension of absoluteness to the certitude he claimed to have already experienced prior to his conversion.

MARCEL ON RELIGION. Arguments for the existence of God inevitably fail when they reduce God to some objectified third party about which one can predicate certain attributes. Whatever logic there is in such arguments can only be found through a dialogical experience of the mystery of Being. But it is precisely such an ontological sense that the modern world has lost, broken as it is by a rationalistic/scientistic spirit of abstraction and a technological, possessive preoccupation with the solving of problems. The innately human demand for transcendence is suppressed under the impression either of total mastery or of utter absurdity. Any attempt to recover it must begin with a search for that which in personal existence does not allow itself to be dissolved by the dialectics of experience (e.g., criticism, tragedy, despair, etc.) — something, in other words, that is eternal and inexhaustible. Only secondary reflection that involves the cognitive feeling humans experience in the light of Being can be of any help in this regard. By such "blinded intuition" individuals experience themselves as incarnate beings in a world of multiple situations that reach their climax in inter-subjectivity.

It is especially these interpersonal relationships that open individuals to the experience of transcendence. By way of becoming spiritually available and unconditionally committed to each other in love, individuals discover a dimension of reality that is indestructible by death. Even nonreligious people who live within such fidelity can be said to have a sort of crypto-faith by which they witness to the Absolute Thou. For whether they acknowledge it or not, the unconditionality of their fidelity and hope toward and for one another both demand and symbolize the presence of a personal God. Theistic religions simply bring this human participation in the mystery of Being into full expression, at least when, eschewing all conceptualization, they address the God they have come to know in prayerful worship alone.

Sources

Marcel, Gabriel. *Being and Having*. Boston: Beacon Press, 1951.
_____. *Creative Fidelity*. New York: The Noonday Press, 1964.
_____. *The Existential Background of Human Dignity*. Cambridge, MA: The Harvard University Press, 1963.
_____. *Homo Viator*. New York: Harper, 1962.
_____. *Metaphysical Journal*. Chicago: Henry Regnery Company, 1952.
_____. *The Mystery of Being*. 2 vols. Chicago: Henry Regnery Company, 1964.
_____. *The Philosophy of Existentialism*. New York: Citadel, 1961.
Blackham, H.J. *Six Existentialist Thinkers*. New York: Harper and Brothers, 1959. 66–85.
Collins, James. *The Existentialists: A Critical Study*. Chicago: Henry Regnery Company, 1952. 115–49.
Keen, Samuel M. *Gabriel Marcel*. Richmond, VA : John Knox Press, 1967.
_____. *The Idea of Mystery in the Thought of Gabriel Marcel*. Unpublished doctoral dissertation. Princeton: Princeton University, 1962.
Schaldenbrand, Sister M. Aloysius. "Gabriel Marcel: Philosopher of Intersubjectivity." In *Twentieth-Century Thinkers*, edited by John K. Ryan. Staten Island, NY: Alba House, 1967. 107–32.
Schilpp, Paul Arthur, and Lewis Edwin Hahn, eds. *The Philosophy of Gabriel Marcel*. LaSalle, IL: Open Court, 1984.

Maritain, Jacques (1882–1973)

Maritain's mother, a lapsed Catholic (like the libertine husband she eventually divorced),

had Jacques baptized a Lutheran, but brought him up in a Parisian environment of liberal Protestantism. While studying natural science at the Sorbonne he met his future wife, Raïssa, who along with her Jewish family had been forced to flee Russia because of anti–Semitic persecution. His initial confidence in the ability of science to explain everything soon dissipated, and following the advice of Charles Peguy, he and Raïssa started attending the lectures of Henri Bergson. This, Maritain claimed, awakened their sense of the absolute, and several years after marrying in 1904, both he and his wife converted to Catholicism, being baptized in a Montmartre church, with Leon Bloy, who had influenced them to make the move, serving as their godfather. Soon thereafter, their spiritual adviser, a Dominican monk named Humbert Clérissac, persuaded them to take up the study of Thomas Aquinas. Maritain was enthused by his reading of Thomas' *Summa Theologiae*, and for the remainder of his life, while writing over sixty books and holding various professorial positions at the Institute Catholíque, the Pontifical Institute of Medieval Studies in Toronto, Princeton University, and elsewhere, became a major advocate for the revival of Thomism.

During several post–World War II years he served as France's ambassador to the Vatican. He was a close friend and mentor of Pope Paul VI. Raïssa, who in the meantime had become a respectable poet, and who had, by Maritain's own account, been a major inspiration in his life and thought, died in 1960. Maritain thereupon decided to live with the Little Brothers of Jesus in Toulouse, a contemplative religious congregation inspired by the ideals of de Foucault to live out the Christian message among members of the working class. Maritain had associated with them from the beginning of their foundation in France. He later became a Little Brother himself.

While living with the Brothers, he continued writing about many subjects relevant to his Catholic faith, including the controversial book entitled *The Peasant of the Garonne*, in which he gave expression to some of his misgivings about the direction being taken by the Catholic Church after the Second Vatican Council. Before dying in the spring of 1973 he received Communion and the last rites of the Catholic Church.

MARITAIN ON RELIGION. There is a prephilosophical natural knowledge which, starting from a primordial intuition of existence and the possibility of not being, perceives the necessary existence of Being-without-nothingness as the cause of all beings. Such knowledge was at the heart of the "primitive tradition" which came to be incorporated in primitive religion, and notwithstanding its corruption by the more degraded forms of religion (polytheism, animism, totemism, etc.) or its subsequent rationalistic distortion by Zoroastrian dualism, Hindu pessimism, Brahmanic pantheistic idealism, Buddha's atheistic evolutionism, Lao Tze's illusory wisdom, and Confucius' ethical positivism, carried over into the best of Greek philosophy (i.e., Aristotle), and later, when elevated by Christian revelation, was woven by the likes of Thomas Aquinas into the fabric of the highest wisdom, the wisdom of man deified by grace.

Thomas' ways of demonstrating the existence and nature of God analogically were simply a development of this natural knowledge. It reaches its climax in the experience of supernatural mysticism, in which the soul enters into the ever-mysterious, unfathomable depths of God and experiences the cognitive union of love. By virtue of this experience of the intimate life of God, Christianity, unlike the pagan religions of antiquity, transcends every civilization and every culture, and rightly subordinates the temporal goals of the latter to the eternal, supernatural life which is the end of true religion. The theocentric, integral humanism resulting therefrom can help cultivate a democratic society in which complete fidelity to truth and fervent love of unity combine to create a fellowship of friendship between humans — Christians, non–Christians, or even atheists — who think very differently on essential matters, but who recognize that beliefs other than their own can include elements of truth and value, and on

that account share invisible membership in the visible Church of Christ.

Sources

Maritain, Jacques. *Approaches to God*. Translated by Peter O'Reilly. New York: Harper and Brothers Publishers, 1954.
_____. *Bergsonian Philosophy and Thomism*. Translated by Mabelle L. Andison. New York: Philosophical Library, 1955.
_____. *The Degrees of Knowledge*. Translated by Gerald B. Phelan. New York: Charles Scribner's Sons, 1959.
_____. *An Essay on Christian Philosophy*. Translated by Edward H. Flannery. New York: Philosophical Library, 1955.
_____. *Integral Humanism*. Translated by Joseph W. Evans. Notre Dame: University of Notre Dame Press, 1973.
_____. *Introduction to Philosophy*. Translated by E.I. Watkin. New York: Sheed and Ward, Inc., 1955.
_____. *On the Church of Christ*. Translated by Joseph W. Evans. Notre Dame and London: University of Notre Dame Press, 1973.
_____. *On the Use of Philosophy: Three Essays* ("The Philosopher in Society;" "Truth and Human Fellowship;" "God and Science"). Princeton: Princeton University Press, 1961.
Cockerham, David. *Toward a Common Democratic Faith; Political Ethics of John Dewey and Jacques Maritain*. Unpublished doctoral dissertation. Indiana University, 2006.
Gallagher, D.A., W. Evans, and W. Sweet. "Jacques Maritain." *New Catholic Encyclopedia*. Vol. 9. Edited by W.J. McDonald. New York: McGraw-Hill, 1967, 2nd ed. 2003. 177–80.
McInerny, Ralph. *The Very Rich Hours of Jacques Maritain: A Spiritual Life*. Notre Dame: University of Notre Dame Press, 2003.
Tong, Paul K.K. "Jacques Maritain: A Christian in Philosophy." In John K. Ryan, ed. *Twentieth-Century Thinkers*. Staten Island, NY: Alba House, 1967. 89–105.

Marx, Karl (1818–1883)

Marx's father and mother were Jewish, both descending from a long line of rabbis. Probably to avoid prevailing anti–Semitic obstacles to the advancement of his legal career and livelihood, the father decided shortly before Marx's birth to convert to Lutheran

Protestantism. He stayed in touch with his brother (the Chief Rabbi of Trier) and other members of the Jewish community, but six years later had his wife and first son, Karl, baptized as Christians. The father, however, was also an admirer of the French Enlightenment, and although he and his wife both would remain believers in God, he spent more time reading to his son from the works of Voltaire, Racine and Rousseau than from the Bible.

Given the predominantly Christian orientation of the educational system at the time, Marx was required before graduating from secondary school at the age of seventeen to write an essay on a Johanine biblical theme extolling union with Christ as a motivating force of social action. He did so dutifully. But while later pursuing his doctorate in philosophy at Berlin, he made the acquaintance of some left-wing Hegelians like Feuerbach, Stirner, and especially Bruno Bauer (a *Privatdocent* at the university who was interpreting Hegel as a cryptic "atheist and anti–Christian") and ended up, in the Preface of his doctoral dissertation on the relation of Democritus and Epicurus, lauding Epicurean atheism. No doubt aware that the espousal of such views would get him blacklisted from professorial appointments, he turned to journalism and socialistic activism over the remaining forty years of his life.

Expelled from one city after another until finally settling in London, he and his wife and children were always on the edge of grinding poverty and fatal illnesses, relying heavily upon the financial support of his friend and collaborator, Friedrich Engels. But his anticapitalist, communistic interpretation of poverty and other social injustices afflicting the proletariat (like the government's slaughter of thousands of Commune supporters in Paris in 1871) was not so much the cause, as it was the outcome and confirmation of his understanding of religion as being both the voice and the opiate of the oppressed masses. His earlier humanistic atheism had simply evolved into, and would remain, a political and economic atheism.

MARX ON RELIGION. As Feuerbach asserted against Hegel, religion gives expression to the alienated self of man, not of God. But religion is more a symptom than a cause of human alienation. Humans dream of gods who might provide them with happiness in the next life only because their world has been rendered unfit for self-realization by a history of class struggle, and never more so than in modern bourgeois society wherein idolization of money has corrupted all the superstructures of social relations. To that extent, religion represents the sigh of the oppressed, the heart of a heartless world. It is an expression of, and a protest against, the real suffering of workers who have been denied a fair share in the fruit of their labor and treated like beasts of burden. And it voices their hope that life will be better in the world to come.

But the realization of the human essence it offers is fantastic; its consciousness of the world is inverted, not real; its promise of happiness, illusory. As such, religion is also the opium of the people. Not only does it allow the bourgeois elite to legitimize their own privileged positions, but by nurturing false dreams of celestial bliss it distracts the masses from the struggle at hand and saps the energy they might otherwise use to quicken the inevitable collapse of the capitalistic system. Among the changes (rather than mere reinterpretations) that will need to be made, therefore, if man is ever to find real happiness, will be the abolition of religion. People will have to be stopped from projecting the fulfillment of their bodily needs onto the supernatural realm, and encouraged to take back what is their earthly due here and now. Whatever is left of religion after such a revolution will simply dissolve, for in a classless, proletariat utopia there will be no exploitation against which to protest. That this will be of no detriment to the state was demonstrated by the fact that the ancient cultures of Greece and Rome reached their zenith when religion was at its lowest ebb.

Sources

Marx, Karl. *Capital; Manifesto of the Communist Party*. Great Books of the Western World. Vol. 50. Edited by R.M. Hutchins. Chicago: Encyclopædia Britannica, Inc., 1952.

_____. *Marx on Religion*. Edited by John Raines. Philadelphia: Temple University Press, 2002.

Carver, Terrell, ed. *The Cambridge Companion to Marx*. Cambridge: Cambridge University Press, 1991.

Collier, Andrew. *Marx*. Oxford: Oneworld, 2004.

Copleston, Frederick, S.J. *A History of Philosophy*. Vol. 7, pt. 2. Garden City, NY: Doubleday and Company, Inc., 1962–77. 73–104.

Dupré, Louis. "Marx, Karl." In *Encyclopedia of Religion*. Vol. 9. Edited by Mircea Eliade. New York: Macmillan and Co., 1987. 238–40.

_____. *The Philosophical Foundations of Marxism*. New York: Harcourt, Brace and World, 1966.

Küng, Hans. *Does God Exist?* Translated by Edward Quinn. Garden City, NY: Doubleday and Company, Inc., 1980. See esp. 217–61.

Niebuhr, Reinhold, ed. *Karl Marx and Friedrich Engels on Religion*. New York: Schocken Books, 1964.

Padover, Saul K., ed. *On Religion: Karl Marx*. New York: McGraw-Hill, 1974.

Merleau-Ponty, Maurice (1908–1961)

When Merleau-Ponty was about the age of seven, his father was killed in action during the First World War. Maurice and his siblings were left to be raised by their mother. The mother, with whom Merleau-Ponty retained exceptionally close ties till her death in 1952, was a devout Catholic. She brought her children up in the same religion. Merleau-Ponty was still practicing his Catholicism when, upon completing his secondary education at several prestigious *lycees* in Paris, he began his philosophical studies at the École Normale Supérieure in 1926. This was evidenced by his subsequent flirtation with journalists involved in the publication of the left-wing French Catholic journal, *L'Esprit*, and the protests he raised, as a member of the *Jeunesse Étudiante Catholique,* against the obscenity of songs traditionally being used to initiate the École's freshmen students.

But soon after graduating in 1930 from the École with the *agrégation de philosophie,* doing a year of mandatory military service, and initiating his teaching career at the secondary level, he began having doubts about institutionalized Catholicism and stopped at-

tending church — to some extent, perhaps, because of his relationship with Sartre (with whom he had become acquainted at the École), or the lectures he was attending by Alexandre Kojève on Hegel's humanistic religious philosophy, or by his disillusionment over the response of Catholic officials to the 1935 shelling of working-class districts in Vienna. When much later, after World War II military service, participation in the *Resistance,* and publication of several phenomenological studies on the structure of human consciousness, he was chosen to succeed to the Chair at the Collége de France previously held by Louis Lavelle and Henri Bergson (both highly respectful of religion), and the traditionalists objected, *Combat* (Sartre and Camus' old *Resistance* publication) rushed to defend Merleau-Ponty as an "atheistic existentialist."

But whether Merleau-Ponty was any more in agreement with, or less disillusioned by, the atheism of Sartre than with or by the latter's radical Marxist views is doubtful. For although in the mid–1930s he may have admitted to being an atheist, he clearly seemed later to have shifted to a more agnostic position. That a Catholic Mass was read at his funeral has been interpreted by some to suggest that he had reached some kind of reconciliation with the Catholic Church before his death in 1961. But the evidence is not conclusive, and he may well have gone to his grave an "agnostic humanist."

MERLEAU-PONTY ON RELIGION. Man's experience is structured by the bodily subjectivity characterizing his being in a world that is, in its totality, a perplexing mix of the visible and invisible, the partly present and the partly absent. Sensations and sensory data giving rise to them are subject to various interpretations, depending upon the context of perceived objects and preconceptions of the perceiver. Everything experienced is ambiguous. Contrary to the presumption of both rationalism and empiricism there is, then, no such thing as perfectly objective knowledge. The search for wisdom never ends, and human consciousness is to that extent transcendent, always questioning and never totally satisfied with the answers it finds. But to suggest that the new philosophies highlighting such transcendence and ambiguity create a fissure through which God can be reintroduced as an absolute goal or necessary being is the height of confusion.

It is characteristic of man to think God, but this does not mean that God exists. Certainly, any notion of a "God of things," who is discovered only by turning away from the world into one's soul, and stands at the beginning and end of time as a separate absolute, cannot be reconciled with the incidence of evil or any conception of the present as a dynamic moment of finite, creative consciousness. But the idea of an exterior "God of men" as "transcendence in immanence" is also contradictory, and ignores the kenotic implications of the Incarnation. Thinking "God" also undermines morality by introducing a Stoic element of indifference and rationalization for whatever humans do. Religion has value only so long as it eschews any claim to a divine perspective and limits itself to the raising of questions about the enigmatic, mysterious nature of human existence. As such, it enjoys a dialectical affinity with philosophy, which by radicalizing the thought of God beyond easy explanation, dismisses any charge of atheism as being irrelevant.

Sources

Merleau-Ponty, Maurice. *The Incarnate Subject.* Translated by Paul B. Milan. Amherst, NY: Prometheus Books, 2001.
_____. *Phenomenology of Perception.* New York: Routledge Press, 1969.
_____. *Sense and Non-Sense.* Translated by Hubert Dreyfus and Patricia Allen Dreyfus. Evanston: Northwestern University Press, 1964.
_____. *Signs.* Translated by Richard C. McCleary. Evanston: Northwestern University Press, 1973.
_____. *The Structure of Behavior.* Translated by Alden L. Fisher. Pittsburgh: Duquesne University Press, 1983.
_____. *The Visible and the Invisible.* Translated by Alphonso Lingis. Evanston: Northwestern University Press, 1968.
Bannon, John F. "Merleau-Ponty on God." *International Philosophical Quarterly* VI, no. 3 (September 1966): 341–65.
Glenn, John D. "Maurice Merleau-Ponty." In *World Philosophers and Their Works.* Vol. 2. Edited by John K. Roth. Pasadena, CA, and Hackensack, NJ: Salem Press, Inc., 2000. 1253–61.
Jolivet, Régis. "The Problem of God in the Philosophy of Merleau-Ponty." *Philosophy Today* 7 (Summer 1963): 150–64.
Matthews, Eric. *The Philosophy of Merleau-Ponty.* Montreal and Kingston: McGill-Queen's University Press, 2002.
Priest, Stephen. *Merleau-Ponty.* London and New York: Routledge, 1998.
Smolko, John F. "Maurice Merleau-Ponty and Philosophy." In John K. Ryan, ed. *Twentieth-Century Thinkers.* Staten Island, NY: Alba House, 1967. 353–84.
Vandenbussche, Frans. "The Idea of God in Merleau-Ponty." *International Philosophical Quarterly* VII, no.1 (March 1967): 45–67.

Mill, John Stuart (1806–1873)

Home-educated by his learned father, Mill had received the equivalent of a university education by the age of thirteen, having already mastered Greek and Latin, algebra and geometry, and much of the classical literature in the fields of history, logic, political economics, and poetry. He would later claim in his *Autobiography,* however, that because his father had long ago abandoned all religious beliefs, he himself had never received any religious education as a child, and on that account was "one of the very few who has not thrown off religious belief, but never had it."

But Mill's memory in this regard may not have been altogether accurate. In the first place, Mill's mother was of a more religious bent than the father, and it is likely she saw to it that, like his sisters, Mill would be baptized and regularly taken to church services during his childhood. Furthermore, although it is true that the father, who had originally been trained to become a Presbyterian minister, did eventually lose his Christian faith over the difficulty of reconciling the existence of an all-powerful God with the prevalence of physical and moral evil in our world and became an agnostic, with hostile feelings toward all religion (except, perhaps, for Manichaeism) as a threat to morality, there is evidence to suggest that he was still accompanying his wife and children to Sunday services until Mill was about ten. But there is no doubt either that Mill early on in his life imbibed his father's agnosticism and came to feel that he had found in Bentham's treatise on legislation the only "creed, doctrine, philosophy, and religion" he would ever need.

Throughout much of his life he would consider the religious beliefs of his countrymen as something of no concern to himself, and in keeping with his father's advice seldom gave expression to his lack of religious conviction. His skeptical attitude toward traditional religious beliefs was apparently reinforced by Harriet Taylor, the woman he had come to idolize shortly after a bout of depression at the age of twenty and years before he actually married her. The study of Coleridge and Comte, however, did awaken in him the hope that religion might at least contribute toward the social well-being of mankind, and later prompted him toward development of the Religion of Humanity which, in its final expression (in the essay on Theism published posthumously), included a qualified assent to belief in a good God of finite power, and "supernatural hope" in human immortality. Avignon's Protestant pastor offered a bedside prayer on the occasion of Mill's death, and then again next day at the grave site.

MILL ON RELIGION. The essence of religion is to be found in an intensely emotional pursuit of an ideal object that is recognized as being more excellent and significant than all objects of selfish desire. But dealing in promises and threats of eternal reward or punishment, what now and in the past has gone by the name of religion, namely the supernatural religions, has generally operated through feelings of self-interest. In one sense, this is an advantage to the supernatural religions, for it not only consoles unselfish souls suffering in this life, but also motivates those individuals who are too self-centered to imagine immortality in any terms other than their own personal survival beyond the grave. On the other hand, it also suggests the radical inferiority of such supernatural religions compared to the

kind of humanism which, by cultivating a sense of unity with mankind and a feeling for the general good, is capable of fulfilling the moral and any other function of religion, and is justly entitled to the name.

Still, there is nothing in scientific experience inconsistent with the theistic belief that the invariable laws of nature are themselves due to specific volitions of a divine power. For although eternal Matter and Force may themselves, rather than God, qualify as First Causes and limit whatever power the Creator might have, it is not absurd to suppose, even in the face of modern evolutionary theory, that the imperfect order of Nature was created by an Intelligent Mind who was somewhat motivated to make his creatures happy by engaging them, as co-creators, in work toward the final victory of good over evil. Natural religion provides no assurance of immortality, but it is not unreasonable or useless to let the example of Jesus' perfect humanity, or any Revelation, inspire an imaginative hope for life after death, especially not if such hope can help the Religion of the Future — the Religion of Humanity — find its due ascendancy over the human mind in an atmosphere of respect for liberty of thought and discussion.

Sources

Mill, John Stuart. *Autobiography*. In the *Harvard Classics*, Vol. 25. New York: P.F. Collier and Son, 1909. 7–199.
_____. *Nature and Utility of Religion*. Edited with an introduction by George Nakhnikian. Indianapolis: The Bobbs-Merrill Company, Inc., 1958.
_____. *On Liberty; Representative Government; Utilitarianism. Great Books of the Western World*. Vol. 43. Edited by R.M. Hutchins. Chicago: Encyclopædia Britannica, Inc., 1952.
_____. *Three Essays on Religion: Nature; The Utility of Religion; And Theism*. London: Longmans, Green and Co., 1923.
August, Eugene. *John Stuart Mill: A Mind at Large*. New York: Charles Scribner's Sons, 1975. See esp. 244–62.
Capaldi, Nicholas. *John Stuart Mill: A Biography*. Cambridge: Cambridge University Press, 2004.
Crimmins, James E., ed. *Utilitarians and Religion*. Bristol, UK: Thoemmes Press, 1998. See esp. 461–93.

Höffding, Harald. *A History of Modern Philosophy*. Vol. 2. New York: Dover Publications, Inc., 1955. 427–33.

Packe, Michael St. John. *The Life of John Stuart Mill*. New York: Macmillan Company, 1954.

Nakhnikian, George. "Editor's Introduction" to John Stuart Mill, *Nature and Utility of Religion*. Indianapolis: Bobbs-Merrill Company, Inc., 1958. vii–xxviii.

Montaigne, Michel de (1533–1592)

Born of a Protestant mother with Jewish ancestry and of a Catholic father, Montaigne grew up, at a time of warlike hostilities between traditionalist and reform-minded Christians, in a family atmosphere of religious toleration. While a brother and sister of his embraced their mother's "new religion," Montaigne himself was raised in the Catholic faith of his father. The profound, lifelong love he had for his father, along with his admiration for the intense, albeit tolerant, Catholic spirituality of his short-lived friend, Étienne de Boétie, no doubt contributed significantly to his decision early on in life to remain true to his Catholic upbringing. When sitting at the age of twenty-nine as a magistrate with the Paris Parlement, for example, he was reported to have gladly sworn the formal profession of Catholic faith required of all its members, even while claiming to respect the right of Protestants to follow their own consciences.

Not long thereafter, at his father's behest, he began working on a translation of the *Theologia Naturalis*, a fifteenth-century, Latin work by the Spanish theologian, Raymond Sebond, which sought to prove the traditional truths of Christianity from the "book of creation" and had long been used to combat supposed heresies. Though later, in one chapter of his *Essays*, Montaigne left some with the impression of advocating a skeptical rebuttal of Sebond's views, it seems more likely that he was actually trying to defend the latter by striking a better balance between faith and reason. In any event, the dedicatory letters he initially attached to his translation suggests that he saw the work as an antidote to Protestantism that might entice straying Catholics to return home.

There is no doubt that as he withdrew from political life to spend all his time and energy painting a verbal picture of himself, he had in mind to spell out the limits of his own knowledge and rational capacity. But this made him neither an absolute skeptic nor a pure fideist. For all his criticism of religious hypocrisy or his indifference to some religious practices, he had every intention, he said, of remaining loyal to "the Catholic, Apostolic, and Roman Church, in which I die and in which I was born." It is reported that as he lay dying, he asked to have a Mass read in his presence, and that as the consecrated host was being elevated, he raised himself on the bed and "gave up his spirit to God."

MONTAIGNE ON RELIGION. To the atheist, all writings tend to atheism, an unnatural and monstrous proposition; relying exclusively on his own rational powers, he corrupts the most innocent matter with his own venom. It is not only the atheists, however, who are wrong to rely exclusively on reason. The dogmatists, who think they can defend religion against the atheists by diving into the divine mysteries with the strength of human reason alone, are equally mistaken. It is a natural disposition of humans arrogantly to set themselves apart from other animals and to attribute to themselves divine wisdom. But he who presumes upon his own wisdom does not yet know what wisdom is, and if man, who is nothing, thinks himself to be anything, he only seduces and deceives himself. For all things produced by our own reasoning and understanding are subject to incertitude and controversy, and it would be folly to think that any purely rational arguments are sufficient to arrive at supernatural knowledge.

In the final analysis, the deep mysteries of religion can be vividly and certainly comprehended only through faith, and then only as the Holy Book containing them has been interpreted by the ecclesiastical authorities, to whom we should submit ourselves wholly and absolutely. It would be a case of overzealous piety, however, to conclude therefrom that it is wrong for religious people to try to use their senses and reason to understand themselves or what they believe. Rational observation of the beautiful design of the world, for example, can reinforce man's faith in God as the eternal, immutable, all-powerful, all-good preserver of all that is. But for reason to be of such help its sterile and undigested matter must be informed, tinted and illustrated by faith and divine grace. One would think that blessed by this ray of divinity, Christianity would excel in the practice of charity, the latter being, unlike the many signs common to all religions (i.e., hope, penance, martyrdom, etc.), that which is unique to itself. But by comparison with Mohammedan or pagan religions, it often falls very short.

Sources

Montaigne, Michel Eyquem de. *The Essays*. Translated by Charles Cotton. *Great Books of the Western World*. Vol. 25. Edited by R.M. Hutchins. Chicago: Encyclopædia Britannica, Inc., 1952.

Brush, Craig B. *Montaigne and Bayle: Variations on the Theme of Skepticism*. The Hague: Martinus Nijhoff, 1966.

Dunn, J. "Montaigne, Michel Eyquem De." *New Catholic Encyclopedia*. Vol. 9. Edited by W.J. McDonald. New York: McGraw-Hill, 1967. 1072–74.

Frame, Donald M. *Montaigne: A Biography*. New York: Harcourt, Brace and World, Inc., 1965.

Sichel, Edith. *Michel de Montaigne*. Port Washington, NY, and London: Kennikat Press, 1911.

Moore, George Edward (1873–1958)

Moore's maternal grandparents had been members of the Society of Friends until their marriage to each other as first cousins got them excommunicated from local meetings. His mother continued going to the meetings on occasion, and no doubt imbibed much of the Quaker tradition. But she had also begun attending Baptist chapel and revivals. By the time of her marriage to Moore's father (a man whose "great aim," she was happy to note, was

to be "useful and conformed to the mind of Jesus"), both were regular attendants at Baptist services. The mother eventually moderated the native penchant for introspection that had been fired by the Quaker emphasis upon the "inner light" and the Baptist insistence upon personal conversion, but the family would remain religiously oriented. Every day before breakfast the father would gather its members for prayer and biblical readings, and twice every Sunday they would all walk to the Baptist chapel in Upper Norwood to attend services and hear the finely honed sermons of its liberal-minded pastor.

After being sent to Dulwich college at the age of eight, Moore developed the habit of reading daily by himself passages from the Bible, and for at least several years never thought of questioning its assertions about the living, divine reality of Jesus. It dawned on him, though, that if such claims were true and he really loved Jesus, then, as he was encouraged to think by a group of young, "ultra-evangelical" missionaries, he ought to conduct himself in accordance with the expectations of Jesus and try to persuade others to do the same. But his proselytizing efforts caused him considerable pain and embarrassment, and his religious beliefs gradually began falling away.

Even before leaving Dulwich in 1892 to enter Trinity College, he had become a complete agnostic, largely, he says, because of the influence of his eldest, poetically inclined brother, Thomas, who (unlike another genuinely religious brother, named Harry) was constantly challenging their father's religious views in mealtime discussions. At Cambridge he was still compelled to attend chapel and even showed at least a perfunctory interest in missionary activities. And for the rest of his life, as a Fellow and Professor at Cambridge, he would respect the right of every man to believe any proposition that could be defended rationally. But neither in himself nor in anyone else would he ever again tolerate blind faith or stubborn adherence to what was shown to be indefensible.

MOORE ON RELIGION. Religion is a very vague word. But whatever else it might be said to include, it does certainly imply a belief in a personal God. The value of religion, therefore, depends largely upon the value of belief in a personal God. By a "God" is meant (at least in Christianity) a being that is more powerful, more wise and better, than we ourselves. To say that God is personal is to imply that God possesses one unique mind. Whether there is any value in believing in such a personal God depends to some extent upon whether God actually exists. Enormous numbers of people have and still do believe in God's existence. But their belief might simply be due to ignorance of natural science. Furthermore, there are now countless people also who either have lost all interest in the question of God's existence, or believe that, even if there is a God, there is no way of knowing that there is one.

It is fair to say, then, that Common Sense has *no* view on the question whether we know that there is a God or not. Nor, contrary to traditional arguments from Design or to a First Cause, is there any evidence that can be inferred from empirical observation that a personal God does or does not exist. The sole ground for asserting the truth of religion, therefore, is an appeal to intuitive faith. With most believers, however, such faith derives not so much from any religious conviction of being unable not to believe, as from the moral conviction that it would be wicked to doubt God's existence, on the assumption that belief to the contrary would encourage confidence in the ultimate triumph of the good. But apart from the disillusioning possibility of discovering that one's belief in the existence of God is false, there is also no reason to think that our universe or its individual inhabitants are going anywhere in the long run. And even if humans derive some inspiration from contemplating God as an imaginary, ideal object, it might be to their advantage to worship the real creature a little more, and his hypothetical Creator a good deal less.

Sources

Moore, George Edward. "Autobiography." In *The Philosophy of G.E. Moore*, edited by Paul Arthur Schilpp. Evanston and Chicago: Northwestern University, 1942. 3–39.

_____. "A Defense of Common Sense." In *Philosophical Papers*. London: Allen and Unwin, 1959.

_____. *Principia Ethica*. Cambridge: Cambridge University Press, 1959.

_____. *Some Main Problems of Philosophy*. London: George Allen and Unwin, Ltd.; New York: The Macmillan Company, 1953.

_____. "The Value of Religion." In *G.E. Moore: The Early Essays*. Edited by Tom Regan. Philadelphia: Temple University Press, 1986. 101–20.

Braithwaite, R.B. "George Edward Moore, 1873–1958." In *G.E. Moore: Essays in Retrospect*. Edited by Alice Ambrose and Morris Lazerowitz. London: George Allen and Unwin Ltd.; New York: Humanities Press, Inc., 1970. 17–33.

Klemke, E.D. *A Defense of Realism: Reflections on the Metaphysics of G.E. Moore*. Amherst, NY: Humanity Books, 2000. 415–33.

Levy, Paul. *Moore: G.E. Moore and the Cambridge Apostles*. New York: Holt, Rinehart and Winston, 1979.

Schilpp, Paul Arthur. *The Philosophy of G.E. Moore*. LaSalle, IL: Open Court, 1993.

Murdoch, Iris (1919–1999)

Born in Dublin, the only child of Anglo-Irish parents, Murdoch had ancestral ties to all of Ireland's religious sects. During her first year, the parents moved to London (possibly to escape the strict form of Protestantism in which they had been raised) and became rather indifferent toward the practice of their religion. They enrolled her at the age of five in the Froebel Demonstration School, which, despite its lack of religious bias, interspersed its liberal education with daily exercises in prayer, the singing of hymns, and Bible reading. Holidays spent in Ireland with her Protestant relatives provided similar opportunities. At thirteen, she won a scholarship to Badminton School, whose motto was "Each for all, all for God," and where, under the stern but loving direction of its Socialist/Quaker headmistress, she was required to engage in daily prayer and periodically to attend a Sunday church service of her own choice.

In 1934, after a religious experience of sorts, she was confirmed into the Anglican

Church. From 1938–1942 she studied "Mods and Greats" at Oxford's Somerville College under the likes of Eduard Fraenkel and the deeply religious Donald MacKinnon. Despite her initial distaste for Plato's seemingly reactionary ideas, MacKinnon's eccentric determination to practice what he was teaching about a morally good life greatly influenced the poetry, novels, and philosophical treatises she would later publish. While at Oxford she also joined the Communist Party and pursued a rather promiscuous, bohemian lifestyle. Little would change during her wartime service in the British Treasury and cohabitation with her friend, Philippa Foot. While serving in Austria and Belgium as an officer in the UN's postwar Relief and Rehabilitation Administration, she had occasion to meet Sartre. But time spent with the Benedictines at Malling Abbey and her reading of Gabriel Marcel and Simone Weil would soon draw her away from Sartre's brand of Existentialism and back toward a more religious and Platonic view of reality.

Although she would go to her grave disclaiming any belief in a personal God and ultimately professed a preference for some Buddhist doctrines (e.g., *sunyata* and *anatta*), it was Marcel's sense of mystery and Weil's Platonic appreciation of *ascesis* (unselfing) that would have the greatest influence in shaping the twenty-six novels and numerous philosophical treatises she would subsequently write while teaching philosophy at Oxford and thereafter. Constantly on guard against the misuse of religion to offer people false consolation, her experience of this world's horrors made her all the more determined to preserve a place for religion on this planet. She died two years after being diagnosed with Alzheimer's Disease, and at her own request, had her ashes scattered without any memorial service.

MURDOCH ON RELIGION. Freud was probably closer to the truth in depicting the human psyche as a fantasizing, muddled, egocentric system of quasi-mechanical sexual energy than were those modern existentialist philosophers whose excessive emphasis upon human freedom has called into question the traditional religious doctrine of original sin. Human nature is indeed fallen and in need of transformation. To meet that need, theistic religions have traditionally invited their followers to look to a personal God as their redeemer, and provided them with devices like prayer and the sacraments by which to purify the states of mind (purity of heart, meekness of spirit) that might energize good, salvific behavior.

Such theistic beliefs were rightly challenged by Kant's exposure of the so-called proofs of the existence of God, and by modern science's cultivation of the idea of human life as self-enclosed and purposeless. Even the most plausible proof for the existence of God, namely, the ontological argument, is really little more than an assertion of faith. But even if there are no grounds for believing in a personal God, some vision of a reality separate from the self, some "single, perfect, transcendent, nonrepresentable and necessarily real object of attention," is essential if man is ever to escape the net of egoism entangling him. For, contrary to what linguistic behaviorism, existentialism, and utilitarianism have claimed, with their denial of the substantiality of the human self and mind, their exaltation of the pure will as the exclusive creator of value, and their exaggerated emphasis upon actions that move things about in the public world, it is the private, attentive state of mind that constitutes the genetic background of action. No better object of such attention can be found than in the Platonic idea of perfection, or the Good. And like metaphysics and art, traditional, and especially Buddhist, religious practices of prayer and meditation can still, so long as they eschew false consolation, provide humans with the metaphorical images needed to sustain a realistic picture of perfection amidst the shadowy details of life in one cave or another.

Sources

Murdoch, Iris. *The Bell*. London: Penguin Books, 2001.

_____. *Henry and Cato*. London: Chatto and Windus, 1976.

_____. *Metaphysics as a Guide to Morals*. London: Chatto and Windus, 1992.

_____. *The Sovereignty of Good*. London and New York: Routledge, 2003.

Antonaccio, Maria, and William Schweiker, eds. *Iris Murdoch and the Search for Human Goodness*. Chicago and London: The University of Chicago Press, 1996.

Conradi, Peter J. *Iris Murdoch: A Life*. New York and London: W.W. Norton and Company, 2001.

_____. *The Saint and the Artist: A Study in the Fiction of Iris Murdoch*. London: HarperCollins Publishers, 2001.

Jacobs, Alan. "Go(o)d in Iris Murdoch." *First Things* 50 (February 1995): 32–36.

Oates, Joyce Carol. "Sacred and Profane Iris Murdoch." *New Republic* 18 (1978). http://www.usfca.edu/fac-staff/southerr/murdoch.html.

Tucker, Lindsey, ed. *Critical Essays on Iris Murdoch*. New York: G.K. Hall and Co., 1992.

Nicholas of Cusa (1401–1464)

The village of Cusa where Nicholas was born lay near Cologne, "the Rome of the North," and no doubt reflected much of the glory and decadence of that city's medieval, Catholic culture. During his early teens he was sent by his parents to study under the Brothers of the Common Life at Deventer. The reputation of the Brethren was not yet what it would become, but it is likely that the spirit of personal, nonascetical piety and reform already animating their *devotio moderna* had some influence on the young student. Two years at the University of Heidelberg exposed him to the *via moderna* of Nominalism and its ingredients of intellectual independence and quasi-skepticism about the truth of metaphysical deductions. He then spent six more years working toward his doctorate in canon law at the renowned University of Padua, where strains of Latin Averroism (with its notion of eternal recurrence and something approximate to a "double truth" theory) could still be heard, along with calls for the implementation of conciliarist theories propounded earlier by William of Ockham and Padua's own Marsilius.

Later, after returning to the Rhineland and using an ecclesiastical benefice to support his study of mathematics and Christian Neoplatonism at the University of Cologne, he would himself champion the conciliarist claim at the 1432 Council of Basel that the authority of a general council is supreme in the Church. But he subsequently shifted his support to the pope, and spent much of the rest of his life as a priest, bishop, and cardinal, serving as a papal legate to Constantinople, Germany, and elsewhere, trying to implement, through reform of the church, the kind of mystical unity of religious, political, and cosmic polarities he was all the while writing about in his *De Docta Ignorantia, De Pace Fidei, De Ludo Globi*, and other treatises.

Evicted from his diocese of Brixen during a nasty battle over property rights with Austria's Duke Sigmund, he retired during his last years to Rome as an adviser to the pope. Except for his heart, which in accordance with his own instruction was returned to the chapel of St. Nicholas in Cusa, his deceased body was buried in Rome's church of St. Peter in Chains.

NICHOLAS OF CUSA ON RELIGION. Upon unfolding Himself in the creation of the world, God informed the body of man with a rational soul, so that in him the image of His own ineffable excellence might shine forth. From this one person, this "human god," a vast multitude has been promulgated over the entire surface of the earth. Such a vast multitude cannot exist without a great deal of diversity. Their lives laden with woes and misery, most individuals are so preoccupied with their physical needs that they have no time to pursue knowledge of themselves or God by relying on their own freedom of judgment. It was on that account that at various times God has sent different prophets and teachers to the various nations to formulate laws and divine cults for the edification of the uneducated. The trouble is that these diverse religious customs gradually came to be defended as immutable truths. Each community preferred its particular beliefs over those of any other, with the result that the diversity of religion has produced much dissension. Unless some kind of union is found between the different religions, persecution will never cease.

But how is such unity to be achieved? Certainly not by eliminating all the diversity. Any attempt to impose conformity in everything will only further disturb the peace. A great deal of latitude will have to be allowed, and various nations will have to be permitted their own religious devotions, even adoration of godlike, cultic figures. What is essential, however, is that they be brought to see that what they are all seeking is the one same triune God (in whom, as the infinite maximum and minimum, all opposites coincide), and that presupposed by the plurality of their religions, therefore, is the one faith or religion of Wisdom that consists of a "learned ignorance" of Christ as the eternal Logos. Such wisdom is the real source of human happiness (allegorically symbolized by the various religions). And it is to help humans find happiness that every religion exists; it is the goal toward which every religion aims.

Sources

Nicholas of Cusa. *Unity and Reform: Selected Writings of Nicholas De Cusa.* Edited by John P. Dolan. Notre Dame: University of Notre Dame Press, 1962.

Copleston, Frederick, S.J. *A History of Philosophy.* Vol. 3, pt. 2. Garden City, NY: Doubleday and Company, Inc., 1962–77. 37–54.

Gilson. Etienne. *History of Christian Philosophy in the Middle Ages.* New York: Random House, 1954. 534–39.

Koch, J. "Nicholas of Cusa." *New Catholic Encyclopedia.* Vol. 10. Edited by W.J. McDonald. New York: McGraw-Hill, 1967. 449–52.

Kremer, Klaus. *Nicholas of Cusa.* Translated by Frankie and Hans-Joachim Kann. Trier: Paulinus Verlag, 2002.

Sigmund, Paul E. *Nicholas of Cusa and Medieval Political Thought.* Cambridge, MA: Harvard University Press, 1963.

Nietzsche, Friedrich (1844–1900)

Thanks largely to his neo–Pietist sentiments, Nietzsche's father (Carl Ludwig) had been appointed pastor of Röcken's (Nietzsche's birthplace) Lutheran church by the Prussian king. The father declared the "glorious moment" of his son's baptism a "divine mystery beyond human comprehension," and Nietzsche himself seemed inclined almost to worship his father after the latter's death only four years later. The mother, herself the Pietistic daughter of a Saxon pastor, took Nietzsche and his sister to live with their grandmother and two aunts in the Lutheran-dominated city of Naumburg. On everyone's assumption that he would follow in his father's footsteps, Nietzsche was nicknamed "the little pastor" at the local grammar school he attended before his grandmother recruited private tutors to take over his preparation for the ministry.

At the age of fourteen he won a scholarship to the renowned Latin school in neighboring Pforta, and for the next two years at least, until his reception of Confirmation in 1860, remained relatively committed to his religious upbringing. But application of historical criticism to both classical and biblical studies by his liberal instructors during his remaining four years at Schulpforta had begun taking a toll on his faith. After a brief attempt at military service, several more years of studying philology at the universities of Bonn and Leipzig, and feverish reading of works by the likes of Feuerbach, Schopenhauer, and D.F. Straus, he was ready, much to the chagrin of his family, to break not only with Pietism but with the Christian religion in general and any thought of ministering to it.

While continuing over the next two decades of his life (first, as a philology professor in Basel and then, before going insane and dying in 1900, as a *fugitivus errans* in Italy and elsewhere) to pay lip service to the example set by the historical Jesus, he would release a flood of writings hostile to religion, contrasting what he bitterly perceived as the resentful slave mentality of Judaeo-Christianity and most other ascetically minded religions with the lust for life and power celebrated by the ancient Greeks and (before being "emasculated" by the monkish missionaries) his Teutonic ancestors, sending his fictional madman out into the streets to declare the "death of God," and having "Zarathustra" spell out how great men (e.g., Goethe) get beyond traditional morality by sublimating their instinctive will to power into life-affirming, creative energy. Paraphrasing his friend, Franz Overbeck, he might have concluded that the lonely struggle to free himself of the Christianity that for a variety of reasons (including problems with his sexual identity) he had never really possessed, had cost him both his sanity and his life.

NIETZSCHE ON RELIGION. Religion originated from a "narcoticizing" error in the interpretation of certain natural events. Primitive man had no concept of natural causality, and explained all natural phenomena as the arbitrary acts of higher spiritual forces — the gods. But even at this primitive stage man does not confront nature as a powerless slave; in his fright and weakness, he engages in a variety of religious ceremonies; but like the practice of magic, from which they all derive, these polytheistic activities originally represented also a feeble attempt on the part of man to control the forces of nature. It was the noble element in early Greek religiosity to pick up on this primeval tendency toward rapprochement with the higher powers by way of balancing Apollonian and Dionysian dimensions of reality in their pursuit of epic and tragic beauty.

With their monotheistic proclivities, however, the Jews came to look upon Yahweh as the master to whom they themselves, as slaves, were forever indebted. This in turn allowed priestly agitators to interpret good fortune as reward and misfortune as punishment for sin. By thus banishing natural causality still further from the world, the Jewish religion spawned a "slave-morality" that out of feelings of resentment and guilt tries to give the mighty elite bad consciences, and champions the antinatural, life-denying sentiments of those who are the weak and despised outcasts of society. Turning away from its founder, Christianity, unlike the more life-affirming religion of Buddhism, also encouraged an ascetical approach to life. But by proving the self-sufficiency of nature, modern science has exposed the great lie underlying all religion. The resulting "death of God" will end in nihilism, however, unless man can come of age and in the face of an eternally recurring universe, affirm the beauty and joy of the natural life that he, as the "overman," can create through poetic sublimation of his natural impulses.

Sources

Nietzsche, Friedrich. *Beyond Good and Evil*. Translated by Walter Kaufmann. New York: Random House, 1966.

_____. *The Birth of Tragedy and The Case of Wagner*. Translated by Walter Kaufmann. New York: Random House, 1967.

_____. *The Gay Science*. Translated by Walter Kaufmann. New York: Random House, 1974.

_____. *Human, All Too Human*. Translated by Marion Faber. Lincoln: University of Nebraska Press, 1986.

_____. *Thus Spake Zarathustra*. Translated by R.J. Hollingdale. Baltimore: Penguin Books, 1967.

_____. *Twilight of the Idols and The Antichrist*. Translated by R.J. Hollingdale. Harmondsworth, UK: Penguin Books, 1979.

_____. *The Will to Power*. Translated by Walter Kaufmann and R.J. Hollingdale. New York: Random House, 1968.

Bergmann, Peter. Nietzsche, *"The Last Antipolitical German."* Bloomington and Indianapolis: Indiana University Press, 1986.

Copleston, Frederick, S.J. *A History of Philosophy*. Vol. 7, pt. 2. Garden City, NY: Doubleday and Company, Inc., 1962–77. 164–94.

Holub, Robert C. *Friedrich Nietzsche*. New York: Simon and Schuster Macmillan, 1995. 128–48.

Jasper, Karl. *Nietzsche: An Introduction to the Understanding of his Philosophical Activity*. Chicago: Henry Regnery Company, 1969.

Kaufmann, Walter. *Nietzsche: Philosopher, Psychologist, Antichrist*. Princeton: Princeton University Press, 1974.

Köhler, Joachim. *Zarathustra's Secret: The Interior Life of Friedrich Nietzsche*. Translated by Ronald Taylor. New Haven and London: Yale University Press, 2002.

Lampert, Laurence. *Nietzsche and Modern Times*. New Haven and London: Yale University Press, 1993. 315–68.

Melchert, Norman. *The Great Conversation*. Boston: McGraw-Hill, 2002. 542–76.

Schacht, Richard. "Nietzsche, Friedrich." In *Encyclopedia of Religion*. Vol. 10. Edited by Mircea Eliade. New York: Macmillan and Co., 1987. 438–41. Also *The Philosophers: Introducing*

Great Western Thinkers. Edited by Ted Honderich. Oxford: Oxford University Press, 1999. 175–80.

Nozick, Robert (1938–2002)

Nozick's father came from Russia at the age of sixteen. The grandparents on his mother's side had also come from Russia. The individualistic anarchical tradition Nozick would later champion in his first book (*Anarchy, State and Utopia*) as well as its anti-coercive, epistemological implications that found expression in a number of his subsequent writings (*Philosophical Explanations*, *The Examined Life*) were rooted not only in Thoreau, but also, to some extent, in that Russian tradition, as represented by Mikhail Bakunin. Nozick's family was also Jewish. He later claimed to have not paid much attention to his Jewish background until the birth of his children, and to have found Jewish philosophy, impregnated as it is with "historical visions," to be prohibitive of every form of the original thinking that he valued so highly. But during a 1976 sabbatical from his teaching at Harvard he did spend a year in Israel lecturing at Hebrew University, University of Tel Aviv, and other Jewish institutions of higher education, where his interest might have been pricked in Jewish thought in general and the Kabbalistic tradition in particular (with its mystical themes of a "limitless" deity and such) which he would later tap in his *Philosophical Explanations* and *Socratic Puzzles* to explore the meaning of evil (like the Holocaust), of Creation, of life, or of God.

Whether God actually exists, or whether moral principles could be justified, were questions, he said in his interview with Giovanna Borradori, that he was already asking himself in his early teens as he pranced around his Brooklyn high school flaunting a paperback copy of Plato's *Republic* and chewing on "big ideas and big themes." His utopian vision of a minimal state, with its libertarian reluctance to impose upon individuals any one ethos, was meant to inspire people of whatever religious views (Jewish, Christian, Muslim, Buddhist, or Hindu) to be true to their own convictions and to live with each other in peace, albeit, perhaps, in their own communities. Although the book he published on the "nature of rationality" shortly after becoming terminally ill with stomach cancer in 1994 may have been somewhat ethnocentric, he had himself become increasingly interested in his latter years in Oriental, Indian thought as expressive of a more global, total, or all-encompassing vision of the pluralistic character of Being.

NOZICK ON RELIGION. The minimal state provides a framework also for multiple religious utopian visions. It can be interesting, or at least a challenging intellectual exercise, for nonreligious people to examine how such religions address questions about evil, the meaning of life, and so on. To explain adequately why God allows evil in the world, it would seem that religions must not only reconcile divine omniscience, omnipotence and goodness, but also say something decent to people who are actually victims of evil, show that the evils of this world (and especially one of such magnitude as the Holocaust) are somehow reflected in the divine realm, and talk about a divine being that relates to its creatures in a way that makes it worthy of religious worship. Most traditional religious attempts to meet these criteria (e.g., explaining evil as a mere privation, a necessary corollary of human freedom, an aesthetic imperfection in a best of all possible worlds, etc.) have failed. Perhaps only the Kabbalist explanation of evil as the result of some tension, conflict, or interactive process within the divine nature will do justice to the religious concept of a God that is real.

Regarding the meaning of life, one way religion can bring questions about it to a halt is to posit a self-sufficient, unlimited being which is its own meaning and with which humans can somehow connect (e.g., through obedience of the divine law) or identify (e.g., atman equals Brahman). But does such a being actually exist? Deductive arguments of a cosmological, teleological sort, or that most famous of all fishy philosophical arguments, the ontological (by which Descartes tried to overcome his methodical doubts), are fruitless. Claims of direct experience of God are also problematic, but combined with the fact that life can be meaningful only if there is such an unlimited being, perhaps some weight can be added to belief in its existence. Or is that merely wishful thinking that should be resisted in the interests of maintaining rigorous intellectual standards by an act that will of itself bring meaning to human life?

Sources

Nozick, Robert. *Anarchy, State, and Utopia*. New York: Basic Books, Inc., 1974.

_____. *The Examined Life: Philosophical Meditations*. New York: Simon and Schuster, 1989.

_____. *Invariances: The Structure of the Objective World*. Cambridge, MA and London: Harvard University Press, 2001.

_____. *Philosophical Explanations*. Cambridge, MA: Harvard University Press, 1981.

_____. *Socratic Puzzles*. Cambridge, MA and London: Harvard University Press, 1997.

Borradori, Giovanna. *The American Philosopher*. Translated by Rosanna Crocitto. Chicago and London: The University of Chicago Press, 1994. 70–85.

Feser, Edward. "Robert Nozick." *The Internet Encyclopedia of Philosophy*. http://www.iep.utm.edu/n/nozick.htm. 1–16.

Halfond, Irwin. "Robert Nozick." In *World Philosophers and Their Works*. Vol. 2. Edited by John K. Roth. Pasadena, CA, and Hackensack, NJ: Salem Press, Inc., 2000. 1398–1412.

Lacey, A.R. *Robert Nozick*. Princeton and Oxford: Princeton University Press, 2001.

Schmidtz, David, ed. *Robert Nozick*. New York: Cambridge University Press, 2002.

Ortega y Gasset, José (1883–1955)

Born in Madrid, Ortega was reared in the Catholic faith. At the age of eight, he was enrolled in the Jesuit College of Miraflores del Pala in Málaga and remained there for the next six years. He would later, in his twenties, criticize the teaching methods of his Jesuit instructors on grounds that they were intellectually incapable and that they had taught him to look down on anyone other than "our people," and to sneer at all the great classical thinkers (Democritus, Descartes, Kant, and Darwin, among others). Partly on that account, he early on lost his Catholic faith. There is no evidence of an abrupt rupture with the faith of his childhood, but rather, as his disciple and biographer Julián Marías put it, a gradual "evaporation of an already outworn faith." His youthful writings, some of which were published before completing his studies at universities in Madrid, Leipzig, Berlin, and Marburg (under Hermann Cohen) and getting his doctorate in philosophy and literature at Madrid in 1904, show little if any positive attitude toward religion. The kind of Catholicism in which he had been educated apparently meant little to him at that time, striking him as something he had received, not chosen.

By the age of twenty-five he was counting himself (in a review of Fogazzaro's *Il Santo*) among those "who are separated from any church." A year later he gave a lecture criticizing dogmatic Catholicism for turning religion into such a divisive, antisocial force, and explicitly stated, "I am not a Catholic, and since my youth I have tried to order my life in a non–Catholic way." In the same lecture, however, he also refused to subscribe to "an archaic anticlericalism," and already in the aforementioned book review he had given expression to a yearning for a more gentle and disciplined form of Catholicism to which he might adhere.

During the subsequent, more mature years of his political involvement and work as a philosophy professor and journalist, writing among many other masterful pieces his bestselling *The Revolt of the Masses*, his personal references to the Christian religion became, according to Marías, "progressively deeper, more profoundly felt and intimate." The world of religion, Ortega would assert in his latter years, cannot be renounced without pain and a serious undermining of one's creative productivity. Ortega "can be seen," Marías concluded, "as one of those who were closest and most friendly to Catholicism, even at the times when he felt most distant from it." Disappointed in his hopes of reforming Spain, he died in 1955, with political parties on both the right and left claiming him as one of their own.

ORTEGA Y GASSET ON RELIGION. The reality which is called "my life" is basic because every other reality, including God, is made known by some modality of my own life. If God exists, He differs from humans to the extent of existing in the most absolute solitude, with nothing like the world to oppose Him. But in order to be God to me, He must reveal Himself to me. *Homo faber* that he is, man has generally interpreted such revelation to mean that god is a wrathful, loving, and mysterious Creator. But lacking any divine perspective on reality, man's view of god, along with the religious conception of life various peoples necessarily built upon it, remained relative to the situation in which humans found themselves. In the century before Christ, for example, the situation of Mediterranean man was one of desperation. Although the Romans were one of the most religious people that ever existed, they and the Greeks were no longer sure about the existence of the gods whom they both had conceived as the superlative degree of natural reality. Like all Asiatic peoples, the Jews had always lived in a state of desperation, relying for direction upon Jehovah as the supernatural Lawgiver. But having despaired of complying with the law, they too were feeling desperate.

Hence, the appeal of Christianity, which, by completely inverting the perspective of desperation, promised salvation to all those who, rejecting this life as but a mask hiding the true reality of life in God, put all their hope and confidence in Him. Such theocentric belief remained at the heart of medieval life until the *devotio moderna* and modern science restored man's confidence in himself, turning him back to the world and pushing God into the background. This anticipated the religious situation of modern man, wherein everyone, Christians and atheists alike, must willy-nilly play a double game of faith and reason. Where it will all lead, no one can say. For shipwrecked though

he may currently be and without any moral compass, man remains as infinite in possibilities as God, if He exists, is infinite in actualities.

Sources

Ortega y Gasset, José. *An Interpretation of Universal History.* Translated by Mildred Adams. New York: W.W. Norton and Company, Inc., 1973.
_____. *Man and Crisis.* Translated by Mildred Adams. New York: W.W. Norton and Company, Inc., 1958.
_____. *The Revolt of the Masses.* New York: W.W. Norton and Company, Inc., 1932.
_____. *What is Knowledge?* Translated by Jorge Garcia-Gomez. New York: State University of New York Press, 2002.
Díaz, Janet Winecoff. *The Major Themes of Existentialism in the Work of José Ortega y Gasset.* Chapel Hill: The University of North Carolina Press, 1970.
Marías, Julián. *José Ortega y Gasset: Circumstance and Vocation.* Norman: University of Oklahoma Press, 1970.
McClintock, Robert. *Man and His Circumstances: Ortega as Educator.* New York: Columbia University Teachers College Press, 1971.
Niedermayer, Franz. *José Ortega y Gasset.* Translated by Peter Tirner. New York: Ungar, 1973.
Raley, Harold. *José Ortega y Gasset: Philosopher of European Unity.* University, Alabama: The University of Alabama Press, 1971.
_____. "Modes of Prediction in Ortega." In *Ortega y Gasset Centennial.* Madrid: Ediciones José Porrúa Turanzas, S.A., 1985. 69–73.
Weigert, Andrew J. *Life and Society: A Meditation on the Social Thought of José Ortega y Gasset.* New York: Irvington Publishers, Inc., 1983.

Parmenides (c. 515–450 B.C.)

The inscription of a statue pedestal found in Elea a number of years ago describes Parmenides, the son of Pyres, as both a doctor and a philosopher. Whether he ever practiced medicine is uncertain. Diogenes Laertius observed that Parmenides was of "illustrious birth" and "possessed of great wealth," and that he used his social status to "serve his city as a legislator." According to Plutarch, the citizens of Elea were still swearing allegiance many years later to the laws supposedly written by Parmenides. Diogenes also noted that Parmenides used some of his wealth to build a shrine to the memory of a philosopher by whom he had been instructed as a young man, namely, Ameinias the Pythagorean.

Parmenides would seem to have later rejected the Pythagorean philosophy, assigning it (along with Hesiod's theogony) to the Way of Opinion, because of its admission of change and movement, but it may well have been his association with Ameinias, rather than any relation with Xenophanes (as Plato wrongly implied), that stirred his interest in philosophy in the first place. It is also likely that Parmenides had become acquainted with the so-called "mystery cults" that were flourishing in southern Italy in his day. For , as some modern scholars (e.g., W. Jaeger) have pointed out, even if the One was ultimately material in the eyes of Parmenides, he sensed its Being also as something mysterious and his vision of it as the climax of a personal religious experience of the kind that one would expect to find only in the rites of the aforementioned mystery cults. Judging from the proem to his poem on Nature, he sees his philosophical vision, in other words, not as something that he could achieve by using his own unenlightened reason, but as a special revelation that he has received from on high.

Far from being a totally secular exercise in pure intellectualism, therefore, his personal trek along the Way of Truth was, at least in his own eyes, a deeply religious venture. He had not just been looking to accumulate information, or to dull his sense of wonder by a final solution of all problems. It was rather salvation that he had been in search of, and to judge from the religious fervor with which he wrote his poem, he no doubt thought that he had found it and that it was his mission to help others find the same.

PARMENIDES ON RELIGION. There is something mysterious about reality; it is more than it seems to be. Relying on their own powers of sense perception, and following the Way of Opinion — the road along which mortals who know nothing wander — the deaf and blind, amazed, undiscerning crowds (that might include Heraclitus or even my former mentor, Pythagoras) deem it the same to be and not to be, and that change, movement, and the many it gives rise to are real. Although it is helpful to learn about their opinions, lest one be taken in by them, they are not worthy of trust, for there is nothing that corresponds to the names they give to that which is not — "night" simply being the absence of Light, "cold" the absence of Heat, "earth" the absence of Fire, and so on.

Any terrestrial process of becoming, therefore, is nothing more than steady degradation of being under the dark influence of Necessity. The best to be hoped for, according to the Orphic view, is that some flame of Love still flickers at the center of Nature, providing a few enlightened souls with some hope of escape. But better to abandon the Way of Opinion altogether and to follow instead the Way of Truth which I was personally allowed to experience when, in a moment of divine inspiration, the goddesses of justice and of law and order (*dike* and *themis*) offered me the torch of reason by which to find my way to the truth. In this light of reason, it became clear to me that Reality arises neither out of what is, nor out of what is not, but simply exists, and cannot not be. If Reality can be thought, then it is, because if it could be and yet were not, it would be nothing, and as such could not be thought. But if what is not cannot be, then, Reality, albeit material and spatially finite, is uncreated and indestructible, enjoying a mysterious, divine oneness, eternity (temporal infinity), and immutability that negates the reality of time, change, and plurality. These truths came to me as a divine revelation, and if, as the Orphics claim, there is a Way of Salvation, it is to be found in this Way of Truth, not in the Way of Opinion or in the religion of the official cults.

Sources

Parmenides of Elea. *Fragments*. A text and translation with an introduction by David Gallop. Toronto, Buffalo, and London: University of Toronto Press, 1984.

Austin, Scott. *Parmenides: Being, Bounds, and Logic.* New Haven and London: Yale University Press, 1986.

Barnes, Jonathan. *Early Greek Philosophy.* Harmondsworth, UK: Penguin Books, 1987. 129–42.

Brandis, Christian A. "Parmenides." In *A Dictionary of Greek and Roman Biography and Mythology.* Vol. 3. Edited by William Smith. New York: AMS Press, Inc., 1967. 123–26.

Burnet, John. *Early Greek Philosophy.* New York: The Meridian Library, 1959. 169–96.

Copleston, Frederick, S.J. *A History of Philosophy.* Vol. 1, pt. 1. Garden City, NY: Doubleday and Company, Inc., 1962–77. 64–70.

Cordero, Néstor-Luis. *By Being, It Is: The Thesis of Parmenides.* Las Vegas: Parmenides Publishing, 2004.

Cornford, F.M. *From Religion to Philosophy.* New York: Harper and Row, 1957. 214–24.

Diogenes Laertius. "Parmenides." *Lives of Eminent Philosophers.* Vol. 2, no. 9. Translated by R.D. Hicks. Cambridge, MA: Harvard University Press, 1972. 428–33.

Jaeger, Werner. *The Theology of the Early Greek Philosophers.* Oxford: At the Clarendon Press, 1948. 90–108.

Melchert, Norman. *The Great Conversation.* Boston: McGraw-Hill, 2002. 24–28.

Wheelwright, Philip, ed. "Parmenides." In *The Presocratics.* New York: The Odyssey Press, Inc., 1966. 90–105.

Pascal, Blaise (1623–1662)

Pascal was baptized a Roman Catholic in the family's parish church, Saint-Pierre (in Clermont-Ferrand). Not long after the death of his mother two years later, he and his two sisters were taken to Paris and home-educated in religion, mathematics, law, and other matters by their learned and devout father. Already in his teens Pascal won renown as a mathematical genius. At the age of twenty-two, while engaged in work on his calculating machine at his new residence in Rouen, he was exposed to the writings of the Abbé of Saint-Cyran and Arnauld expounding the Jansenist emphasis upon conversion from attachment to this world to submission to the will of God. This resulted in what is called his "first conversion" toward a less formal, more interior and personal form of religion. Its emphasis upon self-denial and humility seriously challenged his earlier pursuit of fame through scientific achievement. But a serious illness soon required relaxation of the religious discipline he had undertaken.

For several years thereafter he involved himself again in the worldly activities of his atheistic, free-thinking, libertine friends, and upon their advice, did some reading of the skeptical, fideistic writings of Montaigne. In 1654, however, he confessed confusion to his sister Jacqueline (who had joined the Jansenist-oriented convent at Port-Royal) and had a mystical experience of the living God. His own account of this "second conversion" (the so-called "Mémorial") began with the words, "God of Abraham, God Isaac, God of Jacob, not the God of philosophers or of scientists," and was sown inside the lining of every new piece of clothing he would wear for the rest of his life.

Although he continued to pursue his interests in science and mathematics, he gave away much of his wealth and became increasingly involved in defending the purity of the Christian faith. He never became a Jansenist himself, but certainly did favor their position over what he considered to be the pagan assumptions of Jesuitical, moral casuistry (*The Provincial Letters*). Ongoing contact with his atheistic friends prompted him to undertake the writing of an apology for the Christian religion. The notes he developed for that project have come to be known as the *Pensées*. The recurrence of sickness during the last three years of his life rendered completion of the project impossible. To the end, he prayed that God might "make good use of his illness."

PASCAL ON RELIGION. Religion is absurd and ridiculous if it contradicts reason. But religion is not contrary to reason. In regard to the wager which one has no choice but to make about the existence or nonexistence of God, for example, it is certainly more reasonable to wager that God exists, for "if one wins, one wins all, but if one loses, one loses nothing." The religious belief in the existence of God finds some support also in the traditional, rational arguments of a cosmological, teleological, or ontological sort.

It must be admitted, however, that such arguments are generally so complicated that they have little practical effect in people's lives, and usually evoke nothing but contempt from agnostics and atheists. Furthermore, while it may be wrong to exclude reason from religion, it is also wrong to try basing religion on reason alone. For, as any true religion will attest, God is hidden from rational scrutiny to such an extent that in the end reason by itself can know only a "prime mover" or "author of geometrical truths"(the philosopher's God, or the God of Deism) but never the existence or nature of the one, true God (the God of Abraham, Isaac, and Jacob). Nor, contrary to the pretensions of pagan humanism, can reason tell us anything certain about the real nature of man — his creation, his endowment with soul, his original fall, or his wretchedness. Reason's last step, therefore, is to recognize that there is much that surpasses it and to submit to the judgment of the heart — the heart that has its reasons which reason itself does not know.

That is what Christian faith is: "God felt by the heart," instinctively, intuitively, and not by reason. By thus coming to know God as both his creator and redeemer, fallen man can avoid despair and with the help of divine grace discover the greatness of his own being without succumbing to pride on the one hand, or renouncing all worldly interests on the other. Viewed as part of one's humble service to God's eternal plan, scientific and mathematical research, for example, can be taken all the more seriously.

Sources

Pascal, Blaise. *Pensees and Other Writings*. Translated by Honor Levi; introduction by Anthony Levi. Oxford and New York: Oxford University Press, 1995.

Pascal, Blaise. *The Provincial Letters; Pensees; Scientific Treatises*. *Great Books of the Western World*. Vol. 33. Edited by R.M. Hutchins. Chicago: Encyclopædia Britannica, Inc., 1952.

Cole, John R. *Pascal: The Man and His Two Loves*. New York and London: New York University Press, 1995.

Coleman, Francis X.J. *Neither Angel nor Beast: The Life and Work of Blaise Pascal*. New York and London: Routledge and Kegan Paul, 1986.

Copleston, Frederick, S.J. *A History of Philosophy*. Vol. 4. Garden City, NY: Doubleday and Company, Inc., 1962-77. 161–80.

Küng, Hans. *Does God Exist?* Garden City, NY: Doubleday and Company, Inc., 1980. 42–92.

Morris, Thomas V. *Making Sense of It All*. Grand Rapids, MI: William B. Eerdmans Publishing Company, 1992.

Peirce, Charles Sanders (1839–1914)

After being christened in 1840, Peirce, according to his autobiography, grew up in a Unitarian household. Religion was taken seriously, but with little emphasis upon dogma and sectarian differences. Emerson, whose Transcendentalism Peirce would later describe as having derived from Plotinus, Boehme, Schelling and other minds "stricken with the monstrous mysticism of the East," was an occasional guest of the family. Peirce early on read Emerson, and by his own account became a "transcendentalist" of sorts, modified no doubt by his reading also of Kant. He became a "passionate devotee" of the latter's *Critique of Pure Reason*, but rejected his and Mansel's extreme dichotomy of faith and reason.

After graduating (without distinction) from Harvard and for a brief period teaching mathematics and philosophy there, Peirce, under the influence of the first of his two wives, joined the Episcopal Church. Later he would claim that he had joined without believing anything more than the "essence and spirit" (i.e., the "principle of love") of the Episcopal Creed, having put aside, he said, "anything that tends to separate me from my fellow Christians." It astounded him to read Schaff's *Creeds of Christendom* and not find a single mention of the principle of love in its three volumes. All his life long he would war against unscientific attempts by theologians to immunize themselves from error and set their metaphysical convictions up as a standard of faith. Theology, he said, "derives its initial impulse from a religious wavering," and if he had to make a choice, he would choose "an old-fashioned God" over the theologian's "modern patent Absolute."

Suspicions about the orthodoxy of his religious views and moral practice (not to mention a rather neurotic personality) resulted in his dismissal from a professorial position at Johns Hopkins, and except for a few lectures at Harvard (arranged by William James), the denial of any further academic appointments. Using a small inheritance to retire with his second wife to the northeastern Pennsylvania countryside, he continued producing brilliant, albeit unpublished, manuscripts for the rest of his life — many of them about God and religion. In 1892 he reaffirmed his lifelong membership in the Episcopal Church by returning as a regular communicant.

PEIRCE ON RELIGION. All definitions being hypothetical by nature, the existence of God cannot be deduced from a rational analysis of the definition of God. Nor can reason be used inductively to infer the existence of God from the orderliness of nature. But there is no dichotomy between faith and reason such as might preclude the possibility of rationally defining and knowing God or any other object of faith. Rooted as it is in instinct, the human mind has a natural proclivity toward musing playfully, not about the existence of God (which would reduce God to a polytheistic finite thing) but about his reality (as opposed to fictitious or illusory being). Seeing the beauty of nature, man's imagination becomes excited to the point of gradually giving rise to an anthropomorphic idea of God, which upon the refinement of instinct through reflection upon experience, becomes an hypothesis that can best account for the fortuitous regularity of our evolving universe. The hypothesis is that God is the Infinite, Absolute, Ideal Reasonableness that is both immanent and transcendent to the purposeful, evolving nature of things.

It is the glory of science, through its ongoing, self-correcting, empirical discovery of the general laws of nature, to test the ultimate truth of this hypothesis. But notwithstanding

the superstition of religion *per se,* the various religions also play a role in this regard. For although the nature of God can never be fully comprehended, and positive theology makes no sense, talking vaguely about God as the principle of love can serve as a powerful symbol of cosmic evolution toward the harmonious unity of all things. Such a symbol will have the force of truth, however, only to the extent that it makes a difference in the conduct of those embracing it by inspiring, among other things, their mutual tolerance of conflicting interpretations. Indeed, without the social institution of a "church" that forms a community of interpreters, the religion of love can have but a rudimentary existence.

Sources

Peirce, Charles S. *Collected Papers of Charles Sanders Peirce.* Edited by C. Hartshorne, P. Weiss, and A. Burks. Cambridge, MA: Harvard University Press, 1935, 1958.

_____. "A Neglected Argument for the Reality of God." *Hibbert Journal* 7 (October 1908): 90–112.

_____, and Victoria Welby. *Semiotic and Significs: The Correspondence between Charles S. Peirce and Victoria Lady Welby.* Edited by C. Harwick. Bloomington: Indiana University Press, 1977.

Alexander, G. "The Hypothesized God of C.S. Peirce and William James." *Journal of Religion* 67 (1987): 304–21.

Bernstein, Richard J., ed. *Critical Essays on Charles Sanders Peirce.* New Haven and London: Yale University Press, 1965.

Brent, Joseph. *Charles Sanders Peirce: A Life.* Bloomington: Indiana University Press, 1998.

Burrell, David B. "Knowing as a Passionate and Personal Quest." In *American Philosophy and the Future,* edited by Michael Novak. New York: Charles Scribner's Sons, 1968. 107–37.

Demarco, J.P. "God, Religion and Community in the Philosophy of C.S. Peirce." *Modern Schoolman* 49 (1972): 331–47.

Hartshorne, C. "A Critique of Peirce's Idea of God." *Philosophical Review* 50 (1941): 516–23.

Ketner, Kenneth Laine. *His Glassy Essence: An Autobiography of Charles Sanders Peirce.* Nashville and London: Vanderbilt University Press, 1998.

Levinson, Henry Samuel. "Religious Philosophy." In *Encyclopedia of American Religious Experience.* Vol. 2. New York: Charles Scribner's Sons, 1988. 1194–96.

Mahowald, M. "Peirce's Concepts of God and Religion." *Transactions of the Charles S. Peirce Society* 12 (1976): 367–77.

Orange, Donna A. *Peirce's Conception of God: A Developmental Study. Peirce Studies.* No. 2. Lubbock, TX: Institute for Studies in Pragmatism, 1984.

Pfeifer, David E. "Charles Peirce's Contribution to Religious Thought." In *Proceedings of the C.S. Peirce Bicentennial International Congress* 23, edited by Kenneth L. Ketner et al. (September 1981): 367–73.

Potter, Vincent G., S.J. "'Vaguely like a Man': The Theism of Charles S. Peirce." In *God Knowable and Unknowable.* Edited by Robert J. Roth, S.J. New York: Fordham University Press, 1973.

Raposa, Michael L. *Peirce's Philosophy of Religion. Peirce Studies.* No. 5. Bloomington and Indianapolis: Indiana University Press, 1989.

Sleeper, R.W. "Pragmatism, Religion, and Experienceable Difference." In *American Philosophy and the Future,* edited by Michael Novak. New York: Charles Scribner's Sons, 1968. 277–86.

Smith, J.C. "Peirce's Religious Metaphysics." *International Philosophical Quarterly* 19 (1979): 407–25.

Thompson, Manley. *The Pragmatic Philosophy of C.S. Peirce.* Chicago: The University of Chicago Press, 1963.

Trammel, R.L. "Religion, Instinct and Reason in the Thought of Charles S. Peirce." *Transactions of the Charles S. Peirce Society* 8 (1972): 3–25.

Phillips, D.Z. (1934–2006)

Phillips was born in Morriston, a small, heavily industrialized town on the edge of Swansea in South Wales. With twenty-eight houses of worship (all but five being nonconformist), the town provided a thoroughly religious environment. Its many chapels were often the center of the town's intellectual and cultural activities. As he was growing up Phillips attended Sunday school and church at the nonconformist Horeb chapel, often memorizing the sermons he would hear in the morning service and delivering them verbatim that evening to the aunts and uncles congregated in his family's home. Throughout his teen years he would continue preaching to lay congregations.

After graduating from the religiously nondenominational Bishop Gore Grammar School in Swansea, and pursuing bachelor's and master's degrees in English and philosophy (under the likes of Rush Rhees and Gilbert Ryle) at the University College of Swansea and Oxford University, Phillips followed the example of an older brother and decided to become a full-time minister. Not yet having studied any theology, he was appointed minister at Fabian's Bay Congregational Chapel on a probationary basis in 1958. He (along with his newly wedded wife) served the congregation over the next three years and was well received, notwithstanding his continued attendance on alternate Sundays at Oxford's Pusey House Chapel whose richly "Catholic" liturgy put far more emphasis upon the communion service than was traditional in nonconformist worship.

In 1961 he suspended his pastoral activity to launch an academic career by accepting a teaching post in Queen's College, Dundee. Over the next four and a half decades, he would devote most of his time and energy to writing multiple books and articles (mainly about the philosophy of religion) and teaching philosophy courses at universities in Bangor (North Wales), Swansea, and California. He held the Danforth Chair in Philosophy of Religion at Claremont Graduate University in California and was the Rush Rhees Professor Emeritus at the University of Wales, Swansea.

Throughout those many years, Phillips' views about the nature of religious belief underwent considerable change, so much so in fact that he could no longer identify with any one or another particular creed. On that account, he terminated his membership in the Congregational Church and declined joining any other. He continued, however, to regard himself as a believer, on grounds that the community of true believers cannot be limited only to those who worship according to one or another tradition.

PHILLIPS ON RELIGION. Theists and atheists alike seem to assume that for religious beliefs to be grounded empirical evidence or reasons for such beliefs must be found external to the beliefs themselves. Thus, on the one side, for example, an attempt is made to prove that there is a God by arguing from the motion, contingency, and regularity of the universe that there must be a Prime Mover, a Necessary Being, a Designer, while, on the other side, pursuant to Hume's definitive rejection of any inference of the existence of God from features of the world, it is argued that there is no evidence to support the existence of God, and that religious beliefs are simply the result of ignorance, emotional stress, social pressure, or metaphysical impulse. Both sides, however, are confused to the extent of assuming that religious beliefs are factual, foundational assertions. Neither really understands what it means to believe.

Religious beliefs about the existence of God, the Last Judgment, and so on, do not make factual claims. Contrary to what the Logical Positivists thought, however, Wittgenstein did not mean thereby that religious beliefs can be reduced to nothing but an expression of emotion. What he meant was that religious beliefs can only be properly understood as mental pictures that the believer brings to bear upon life in a way that differentiates his or her attitudes and behavior from that of nonbelievers. Coming to believe that there is an eternal God, then, is not like coming to see that an additional being exists, but that one's life has a new, deeper meaning; it provides a picture to live by, or by which to judge oneself in terms of the possibility of eternal love. In such a context, belief in eternal life would refer to the quality of this life, not to life beyond the grave. To discover the meaning of religion, therefore, is to discover a new universe of discourse, a new language-game, which, as part of a unique form of life, has its own internal criteria for assessing the truth and value of its assertions.

Sources

Phillips, D.Z. *Faith After Foundationalism*. London and New York: Routledge, 1988.
_____. *Faith and Philosophical Enquiry*. London: Routledge and Kegan Paul, 1970.
_____. *Recovering Religious Concepts*. New York: St. Martin's Press, Inc., 2000.
_____. *Religions Without Explanation*. Oxford: Basil Blackwell, 1976.
_____. *Wittgenstein and Religion*. New York: St. Martin's Press, 1993.
Alston, William. "Taking the Curse off Language-Games." In *Faith and Reason*, edited by Paul Helm. Oxford and New York: Oxford University Press, 1999. 313–14.
Diamond, Malcolm L., and Thomas V. Litzenburg, Jr., eds. *The Logic of God: Theology and Verification*. Indianapolis: The Bobbs-Merrill Company, Inc., 1975. 309–10.
Geivett, R. Douglas, and Brendan Sweetman, eds. *Contemporary Perspectives on Religious Epistemology*. New York and Oxford: Oxford University Press, 1992. 8–9.
Hick, John. *Philosophy of Religion*. 3rd ed. Englewood Cliffs, NJ: Prentice-Hall, Inc., 1983. 90–93.
Rowe, William L., and William J. Wainwright, eds. *Philosophy of Religion: Selected Readings*. Fort Worth, TX: Harcourt Brace and Company, 1998. 288–312.
Verkamp, Bernard J. *The Senses of Mystery: Religious and Non-Religious*. Scranton, PA: University of Scranton Press, 1997. 57–59.
Whittaker, John H., ed. *The Possibilities of Sense*. New York: Palgrave, 2002. See esp. 1–9; 131–218.

Plantinga, Alvin (1932–)

Plantinga's parents were deeply committed to the Dutch Calvinist religious faith of their ancestors and insisted upon his attendance at Sunday school and church, summer Bible camps, weekly catechism classes and Christian youth meetings that were occasionally under the direction of his own father, who in addition to being a professor of philosophy, often preached and taught at local churches. He remained staunch in his faith throughout his high school years, despite the fact that already by the age of nine he had begun asking serious questions about predestination and other troubling Calvinist doctrines.

After a year at Calvin College, where his father had landed a professorial position, he won a scholarship to Harvard. There he attended a Methodist church and a Sunday-school class taught by Peter Bertocci, but also encountered for the first time "serious non–Christian thought" and an "enormous variety of spiritual opinion." Whatever doubts he felt were soon vanquished, however, by a quasi-mystical experience of God's presence he had one gloomy evening walking across Harvard Yard. Along with an opportunity during spring break to attend some philosophy classes taught at Calvin College by "a magnificently thoughtful Christian," William Harry Jellema, it convinced him to return to Calvin. His further study under Jellema in that school's splendid, albeit rather religiously exclusive, intellectual environment, he says, was what preserved his Christian faith and made it the focal point of his intellectual life.

Marriage to a good Calvinist Christian woman and frequent treks into the mountains reinforced that faith as he pursued graduate studies under Alston and Frankena at the University of Michigan, acquired his Ph.D. at Yale and spent six years at Wayne State in the company of Nakhnikian, Castañeda, and other professors who had "turned their backs on Christianity," before being invited to succeed a retiring Professor Jellema at Calvin. Teaching and writing there for the next nineteen years, and then at Notre Dame after 1982, he devoted himself to fulfilling what he perceived to be the mission of a "Christian philosopher" by developing new epistemological and metaphysical lines of thought that challenged prevailing Positivist antireligious assumptions, reinforced traditional theism, and helped rally professors and students alike from around the country into the formation of a Society of Christian Philosophers. He finds this revival of Christian philosophy "a source of amazement, delight and gratitude."

PLANTINGA ON RELIGION. As most religious people have known all along, there are many religions other than their own. What is new is the widespread sympathy and solidarity some now feel toward other religions. But given the conflicting beliefs among theistic and nontheistic religions about the existence and nature of an omnipotent, omniscient, perfect, and personal God, the plurality of religions is problematic.

So how is someone who becomes aware of all this religious plurality supposed to react? Among many possible reactions, one called exclusivism claims that one should continue to believe what one has always believed, on the assumption that the tenets of one's own religion are true and that any other religious beliefs contradicting them are false. Such a reaction would be no more morally suspect (arbitrary, arrogant, or imperialistic) than for radical pluralists themselves to claim privilege for their own dissenting views. Nor is exclusivism epistemically unjustified or irrational. For one thing, good arguments could be made that the existence of God is necessary if God has the property of maximal greatness (as is at least possible), and that there is nothing logically impossible about God coexisting with evil in a world that contains free creatures.

But objection to exclusivism is not really about the truth of one's religious belief; it is rather about the propriety or rightness of adhering to such beliefs. It would not be unjustified, exclusivists could argue, if, after careful, prayerful consideration one is still convinced of the truth of one's beliefs, and one does not think one's own beliefs are on an epistemic par with those of other religions. It would not be irrational, they could claim, if such beliefs were not demonstrably false or contrary to self-evident truths, or if true, could conceivably have been produced in one and warranted as properly basic beliefs by some reliable belief-producing process like Calvin's *Sensus Divinitatis,* without any propositional evidence.

Sources

Plantinga, Alvin. *God, Freedom, and Evil.* Grand Rapids, MI: William B. Eerdmans Publishing Co., 1977.

_____. "Pluralism: A Defense of Religious Exclusivism." In *The Philosophical Challenge of Religious Diversity,* edited by Philip L. Quinn and Kevin Meeker. New York and Oxford: Oxford University Press, 2000. 172–92.

_____. "Reason and Belief in God." In *Faith and Rationality: Reason and Belief in God,* edited by Alvin Plantinga and Nicholas Wolterstorff. Notre Dame: University of Notre Dame Press, 1983. 16–93.

_____. "The Reformed Objection to Natural Theology." *Christian Scholar's Review* 11.3 (1982): 187–98.

_____. *Warranted Christian Belief.* New York: Oxford University Press, 2000.

Clark, Kelly James, ed. *Philosophers Who Believe: The Spiritual Journeys of 11 Leading Thinkers.* Downers Grove, IL: InterVarsity Press, 1993. 45–82.

Peterson, Michael, William Hasker, Bruce Reichenbach, and David Basinger, eds. *Reason and Religious Belief.* 3rd ed. New York and Oxford: Oxford University Press, 2003. See esp. 112–17; 120–23; 130–33.

Sennett, James F., ed. *The Analytic Theist: An Alvin Plantinga Reader.* Grand Rapids, MI, and Cambridge, UK: William B. Eerdmans Publishing Company, 1998.

Plato (429–347 B.C.)

At the time of Plato's birth into an aristocratic Athenian family, Greek life was dominated by a plethora of religious beliefs, rites, festivals, oracles, and temples. Everything in the life of the average citizen, from birth to death, was perceived in religious terms. It is hardly surprising, then, that some of Plato's admirers would claim that he was, if not the son of the divine Apollo, at least the grandson, on his father's side, of Poseidon. Of course, Plato himself would never have given any more credence to such talk than he gave to the "*polis* religion" in general. It is true that despite his protest against Homer's unedifying depiction of immorality on the part of the Olympian pantheon, or against the tendency of the masses to rely superstitiously on the efficacy of religious rituals, Plato clearly saw popular piety as a bulwark of civic order, and all the more so given the anxieties he must have been feeling in the course of Sparta's defeat of Athens, the reign of the Thirty Tyrants, the execution of Socrates, and other horrors that eventually led him to disengage himself completely from political affairs.

In *The Republic, The Laws,* and other of his writings, he emphasized how important it was for the masses to adhere to the traditional rites and defended the prerogative of the oracles to direct temple worship and the celebration of sacred festivals. But how much, beyond perfunctory attendance at official celebrations, Plato himself participated in this popular religion, with its Delphic emphasis upon the "otherness" of the gods, is doubtful. More likely, the religion he practiced personally was along one or another alternate route offered by Orphism, the Eleusinian Mysteries, Pythagorean and other novel forms of religion that had proliferated in fifth-century Athens in response to the trauma of war and plague. Resonating to their insistence upon continuity between the human and the divine and all their talk about becoming like the gods, but replacing the highly emotional character of their purificatory, ecstatic rituals with an emphasis upon purification of the soul through the process of knowing, Plato basically turned philosophy itself into something of a religion, if not for everyone, at least for himself and others who are capable of sustained intellectual reflection on the divine reality. In any event, after much travel to avoid a fate similar to that of Socrates and the failure of his attempt to turn Dionysius II into the philosopher-king of Syracuse put an end to whatever political aspirations he still harbored, he returned to Athens and founded the Academy, where for the rest of his life he made the quest for wisdom the ultimate concern of all his lecturing and writing.

PLATO ON RELIGION. Egged on by those who claim that the gods are nothing but the relativistic products of culture, and that "all religion is a cooking up of words and a make-believe," it is not unusual for young people to suppose that there is no god. Few, however, remain atheistic into their old age, for upon rational reflection it becomes clear that to explain the being and harmonious movement of material entities that cannot move themselves there must be posited the existence of a supremely intelligent, self-moving, spiritual being. Motivated by the goodness and oneness of its being, God, as the Divine Craftsman or Demiurge, creates the material universe after the model of the Ideal Forms, and moves to bring order out of the primordial chaos by first creating a world soul, next the star souls, then human souls. The irrational part of the latter, however, was created by the celestial gods, as was also the body into which the soul eventually fell under the influence of the un-ruly, downward thrust of its appetitive side.

The goal of human life is to become like God by taking care of one's soul through the pursuit of wisdom and the practice of virtue. Those who do evil, do so because they think that God either does not exist, or is indifferent, or is easily appeased by sacrifices. Belief in the existence of a caring and just God, therefore, is the foundation of all morality and the source of happiness, both here and beyond, and those who persist in their atheism should be punished. Evidence of the pre-existence of the human soul, its simplicity, its vitality, and its domination of the body, clearly refutes any and all doubt about its immortality. Faith in that and other religious doctrines can be reinforced by respectful attention to prayer and the traditional incantation of mythology. Upon death, the souls of the wicked linger in their bodies, and eventually are reincarnated in one or another animal body corresponding to the nature of their deeds in this life. The just souls, on the other hand, having been purified by the pursuit of wisdom, will escape such reincarnation and enter into the communion of the gods.

Sources

Plato. *The Dialogues of Plato*. Translated by Benjamin Jowett. *Great Books of the Western World*. Vol. 7. Edited by R.M. Hutchins. Chicago: Encyclopædia Britannica, Inc., 1952.

Carmody, John. "Plato's Religious Horizon." *Philosophy Today* 15.1 (1971): 52–67.

Chroust, Anton-Hermann. *Socrates: Man and Myth. The Two Socratic Apologies of Xenophon*. Notre Dame: University of Notre Dame Press, 1957.

Copleston, Frederick, S.J. *A History of Philosophy*. Vol. 1, pt. 1. Garden City, NY: Doubleday and Company, Inc., 1962–77. 151–291.

Gadamer, Hans-Georg. *Dialogue and Dialectic: Eight Hermeneutical Studies on Plato*. New Haven and London: Yale University Press, 1980. 21–38.

Gooch, Paul W. *Reflections on Jesus and Socrates. Word and Silence*. New Haven and London: Yale University Press, 1996. See esp. 93–106; 140–46; 168–75; 182–83; 275–305.

Lefkowitz, Mary. "Comments on Vlastos' 'Socratic Piety.'" *Proceedings of Boston Area Colloquium in Ancient Philosophy* 5 (1989).

Lefkowitz, Mary. "Impiety and Atheism." *The Classical Quarterly* 39 (1945): 70–82.

Merlan, Philip. "Religion and Philosophy from Plato's *Phaedo* to the Chaldean Oracles." *Journal of the History of Philosophy* 1 (1963): 163–76.

Morgan, Michael L. "Plato and Greek Religion." In *The Cambridge Companion to Plato*, edited by Richard Kraut. Cambridge: Cambridge University Press, 1992. 227–47.

Reale, Giovanni. *A History of Ancient Philosophy. II. Plato and Aristotle*. Albany: State University of New York Press, 1990.

Shorey, Paul. *What Plato Said*. Chicago: The University of Chicago Press, 1933. 74–83; 198–207; 169–84.

Taylor, A.E. *Plato, The Man and His Work*. New York: The Dial Press, Inc., 1936.

Vlastos, Gregory. *Socrates, Ironist and Moral Philosopher*. Ithaca, NY: Cornell University Press, 1991. 157–78.

Plotinus (205–270)

Apart from the fact that as a young boy he attended grammar school in what was probably the city of his birth (Lycopolis, Egypt), little is known about Plotinus' youth. In his late twenties he shows up in Alexandria. There, after failing to find any satisfaction in what he was hearing at the schools he attended, he was introduced to the "God-taught," former Christian thinker, Ammonius Saccas, and convinced that "he had found the man he was seeking," stayed on with him for the next eleven years. It is possible that the "Christian Origen" Porphyry refers to in his *Life of Plotinus* as a fellow student of Plotinus at that time was the future Christian theologian of Alexandria by that name.

At the age of thirty-nine Plotinus left Ammonius to join an imperial expedition to the East in hopes of learning something about Persian and Indian philosophy. The project failed, and Plotinus barely escaped with his life before finding his way to Rome, where he stayed for the next twenty-six years, teaching a syncretistic version of Platonic, Aristotelian, Stoic, and Pythagorean thought, spiritually counseling many of Rome's leading citizens, meditating daily, practicing vegetarianism and other forms of asceticism, and finally, after shelving a pledge to keep secret his master's teaching, writing the many treatises that Porphyry would eventually arrange in groups of nine under the title, *The Enneads*.

Porphyry and other of his students, like Amelius, tended to worship him as a quasi-divine figure. Fascinated by the many religious movements then popular in Rome, these same students often tried to lure their teacher into accompanying them to the sacrificial rites being performed at various religious festivals around the city. But Plotinus would have nothing of it. "The gods should come to me, not I to them," he once rebuffed a pleading Amelius.

He had no use for the divination, sacrificial rites, and prayerful worship associated with Rome's popular religion. Nor did he have any taste for the religious movement Christians were calling the "heresy" of Gnosticism, dismissing it as an "arrogant and perverse reading of Plato." As for Christianity itself, his student Porphyry would later publish an attack on the Christian religion, but it is not certain whether Plotinus himself ever openly criticized the Christian religion. His own personal religion inclined toward mysticism. Porphyry tells us that at least four times in his life Plotinus succeeded in experiencing the ecstatic bliss of "intimate union with the God who is above all things." It is reported that on his deathbed his last words were about "leading the god in [me/you] up to the divine in the universe."

PLOTINUS ON RELIGION. The efficacy of traditional religious activities, such as the observance of holy days, or prayer and ritualistic sacrifice to the astral divinities, is due, not to some divine memory, intention, or will, but, like magic, to the "sympathy" or interconnectedness of the multiple parts of the cosmos resulting from the presence of the One in the All. But there are other laws operative in the universe also, like the laws that decree victory only to those who fight bravely, promise a harvest only to those who toil the fields, or guarantee the punishment of evildoers. It would be childish, therefore, to expect that while ignoring the laws they have prescribed for our well-being, we can incline the gods by prayer to keep all well for us. Furthermore, the truly wise man will likely have little interest in the religious and magical activities preoccupying the general public, and will be drawn instead to the higher level of contemplation of the One.

As their ultimate Source, the One is transcendent to the All emanating from It (*Nous*, the World Soul, human souls, matter). But the One is also immanent, always present on the horizon of human experience to be contemplated like the rising of the morning sun. Such contemplation will be the highest form of prayer, consisting as it does, not in the mouthing of loud incantations, but in the silent, lonely leaning of the soul toward a vision of the One that reunites the One within man with the One in Itself, even while preserving the otherness of the former and the incomprehensibility of the latter. To achieve this difficult ascent back to the Source of its being, the soul, eschewing any Gnostic, pantheistic antinomianism, must cultivate all the moral and intellectual virtues, renounce its selfish attachment to the body and evil-producing matter, and finally leap beyond the intellectual level of *Nous* into the realm of the unknown. Any failure to do so will result in a weary cycle of reincarnation. Success will mean salvation, with the soul escaping its bodily imprisonment and basking forever in blissful contemplation of the beautiful simplicity and goodness of the One.

Sources

Plotinus. *The Six Enneads*. Translated by Stephen MacKenna and B.S. Page. *Great Books of the Western World*. Vol. 17. Edited by R.M. Hutchins. Chicago: Encyclopædia Britannica, Inc., 1952.

Armstrong, A.H. "The Gods in Plato, Plotinus, Epicurus." *The Classical Quarterly* 32 (1938), 190–96.

Clark, Mary T. "Plotinus." In *Encyclopedia of Religion*. Vol. 11. Edited by Mircea Eliade. New York: Macmillan and Co., 1987. 268–69.

Gerson, Lloyd P., ed. *The Cambridge Companion to Plotinus*. Cambridge: Cambridge University Press, 1994.

Inge, William Ralph. *The Philosophy of Plotinus*. 2 vols. London: Longmans, Green and Co., 1918.

Mayhall, C. Wayne. *On Plotinus*. Belmont, CA: Wadsworth Press, 2004.

O'Meara, Dominic J. *Plotinus: An Introduction to the Enneads*. Oxford: Clarendon Press, 1995.

O'Neill, W.H. "Plotinus." *New Catholic Encyclopedia*. Vol. 11. Edited by W.J. McDonald. New York: McGraw-Hill, 1967. 443–44.

Porphyry. *On the Life of Plotinus and the Arrangement of his Works*. Translated by Mark Edwards. Liverpool: Liverpool University Press, 2000.

Rist, J.M. "Mysticism and Transcendence in Later Neoplatonism." *Hermes* 92 (1964): 213–25.

_____. *Plotinus: The Road to Reality*. Cambridge: At the University Press, 1967.

_____. "Theos and the One in Some Texts of Plotinus." *Mediaeval Studies* 24 (1962): 169–80.

Stumpf, Samuel Enoch. *Socrates to Sartre. A History of Philosophy*. New York: McGraw-Hill Book Company, 1982. 119–25.

Plutarch (c. A.D. 46–120)

Born in the "poor, little town" of Chaeronea, Plutarch was Boeotian, but hardly the "dull, stupid person" the name has come to connote in modern times. Judging from the respect he got while still living, and the acclaim some of his works (notwithstanding their occasional superficiality and lack of historical accuracy) were afforded down through the centuries, he was one bright and witty fellow—so much so, in fact, that Montaigne would later claim that it was by reading Plutarch's *Lives* that the rest of us "dunces" are "raised out of the dirt." He apparently received much of his early education from the reputedly Egyptian philosopher, Ammonius, with whom he lived during an extended stay in Athens as a young man of twenty years. In addition to giving Plutarch instructions in philosophy, Ammonius may also have been the one from whom Plutarch gained the astute understanding of Egyptian religion he would later display in the treatise about Isis and Osiris he addressed to the learned lady Clea.

One way or the other, either with the help of others or by teaching himself, by the time he was an older man he had a reputation of being a very learned and wise man. Much of his adult life was devoted to social, civic and literary activities, fathering five children by his beloved wife Timoxena, serving as a magistrate in Chaeronea, representing his hometown and country on various missions to Rome (where he also briefly gave lectures on philosophy), and producing an exceptionally large body of writings (most notably, the *Parallel Lives*). But all the while he also remained keenly interested and involved in religion. As indicated in the touching consolation he wrote to Timoxena on the occasion of their young daughter's death, both he and his wife had been initiated into the secret mysteries of Dionysius and convinced thereby of the soul's immortality.

After asserting in his treatise *On the E at Delphi* that there is no reason to doubt the existence or oneness of Apollo, he encouraged his readers to worship the god of Delphi accordingly. In another of his essays, "Whether an Old Man should continue in Public Life," he acknowledged the fact that he had chosen to become one of the two priests of Apollo at Delphi whose function it was to transcribe and interpret the divinatory utterances made during an elaborate ritual by a chief priestess (called Pythia after the monster slain by Apollo on Parnassus), adding that he had "served the Pythian God for many *pythiads* past" by repeatedly taking part in the ritualistic "sacrifices, processions, and dances."

PLUTARCH ON RELIGION. It is probably best to remain silent about one's experience of the Mysteries in which the truth about the gods are to be found, but anyone, like myself, who has served Pythian Apollo for so many years as a priest, knows full well the hidden meanings that can be discerned in religious mythology, ritual, and symbolism, when these are subjected to rational interpretation. One can, in other words, find good reason to avoid both atheism and superstition.

Atheism springs from the ignorance of the gods on the part of hard-minded people who assign natural causes to everything, sarcastically dismiss all religious ceremonies, undermine belief in immortality (the sweetest and greatest hope of mankind), and degrade the traditional gods either to the level of outstanding human beings or, in a dualistic attempt to explain the presence of good and evil in our world, to mere physical and astronomical allegories (Isis equals earth, Typhon equals sea, Osiris equals moon, etc.). Philosophical/theological reflection will show, however, that a supreme God (Zeus/Apollo) exists eternally, and that this God is One, Intelligent, Good, and Personal, appointing other intermediary, quasi-divine beings (*daemons,* the more benevolent of which carry the names and missions of the different gods of different peoples, the more malevolent causing all the evil in the world, including the perversely religious sacrifice of Iphigenia) to execute His paternal Providence among humans. More threatening to true religion (our national Faith) than the intellectual error of atheism, however, is the emotionally tinged, moral evil of superstition, which inclines the weak-minded to fear everything in this life and the next because of their ignorant fear of God. Such superstition is repugnant to the conception of a good God, who, if provident, not only looks after man in this life, but will surely not let the good souls of the dead perish without reward, or the bad without finally being punished by the relentless pangs of their own awakened consciences.

Sources

Plutarch. *De Iside et Osiride.* Translated by J. Gwytn Griffiths. Cardiff: University of Wales Press, 1970.

_____. *The Lives of the Noble Grecians and Romans.* Translated by John Dryden and revised and introduced by Arthur Hugh Clough. New York: Modern Library, 1932. See esp. ix–xv.

_____. *The Moralia.* Vols. 14: *Superstition*; 23: *Isis and Osiris*; 26: *The Decline of Oracles*; 41: *God's Slowness to Punish*; 60: *The Face of the Moon.* Edited with translations by Frank Lloyd Babbitt et al. Boston: Loeb Classics, 1927ff.

Dillon, John. "Plutarch and God: Theodicy and Cosmogony in the Thought of Plutarch." In Dorothea Frede, and Andre Laks, eds. Traditions of *Theology: Studies in Hellenistic Theology, Its Background and Aftermath.* Leiden and Boston: Brill, 2002, 2002:223–37.

Lamberton, Robert. *Plutarch.* New Haven and London: Yale University Press, 2001. See esp. 52–59.

Oakesmith, John. *The Religion of Plutarch.* New York and Bombay: Longmans, Green, and Co., 1902.

Russell, D.A. *Plutarch.* London: Duckworth and Company, Ltd., 1973. See esp. 63–83.

Porphyry (A.D. 233–c. 305)

Porphyry called himself a Tyrean, not because, as implied by the early Christian historian Socrates, he was an apostate from Christianity who was trying to conceal his Jewish roots, but simply because he was born into a distinguished family in Tyre, a great Phoenician seaport of antiquity. Playing off the kingly connotation of his original name, Malchus, and alluding to the usual color of royal robes, a future teacher of his (Longinus) would later give him the name by which he has come to be identified historically (i.e., Porphyry). He claimed that as a very young man he received some instruction from Origen (possibly the renowned Christian theologian), and then studied rhetoric and grammar under Longinus, before finally, at the age of twenty going to Rome and striking up an acquaintance with Plotinus. The latter soon thereafter had to leave Rome and it was not until ten years later that Porphyry would become his full-time student and disciple.

He did not always agree with his teacher, but during the six years he would spend with him, he won the confidence of Plotinus to such an extent that he was often assigned the task of refuting opponents and eventually of editing his master's writings. When, in 268, he began suffering from severe depression and was toying with the thought of suicide, Plotinus counseled him to leave Rome and to go south to Sicily. Eusebius claimed that it was while Porphyry was in Sicily that he wrote his diatribe against the Christian religion, a work consigned to the flames by the emperor Theodosius and lost but for fragments cited in the multiple refutations it evoked from Christian apologists. Sometime after the death of Plotinus in 270, he returned to Rome, where he apparently stayed for most of the last three decades of his life, teaching, getting married for a brief time, completing the publication of Plotinus's works, and writing multiple treatises of his own, including several biographies that are as much about himself as about those of whom he is writing (e.g., Pythagoras and Plotinus).

Notwithstanding his vigorous attack against what he considered to be the superstitious nature of the theurgic rites or of popular religion in general, he certainly was not adverse to practicing religion in what he perceived to be its purest form. To advance the virtuous pursuit of wisdom that he associated with true piety, he not only strove to purge himself of all sensual desires by various ascetical practices (like refraining from the eating of meat), he also (as indicated in his letter to his former wife) devoted much of his time to prayer and mystical contemplation. In his *Life of Plotinus* he writes that, like his former teacher, he himself, at the age of sixty-eight, was blessed with an ecstatic vision of the eternal Deity.

PORPHYRY ON RELIGION. Although there is no one universal way of salvation, those who deny the existence and providence of God and try to destroy men's conception of God — as if the universe is carried along by a blind irrational force — expose themselves to unspeakable danger and will not escape divine justice. But those who hold that God exists know God as an undetermined Being-by-itself that is everywhere and rules everything. Under the watchful eyes of angelic intermediaries — the invisible good daemons emanating, along with the visible astral gods, through the power and wisdom of this "God-over-all"–believers will attain to a well-ordered life.

Essential to such a life is the paying of proper homage to the Deity. Care must be taken to avoid the kind of superstitious incantations and animal sacrifices practiced by people trying to appease the malevolent daemons who have deceived the masses into thinking that evil is caused by God and the good daemons. For wrath is alien to God. Nor does God have any need for religious adoration, sacrifices, or prayers. While prayer and the traditional practice of religion can be fruitful,

therefore, it will be so only because those worshiping feel within themselves a need to honor the divine majesty. God is truly pleased only by the purity of mind that one acquires through honest, faithful, loving, and hopeful thought of God and the free cultivation of political, cathartic, and paradigmatic virtues which incline one toward social moderation, the purgation of bodily appetites, and contemplation of *Nous* and its ideal Forms. This leads to knowledge of oneself as a godlike, spiritual being. Therein, contrary to Gnosticism and Christian talk of Incarnation and bodily resurrection, lies salvation. Transmigrating through different human bodies, the purified soul, with the help of its natal daemon, finally finds union with God, joining the daemonic commonwealth of friendship peopled by Plato, Pythagoras, Plotinus and other philosophers of highest virtue who have set going the dance of immortal love.

Sources

Porphyry. *De Abstentia.* In Edwyn Bevan. *Later Greek Religion.* London and Toronto: J.M. Dent and Sons, Ltd.; New York: E.P. Dutton and Co., 1827. 204–10.

_____. *Ad Marcella.* In Edwyn Bevan. *Later Greek Religion.* London and Toronto: J.M. Dent and Sons, Ltd.; New York: E.P. Dutton and Co., 1827. 210–18.

_____. *Against the Christians.* In Eusebius, *The History of the Church.* Translated by G.A. Williamson. New York: Dorset Press, 1965. 258–59.

_____. *On the Life of Plotinus and the Arrangement of His Works.* In *Neoplatonic Saints: The Lives of Plotinus and Proclus by Their Students.* Translated by Mark Edwards. Liverpool: Liverpool University Press, 2000. 1–53.

_____. *Sententiae ad Intelligibilia Ducentes.* Leipzig: Teubner, 1975.

Barnes, Jonathan. *Porphyry: Introduction.* Oxford: Clarendon Press, 2003.

Bevan, Edwyn. *Later Greek Religion.* London and Toronto: J.M. Dent and Sons, Ltd.; New York: E.P. Dutton and Co., 1827. 204–18.

Copleston, Frederick, S.J. *A History of Philosophy.* Vol. 1, pt. 2. Garden City, NY: Doubleday and Company, Inc., 1962–77. 216–18.

Edwards, Mark. "Introduction." *Neoplatonic Saints: The Lives of Plotinus and Proclus by Their Students.* Liverpool: Liverpool University Press, 2000. xxx–xxxix.

Hadot, P. "Porphyry." *New Catholic Encyclopedia.* Vol. 11. Edited by W.J. McDonald. New York: McGraw-Hill, 1967. 593–94.

Mason, Charles Peter. "Porphyrius." In *A Dictionary of Greek and Roman Biography and Mythology.* Vol. 3. Edited by William Smith. New York: AMS Press, Inc., 1967. 498–507.

Rist, J.M. *Plotinus: The Road to Reality.* Cambridge: At the University Press, 1967. 2–20; 34–37.

Whittaker, Thomas. T*he Neo-Platonists: A Study in the History of Hellenism.* Cambridge, UK: University Press, 1928. 107–20.

Proclus (c. A.D. 411–485)

Proclus was born in Byzantium. His father was a successful lawyer and devoted "Hellene" or adherent to the traditional religion of ancient Greece and Rome. While Proclus was still a child the parents moved their family back to their prosperous, seaside hometown of Xanthus, probably to avoid becoming a target of persecutions initiated by the fanatically Christian, Byzantine regent, Pulcheria. After being tutored there, Proclus was sent to Alexandria to prepare for a career in law. But during a trip to Byzantium he had a dream of Athena, the goddess of wisdom, telling him to take up the study of philosophy in Athens. He returned to Alexandria, abandoned his legal studies, and briefly studied Aristotelian logic and Neo-Pythagorean religion, before finally, at the age of nineteen, sailing to Athens. There, having severed all ties with his parents, he completed his study of Aristotle and Plato under the guidance of Syrianus, the acting head of the Academy, and was initiated into the secret rites of "theurgic" Neo-Platonism. Within six years he would succeed Syrianus as head of the school, an administrative position he would hold for the remaining fifty years of his life.

Notwithstanding what, by his own account, were "strong carnal desires" and (according to his biographer, Marinus) numerous "matrimonial opportunities," he never married. He dedicated himself instead to teaching and preaching the Neo-Platonic (less Plotinian, and more Iamblichian) philosophy he had come to embrace, every day lecturing five

times and writing at least seven hundred lines of the many commentaries he would eventually publish on the works of Plato, the Chaldean oracles, Euclid, Hesiod, and others. All the while, according to Marinus, Proclus was most assiduous in practicing the Orphic and Chaldean mystic rites of purification to which he had earlier been initiated. He would fast and keep vigils with "scrupulous exactitude," abstain from the eating of all meats, pay constant reverence to the sun and moon, and celebrate the important religious festivals of all nations, often composing hymns in honor of their various gods. Conceiving of himself as the "hierophant of the whole world," he would perform sacred rites in order to venerate, not only departed heroes and philosophers, but also the departed spirits of the entire human race. Despite his openness to the worship of all forms of the one God, he would express some hostility toward the Christian religion, probably because of the threat of persecution he and other "pagans" were constantly being subjected to by Christian authorities.

PROCLUS ON RELIGION. Beyond the One there is no further principle. The One is identical with the Good, and as such the formal and final cause of the universe. There is no vacuum, however, between the One and the multiplicity of beings processing therefrom. Whatever proceeds from the principle participates in that principle as its potentiality, and remains partly similar to it. Essential, therefore, to all the actual levels of being proceeding eternally from the One (*Nous*, Soul, Nature, Matter) are not only primal Limit and Limitlessness, but also a multiplicity of Unit-Henads, through participation in which anything that is acquires its unity of being, its wholeness, its divine spark. To the extent that they are self-complete (in contrast to being mere irradiations of unity) and exist eternally alongside the One as its personifications, such Henads are identical with the *theoi,* the providential gods adored and worshiped in the many diverse, traditional religions.

To be purified of the relative evils resulting from past failures to be good, a philosopher, therefore, ought not to worship only at the local temple, but should be a minister of the whole world in common, performing perhaps the rites of Isis and the Great Mother, practicing Pythagorean vegetarianism, observing the feasts of the Olympian gods, reciting the Chaldean Oracles, or singing the Orphic hymns. The reversion by which an entity completely actualizes its potential unity also involves getting to know the nature of things through sense perception, logical thought and rational conceptualization. But ultimately the divine can be reached only by grasping intuitively the divine spark within oneself through a loving, honest, and supra-intellectual leap of faith. For this to happen, however, the soul must be lifted up by the gods themselves. The souls so gifted through their participation in the theurgic rites, will be carried by their purified vehicles back to where they came from, there to rest forever in silent, ecstatic contemplation of, not only the fiery Hecate (as in the past), but the One Itself.

Sources

Proclus. *Commentary on Plato's Parmenides*. Translated by Glenn R. Morrow and John M. Dillon. Princeton: Princeton University Press, 1987.

_____. *The Elements of Theology*. Translated by E.R. Dodds. Oxford: At the Clarendon Press, 1963.

_____. *On the Eternity of the World*. Translation by Helen S. Lang and A.D. Macro. Berkeley, Los Angeles, and London: University of California Press, 2001.

_____. *On the Existence of Evils*. Translated by Jan Opsomer and Carlos Steel. Ithaca, NY: Cornell University Press, 2003.

Copleston, Frederick, S.J. *A History of Philosophy*. Vol. 1, pt. 2. Garden City, NY: Doubleday and Company, Inc., 1962–77. 221–25.

Dillon, John M. "Introduction and Notes." In Proclus, *Commentary on Plato's Parmenides*. Princeton: Princeton University Press, 1987. xi–xliv; 3–18; 93–100; 145–56; 195–209; 324–31; 385–99; 474–91.

Dodds, E.R. "Introduction and Commentary." In Proclus, *The Elements of Theology*. Oxford: At the Clarendon Press, 1963. ix–xlvi; 187–310.

Marinus of Neapolis. *Proclus, or On Happiness*. Translated by Mark Edwards. Liverpool: Liverpool University Press, 2000. 58–115.

Mason, Charles Peter. "Proclus." In *A Dictionary of Greek and Roman Biography and Mythology*.

Vol. 3. Edited by William Smith. New York: AMS Press, Inc., 1967. 533–37.

Rist, J.M. *Plotinus: The Road to Reality*. Cambridge: At the University Press, 1967. 188–96; 238–48.

Siorvanes, Lucas. *Proclus: Neo-Platonic Philosophy and Science*. New Haven and London: Yale University Press, 1996.

Sweeney, L. "Proclus." *New Catholic Encyclopedia*. Vol. 11. Edited by W.J. McDonald. New York: McGraw-Hill, 1967. 825.

Proudfoot, Wayne (1939–)

Proudfoot was brought up in the Methodist Church. His father, who had been trained in a liberal tradition reminiscent of the Social Gospel movement, was a Methodist minister, first in New Hampshire and Massachusetts, and then in the state of Washington. Proudfoot did his undergraduate studies at Yale University, majoring in physics and successfully graduating in 1961 with a B.S. degree in that field. While studying at Yale, he was active in the Methodist Student Movement and eventually became its national president. This activity, combined with his involvement in social action during the early days of the civil rights movement, inclined him, after graduation from Yale, to enroll in Harvard's Divinity School.

For a time he considered following in the footsteps of his father to become a minister, and toward that end received a Bachelor of Divinity degree in 1965 and a Master of Theology degree in the following year. By that time, however, his interest in religion had become increasingly academic. So, instead of pursuing a ministerial career, he decided to stay on at Harvard and entered its Ph.D. program in the study of religion, specializing in theology and the philosophy of religion. He received the Ph.D. from Harvard in 1972.

After teaching for a year at Andover Newton Theological School and for another two years at Fordham University, he joined the Department of Religion at Columbia University. As a professor there he has taught courses on eighteenth- and nineteenth-century European religious thought, theories and methods for the study of religion, philosophy of religion, and pragmatism and religion. His research interests have included contemporary philosophy of religion, the ideas of religious experience and mysticism, classical and contemporary pragmatism (especially James and Peirce), modern Protestant thought, and the relation of science and religion. Among his many articles and books was the 1985 publication, *Religious Experience*, in which he applied psychology's "attribution theory" to the study of religion, and for which he won the American Academy of Religion Award for Excellence. Although he has not had membership in any church since graduation from Harvard, and disclaims any longer being religious, he remains very much interested in religion.

PROUDFOOT ON RELIGION. With the metaphysical and teleological arguments traditionally used to justify religious beliefs being dismantled by Kant and Hume, and the authority of the Bible and the Church's *magisterium* being undercut by historical criticism, Schleiermacher, Rudolf Otto, Mircea Eliade and others have tried to rescue religion by claiming that it is grounded in the human experience of dependency, stupor, or some other feeling about the sacredness, the infinite depth, or the mystery of reality. Such a religious experience, they say, is altogether autonomous (in the sense of standing on its own, independent of any concepts, beliefs, grammatical rules, and practices), and to that extent is irreducible to any cluster of phenomena that can be explained in historical, psychological, or sociological terms. This might make for a good apologetic strategy, since it implies that the religious experience is totally immune to scientific scrutiny and can be understood only by those who have somehow or other shared in the experience. But it is based on a failure to distinguish properly between a description of the religious experience and its explanation.

To describe the religious experience adequately one must take into account the belief of the person having the experience that it is of supernatural origin. It is such belief, and not (as Alston claims) a raw perception of a presumably existing, divine object, that constitutes the experience religious. But an explanation of the experience is another matter. Here the concern is no longer for what the religious person believes to be the cause of his or her experience, nor necessarily for determining whether there are any grounds for such belief. The concern is rather for why the individual believes as he or she does, and how historical, psychological, or sociological factors might have inclined him or her to interpret as religious an experience that might in fact be a symbolic mapping of reality in terms of self-knowledge, or nothing more, perhaps, than an exercise in wishful thinking, an hallucination, an error in judgment, or whatever, depending upon the evidence at hand.

Sources

Proudfoot, Wayne. *God and the Self: Three Types of Philosophy of Religion*. Lewisburg, PA: Bucknell University Press; London: Associated University Presses, 1976.
_____. *Religious Experience*. Berkeley, Los Angeles, and London: University of California Press, 1985.
Peterson, Michael, William Hasker, Bruce Reichenbach, and David Basinger. *Reason and Religious Belief: An Introduction to the Philosophy of Religion*. New York and Oxford: Oxford University Press, 2003. 24–27.

Pythagoras (c. 570? B.C.)

By many of his followers Pythagoras was reported to have been a Hyperborean, quasi-divine, shaman-like figure with a golden thigh, who had been fathered by Apollo and who, like his Olympian cousins, could bi-locate, be adulated by the river Casas, and have the animal kingdom at his beck and call. More reliable, however, is the information that after being born and spending the first thirty years of his life on the island of Samos, he migrated to Croton (in southern Italy) and stayed there for about twenty years, before finally being forced to flee to Metapontum, where he remained until his death.

His flight from Croton was precipitated by a popular reaction against the exclusive, semi-monastic brotherhood he had formed in that city with three hundred of his followers who had been willing to swear allegiance to him and devote their lives to the study and practice of his mathematical, philosophical and religious views, all the while maintaining the strictest secrecy about what they were hearing from their master (who himself, for all that is known, never wrote anything). What they were hearing basically was that to find salvation and escape reincarnation their souls would have to be purified not only by inquiry into the harmonic nature of the cosmos, but also through the application of such knowledge to the practical conduct of their lives. This meant, among other things, abandoning their previous hedonistic manner of living and observing periods of silence, solitary walking, communal dining, certain dietary rules and any other ascetical regulations enjoined by Pythagoras.

Given the high respect in which he was held by his followers, there is no reason to suspect that he did not himself practice what he preached. Isocrates would later comment, rather cynically, that Pythagoras was "more conspicuous than anyone else" in the performance of "sacrifices and temple purifications." If he was eventually driven from Croton, it was more for political than religious reasons. Most of his early adherents were from noble and wealthy classes. Like them, Pythagoras apparently harbored rather aristocratic ideas about how to organize the *polis*. This did not set well with Croton's democratic party, and under the leadership of Cylon (who may still have been smarting also over being excluded from the brotherhood), its members attacked the Pythagorean community, burning down its meeting place and killing many of its members. Arnobius claimed that their leader perished with them in the flames. But most later accounts have him escaping, first to Tarentum, and then to Metaponton, where he eventually died from what, according to some questionable reports, was a Jain-style quest for spiritualization by way of self-starvation.

PYTHAGORAS ON RELIGION. If life in this world is as good as Homer would have us believe, one could readily understand why he would have Achilles say that he would prefer being a slave among the living than the lord of those pale, bloodless ghosts sitting around Hades gloomily bemoaning their loss of terrestrial delights. But life may not be so good here and now, nor so bad after death, as Homer presumed. And motivated by discontent with the daily frustrations of this life, we might all yearn to become like the gods and place our hope in the immortality of our souls. To find such salvation, however, our souls will first have to be purified. And for that to happen, it will not be enough merely to perform a few Dionysian or Orphic rituals.

As the sages of ancient India have taught us, the future plight of our souls is altogether tied to our deeds, to the way we live, in this life. If our deeds are bad, our souls will be subjected to a cycle of reincarnations in the form of one animal species or another. If, upon taking human form again, our souls are finally purified, they will be released from the tomb of their bodies and return to the starry heavens, there to enjoy, if not deathless continuation of personal identity, at least the preservation of the group-soul's memory throughout an eternally recurring process of universal events. Abstaining from the eating of meat, along with obedience of all the other communal precepts, is important. But the best way to purify the soul is through cultivation of a love of wisdom. Like spectators at the Olympian games who rise above the commercial and competitive interests of the hawkers and athletes to focus instead upon an analysis of what is happening around them, the philosopher's theoretical thinking liberates him from preoccupation with the particular details of life, setting him free to focus on what is really real, namely, the numerical forms (e.g., the *tetraktys*) by which the universal polarities (e.g., male/female, one/many) are defined (i.e., delimited) in a harmonious way. The study of mathematics is essential, therefore, to a religious appreciation of the music of the spheres that sets the soul free.

Sources

Barnes, Jonathan. *Early Greek Philosophy*. Harmondsworth, UK: Penguin Books, 1987. 81–88; 202–13.

Cornford, F.M. From *Religion to Philosophy*. New York: Harper and Row, 1957. 194–212.

_____. "Mysticism and Science in the Pythagorean Tradition." *The Classical Quarterly* XVI (1922): 137–50.

Diogenes Laertius. *Lives of Eminent Philosophers*. Translated by R.D. Hicks. Cambridge, MA: Harvard University Press, 1972. 321–67.

Gorman, Peter. *Pythagoras: A Life*. London: Routledge and Kegan Paul, 1979.

Iamblichus. *On the Pythagorian Way of Life*. Translated by John Dillon and Jackson Hershbell. Atlanta, GA: Scholars Press, 1990.

Jones, W.T. *The Classical Mind: A History of Western Philosophy*. New York: Harcourt, Brace and World, Inc., 1969. 31–39.

Kahn, Charles H. *Pythagoras and the Pythagoreans*. Indianapolis and Cambridge: Hackett Publishing Company, Inc., 2001.

Mason, Charles Peter. "Pythagoras." In *A Dictionary of Greek and Roman Biography and Mythology*. Vol. 3. Edited by William Smith. New York: AMS Press, Inc., 1967. 616–25.

Philip, J.A. *Pythagoras and Early Pythagoreanism*. Toronto: University of Toronto Press, 1966.

Ramsey, Bennett. "Pythagoras." In *Encyclopedia of Religion*. Vol. 12. Edited by Mircea Eliade. New York: Macmillan and Co., 1987. 113–15.

Stumpf, Samuel Enoch. *Socrates to Sartre. A History of Philosophy*. New York: McGraw-Hill Book Company, 1982. 8–12.

Waterfield, Robin. *The First Philosophers: The Presocratics and Sophists*. Oxford: Oxford University Press, 2000. 87–99.

Wheelwright, Philip, ed. "Pythagoreanism." In *The Presocratics*. New York: The Odyssey Press, Inc., 1966. 200–34.

Radhakrishnan, Sarvepalli (1888–1975)

Radhakrishnan was born in Tirutani, a pilgrimage center close to Madras in southeast India. His relatively poor parents belonged to the Brahmin class and would pass on to their son their special devotion to the god Krishna. Much of his early education was received in Christian missionary schools whose German, Dutch, and Scottish teachers were generally very critical of what they considered to be the primitive and idolatrous polytheism rampant at the pilgrimage centers. Though tolerant of the religious traditions of their students, they thought of Hinduism as being at best God's way of preparing individuals for the superior religion of Christianity.

Smarting from the constant criticism, but suspecting its legitimacy, Radhakrishnan determined to make a closer study of his native religion while pursuing B.A. and M.A. degrees in philosophy at the Madras Christian College. An ethics professor at the college (A.G. Hogg) taught him to distinguish the experience that lay at the heart of various religions from all their doctrinal and ritualistic trappings. Under the influence of his reading of works by Swami Vivekananda, he came to view the Advaita Vedanta as precisely such an experiential essence of Hinduism, and in the thesis he wrote for his master's degree he insisted that, contrary to the claims of some, Hinduism, with its emphasis upon the law of Karma and rebirth, was actually rich in sound ethical implications.

The thesis was only the first in the long list of works he would subsequently publish in defense of "the religion of the Upanishads" while serving for many years as a professor of philosophy at various Indian universities, lecturing around the world, and eventually becoming his liberated country's president in 1962. In one of his earliest books he strongly objected to religious philosophy or the intrusion of authoritarian religion into contemporary philosophy, and throughout his life he would insist upon the independence of philosophy and the separation of religion from the state and other secular institutions. But he also remained convinced that any genuine philosophy or political system would be open to the kind of monistic idealism or philosophical religion found in the Vedanta and at the heart of every religion (as exemplified by the Christian mystical tradition in which he developed an especial interest after retiring). Shortly before his death and cremation in 1975, he became the first non–Christian to receive the Templeton Prize for Progress in Religion.

RADHAKRISHNAN ON RELIGION. What Kant said of metaphysics is equally true of religion. The instinct for it is indestructible. Mankind must and will have religion. Because of the difficulties of traditional religious belief— its conflict with the empiricism and determinism of modern science and technology, its dogmatic authoritarianism, its bewildering variety, its dualism, and its divisive exclusivism — many people in recent centuries have turned to neo-pagan, naturalistic, humanistic, and nationalistic forms of worshiping man himself. But these new loyalties only breed new illusions. They cannot satisfy man's instinctive need for an experience of ultimate reality as a whole.

Only philosophically grounded religion, through intuitive experience of the identity of the True Self with the Transcendent Supreme (either as the Supra-personal Absolute or, at a lower level, as the Personal God), can meet such a need. But for that to happen, the various particular religions must be transformed to reflect the kind of monistic view of reality revealed in the Vedanta, the "eternal religion of the spirit" that transcends every race and creed, and conceives of the spiritual unity of mankind as the "goal of history." So transformed, the particular religions will respect the freedom of the individual as a manifestation of the Supreme, and aim, not at the mere conformity of minds to inherited doctrine or ritualistic piety, but at a renewal of consciousness such as might awaken individuals to their connection with the ultimate sources of reality, integrate their personalities by fusing intellectual, emotional, and volitional powers, spawn in them a fresh ethical sense of truth and social justice, and make the divine in them manifest. Given its traditional tolerance of views other than its own, Hinduism especially has displayed a capacity for such ongoing transformation. But every religion is capable of it, and all the particular religions can best be seen as "parts of an evolving revelation" that might in time be "taken over into the larger religion of the spirit."

Sources

Radhakrishnan, S. *The Hindu View of Life*. New York: The Macmillan Company, 1962.
_____. *An Idealist View of Life*. London: Allen and Unwin, Ltd., 1932.
_____. *Indian Philosophy*. 2 vols. New York: The Macmillan Company, 1927.
_____. *Recovery of Faith*. London: George Allen and Unwin, Ltd., 1956.
_____. *Religion and Society*. London: George Allen and Unwin, Ltd., 1948.
_____. "The Religion of the Spirit and the World's Need: Fragments of a Confession." In Schilpp, *The Philosophy of Sarvepalli Radhakrishnan*. 5–82.
Aubrey, Bryan, and Roy Wood Sellars. "Sarvepalli Radhakrishnan." In *World Philosophers and Their Works*. Vol. 3. Edited by John K. Roth. Pasadena, CA, and Hackensack, NJ: Salem Press, Inc., 2000. 1594–1603.
Minor, Robert N. *Radhakrishnan: A Religious Biography*. Albany: State University of New York Press, 1987.
Schilpp, Paul Arthur. *The Philosophy of Sarvepalli Radhakrishnan*. New York: Tudor Publishing Co., 1952.

Rand, Ayn (1905–1990)

Alisa Zinovievna Rosenbaum (as Rand was named at birth) was born into an affluent Jewish family in St. Petersburg, Russia. Neither of her parents, however, took their Jewish faith seriously. With the father having disengaged himself from religion altogether, and the mother practicing it in only a perfunctory manner, the family was Jewish in name only. As a result, Rand received almost no formal religious training while growing up in the city of her birth during the tumultuous years of the Communist Revolution. At the young age of thirteen she made an entry in her diary declaring that "today I decided that I am an atheist," because "there are no reasons or rational proof for believing in God," and because the concept of God is "morally evil" to the extent that it implies a need on the part of humans to worship an ideal they cannot themselves achieve.

During her first year (1921) at the University of Petrograd she developed a profound respect for Aristotelian logic and epistemology, considered Nietzsche as a possible spiritual ally before becoming disappointed by his antirationalism, and was completely put off by the philosophy of Plato, on the same grounds basically that she had also come to despise all religions and her own country, namely, what she perceived to be their inveterate mysticism and their spirit of collective altruism. Jumping at an opportunity to flee the spiritual constrictions of her native country's Communist regime, she came to the United States in 1926, changed her name, and while working in Hollywood met Frank O'Connor, who, because of its supposedly "nonsensical" doctrine of original sin, had himself become disillusioned with the Christian religion into which he had been born. Impressed by his intellectual independence and rationality, she found him the perfect "soul mate," and entered into a fifty-year marriage to him, notwithstanding an alleged extramarital affair with the leading figure among the Objectivist "disciples" (the "class of '43," as she called them) that had begun flocking around her in the 1950s after publication and filming of her novel, *The Fountainhead*. Her next major work, another piece of fiction entitled *Atlas Shrugged*, was rightly perceived and often criticized as a moral defense of capitalism that challenged "the entire tradition of Judeo-Christian [altruistic] ethics." She went to her death in 1982 adhering to her conviction that there is no afterlife.

RAND ON RELIGION. Man's distinctive characteristic and basic means of survival is his particular type of consciousness, namely, the faculty of reason. It is man's only means of perceiving reality, which as an objective absolute consists of facts that are independent of man's feelings, wishes, hopes, or fears. This supremacy of reason constitutes the essence of Objectivism. Religion, by cultivating a belief that is unsupported, or contrary to, the facts of reality and the conclusions of reason, is of no real value. True, as a primitive form of philosophy, it tried to develop a comprehensive view of reality and code of morality. But it was only a helplessly blind groping. And when, thanks mainly to Aristotle, philosophy finally did come of age, it rightly claimed for itself (notwithstanding the skepticism of some) the grand dedication to the pursuit of truth once associated with religion.

Religious faith is, in fact, a negation of reason. To exist is to possess an identity. But all the religious identifications of God consist of negating. Lacking any valid metaphysical reason for identifying God as infinite, omnipotent, and so on, religious faith ends up telling us that God is that which no human can know, and then asking us to consider such negation knowledge. So, too, in regard to the supernatural realm in general. Against the evidence of one's reason, mystical faith claims to perceive — intuitively or through divine revelation — some other reality whose definition is only that it is not natural. Such faith in the supernatural began as faith in the superiority of others when, in the clash of diverse opinions, some became afraid of thinking for themselves and supposed that others possessed a mysterious knowledge which they themselves lacked. In the process, they became enslaved to religious authorities, who proceeded to forbid everything (capitalistic production, sexual love, etc.) that makes existence on earth enjoyable. To redeem themselves, people need to start trusting their own minds again and realize that an error made on one's own is safer than ten truths accepted on faith.

Sources

Rand, Ayn. *Atlas Shrugged*. New York: Plume, 1999.
_____. *For the New Intellectual*. New York: Random House, 1961.
_____. *Introduction to Objectivist Epistemology*. New York: Meridian, 1990.
_____. *The Objectivist*. New York: The Objectivist, 1966–1971.
_____. *Philosophy, who needs it?* Indianapolis: Bobbs-Merrill, 1982.
_____. *The Romantic Manifesto*. New York: New American Library, 1975.
Binswanger, Harry, ed. *The Ayn Rand Lexicon: Objectivism from A to Z*. New York: New American Library, 1986.
Branden, Barbara, and Nathaniel Branden. *Who is Ayn Rand?* New York: Random House, 1962. See esp. the "Biographical Essay," 149–239.
Gladstein, Mimi Reisel. *The New Ayn Rand Companion*. Revised and expanded edition. Westport, CT, and London: Greenwood Press, 1999.
Peikoff, Leonard. *Objectivism: The Philosophy of Ayn Rand*. New York: Dutton (New American Library), 1991.

Randall, John Herman, Jr. (1899–1980)

Randall's ancestors were Calvinists. His father was a Baptist minister who had taken his training at the Chicago Divinity School back in the 1890s. To provide better educational opportunities for his son, the father moved the family from Grand Rapids, Michigan, to New York City. Randall graduated Phi Beta Kappa from Columbia University with a B.A. in 1918 and an M.A. the following year. While at Columbia he attended Sunday services at a nearby church on Convent Avenue to which his father had been appointed pastor. He no doubt heard many a sermon and got no little theological tutelage from his father. Later he would chide his father for having led him to underestimate the Apostle Paul's version of the Christian message, but he also collaborated with him in the writing and 1929 publication of *Religion and the Modern World*.

While still working on his Ph.D., Randall was hired to lecture in Columbia's philosophy department, alongside the likes of John Dewey and Frederick J.E. Woodbridge. After completing his doctoral work in 1922 and getting married, he decided to stay on at Columbia. And he would, in fact, teach there for the next half-century, eventually working his way up through the professorial ranks to become the Woodbridge Professor of Philosophy in 1951. In addition to the numerous books and articles he would publish over those years on the history of philosophy and the making of modern science were also many on the subject of religion. His interest in religion was more than theoretical. He undoubtedly shared the disillusionment of his generation over the seemingly senseless slaughter of lives in World War I and early on developed a sympathy for Quaker pacifism.

It is said that, after drifting from the religion of his childhood, Randall aligned himself with three different religious groups: the Universalist Church, the Society of Ethical Culture, and the Quakers. His affinity with the latter group became especially pronounced during World War II. Already in 1933 he had signed a faculty statement issued by the Columbia Socialist Club denouncing "rampant economic nationalism and individualism which threaten to sweep the world into another war." But when the war came, he refused, despite Hitler's obvious threat to democracy, to condone the use of military force against Germany's Nazi regime. He conceived it as part of his mission as a philosopher to challenge the basic assumptions underlying all intellectual traditions. This included occasionally calling into question the fundamental beliefs of one or another religion, not because of any hostility toward religion in general, but as his writings on the subject clearly indicate, because he wanted to help keep religion alive in the modern world.

RANDALL ON RELIGION. Religion, like every other human activity (art, physics, etc.), is part of the subject matter of existence which philosophy must try to understand. To do so, it is necessary to move beyond the old conflict between science and religion. That conflict had grown out of the traditional interpretation of religion as a form of knowledge that contains verifiable truths about the existence and nature of God, and so forth. As the cultural sciences of anthropology, history, and sociology have themselves shown, however, religious beliefs are without exception mythological and as such lack the literal truth of scientific, factual statements. They are symbols which, instead of being interpreted as sources of knowledge and truth, should be evaluated in non-cognitive terms of what they do, how they function. One way they function is to provoke an emotional response and to motivate appropriate human activities. A second way they function is, as Dewey has emphasized, to contribute to the building up of community life by provoking common or shared experiences. They also function like artistic symbols (as opposed to mere signs) and communicate certain ineffable aspects of the shared experiences that are hard to put into the precise words or statements of everyday language. Finally, and most importantly, religious symbols reveal something about the world; they do not tell us anything that is verifiably so, but they help us see the divine splendor of our experienced world; they provide us with an imaginative insight into or a vision of the powers and possibilities inherent in the nature of things — what Tillich calls the "power of Being" or, insofar as it pertains to the potential of human existence, man's "ultimate concern." God and other religious symbols exist, therefore, only as products of the human imagination, and religion, far from being a mystic intuition of some supernatural realm, consists rather of the art of knowing how to open one's heart for seeing the Divine in the midst of human life in the natural world.

Sources

Randall, John Herman, Jr. *The Irrepressible Conflict in Religion.* New York: Dodge Publishing Company, 1925.

_____. "The Religion of Shared Experience." In John Herman Randall, Jr., *Philosophy After Darwin: Chapters for the career of Philosophy,* volume III, and other essays. New York: Columbia University Press, 1977. 241–67.

_____. *The Role of Knowledge in Western Religion.* Boston: Starr King Press; Boston: Beacon Hill, 1958.

Anton, John P., ed. *Naturalism and Historical Understanding: Essays on the Philosophy of John Herman Randall, Jr.* Albany: State University of New York Press, 1967.

Anton, John P. "Randall, John Herman, Jr." In *American National Biography.* Vol. 18. Edited by John A. Garraty and Mark C. Carnes. New York and Oxford: Oxford University Press, 1999. 113–14.

Arnett, Willard E. "Are the Arts and Religions Cognitive?" In Anton, *Naturalism.* 232–42.

Friess, Horace L. "A Naturalistic View of 'Functioning Religiously.'" In Anton, *Naturalism.* 243–51.

Hick, John. *Philosophy of Religion.* 3rd ed. Englewood Cliffs, NJ: Prentice-Hall, Inc., 1983. 83–86.

Juffras, Angelo. "John Herman Randall, Jr." *American Philosophers,* 1950–2000. Edited by Philip B. Dematteis and Leemon B. McHenry. Detroit: Thomson/Gale, 2003. 273–84. (Includes an extensive bibliography of Randall's books and articles).

New York Times, "Obituary," December 3, 1980, B11.

Smith, John E. "Randall's Interpretation of the Role of Knowledge in Religion." In Anton, *Naturalism.* 252–61.

Rawls, John (1921–2002)

His father a self-taught lawyer, and his mother an activist championing voting rights for women, Rawls' eventual engagement in political philosophy came naturally. His original interest, however, lay elsewhere. After first attending Baltimore elementary public schools, Rawls transferred to the renowned preparatory boarding school in Kent, Connecticut, which, founded in the Episcopal tradition, actively encouraged moral and spiritual growth and a sense of community on the part of its ninth- to twelfth-grade students by requiring attendance at Sunday and two weekday chapel services and enrollment in introductory theology and comparative religion courses.

There, and at Princeton University where he went next to pursue an undergraduate degree, Rawls gradually made up his mind to become a minister. But with World War II still raging when he graduated from Princeton in 1943, he enlisted instead in the army and was still serving as an infantryman in the Pacific arena when the U.S. dropped atomic bombs on Hiroshima and Nagasaki in 1945. He later observed that the war overshadowed everything he had experienced as a student and aroused his interest in questions about international justice. But it apparently also nipped in the bud his earlier intention to become an Episcopalian priest and raised serious doubts about his religious beliefs in general. For upon returning from military service, Rawls, according to his future wife, simply gave up (without telling anyone why) his ministerial aspiration and resumed instead his pursuit of a Ph.D. at Princeton, writing a doctoral dissertation in moral philosophy.

Over the remaining years of his life — marrying and raising a family, winning a Fulbright Scholarship to Oxford, teaching at Princeton, Cornell, MIT, and Harvard, and writing multiple articles on political philosophy, but waiting until 1971 to publish his first book (the bestselling *A Theory of Justice*) and another twenty before issuing several more (e.g., *Political Liberalism* and *Justice as Fair-*

ness) in defense of the first against considerable criticism — he would leave colleagues and friends (like Hilary Putnam and Ben Rogers) with the impression of being a "profoundly wise and good person," albeit also "a very complex and troubled man, who, although not a believer, had retained an essentially religious outlook." Following a series of strokes, he died of a heart attack at the age of eighty-one. A memorial service was held at the First Parish Unitarian Universalist Church in Lexington.

RAWLS ON RELIGION. Contrary to supposedly enlightened expectations, the vast majority of Americans still profess to be religious. Unlike the ancient world that knew nothing of the clash between salvationist, creedal, and expansionist religions, this profession of religion in America is very pluralistic. The question arises then about how in a constitutional democracy such as our own, all the different religions, each with its own comprehensive doctrine, can cooperate in running a reasonably just and effective government. Fighting it out, or settling for a mere *modus vivendi* between warring parties, as they did in sixteenth-century Europe, obviously will not work. And thanks to James Madison's insistence upon the separation of church and state, the attempt to allow individual states to establish one or another religion did not prevail in our own country. Nor is the solution to be found in trying to present the conception of justice as fairness (with its two principles of liberty and difference arising out of the original position of veiled ignorance) as a comprehensive doctrine that might serve as an alternative to Utilitarianism or any other moral, philosophical, or religious comprehensive theory. That would only add to the instability.

What is needed is a noncomprehensive, freestanding, political conception of justice that applies only to the basic constitutional structure of a democratic society (right to vote, etc.), and upon which citizens profoundly divided by reasonable though incompatible religious doctrines can achieve an overlapping consensus on the basis of public reasoning about certain latent fundamental ideas (e.g.,

citizens as free and equal persons) that is independent of any commitment to their comprehensive religious views. For the sake of mutual civility, trust, and respect, and depending on the issue at stake and the parties involved, this will impose certain restrictions upon any appeal to religious beliefs in public debate, but it need not result in their complete prohibition or privatization if presented as public reasons.

Sources

Rawls, John. *Collected Papers*. Cambridge, MA, and London: Harvard University Press, 1999.

———. *Political Liberalism*. New York: Columbia University Press, 1993.

———. *A Theory of Justice*. Cambridge, MA: Harvard University Press, 1971.

Dombrowski, Daniel A. *Rawls and Religion: The Case for Political Liberalism*. Albany: State University of New York Press, 2001.

Feeney, Mark. "John Rawls, Towering Figure of Political Philosophy." Obituary in *Boston Globe*, November 26, 2002. http://nl.newsbank.com/nl-search/we/Archives. 1–3.

Fern, Richard L. "Religious Belief in a Rawlsian Society." *The Journal of Religious Ethics* 15 (1987): 35–58.

Hollenbach, David. "Public Reason/Private Religion? A Response to Paul J. Weithman." *Journal of Religious Ethics* 22.1 (1994): 39–46.

Langan, John, S.J. "Overcoming the Divisiveness of Religion: A Response to Paul J. Weithman." *Journal of Religious Ethics* 22.1 (1994): 47–51.

———. "Rawls, Nozick, and the Search for Social Justice." *Theological Studies* 38.2 (June 1977): 346–58.

Martin, Douglas. "John Rawls, Theorist on Justice, Is Dead at 82 [81]." Obituary in *The New York Times*, November 26, 2002. http://query.ny times.com/search/restricted/article. 1–3.

Owen, J. Judd. *Religion and the Demise of Liberal Rationalism: The Foundational Crisis of the Separation of Church and State*. Chicago and London: The University of Chicago Press, 2001. See esp. 97–128.

Prusak, Bernard G. "Politics, Religion and the Public Good: An Interview with Philosopher John Rawls." *Commonweal* (September 25, 1998). 12–17.

Rogers, Ben. "John Rawls." Obituary in *The Guardian*, November 27, 2002. http://www.guardian.co.uk/obituaries. 1–7.

Sterba, James P. "Rawls and Religion." In *The Idea of a Political Liberalism*. edited by Victoria Davion and Clark Wolf. Lanham: Rowman and Littlefield Publishers, Inc., 2000. 34–45.

Weithman, Paul J. "Rawlsian Liberalism and the Privatization of Religion." *Journal of Religious Studies* 22.1 (Spring 1994): 3–28.

Reid, Thomas (1710–1796)

Reid grew up in the small, rural Scottish town of Strachan. The Gregory family from which his mother came included a long line of distinguished professors of mathematics, history, and science. But his tendency to view the world in terms of its moral and religious dimensions was probably inherited from his father, the Reverend Lewis Reid, a devout, highly respected and longtime pastor of the parish of Strachan. Many of the father's ancestors had been ministers of the Church of Scotland from the time of the Reformation. After years of being home-educated, Reid spent two years in the parish school of neighboring Kincardine. Then, at the age of twelve, he was enrolled at Marischal College in Aberdeen, a town that had outgrown its religiously spawned, anti-intellectual past by allying its religion with a more progressive and enlightened culture. His regent there was George Turnbull, the son of a Presbyterian minister and himself later an ordained Irish-Anglican minister. His instruction of Reid in moral philosophy, notwithstanding a resemblance to Berkeley's views, played up the role of common sense in determining one's obligations to God and fellow humans and favored an empirical approach over any kind of rationalistic apriorism.

Upon graduation from Marischal in 1726, Reid took up the study of theology, and was eventually licensed "to preach the Gospel of Christ, and to exercise his gifts as a probationer for the [Presbyterian] holy ministry." After a number of years serving as Clerk to the Presbytery and librarian at Marischal College and traveling to England, he was appointed pastor of New Machar (Northwest of Aberdeen). Despite initial problems resulting from the parishioners' suspicion of nepotism, he and his newly wedded wife won the parish over by their gentle religiosity. An indication of Reid's own deep spirituality can be found in the prayer he offered on an occasion of his wife's serious illness. A reading of Hume's *Treatise of Human Nature* in 1739 alerted him to the dangers of modern agnosticism, and much of Reid's subsequent writing (e.g., the *Inquiry*) as a professor of philosophy at King's College in Aberdeen and at the University of Glasgow (where he succeeded Adam Smith) would concern itself with calling into question the epistemological foundation of Hume's skepticism. He remained true to his "rational piety" till the day he died in 1796, and was buried in Glasgow's College Church cemetery.

REID ON RELIGION. Some persons seem to think that religion is an unnecessary encumbrance to an active and virtuous life. But such individuals must either be hypocrites or grossly deluded. For if it makes sense to honor parents or to be grateful to benefactors, it is all the more reasonable to reverence our heavenly Father, whose offspring we are in a stricter sense than of our earthly parents, or to thank the Almighty upon whose protection we are more dependent than upon any other benefactor. Furthermore, Jews, Christians, and heathens alike all testify to the joy and consolation that religion can bring in times of greatest distress. There are, of course, empty forms of religion that consist only in the performance — often hypocritical — of external rites and ceremonies. But a religion that is without any articles of faith is a contradiction in terms. While, therefore, the State should be tolerant of a diversity of religious views and not try to use religion to justify tyranny, it also has the duty to provide its citizens with religious instruction in the articles of belief that are essential to any religion it might establish.

The primary source of such beliefs is revelation, which discloses truths that lie beyond reason. But revelation also teaches a natural religion, further elucidating truths which reason — being no less a gift from God than revelation — discovers on its own. Among such truths is belief in the existence of God as the eternal and perfect First Cause whose Supreme Intelligence and Goodness is everywhere evident in nature's design, notwithstanding imperfections and evils of a natural or — because of human freedom — a moral sort. But being less innate, universal and automatic than the First Principles of knowledge (e.g., "the natural faculties by which we distinguish truth from error, are not fallacious"), such a belief in God is not necessarily basic, and however helpful in grounding the reliability of the First Principles, need not be deemed essential to the same in any Common Sense, nonidealistic approach to philosophy.

Sources

Reid, Thomas. *Essays on the Intellectual Powers of Man.* Edited by A.D. Woozley. London: Macmillan and Company, Limited, 1941.
_____. *Practical Ethics: Being Lectures and Papers on Natural Religion, Self-government, Natural Jurisprudence, and the Law of Nations.* Princeton: Princeton University Press, 1990.
Bary, Philip de. *Thomas Reid and Scepticism: His reliablist response.* London and New York: Routledge, 2002. See esp. 64–89; 165–91.
Copleston, Frederick, S.J. *A History of Philosophy.* Vol. 5, pt. 2. Garden City, NY: Doubleday and Company, Inc., 1962–77. 167–76.
Fraser, Alexander Campbell. *Thomas Reid.* Edinburgh and London: Oliphant Anderson, 1898.
Haldane, John, and Stephen Read, eds. *The Philosophy of Thomas Reid: A Collection of Essays.* Oxford: Blackwell Publishing, 2003.
Lehrer, Keith. *Thomas Reid.* London and New York: Routledge, 1991.
Stewart, Dugald. "Account of the Life and Writings of Thomas Reid, D.D. F.R.S." In *Works.* Vol. VII. Cambridge, UK: Hilliard and Brown, 1829. 205–89.
Tuggy, Dale. "Reid's Philosophy of Religion." In *The Cambridge Companion to Thomas Reid,* edited by Terence Cuneo and René Woudenberg. Cambridge: Cambridge University Press, 2004. 289–312.

Rescher, Nicholas (1928–)

The Westphalian family into which Rescher was born had nominal membership in Germany's predominant Lutheran-Evangelical Church. Rescher himself was baptized and confirmed, but by his own account, religion played only a marginal role in his life as a child. Little changed when, at the age of

nine, he and his mother immigrated to New York to rejoin his father (a lawyer whose hostility to Nazism had earlier inclined him to flee Germany). Preoccupation with his study of mathematics and philosophy during teenage student days precluded any "serious engagement in religious concerns." It was not until 1952 when, after graduating from Princeton University with a doctorate in philosophy, he began a two-year, noncombative stint in the military during the Korean War and became aware of how uncertain and contingent human life can be, that he became "more open-minded toward religion."

With the death of his father at about the same time, his mother had become active in the California branch of the Quaker religion. Influenced by her example, Rescher himself began attending Meetings of the Friends in Santa Monica (where he was employed by the Rand Corporation). Impressed by their lack of a dogmatic creed, their quiet manner of worship, and their compassionate humanity, he finally joined their community. He continued attending Quaker Meetings and even became one of that religion's "overseers" after accepting a professorial position at Lehigh University.

Upon his appointment as a professor of philosophy at the University of Pittsburgh in 1961, however, his attachment to the Quaker community began to wane. He started attending Mass with his Roman Catholic wife, and eventually, in 1981, joined her church — not by reasoning, but as Pascal had recommended, by association. Faced with a choice of whether to align himself with "religion-disdaining" Voltaires, Humes, Nietzsches, and Russells, or with "theistically committed" Platos, Anselms, Aquinases, Leibnizes and Hegels, he chose the latter as his "spiritual kindred" because of their "transcendent aspirations" and the seriousness of their worship and thought. While publishing hundreds of articles and books in every field of philosophy, launching and editing several scholarly journals, providing leadership to a number of philosophical societies, and winning multiple awards, he continues teaching philosophy at the University of Pittsburgh and remains as committed as ever to his Catholic faith.

RESCHER ON RELIGION. Contrary to what the Post-modernists and other skeptics and relativists have suggested, there is an objective reality that, through the use of reason, can be known well enough to realize certain human ends. It is conceivable, for example, that nature may prove to be explanatorily self-contained and that science might, therefore, someday come up with a very useful explanation of all this world's phenomena in terms of nature's own processes. But there are limits to human knowledge. Even if science can "explain" the causal connections of natural phenomena, it cannot apprehend their value and meaning. For an appreciation of the latter, science must be complemented by philosophy and theology.

It is a hopeless proposition, of course, to try inferring God's existence and nature from the order of the universe, as though God were the "maker of heaven and earth" in the sense of being "part of the world's causal machinery." But philosophical and theological lines of reasoning, like Pascal's Wager Argument or, more recently, those being pursued by Whitehead and other Process thinkers, can provide at least a starting point for the discovery of value and meaning by meeting rational people where they are and appealing to their personal, long-term advantage in working along with a temporally participatory, but nonsubstantial and nonomnipotent, God toward goals that have not been preestablished. Such arguments can help induce humans to believe in a God of hope and the ultimate meaningfulness of human endeavor; it can incline individuals to take the initial step of enrolling in the community of believers, on the assumption that without religion the prospects of realizing their desired ends are greatly diminished. In the final analysis, however, access to the loving and merciful God of the Bible can only be gained through grace and the heart. Such religious faith is not irrational, for as Pascal pointed out, "the heart has its reasons too," reasons "of which Mind knows nothing."

Sources

Rescher, Nicholas. *Enlightening Journey: The Autobiography of an American Scholar.* Lanham, Boulder, New York, and Oxford: Lexington Books, 2002.

_____. *Objectivity: The Obligations of Impersonal Reason.* Notre Dame: University of Notre Dame Press, 1997.

_____. *Pascal's Wager: A Study of Practical Reasoning in Philosophical Theology.* Notre Dame: University of Notre Dame Press, 1985.

_____. *Process Metaphysics: An Introduction to Process Philosophy.* Albany: State University of New York Press, 1986.

Clark, Kelly James, ed. *Philosophers Who Believe: The Spiritual Journeys of 11 Leading Thinkers.* Downers Grove, IL: InterVarsity Press, 1993. 127–36.

Cobb, John B., Jr. "Process Philosophy." In *After Whitehead: Rescher on Process Metaphysics,* edited by Michel Weber. Frankfurt and Lancaster: Ontos Verlag, 2004. 211–21.

Hall, Richard A. Spurgeon. "Nicholas Rescher." In *World Philosophers and Their Works.* Vol. 3. Edited by John K. Roth. Pasadena, CA, and Hackensack, NJ: Salem Press, Inc., 2000. 1627–33.

Marsonet, Michele. *The Primacy of Practical Reason: An Essay on Nicholas Rescher's Philosophy.* Lanham, New York, and London: University Press of America, Inc., 1996.

Ricoeur, Paul (1913–2005)

After the death of his mother when he was only seven months old and the loss of his father two years later in the Battle of the Marne, Ricoeur went to live with his paternal grandparents. The latter belonged to a strong Huguenot tradition that reflected a mixture of liberal and Pietistic Protestantism. They preferred private biblical reading (especially the Psalms, the Book of Wisdom, and the Beatitudes), prayer, and examination of conscience over any intellectual concern about dogma. Throughout his life Ricoeur would adhere to the practice he had developed as a youth of regularly reading the Bible. The grandparents lived in the Catholic stronghold of Rennes where Protestants were perceived as outsiders — a situation, Ricoeur noted, similar to that of "Jews in a Christian milieu" that left him with the feeling of being considered a heretic by the majority. Encouraged by a philosophy teacher (Roland Dalbiez) at Rennes' secondary school not to see rational criticism as a threat to his religious convictions, Ricoeur began what would become a lifelong attempt to reconcile his Protestant upbringing on the Word of God with philosophical reflection upon the word of man.

Already in his undergraduate days he was wrestling with the duality of Bergsonian and Barthian lines of thought. At the Sorbonne, where he enrolled in 1934, Ricoeur was further challenged to engage in original thinking by his participation in the Friday evening discussions sponsored by Gabriel Marcel. Five years in a German prisoner of war camp had given him time to read the works of Husserl, Jaspers and other great philosophers who would figure into his postwar doctoral studies and publications. He became a professor at the Sorbonne in 1956 and (before ever meeting Lacan) began trying to fit Freud into "the dialectic between suspicion and faith." At the same time, he and his wife and children moved into *Les Murs Blanc*, a commune created by Emmanuel Mounier, the Catholic founder of the journal *Esprit*, to whose concern for democratic socialism he was greatly attracted.

Disillusioned with the Sorbonne and frustrated as dean of the new university at Nanterre by the student uprisings, Ricoeur eventually succeeded Paul Tillich to a chair in the Divinity School at the University of Chicago and jointly taught several courses there with his old friend Mircea Eliade, while also lecturing periodically around the world. To the end he remained a thinking Protestant, respectful of and deeply involved with other religions, but opposed to "institutional ecumenism" because of his belief in "the originally plural destination of Christianity."

RICOEUR ON RELIGION. Ignoring arguments about the existence of God, the external critique of religion propounded by the modern masters of suspicion — Marx, Nietzsche, and Freud — is an attempt to demystify religious language by exposing its underlying false or masked consciousness and deciphering its apparent message as either a coded language of domination and submission originating in the capitalistic money fetish, the expression of a slave mentality projecting its moralistic, nihilistic scorn for life into some ideal, supernatural realm, or the totemic drama of an eternal struggle of *Eros* with *Thanatos* around the father figure. This atheistic, deconstructive hermeneutics has shown religion, with its two main aspects of taboo and refuge, to be a primitive structure of life that is grounded in the fear of punishment and the desire for protection. In the process, it has smashed the illusory idols of religion (e.g., the authoritarian, provident Father-God of Retribution) and allowed for their recovery as symbols of faith (e.g., God the Father as a figure of creative love). For that to happen, however, there must also occur an internal critique of religion by way of the demythologization of the cultural vehicle (literal narrative, prophecy, hymn, etc.) in which the original expression of faith (the symbolic *kerygma,* the word "God") has been embedded.

This is a task for theologians and preachers. But Heidegger has identified the kind of being that would make something like the word of God existentially possible (i.e., one, whose essence it is, prior to all moralistic accusations or threats, to listen silently to Being, and like Job, consent to the mysterious unity of its own broken existence). Philosophy can also facilitate the faithful overcoming of religion by deconstructing modern scientistic assurances and opening a new horizon of human possibility beyond the affirmative, but deterministic, dimensions of Feuerbachian humanism.

Sources

Ricoeur, Paul. *Critique and Conviction: Conversations with François Azouvi and Marc de Launay.* Translated by Kathleen Blamey. New York: Columbia University Press, 1998.

_____. "The History of Religions and the Phenomenology of Time Consciousness." In *The History of Religions: Retrospect and Prospect*, edited by Joseph M. Kitagawa. New York: Macmillan Publishing Company, 1985. 13–29.

_____. "Philosophy and Religious Language." *The Journal of Religion* 54 (1974): 71–85.

_____. "Religion, Atheism, and Faith." In Paul Ricoeur, *The Conflict of Interpretations: Essays in Hermeneutics*, edited by Don Ihde. Evanston: Northwestern University Press, 1974. 440–67.

_____. "Reply to David Detmer's 'Ricoeur on Atheism: A Critique.'" In *The Philosophy of Paul Ricoeur*, edited by Lewis Edwin Hahn. Chicago and LaSalle, IL: Open Court, 1995. 494–97.

_____. "Response to Karl Rahner's Lecture: On the Incomprehensibility of God." *The Journal of Religion* 58, Supplement, (1978): S126–31.

_____. "Two Essays by Paul Ricoeur: The Critique of Religion and The Language of Faith." *Union Seminary Quarterly Review* XXVIII, no. 3 (Spring 1973): 203–24.

Gerhard, Mary. "Paul Ricoeur." In *A Handbook of Christian Theologians*, edited by Martin E. Marty and Dean G. Peerman. Nashville: Abingdon Press, 1984.

Hahn, Lewis Edwin, ed. *The Philosophy of Paul Ricoeur*. Chicago and LaSalle, IL: Open Court, 1995.

Ihde, Don. *Hermeneutic Phenomenology: The Philosophy of Paul Ricoeur*. Evanston: Northwestern University Press, 1971.

Klemm, David E., and William Schweiker, eds. *Meanings in Texts and Actions: Questioning Paul Ricoeur*. Charlottesville and London: University Press of Virginia, 1995.

Reagan, Charles E. *Paul Ricoeur: His Life and His Work*. Chicago and London: The University of Chicago, 1996.

Spiegelberg, Herbert. *The Phenomenological Movement*. The Hague: Martinus Nijhoff Publishers, 1982. 584–600.

Vanhoozer, Kevin J. *Biblical narrative in the philosophy of Paul Ricoeur*. Cambridge: Cambridge University Press, 1990.

Wall, John, William Schweiker, and W. David Hall, eds. *Paul Ricoeur and Contemporary Moral Thought*. New York and London: Routledge, 2002.

Rorty, Richard (1931–2007)

Rorty was the grandson of Walter Rauschenbusch, the renowned Baptist minister and Socialist theologian of the late nineteenth and early twentieth centuries. But he had no religious upbringing. Communism, he observed, was "the faith of the household." And although his parents had broken with the Communist Party the year after Rorty's birth,

he was still "brought up a Trotskyite, the way people are brought up Methodists or Jews." As an adolescent he was momentarily attracted by his reading of Augustine's *Confessions*, Bonaventure's *Itinerary of the Mind to God*, and Spinoza's *Tractatus on the Emendation of the Intellect* to an ethic of intellectual ascent via purification of the soul, and tried unsuccessfully linking it to a religious view. He "dropped the religious view" altogether, and while pursuing degrees thereafter at the universities of Chicago and Yale, teaching at Wellesley, Princeton, Virginia, and Stanford, and publishing a variety of works he humbly referred to as a crafty mix of "bits of Derrida, Dewey, Davidson, and Wittgenstein," never attached himself to any religious tradition.

Finding it impossible to "believe that God had actually been incarnated in one person," he early on began referring to himself as an atheist. But more recently, on the occasion of his being awarded the Meister Eckhart Prize in Berlin, he distinguished between two sorts of philosopher-atheists: those who, contrary to Hume's and Kant's conclusions about the irrelevance of empirical evidence to talk about God, unprofitably persist in rejecting the existence of God as an empirical hypothesis, and those who apply the term atheist to themselves only in the political sense that their anticlerical and secularist attitudes incline them to think that ecclesiastical institutions, "despite all the good they do, are dangerous to the health of democratic societies," and should be excluded from public policy-making. Having become an "intellectual pluralist" who no longer felt a need for any metaphysical, all-embracing frame of reference, Rorty regretted ever having counted himself among the former type of atheists, and preferred to be identified by the latter type, along with Gianni Vattimo and other philosophers who, while "moving religion out of the epistemic arena," and denying it any public role, might still value a privatized form of religion that celebrates secularization as the kenotic fulfillment of Christian revelation.

RORTY ON RELIGION. De-divinization of the world and the self spurred by the likes of

Darwin, William James, and Nietzsche, gives rise to a culture where there is no room for nonhuman forces, where everything is treated as a product of time and chance, and nothing is worshiped as quasi-divine. This implies also that there is nothing absolute about the nature of man and the world that might be mirrored in the language used to describe them. Both Cartesian Rationalism and scientistic empiricism are wrong, therefore, in trying to supplant the religious quest for dogmatic certainty in the past with attempts to found knowledge on either innate, *a priori* truths or the privileged experience of sense data.

Language is wholly contingent and ironic, lacking any religious, metaphysical or scientific criteria by which its absolute truth might be judged. If true, it is only in the sense of being useful in weaving or repairing an imaginative, Quinian "web of beliefs" by which humans try to satisfy their basic desires without interfering with the freedom of others. In the public forum, this will mean trying to reach an ever-evolving democratic consensus on how best to minimize the amount of cruelty in the world by expanding the sense of community to include marginalized people.

Institutionalized forms of religion are dangerous to the health of such democratic societies when they try to set their members apart as an elite whose views must be embraced by everyone, or when they encourage people to wait for some external power to do the work they are themselves responsible for doing. So long as it is privatized, however, and regarded as irrelevant to public policy, religion is entirely unobjectionable. Addressing other than epistemic needs, it not only is not in conflict with science or secularism, but by its pluralistic expressions of unjustifiable hope in a more loving human future, can also expand on the creation of new kinds of human beings.

Sources

Rorty, Richard. *Contingency, irony, and solidarity.* Cambridge: Cambridge University Press, 1989.

_____. "Meister Eckhart Prize Speech." Dewey List Serve.

_____. *Philosophy and the Mirror of Nature.* Princeton: Princeton University Press, 1979.

_____. *Philosophy and Social Hope.* London: Penguin Books, 1999.

_____. "Religious faith, intellectual responsibility, and romance." In *The Cambridge Companion to William James,* edited by Ruth Anna Putnam. Cambridge: Cambridge University Press, 1997. 84–102.

_____. "Remarks at the Eckhart-Prize Ceremony." Speech delivered on October 29, 2001. Dewey List Serve. Archives: March 2002, Week 1, Entry 5. http://listserv.sc.edu/cgi-bin/wa?A2=ind0203a&L=dewey-l&D=1&O=D&P=74.

Christie, Drew. "Richard Rorty." In *World Philosophers and Their Works.* Vol. 3. Edited by John K. Roth. Pasadena, CA, and Hackensack, NJ: Salem Press, Inc., 2000. 1634–42.

Isenberg, Sheldon R., and Gene R. Thursby. "A Perennial Philosophy Perspective on Richard Rorty's Neo-Pragmatism." *International Journal for Philosophy of Religion* 17 (1985): 41–65.

Knobe, Joshua. "A Talent for Bricolage: An Interview with Richard Rorty." *The Dualist* 2 (1995): 56–71. http://www.princeton.edu/~jknobe/rorty.html.

Lauritzen, Paul. "Philosophy of Religion and the Mirror of Nature: Rorty's Challenge to Analytic Philosophy of Religion." *International Journal for Philosophy of Religion* 16 (1984): 29–39.

Melchert, Norman. *The Great Conversation.* Boston: McGraw-Hill, 2002. 712–23.

Vaden House, D. *Without God or His Doubles: Realism, Relativism and Rorty.* Leiden: E.J. Brill, 1994.

Rousseau, Jean-Jacques (1712–1778)

Born in Calvin's city of Geneva where Catholicism was represented as the "blackest idolatry," Rousseau lost his mother (the daughter of a religious minister) a few days after his birth, at the age of ten was reluctantly abandoned by his father (a "pleasure-loving," but "good Christian" at home), and was placed under the care of the pastor of rural Bossey for several years before returning to Geneva. At the age of sixteen, he fled from Geneva to Consignon in Savoy, where a fanatical Catholic priest, trying to "pluck his soul from heresy," recommended that he go to Annecy and seek out Mme. de Warens, herself a recent and sincere convert to Catholicism. She, in turn, consented to having Rousseau sent to Turin for the sake of being instructed into the Catholic faith. Despite initial resistance and a dreadful experience in the hospice there that included exposure to homosexual harassment, he finally made a solemn abjuration of the "religion of his fathers," and received a "supplementary baptism."

Upon returning to Annecy, his beloved Mme. de Warens got the impression that he might be suited for the priesthood and had him enrolled at the seminary. It was soon determined, however, that he was not fit for such a vocation. During several decades of pursuing an interest in music, he became involved with a circle of French philosophers, befriending especially Denis Diderot, the anticlerical ex-seminarian and future editor of the *Encyclopédie* who encouraged Rousseau to pen his prize-winning essay on how a revival of the arts and sciences had corrupted morality. But despite his own contributions to the *Encyclopédie*, Rousseau developed as keen a distaste for the dogmatic atheism of the *philosophes* as he had for any kind of authoritarian religion.

Although he reconverted to Calvinism in 1754, his subsequent publication of *The Social Contract* and *Émile* (whose "Creed of a Savoyard Priest," some would claim, summarized his own mature and conscientious views about "natural religion") drew condemnation from Protestants, Catholics, and *philosophes* alike. Until the day he died, however, Rousseau saw himself as a champion of genuine religion, and in response to the Archbishop of Paris, asserted that he was a "sincere Christian," not as a "disciple of the priests, but as a disciple of Jesus Christ." Because of all the persecution, loneliness, physical and mental illness he had experienced in this life, he felt that he, no less than other good and honest men, deserved a better life beyond the grave, and had no doubt that his immortal soul would find it.

ROUSSEAU ON RELIGION. Religion can never be contrary to reason. In fact, its grandest ideas about God as the First Cause of universal harmony — which eventually supplanted primitive, animistic polytheism — or about the natural goodness and immortality of the human soul, came from reason, not from revelation. Except for the Gospels, whose simple but profound message about Jesus is so consistent with the tenets of natural religion and law, most of the books supposedly based on revelation not only defy verification, but are often also the cause of religious intolerance and fanaticism. To appreciate the reasonableness of natural religion and what it tells us about man's place in the cosmic order, however, one must also put aside the rationalistic speculations of the metaphysicians. Their subtle abstractions are nothing but an exercise in obscurantism, motivated more often than not by an egoistical and inhumane desire to differentiate their own views from the religious beliefs of poor, ordinary folk.

Reason must always be complemented by cognitive feeling. When it is, no rationalistic argument can prevail against its conclusions. Thus, the intuitive sense one has of an intelligent, provident God or of human freedom and immortality, speaks to one more forcibly than any metaphysical subtleties or empirical facts — like the Lisbon earthquake — that might call its reliability into question. Such truths constitute the heart of not only the private person's "religion of the Gospel," but also, when combined with belief in the sanctity of social contracts and laws that recognize the divine right of the sovereign to rule by the will of the people, of that "civil religion" which is essential to any community life. All religions must be tolerated by the state, so long as they themselves are tolerant and their dogmas contain nothing contrary to the duties of citizenship.

Sources

Rousseau, Jean-Jacques. *The Confessions*. Translated by J.M. Cohen. Harmondsworth, UK: Penguin Books, 1953.

_____. *Émile*. Translated by Barbara Foxley. London: J.M. Dent, 1993.

_____. *La Nouvelle Héloïse*. Translated by Judith H. McDowell. University Park and London: The Pennsylvania State University Press, 1968.

_____. *On the Origin of Inequality; On Political Economy; The Social Contract. Great Books of the Western World.* Vol. 38. Edited by R.M. Hutchins. Chicago: Encyclopædia Britannica, Inc., 1952.

_____. *The Reveries of the Solitary Walker.* Translated by Charles E. Butterworth. Indianapolis and Cambridge: Hackett Publishing Company, 1992. See esp. 27–42.

_____. *The Social Contract.* Translated and introduced by Maurice Cranston. Harmondsworth, UK: Penguin Books, 1981.

Copleston, Frederick, S.J. *A History of Philosophy.* Vol. 6, pt. 1. Garden City, NY: Doubleday and Company, Inc., 1962–77. 75–118.

Gourevitch, Victor. "The Religious Thought." In *The Cambridge Companion to Rousseau*, edited by Patrick Riley. Cambridge: Cambridge University Press, 2001. 193–246.

Grimsley, Ronald. *Rousseau and the Religious Quest.* Oxford: Clarendon Press, 1968.

O'Hagan, Timothy. *Rousseau.* London and New York: Routledge, 1999. See esp. 235–72.

Royce, Josiah (1855–1916)

Originally a Baptist in the habit of reading the Bible daily and memorizing numerous passages from it, Royce's father joined the Disciples of Christ in 1857. His seminary-trained mother, with her mystical, evangelical sense of the divine presence, preferred the quiet devotions of the Congregational Church, but helped her husband all the same in organizing the Disciples' congregation. With the father often on the road in a mostly futile pursuit of the American dream, Royce's religious upbringing was directed mainly by his mother. His lifelong intimacy with the Scriptures owed much to the fascination he experienced as a child listening to his mother reading stories to him from the Bible. The first book he remembered reading independently was the Apocalypse from the copy of the New Testament on display in the family's living room. When home, the father strictly supervised the biblical readings, prayers, and singing of evangelical hymns. This paternal regimen, along with the excessive dogmatism and formality of the organized church services Royce was made to attend as a child and teenager, soon evoked the stubborn rejection of external religious observances that would mark the rest of his life.

Undergraduate study at the University of California under the Darwinian Joseph LeConte and his reading of Mill and Spencer triggered doubts about personal immortality and other religious doctrines. His childhood faith was further challenged by exposure to the indifference and hostility toward traditional religion he later encountered during a year abroad studying the continental philosophers (e.g., Kant, Fichte, Hegel) at several German universities, before finally getting his doctorate at Johns Hopkins and (thanks to William James) eventually landing a professorial position at Harvard. Discovering in the possibility of human error a new argument for the existence of God gave his native religiosity an absolute grounding that it would never lose as he spent the last thirty years of his life expounding in the classroom, lecture hall, and print how best (along Kantian, Hegelian, and Peircean lines) to resolve religious problems and to reconcile religion and science. He resumed his reading of the Bible, and developed a prayer life of sorts ("communing with the divine"), but seldom attended "stifling and divisive" church services, never again joined any religious body, and along with his formerly Episcopalian wife, decided against having their children attend church or denominational schools.

ROYCE ON RELIGION. The deepest religious aspect of reality is furnished not by what the present world has come from, nor by what it is becoming, but by what it eternally is. And what the whole of our universe is, eternally, is "one live thing, a mind, one great Spirit," variously interpreted as the Absolute and Universal Intelligence that grounds the pursuit of both truth and goodness, or the Infinite Self, whose omniscient will and purposeful loyalty constitute the transcendent ideal toward and in which all individual lives are directed and find their freedom and identity. It is the possibility of error, rather than any pantheistic monism or empirical, teleological theism, that provides the best rational support for the reality of such an eternal dimension. For without the actuality of Infinite Thought within which to relate all isolated judgments to each other, actual error is impossible to conceive.

But if reason can help in resolving the religious paradox of being sure of God's presence or revelation despite man's natural ignorance, it is, nonetheless, only one of the many sources of insight into what is the essential feature of the higher religions, namely the need for and interest in finding salvation. Individual and social experiences of the Ideal (by which to judge the value of personal lives), the Need (the falling short of the Ideal), and the Deliverer (the superhuman, salvific power) precede such rational reflection. Subsequent, complementary sources of religious insight are the aim of the will to conform itself freely to the Supreme Will, loyalty to the cause of all loyal people (i.e., unity), patience in the face of human tragedy, and especially, communion with the invisible church of all who are devoted to the common cause of resolving conflicting interpretations of how best to save mankind. Among the religions of loyalty constituting the precious, visible parts of this invisible community, Christianity is the most highly developed.

Sources

Royce, Josiah. *The Conception of God*. Berkeley: Executive Council of the Philosophical Union of the University of California, 1895.

_____. *The Problem of Christianity*. 2 vols. New York: Macmillan, 1913.

_____. *The Religious Aspect of Philosophy*. Boston: Houghton, Mifflin and Company, 1900.

_____. *The Sources of Religious Insight*. New York: Charles Scribner's Sons, 1912.

_____. *The World and the Individual*. 2 vols. New York: Macmillan, 1899–1901.

Clendenning, John. *The Life and Thought of Josiah Royce*. Nashville and London: Vanderbilt University Press, 1999.

Collins, James. "Josiah Royce: Analyst of Religion as Community." In *American Philosophy and the Future*, edited by Michael Novak. New York: Charles Scribner's Sons, 1968. 193–218.

Hartshorne, Charles, and William L. Reese. *Philosophers Speak of God*. Chicago and London: The University of Chicago Press, 1963. 197–208.

Hine, Robert V. *Josiah Royce: From Grass Valley to Harvard*. Norman and London: University of Oklahoma Press, 1992.

Levinson, Henry Samuel. "Religious Philosophy." In *Encyclopedia of American Religious Experience*. Vol. 2. New York: Charles Scribner's Sons, 1988. 1196–97.

Oppenheim, Frank M. "Graced Communities: A Problem in Loving." *Theological Studies* 44.4 (December 1983): 604–24.

_____. *Royce's Mature Philosophy of Religion*. Notre Dame: University of Notre Dame, 1987.

Peterfreund, Sheldon P. *An Introduction to American Philosophy*. New York: The Odyssey Press, Inc., 1959. 121–65.

Smith, John E. "Royce, Josiah." *Encyclopedia of Philosophy*. Vol. 7. Edited by Paul Edwards. New York: Macmillan and Co. and The Free Press, 1967. 225–29.

Ruse, Michael (1940–)

Ruse was born in Birmingham, England, at the start of World War II. His father became a conscientious objector during the war and associated closely with the Religious Society of Friends. Ruse claims that the "loving Christian atmosphere created by my parents and their co-religionists in the Warwickshire Monthly Meeting" of the pacifist Quakers was one of the "deepest influences" on his life. But after the war, his father "drifted from one religion to another," and finally settled into "a kind of Voltaire situation," like that of a Candide working his garden. As for himself, Ruse says he grew up always thinking of God as "a bit of a Presbyterian," or a God, in other words, who "after creating humans, spends the rest of creation hating them and making life miserable for them."

After acquiring his Ph.D. from Bristol University, teaching for some forty years at the University of Guelph (Canada) and Florida State University, writing hundreds of scholarly articles and books on the relation of evolutionary science and religion, and lecturing around the world, he became a "nonbeliever," and now finds it a "great relief no longer to have that kind of God hovering over me" and "producing a fair number of heavy-duty psychological stresses and strains." Eschewing the label of an agnostic because of its connotation of indifference, he prefers to identify himself as a "theological skeptic." He has little but scorn, however, for the likes of his "friend" Richard Dawkins and others who, in the name of Darwinism, have launched a "crusade of nonbelief" against religion in general, and Christianity in particular, sneering for example at Catholic beliefs about the Virgin Mary or Evangelical theories about Intelligent Design. While sharing much of Dawkins' nonbelief, Ruse reminds him and his kind that, as the Post-Modernists and Alvin Plantinga have pointed out, Darwinism is infiltrated with culture and epistemological "leaps of faith," rendering evolutionary theory itself thereby something of a religion.

Co-testifying earlier with the biblical exegete Bruce Vawter and ongoing dialogue with other scholars like the Catholic Ernan McMullin, the Anglican Arthur Peacocke, the Lutheran Philip Hefner, or the Presbyterian Ursula Goodenough have convinced Ruse that not only do the questions raised by religion deserve to be respected for the sense of mystery they spawn, but clearly evidence the fact that "a Darwinian can be a Christian." Committed as he is to the "sacred obligation" to do scientific research and to pass its conclusions and methodology (along with consideration of creationist and ID theories in comparative religion classes) to future generations, he sustains the hope that if there is an afterlife, it will be filled with ever-new Mozart operas and an endless supply of fish and chips at intermissions.

RUSE ON RELIGION. While organizing their members socially, and imposing upon them divinely sanctioned moral prescriptions, religions are especially concerned with explaining ultimate reality and the place and role humans have in it. Religion may very well be a part of the adaptive design of human nature. Far from being a *tabula rasa*, the human mind is structured according to various innate dispositions which have proven valuable in the past struggle for survival. That religion, notwithstanding its long tradition of nonscientific doctrine, has conferred biological advantage to the human species in the past by congealing identity and providing group cohesion, is, as E.O. Wilson and others have pointed out, beyond doubt. However irrational, a religious taboo against the slaughter of cows, for example, might well have contributed to survival of the people of India.

Clearly, success in the struggle for survival required more than that which could be provided by philosophical and scientific proclivities. Other aspects of human experience also needed to be addressed. It is conceivable, therefore, that just as the process of natural selectivity has left human minds imprinted with certain regularities or epigenetic rules that govern the inductive/deductive methodology of science or the laws of logical argumentation, so it might also have given rise to religious propensities to wonder about the unseen and unseeable ultimate reality. Whether by having been explained naturally, traditional religion has outlived its evolutionary usefulness and needs to be replaced, as Wilson thinks, by a new, less illusory, but still emotively and socially powerful, secular religion of "scientific materialism" is debatable. An explanation of how humans came to their religious beliefs does not in and of itself debunk the latter's veracity. Other factors also need to be considered. And, in fact, it is not inconceivable that a religion like Christianity, with its doctrines of the soul, freedom, teleology, and so forth, could be reconciled with a Darwinian version of evolution.

Sources

Ruse, Michael. *Can a Darwinian Be a Christian? The Relationship between Science and Religion.* Cambridge: Cambridge University Press, 2001.

_____. *The Darwinian Paradigm: Essays on its history, philosophy, and religious implications.* London and New York: Routledge, 1989.

_____. "Response to Lothar Shafer." *Science and Theology News* (December 2001). http://www.stnews.org/archives/2001/Dec_editorial.html.

_____. *Taking Darwin Seriously.* Oxford: Basil Blackwell, 1986.

_____. "Through a Glass, Darkly." A review of Richard Dawkins' *A Devil's Chaplain.* American Scientist, Online, November–December 2003. http://www.americanscientist.org. 1–4.

Moore, Maynard E. "Real Calvinism: A Review of Michael Ruse's *Can a Darwinian Be a Christian?*" Metanexus: Views, August 5, 2002. http://www.metanexus.net. 1–2.

Sommer, Tamler. "Interview with Michael Ruse reprinted from *The Believer* 1.4 (July 2003)." http://evans-experientialism.freewebspace.com/ruse.htm. 1–14.

Verkamp, Bernard J. *The Sense of Religious Wonder: Epistemological Variations.* Scranton, PA: The University of Scranton Press, 2002. 9–17.

Russell, Bertrand (1872–1970)

Russell's mother died when he was only two. The father, who was a freethinking author of *An Analysis of Religious Belief,* died the following year and had tried to protect Russell and his older brother from "the evils of a religious upbringing" by leaving them in the hands of two atheistic guardians. The paternal grandparents stepped in, however, and rescued the children from the clutches of these "intriguing infidels." The Anglican grandfather also died three years later, but the grandmother, a liberal-minded Scotch Presbyterian who late in life would switch to the Unitarian religion, provided Russell with a Bible, took him to church every Sunday, and taught him the Unitarian version of Christian doctrine.

At the age of fifteen, determined to follow reason wherever it might lead him, Russell began systematically investigating the arguments for the Christian beliefs he (unlike his brother who had already converted to Buddhism) had held up to that point in his life. Within two years he lost his belief in human immortality, but still found the First Cause argument for God's existence irrefutable. But after enrolling at Trinity College (Cambridge) and reading in J.S. Mill's *Autobiography* about how the question of "Who made me?" suggests the further question of "Who made God?," he was led to abandon the argument and to become an atheist. At first this gradual loss of faith had caused him acute pain, fearing as he had that it would shock his beloved grandmother and make him unhappy. But in the end he was surprised to find that he was "glad to be done with the whole subject."

Of course, that was hardly the end of his dealing with the question of religion. Throughout the remainder of his life, while finishing his study of philosophy and mathematics, working with Whitehead at Cambridge to lay the foundations of modern symbolic logic, championing pacifism and nuclear disarmament, lecturing at home and abroad, and marrying three times, he became openly hostile to any form of institutionalized religion and published multiple articles and books that challenged the rational foundation of religious beliefs and encouraged his fellow humans to stop worshiping the "false gods" and to devote themselves, as free men, instead to the pursuit of the humanistic values of truth, beauty, and goodness. His views on religion and morality were very controversial and occasionally resulted in his being imprisoned or denied the right to lecture. After his death at the age of ninety-eight, his body was cremated.

RUSSELL ON RELIGION. People are religious mainly because they are taught to be so from early infancy. But religion has no rational foundation. Against the cosmological, teleological, moral, and ontological arguments for the existence of God, one can ask in the end "Who made God?" and point to defects and decay of the universe, the great deal of injustice in this world, and the lack of independent existence of even mathematical ideas. What science cannot discover, mankind cannot know. But notwithstanding recent claims, modern science offers no convincing support for belief in freedom of the will, the reality of the soul or its immortality, the possibility of a spiritual realm, or a creative purpose behind evolution. Science also challenges what is the second most powerful reason for popular religious belief, namely the emotional fear of the unknown and the wish for safety.

Instead of offering the masses genuine solace or promoting public morality, popular religion, under the influence of beliefs in hell preached by the likes of Jesus (whose wisdom and virtue pale by comparison to Socrates), has only spawned greater fear, anthropic conceit, and hatred. Still, there is something about the essence of religion (that quality of infinity that directs man toward a life in the whole, free from the finiteness of self and the tyranny of petty desires and thoughts) that can and should be retrieved by abandoning belief in the false gods and impartially worshiping the human ideals of truth, beauty, and goodness. The feelings of resignation and liberation resulting from such a life of the spirit will enlarge the self, adding depth to common human experiences of sex, parenthood, and patriotism, and engaging one in projects bigger than one's own ego (e.g., the pursuit of peace and social justice), thereby making this world a more fit and meaningful place to live in now, even though it may be heading for doomsday.

Sources

Russell, Bertrand. *The Autobiography of Bertrand Russell, 1872–1914.* Boston and Toronto: Little, Brown and Company, 1967.

_____. *Russell on Religion: Selections from the writings of Bertrand Russell.* Edited by Louis Greenspan and Stefan Andersson. London and New York: Routledge, 1999.

Brightman, Edgar Sheffield. "Russell's Philosophy of Religion." In *The Philosophy of Bertrand Russell,* edited by Paul Arthur Schilpp. New York: Tudor Publishing Company, 1951. 539–56.

Clark, Ronald W. *The Life of Bertrand Russell.* New York: Alfred A. Knopf, 1976.

Harwood, Larry D. "Russell's Reticence with Religion." *The Journal of the Bertrand Russell Archives,* n.s., 17 (Summer 1997): 27–41.

Jager, Ronald. *The Development of Bertrand Russell's Philosophy.* London: George Allen and Unwin Ltd.; New York: Humanities Press Inc., 1972.

Santayana, George (1863–1952)

Although born in Madrid as the only son of a father who claimed to have no ideals and dismissed religion as a sham, and of a mother who had little taste for religious piety, Santayana was baptized a Catholic in accordance with Spanish tradition. While growing up in Avila he had occasion annually to experience and be fascinated by the religious celebration of *Corpus Christi* and other Catholic feastdays, like that of *Santa Teresa.* At the age of eight he moved to Boston to join his mother (who had separated from his father) and her children by a previous marriage. One of the latter, a half-sister by the name of Susana, had also served as his godmother. The mother blamed her for instilling in Santayana his adolescent attraction to religious imagery and ritual. Taking seriously the spiritual relationship and duties of her role as godmother, she had indeed taken it upon herself to teach Santayana his prayers and advanced catechism. But Santayana claims to have early on moved beyond his godmother's religious literalism and to have come to see religion as something invented for moral reasons.

As a teenager, he continued to go to Mass on Sundays, sometimes alone at the Jesuit-run, German church whose communal, religious atmosphere excited him, and sometimes in the company of his godmother at the Church of the Immaculate Conception whose less than superb architecture and music seemed to help him escape to another world. He had no wish to go to confession or to partake of communion, but liked religion more than business, he said, because, "like poetry, [it] was more ideal, more freely imaginary." Later, after graduating from Harvard College, studying for two years in Germany, and returning to Harvard to take his doctoral degree, he was appointed a professor of philosophy and over the next twenty years settled into what he would describe as Harvard's "unintelligible, sanctimonious and often disingenuous," predominantly Protestant environment as a professor of philosophy.

He claimed that in his first book *(Interpretations of Poetry and Religion)* he "disregarded or defied public opinion ... by being indiscernibly a Catholic or an atheist." He never practiced his Catholic religion in the sense of actually using it as a means of getting to heaven or avoiding hell, and argued that the Christian *Weltanschauung* is pregnant with catastrophe if it is taken "for history and cosmology, and not for a symbolic myth." His last days were spent in Rome, and at his own request, he was buried in a plot of unblessed ground in that city's Catholic cemetery, Campo Verano.

SANTAYANA ON RELIGION. Religious creeds originated in historic facts and in doctrines literally meant by their authors. So, too, most religious people believe in the literal and empirical reality of their dogmas. This is what has given rise to sectarian controversies and conflict between religion and science. If taken literally, however, and treated as science that explains the universe by referring things to their causes or interprets the gods as supernatural powers that actually exist and work in the world, religion is, as the Positivists claim, necessarily false and no different from superstition.

But contrary to what both religious conservatives (with their fundamentalist literalism) and liberals (with their attempt to strip religion down to some demythologized core) might claim, religion has nothing to do with matters of fact. Its function is rather to idealize human experience, providing man with a total vision, a grasp of the whole. In that, it is like poetry; both consist in what the imagination adds to science, history, and morals. Religion differs from poetry, however, in that it tends toward application in practice, affecting human conduct by cultivating dispositions of piety, spirituality, and charity, finding expression in worship and dogma, and generating metaphysical illusions. While every person's religion is as historically conditioned and unique as his language, all religions (but especially Christianity with its image of the Cross) try to bring people face to face with the mystery and pathos of mortal existence (its apparent absurdity, pain, and evil), and through its sacred rites and ceremonies lead them into another world, where, even while fully aware of the limits of a life of reason, they can bask festively in the ideal beauty and perfection of this world. Even if its prayers and burial rites fail to negate the law of gravity, religion can still help people find an ideal immortality by inclining them to appreciate the eternal dimension of what they have done and thought, and the example they have set thereby for future generations.

Sources

Santayana, George. *The Idea of Christ in the Gospels or God in Man*. New York: Charles Scribner's Sons, 1946.
_____. *Interpretations of Poetry and Religion*. Co-edited by William G. Holzberger and Herman J. Saatkamp, Jr. Cambridge, MA, and London: MIT Press, 1989.
_____. *Persons and Places: Fragments of Autobiography*. Cambridge, MA: MIT Press, 1986.
_____. *Reason in Religion*. New York: Dover Publications, Inc., 1982.
_____. "Ultimate Religion." In *Obiter Scripta: Lectures, Essays and Reviews*, edited by Justus Buchler and Benjamin Schwartz. New York: Charles Scribner's Sons, 1936. 280–98.
Friess, Horace L., and Henry M. Rosenthal. "Reason in Religion and the Emancipated Spirit." In *The Philosophy of George Santayana*, edited by Paul Arthur Schilpp. Evanston and Chicago: Northwestern University, 1940. 353–76.
Levinson, Henry Samuel. "Religious Philosophy." In *Encyclopedia of American Religious Experience*. Vol. 2. New York: Charles Scribner's Sons, 1988. 1199–1201.
_____. *Santayana, Pragmatism, and the Spiritual Life*. Chapel Hill and London: The University of North Carolina Press, 1992.
Olafson, Frederick A. "Santayana, George." *Encyclopedia of Philosophy*. Vol. 7. Edited by Paul Edwards. New York: Macmillan and Co. and The Free Press, 1967. 282–87.
Peterfreund, Sheldon P. *An Introduction to American Philosophy*. New York: The Odyssey Press, Inc., 1959. 166–201.

Sartre, Jean-Paul (1905–1980)

Baptized a Roman Catholic, Sartre was raised (after the death of his father a year later) in the Catholic faith by a mother who had "her own God," a disgustingly "mystical" and anticlerical grandfather, and a skeptical grandmother who, though she "believed in nothing," professed, like the rest of the "de–Christianized" family, a belief in God as a "matter of discretion" and looked down on atheists as "wild and fanatical characters." He grew up saying his daily prayers, now and then accompanying his mother to Sunday Mass, receiving religious instruction from one or another Abbé, and once, before reaching his teen years, imagining God watching him trying to cover up a petty crime of setting a small rug on fire. Sensing the "divine gaze," he flew into a rage of blasphemous cursing, and not long thereafter, was struck, in the form of a momentary intuition, by the notion that "God does not exist!" Sartre claimed that in all his remaining sixty-some years he never once called into question the truth of that juvenile flash of insight.

As he grew older and enrolled at the age of nineteen to study philosophy at the École Normale Supérieure, he gradually shifted from an idealist to a materialist atheism in a long-term attempt to develop a philosophical vision of a world that is without God, or in other words, "a philosophy of man in a material world." Along with his lifelong soulmate, Simone de Beauvoir, he passed on his second try the *agrégation* that qualified him to teach. He began teaching at Le Havre, Laon, and the *Lycée Pasteur* in Paris, and then again at the latter school after returning in 1941 from military service in the ambulance corps and ten months of captivity in a Nazi POW camp.

In the prison some of his "best friends" were Jesuit priests, whose intelligence and tolerance impressed him, but whose belief in God struck him as "old-fashioned and outworn," a "relic of the seventeenth century," and something that he himself had dismissed while still a child as "just a story." But in the multiple novels, plays, and philosophical treatises he would produce both before and after his retirement from teaching in 1945 he often tried to vindicate philosophically his own disbelief in God on grounds (among others) that just as the early death of his father had spared him the loss of his freedom, so the "death of God" was a necessary corollary of his own pure subjectivity. Toward the end of his life he claimed that he had become "exactly what [he] wanted to be," that he "would die content" as an "atheist who has always thought there was nothing after death." A crowd of about fifty thousand people followed the hearse that carried his (later to be cremated) deceased body in 1980 to its burial site in Montparnasse graveyard.

SARTRE ON RELIGION. Given their own quest for an ever more substantial mode of being, humans are naturally inclined to posit the existence of a transcendent God, who as a Necessary Being can ground transphenomenal being-in-itself, or as an almighty, all-seeing Absolute Thou provide a divine synthesis of the world as a whole. Were such a Creator God actually to exist, man's essence would be preconceived prior to his existence, and he would not be free. But the idea of God is self-contradictory, since the negating of being involved in consciousness precludes by its very nature the union of being-for-itself and being-in-itself. Apart from its phenomenal instrumentality, therefore, the being of the world in-itself has no ultimate meaning; it simply is, without any real necessity, divine oversight, or communal depth.

The nauseous experience of this superfluity of being-in-itself, climaxing in an anxious awareness of human mortality, impresses upon humans all the more the need to take responsibility for their own being. For if there is no God to predetermine their essence, and they are nothing by birth, humans have no choice — if they want to live authentically — but to make something of themselves. It is a useless passion for humans to try, as they do, to become God by metamorphosing their own for-itself into an In-itself–For-itself or by appropriating the world as a totality of being-in-itself. But by denying the existence of God and putting aside the illusions of religious belief, humans are more free than ever to discover their own true selves and to relate more directly to each other. They don't need God to love one another. Even without God, they can build up a human race that will have its own principles, aims, and unity. Materialistic, as opposed to idealistic, atheism goes beyond ridding the mind of the abortive idea of God's existence to a new conception of man as a being who, while alone and lost in the world, can nonetheless recreate the world, make it his own, and in death return to the nature from which he came.

Sources

Sartre, Jean-Paul. *Being and Nothingness*. New York: Philosophical Library, 1956.
_____. *Existentialism*. New York: Philosophical Library, 1947.
_____. *Situations*. New York: George Braziller, 1965.
_____. *Words*. New York: George Braziller, 1964.
Beauvoir, Simone de. *Adieux. A Farewell to Sartre*. New York: Pantheon Books, 1984.
Blackham, H.J. *Six Existentialist Thinkers*. New York: Harper and Brothers, 1959. 110–48.
Collins, James. *The Existentialists*. Chicago: Henry Regnery Company, 1952. 38–79.
Copleston, Frederick, S.J. *A History of Philosophy*. Vol. 9, pt. 2. Garden City, NY: Doubleday and Company, Inc., 1962–77. 135–63.
Sienkewicz, Ann W. "Jean-Paul Sartre." In *World Philosophers and Their Works*. Vol. 3. Edited by John K. Roth. Pasadena, CA, and Hackensack, NJ: Salem Press, Inc., 2000. 1720–23.

Scheler, Max (1874–1928)

Scheler's mother and her brother (in whose house he would be forced to live after the early death of his Lutheran father) were Orthodox Jews, and Scheler was often made to join in their observance of the Sabbath and Jewish rituals. While attending a Catholic high school, however, he was impressed by the sense of community engendered by the school's Catholic rituals and decided, much to the chagrin of his mother and uncle, to join the Catholic Church. His scholastic record being very poor, he was sent to a private tutoring school, whereupon another uncle who had abandoned Judaism and assimilated to German culture, took him under his wing and introduced him to the writings of Nietzsche.

While vacationing in the Austrian Tyrol during the summer following graduation from high school, he met and eventually married an older, married woman, the first of multiple sexual liaisons a frenzied libido would eventually drive him into in later years. Despite the disruptive impact this had upon his subsequent studies at the universities of Munich, Berlin, and Jena, he was recognized as being something of a genius, and at the age of twenty-three did earn a doctorate in philoso-

phy. He began his teaching career at Jena, and became a close associate there of Husserl and had occasion to meet Heidegger. But after being accused of adultery by his wife, he was forced to seek a professorial position in Munich, and then, upon being accused of borrowing money from a student, lost it too (along with his license to teach in any German university).

Though impoverished by this loss and the cost of divorcing his first wife, he and the woman he next married managed to survive on the meager income he earned from the spellbinding lectures and writing he had begun delivering and publishing. These (culminating in the publication of *On the Eternal in Man*) soon identified him as a leading apologist for Catholicism, and in 1919 he was again allowed to teach at the University of Cologne. By 1922, however, at a time when he was trying to get the Church's permission to divorce his second wife and to marry a much younger woman, he had let it be known, much to the dismay of his Catholic admirers, that he no longer subscribed to theism in the usual sense. Despite an earlier heart attack, heavy drinking, chain-smoking and a troubled third marriage, he succeeded over the next six years in fleshing out in multiple books and articles the more panentheistic implications of his new religious focus. He died of another heart attack a few days after accepting an appointment to teach at the University of Frankfurt. He was given a Catholic burial in Cologne.

SCHELER ON RELIGION. The existence of a personal God cannot be proven, since proofs start with facts of the world, and there is no such factual evidence regarding the existence of a supernatural, divine, personal Being. But sensory perception is neither the only nor the most original experience. Thus, even though the existence of a personal God cannot be proven, it is conceivable that it can be detected and authenticated by a phenomenological analysis of the religious act of faith that arises within the "divine sphere" of human consciousness whereby every human is directed toward the absolute. Neither nothingness, nor money, nor the state, nor any other idolized earthly object can serve as an adequate correlate for religious consciousness.

Only an infinite and transcendent, personal God, who unites all objects into one whole and alone is capable of fulfilling the yearning of the human heart by giving and unfolding Himself in the religious acts of individuals and collective persons (e.g., churches), would seem, at first blush, to meet that need. But it is hard to see how such an omnipotent, omniscient, and all-good God could create a world so full of evil. Rather than conceiving of God as a real and personal Being existing prior to and beyond Nature, therefore, it might be better to think of God as the terminal point of a process of becoming through the intersection in the human person of the two attributes of the metaphysically discernible "Ground of Being," the *ens a se*, namely, *Geist* ("mind/spirit" that envisions or sketches possibilities it is powerless to realize) and *Drang* (the initially blind "impulse/force" that energizes the conversion of ideals into reality). It is nonspiritualized *Drang* that accounts for the initially "evil, lower forms of being" in the world. God only "becomes" by harvesting through death the good of individual human lives. With the knowledge that in dying he is giving birth to God, man can die in peace, knowing that he will live on in the "divine All-life" of our evolving universe.

Sources

Scheler, Max. *Man's Place in Nature.* Translated by Hans Meyerhof. New York: Noonday Press, 1971
_____. *On the Eternal in Man.* Translated by Bernard Noble. Hamden, CT: The Shoe String Press, Inc., 1972.
_____. *Problems of a Sociology of Knowledge.* London: Routledge and Kegan Paul, 1980.
_____. *Selected Philosophical Essays.* Translated by David R. Lachterman. Evanston, IL: Northwestern University Press, 1973.
Dunlop, Francis. *Thinkers of Our Time.* London: The Claridge Press, 1991.
Frings, Manfred S. *Max Scheler.* Pittsburgh, PA: Duquesne University Press, 1965.
_____. *The Mind of Max Scheler.* Milwaukee: Marquette University Press, 1997.
Spader, Peter H. *Scheler's Ethical Personalism.* New York: Fordham University Press, 2002.

Staude, John Raphael. *Max Scheler: An Intellectual Portrait.* New York: The Free Press, 1967.

Schelling, Friedrich (1775–1854)

With eleven designated godparents in attendance, Schelling was baptized one day after his birth in Leonberg. His father, who at the time was a scholarly deacon and preacher at the local Lutheran church, had published some well-received articles on theology and Oriental thought, and two years later would be appointed a professor of Old Testament studies at the Seminary in Bebenhausen. Growing up in this small city and its surrounding countryside, Schelling developed the love of nature that was reflected in his later work, and at its seminary and a Latin school nearby honed his knowledge of classical and Oriental languages.

At the age of fifteen, he composed an "elegy to death" that revealed something of the lifelong respect he would have for the theosophical pietism of Pastor Johann Hahn, to whom he had been introduced by his father. At about the same time his father had him enrolled in the University of Tübingen. There, while rooming with Hegel and Hölderlin and sharing their enthusiasm for the French Revolution, he studied philosophy (especially Kant) for two years, and then, for the next three, theology (with a special interest in Gnostic literature), resulting (especially after his encounter with Fichte) in his abandonment of any orthodox form of theistic supernaturalism. Instead of becoming a pastor upon graduation, he took a position as a private teacher, and having already published a number of works (like the Fichtean-inspired *On the Possibility of a Form of Philosophy in General*), promptly began seeking a professorial appointment.

Impressed by Schelling's *On the World Soul*, Goethe recommended him for a chair at the University of Jena, which he got in 1799 at the age of twenty-three and held for about six years (while living with Wilhelm Schlegel and betimes flirting with the latter's wife whom he would eventually marry) before moving on to spend the rest of his years lecturing (to Kierkegaard among others) at Würzburg, Munich, Erlangen, and finally Berlin. In addition to expounding a positive philosophy of mythology and revelation during these latter decades, Schelling continued working under the influence of Franz von Baader's rehabilitation of mystics like Eckhart and Boehme toward a dynamic Trinitarian conception of a final divine self-revelation in a future, spiritualized Johannine Church that would synthesize Petrine Catholicism of the past with the present Pauline version of Protestant Christendom. After Schelling's death in 1854, the Bavarian king, Maximilian II, erected a monument with an inscription hailing him as "the foremost thinker of Germany."

SCHELLING ON RELIGION. To appreciate why there is something rather than nothing, the existence of our universe must be grasped intuitively as an ongoing process of freely falling away and returning to God, paralleling analogously the eternal becoming of divine self-consciousness. In the process of overcoming its dark, undifferentiated, and unconscious *Ungrund* (the impersonal, contractive and egoistic yearning that would negate all other being), Divine Being, as the Absolute Subject, freely wills to tap its expansive, conscious, loving, altruistic and personal power by way of positing its own being as the Absolute Object of its consciousness. In the Infinite Other or Self-differentiated thereby is also born the eternal Idea, out of which spontaneously fall or leap in turn the ideal images that constitute the essence of all finite, sensible objects, and manifest — especially in their artistic expression — the truth and beauty of Divine Being.

Participating as they do in God's own being, natural phenomena are also caught up in the eternal struggle between necessity and freedom. But the human mind upon which they all rely for ideal transformation lacks the perfect unity of Absolute Reason, and to that extent can freely choose to keep them locked within the vicious circle of its own primordial egoism. For humans and their world to escape

this grip of evil, there must be not only an idea of God, but a personal Absolute that actually exists and out of love reveals itself, along with the eternal process of its becoming an integrated personality, in and through human history. That such a revelation has actually occurred can be documented in the history of mythology and its final sublation in the more conscious and free manifestation of the divine reality in the person of Jesus. While all religions, therefore, contain an inner truth to the extent of recognizing the need for a personal God who can redeem mankind, it is in Christianity, and especially in its Johannine version, that divine wisdom has found its clearest expression.

Sources

Schelling, Friedrich W.J. *Clara.* Translated and introduced by Fiona Steinkamp. Albany: State University of New York Press, 2002.
_____. *On the Natural and the Divine Principle of Things.* Translated by Michael G. Vater. Albany: State University of New York Press, 1984.
_____. *Philosophical Inquiries into the Nature of Human Freedom.* Translated and introduced by James Gutmann. LaSalle, IL: Open Court, 1936.
_____. *Philosophie und Religion.* Tübingen: I.G. Cotta, 1804.
_____. *Urfassung der Philosopher der Offenbarung.* Hamburg: F. Meiner Verlag, 1992.
Arndt, Martin. "Schelling." In *Biographisch-Bibliographisches Kirchenlexikon.* Vol. 9. Verlag Traugott Bautz, 1999. http://www.bautz.de/bbkl/. 104–38.
Beach, Edward Allen. *The Potencies of God(s): Schelling's Philosophy of Mythology.* Albany: State University of New York Press, 1994.
Brown, Robert F. *The Later Philosophy of Schelling: The Influence of Boehme on the Works of 1809–1815.* London: Bucknell University Press, 1977.
_____. *Schelling's Treatise* on "The Deities of Samothrace" Missoula, MT: Scholars Press, 1977.
Copleston, Frederick, S.J. *A History of Philosophy.* Vol. 7, pt. 1. Garden City, NY: Doubleday and Company, Inc., 1962–77. 121–82.
Fackenheim, Emil L. *The God Within: Kant, Schelling, and Historicity.* Toronto: University of Toronto Press, 1996. 50–121.
O'Meara, Thomas F. *Romantic Idealism and Roman Catholicism: Schelling and the Theologians.*

Notre Dame: University of Notre Dame Press, 1982.

O'Meara, Thomas F. "Schelling, Friedrich." In *Encyclopedia of Religion*. Vol. 13. Edited by Mircea Eliade. New York: Macmillan and Co., 1987. 97–8.

Sandkühler, Hans Jörg. *Friedrich Wilhelm Joseph Schelling*. Stuttgart: J.B. Metzlersche Verlagsbuchhandlung, 1970.

Tillich, Paul. *The Construction of the History of Religion in Schelling's Positive Philosophy*. Lewisburg, PA: Bucknell University Press, 1974.

Zizek, Slavoj, and F.W.J. Von Schelling. *The Abyss of Freedom/Ages of the World*. Ann Arbor: University of Michigan Press, 1997.

Schleiermacher, Friedrich (1768–1834)

Originally an "enlightened" Reformed pastor and Prussian army chaplain, Schleiermacher's father later experienced a spiritual reawakening in the company of the Pietistic Moravian community in Gnadenfrei. Schleiermacher himself, after undergoing a similar religious experience at the age of fourteen, enrolled in the Herrnhutters' school at Niesky and their seminary at Barby, and was deeply impressed and influenced by their mystical devotion to Jesus as their personal Savior. Reading Goethe and other modern thinkers soon inclined him, however, to break with the Moravians to study theology and philosophy (especially Plato, Spinoza, and Kant) at the University of Halle. Following ordination he received appointments as a pastor and preacher at several places, including the Charité Hospital in Berlin, where he also joined the circle of literary Romanticists to whom, as the "cultured despisers of religion," he would address his first major book, *On Religion*, in 1799.

An unrequited love affair with the wife of another minister prompted his departure from Berlin to take a pastorate in Stolp. During a subsequent two-year stint (1804–1806) as professor and preacher at the University of Halle he published an undogmatic dialogue on the celebration of Christmas in which the significance of Christ's birth is reinterpreted in terms of the Christian community's experience of redemption that further revealed his philosophically inspired humanistic sensitivity as well as his remaining indebtedness to the Pietists. A few years later he married and fathered a family.

Upon returning to Berlin in 1810, as pastor at its Trinity Church and professor of theology at its university, Schleiermacher continued preaching to huge audiences the sermons (not a few of a political nature challenging Prussia's peace with Napoleonic France or, on a more ecclesiastical level, appealing for a reunification of Reformed and Lutheran branches of Protestantism) that would eventually fill ten volumes, finished the translation of the Platonic dialogues he and Friedrich von Schlegel had started earlier, and alongside Hegel in the philosophy department, delivered the theological lectures that would result in publication of *The Christian Faith* and his future acclamation as "the father of modern Protestant theology." He died of pneumonia on February 12, 1834, surrounded by the friends who had just joined him in the celebration of the Lord's Supper. Some twenty to thirty thousand people turned out for his Christian burial.

SCHLEIERMACHER ON RELIGION. Were religion nothing more than a set of doctrines and ceremonies, it might deserve the contempt of cultured people for being only an empty pretense that obscures the truth. But that is not what religion is. Such dogmas and usages are merely its shell, not its kernel, and have rightly been regarded with indifference by all the great religious figures. It is also futile, however, to try defending religion as a moral derivative of the coincidence of virtue and happiness. For the will is no more the ultimate seat of religion than is the mind. The essence of religion is to be found rather in an autonomous realm of feeling. Upon becoming conscious of their selves, humans awaken naturally to a pious "sense of absolute dependency." Not through discursive thinking, but immediately or intuitively, they become aware of "the universal existence of all finite things, in and through the Infinite, and of all temporal things in and through the Eternal." They immediately sense the ultimate unity or wholeness of reality, and experience themselves as parts of that Whole.

Although affective in nature, such consciousness is genuinely cognitive in a nonreflective, nonconceptual way. It tells us something about our place in the world and our relation to the whole of reality. It tells us that as parts of the Whole, we are absolutely dependent. And to say that we feel absolutely dependent, is one and the same thing as saying that we are in relation to God. There is no need, then, to try proving that it is God upon whom humans feel absolutely dependent, for the term God is simply the co-determinant of such a feeling. Every religion, upon reflection, tends to conceive of this feeling and its concomitant notion of God in its own unique way, giving rise thereby to "endless variety, down even to the single personality." No one religion can rightly claim to be absolute, but with its imaginative portrayal of "creature-consciousness" Christianity is likely to sublate all other forms of religion in the end.

Sources

Schleiermacher, Friedrich. *The Christian Faith.* Vol. 1. Edited by H.R. Mackintosh and J.S. Stewart and introduced by Richard R. Niebuhr. New York and Evanston: Harper and Row Publishers, 1963.
_____. *Christmas Eve: A Dialogue on the Celebration of Christmas.* Translated by W. Hastie. Edinburgh: T. & T. Clark, 1890.
_____. *On Religion: Speeches to its Cultured Despisers.* Translated by John Oman. New York: Harper and Row Publishers, 1958.
Demm, Charles. "Friedrich Daniel Ernst Schleiermacher." In *Boston Collaborative Encyclopedia of Western Theology.* http://people.bu.edu/wwildman. 28–37.
Dilthey, Wilhelm. *Leben Schleiermachers.* Berlin: Walter de Gruyter & Co., 1970ff.
Gerrish, B.A. *A Prince of the Church: Schleiermacher and the Beginnings of Modern Theology.* Philadelphia: Fortress Press, 1984.
_____. "Schleiermacher, Friedrich." In *Encyclopedia of Religion.* Vol. 13. Edited by Mircea Eliade. New York: Macmillan and Co., 1987. 108–13.
Niebuhr, Richard R. "Friedrich Schleiermacher." In *A Handbook of Christian Theologians,* edited by Dean G. Peerman and Martin E. Marty. Cleve-
land and New York: The World Publishing Company, 1967. 17–35.
_____. *Schleiermacher on Christ and Religion.* New York: Charles Scribner's Sons, 1964.
Otto, Rudolf. *Das Gefühl des Überweltlichen.* München: C.H. Beck'sche Verlagsbuchhandlung, 1932.
_____. "Introduction." In Schleiermacher, *On Religion: Speeches to its Cultured Despisers.* vii–xx.
_____. *The Philosophy of Religion.* London: Williams and Norgate, 1931.
Redeker, Martin. *Schleiermacher: Life and Thought.* Translated by John Walhausser. Philadelphia: Fortress Press, 1973.
Selbie, W.B. *Schleiermacher: A Critical and Historical Study.* New York: E.P. Dutton and Co., 1913.
Verkamp, Bernard J. *The Evolution of Religion: A Re-Examination.* Scranton, PA: University of Scranton Press, 1995. 170–72.
_____. *The Sense of Religious Wonder: Epistemological Variations.* Scranton, PA: University of Scranton Press, 2002. 33–37.

Schopenhauer, Arthur (1788–1860)

After the return of his bourgeois parents from travel to Belgium, France and England, Schopenhauer was born in Danzig and baptized in that city's beautiful, old Marienkirche. In 1804, after returning from the European travels into which his father had lured him in exchange for his commitment to become a merchant rather than a scholar, Schopenhauer would return to the same church to receive the sacrament of Confirmation. Before his possibly suicidal death several years later, the father had given Schopenhauer a little book by Matthias Claudius, entitled *An meinen Sohn,* in which the eighteenth-century Hamburg poet expounded a version of Pietistic mysticism that encouraged a certain aloofness from and overcoming of this world even while acknowledging one's responsibilities to it. Schopenhauer treasured the book and read it frequently throughout his life, but troubled by the human suffering, poverty, and immorality (not to mention the bigotry of English Protestants) he had witnessed during his travels, he was already at the age of eighteen beginning to question its underlying Pietistic "earthly delight in God."

It is generally assumed that, after terminating his merchant apprenticeship, studying the classics and languages at a gymnasium (where he was required to attend church services), pursuing a doctoral degree in philosophy at the universities of Göttingen and Berlin (attending lectures by Fichte and Schleiermacher), lecturing briefly as a *Privatdocent* in Berlin, breaking completely with his mother, and finally publishing his masterpiece (*The World as Will and Representation*) in 1819, Schopenhauer became, as Nietzsche would put it, "the first admitted and inexorable atheist among us Germans." And to the extent that he rejected belief in a personal Creator-God, doubted personal immortality, and constantly railed against "optimistic Jewish and Islamic superstition," "Greek heathenism," and any philosophy like Hegel's that tried to make theism acceptable to human reason, there is certainly some truth in such a conclusion.

But in addition to his fascination with Catholicism and certain of its more mystical and ascetical figures (Francis of Assisi, Abbe Rancé, Madame Guyon, and Meister Eckhart), Schopenhauer had also developed a keen appreciation for Hindu and Buddhist writings on the assumption that they vindicated his own pessimistic conception of religion as an ethical exercise in renunciation of desire, self-denial, and concern for suffering. Every night before retiring, he would meditate on a passage from the Upanishads. At the time of his death in 1860, a Protestant Evangelical service was performed at his gravesite.

SCHOPENHAUER ON RELIGION. If ours is not the worst of all possible worlds, it is, as anyone who has seen through the egoistic veil of Maya will attest, subject to constant passing away, futile striving, inner conflict, and endless suffering. Such knowledge of the "inner nature of the thing-in-itself," or of the "world as will," leaves an impression of ultimate meaninglessness and gives rise to a strong aversion to the will to live. This in turn generates a voluntary selfrenunciation that expresses itself not only in disinterested aesthetic appreciation of the arts, but also and especially in the practice of religious asceticism. For,

with the possible exception of Judaism and Islam, whose basic character is realism and optimism, most religions, including Christianity (except for modern Rationalistic Protestantism), encourage indifference to things of this world, mortification of the will through voluntary chastity, intentional poverty, fasting, self-chastisement, and, if not suicide, the cheerful acceptance of suffering and death.

With desire burning ever afresh in the human body and spirit, it is a constant struggle to sustain such a denial of the will to live, but examples abound of individuals like the Buddha and Francis of Assisi, who, if only after the experience of great personal misfortune, have conquered all desire and already in this life have found true heavenly peace. By thus encouraging the ascetical spirit, the various religions and their priests have striven to satisfy through revelations clothed in mysterious allegory and myth what they have astutely perceived to be the ineradicable, metaphysical need of the masses (who cannot comprehend the abstractions of philosophy) to know the aim of their existence or that of their world. The problem is that most religions never dare to confess to being allegorical, and by insisting instead upon the truth of their doctrines in *sensu proprio*, spawn perpetual, and perhaps indispensable, deception that may result in their demise when the allegorical nature of their doctrines does become known.

Sources

Schopenhauer, Arthur. *Essays and Aphorisms.* Translated by R.J. Hollingdale. Harmondsworth, UK: Penguin Books, 1970.

_____. *The World as Will and Representation.* 2 vols. Translated by E.F.J. Payne. New York: Dover Publications, Inc., 1958 and 1969.

Copleston, Frederick, S.J. *Arthur Schopenhauer: Philosopher of Pessimism.* Introduced by R.J. Hollingdale. London: Burns Oates and Washbourne Ltd., 1947.

Mannion, Gerard. Schopenhauer, *Religion and Morality: The Humble Path to Ethics.* Hants, UK, and Burlington, VT: Ashgate Publishing Company, 2003. See esp. 39–90.

Reinhardt, K.F. "Schopenhauer, Arthur." *New*

Catholic Encyclopedia. Vol. 12. Edited by W.J. McDonald. New York: McGraw-Hill, 1967. 1176–78.

Safranski, Rüdiger. *Schopenhauer and the Wild Years of Philosophy.* Translated by Ewald Osers. London: Weidenfeld and Nicolson, 1989.

Wallace, William. *Life of Arthur Schopenhauer.* London: Walter Scott, 1890.

Zimmern, Helen. Schopenhauer: *His Life and Philosophy.* London: George Allen and Unwin Ltd., 1932.

Seneca, Lucius Annaeus (c. 4 B.C.–A.D. 65)

Born in the Spanish city of Córdoba, Seneca was already eight or nine years of age when his aunt brought him to Rome to rejoin his father. The father was a scholar of sorts (later writing a history of Rome) but hated philosophy. All the same, in addition to his study of grammar and rhetoric, Seneca early on became interested in philosophy. Under the influence of his teachers, Sotion and Papirius Fabianus (followers of Q. Sextius), he flirted in his youth with Pythagoreanism. At twenty he was still following certain of its practices, like the daily examination of conscience and vegetarianism. Soon thereafter, however, the emperor Tiberius decreed that Jewish and Egyptian rituals were to be expelled from Rome, and on grounds that vegetarianism smacked of Jewish superstition, Seneca was advised by his father to give it up. Seneca did. But as M.L. Clarke has observed, neither the father nor the son, given their Spanish origin, had "any natural inherited sympathy with Roman religion." So, instead of embracing the popular religion after severing his Pythagorean ties, Seneca was inspired by another teacher, Attalus, to turn to Stoicism, a school of thought that had its own religious views and little respect for the traditional practices of ancient Roman religion.

Throughout the hectic years of his political involvement, before finally in the year 65 his growing wealth and popularity, along with suspicions of his complicity in the conspiracy of Piso, inclined the emperor Nero to call upon him to commit suicide, Seneca penned hundreds of letters and essays expounding his modified version of Stoicism. All the while he had also been trying to bring his own life into line with Stoic doctrine. Imitating Attalus' minimalist philosophy of life and asceticism, he cultivated an attitude of indifference toward material goods and creature comforts. And although he would observe whatever religious rituals of sacrifice and worship civil law required, he had next to no confidence in their efficacy.

Consistent with the Stoic identification of God with Fate and/or the Law of Reason operating in Nature, he preferred to worship by trying to live a life of virtue, constantly hymning and praising the divine reason immanent in the universe out of gratitude for all the benefits it has bestowed upon mankind. When denied an opportunity to write a last will by which to reward his loyal servants with shares in his wealth, he told them he would leave them the only and best thing he had left to give, the example of his own life. It was an example which, even apart from the spurious letters between him and the Apostle Paul, many Christians would in later centuries find very inspiring.

SENECA ON RELIGION. Although the religious rites dedicated to the ignoble crowd of gods that the superstition of ages has amassed ought to be observed in accordance with civil law, they do not really deserve any heartfelt respect. For such gods are only popular names for the Eternal Reason which, like a good and provident Father, created order out of inert matter by decreeing a necessary and unalterable course of events (Fate), without any thought of being rewarded by sacrificial rites and prayers. The latter cannot change the mind of God, and can be helpful, therefore, only when they reflect a pious attitude of submission to the God dwelling within all rational creatures.

As a divine spark of the Eternal Fire that burns at the heart of the universe, the soul, with its faculty of reason, empowers humans to help themselves. It would be foolish, therefore, to pray to temple images for wisdom, when, by using one's reason to pursue philosophy, it can be acquired from one's own self. One of the great gifts of philosophy is to unlock the temple of the universe, revealing it to be a product of design rather than mere chance. But philosophy can also help humans live well by fostering a godlike freedom from care. And such, indeed, is the disposition of the truly wise man. Refusing to be enslaved to a puny, burdensome body, and giving undivided authority to his soul, he is free and autonomous, fearing neither wounding, imprisonment, poverty, persecution, old age, nor even death. He lives serenely and conscientiously, as though under constant scrutiny by God and mankind, all the while fully aware of his own sins. Recognizing the universal brotherhood of man, he imitates God by extending a helping hand to all humans, slave and freeman alike. Satisfied that virtue is its own reward, he will, in the end, let nature take its course, taking his own life if necessary, and suffering unhesitatingly whatever Fate thereafter ordains, be it a better, purely spiritual life or reabsorption into the matter from which the next universe will be born.

Sources

Seneca, L. Annaeus. *Ad Lucilium Epistulae Morales.* Translated by Richard M. Gummere. 3 vols. London: William Heineman; New York: G.P. Putnam's Sons, 1920–1925.
_____. *Letters from a Stoic (Epistulae Morales ad Lucilium).* Translated by Robin Campbell. Harmondsworth, UK: Penguin Books Ltd., 1985.
_____. *Moral Essays.* Translated by John W. Basore. London: William Heinemann, Ltd.; New York: G.P. Putnam's Sons, 1928.
_____. *On Benefits.* Translated by Aubrey Stewart. London: George Bell and Sons, 1887.
Augustine, Saint. *The City of God.* Translated by Marcus Dods. New York: The Modern Library, 1950. 201–5.
Bonhöffer, Adolf Friedrich. *The Ethics of the Stoic Epictetus.* Translated by William O. Stephens. New York: Peter Lang, 1996. 122–23.
Braginton, Mary V. *The Supernatural in Seneca's Tragedies.* Menasha, WI: The Collegiate Press, c. 1993.
Clarke, M.L. *The Roman Mind: Studies in the History of Thought from Cicero to Marcus Aurelius.* Cambridge, MA: Harvard University Press, 1956. 116–23.
Copleston, Frederick, S.J. *A History of Philosophy.* Vol. 1, pt. 2. Garden City, NY: Doubleday and Company, Inc., 1962–77. 172–75.
Farrar, R.W. *Seekers after God.* London: Macmillan and Co., 1890. 167–85.
Griffin, Miriam T. *Seneca: A Philosopher in Politics.* Oxford: Clarendon Press, 1992.
_____, and Jonathan Barnes, eds. *Philosophia Togata I: Essays on Philosophy and Roman Society.* Oxford: Clarendon Press, 1997. See esp. 189–91.
Gummere, Richard Mott. *Seneca the Philosopher and His Modern Message.* Boston: Marshall Jones Company, 1922.
Inwood, Brad. "God and Human Knowledge in Seneca's *Natural Questions.*" In Dorothea Frede, and Andre Laks, eds. *Traditions of Theology: Studies in Hellenistic Theology, Its Background and Aftermath.* Leiden and Boston: Brill, 2002. 119–58.
Morford, Mark. *The Roman Philosophers from the Time of Cato the Censor to the Death of Marcus Aurelius.* London and New York: Taylor and Francis Group, 2002. 161–73.
Sevenster, J.N. *Paul and Seneca.* Leiden: E.J. Brill, 1961.
Sørensen, Villy. *Seneca: the humanist at the court of Nero.* Chicago: The University of Chicago Press, 1984.
Turcan, Robert. *Sénèque et les religions orientales.* Bruxelles: Latomus Revue D'Études Latines. 1967.

Sextus Empiricus (fl. early A.D. 200s)

Sextus was probably born in the early third century A.D. Where he was born is not known. Certain references in his writings, along with their pervasive medical flavor, suggest that he was himself a physician. It is conjectured that he received the addition to his name from ties which, according to Diogenes Laertius, he had with the Empirical school of medicine. Where he practiced medicine and did his philosophical writing, however, is also uncertain. Some think it probable that he lived at various times in all three cities of Athens, Alexandria, and Rome. Who his teachers were, or who it was that might have prompted him to embrace the skepticism propounded five hundred years earlier by an obscure, ancient Greek philosopher named Pyrrho, is also unknown. But one way or another he became cognizant of many different schools of thought, and it was probably the disagreement he found among them that inclined him to agree with Pyrrho that a philosophical quest for certitude is not only futile, but a positive threat to an ataraxic enjoyment of life.

His skeptical appraisal was applied to religion also, to its practice no less than to its beliefs. He repeatedly called attention not only to differences of opinion about the existence and nature of the gods, but also to the great amount of anomaly in the performance of sacrificial rites and other religious ceremonies. In some rites, he points out for example, the eating of fish is sanctioned, in others it is considered sacrilegious; some people consider it sacrilegious to expose deceased bodies to the light of day, while others put them out as food for dogs or vultures; and so forth, *ad infinitum.*

He clearly had in mind to suggest that there are no more absolute standards of belief and practice in the realm of religion than anywhere else. But how such a skeptical view impacted upon his own personal beliefs and practice is hard to say, given the scarcity of details about all aspects of his life. The general impression one gets from his writings, however, is that he believed in a God whose nature is totally incomprehensible, and participated in whatever religious ceremonies were customary wherever he happened to be.

SEXTUS EMPIRICUS ON RELIGION. Pyrrho's disciple Timon praises Protagoras for writing that "he did not know and could not observe what any of the gods are like and whether there are any," and Pyrrho himself probably subscribed to the same view, rather than contradicting his doctrine of the indeterminacy of all things by suggesting that the divine could be hypostasized as an eternal entity. But be that as it may, the popular and dogmatic arguments for the existence of God or the gods do not hold up. In the first place, lacking any adequate criterion of truth, it is not of itself pre-evident that God exists nor provable from something else. Secondly, if God exists, He will either take care of everything and be responsible also for all the evil in the world, or wishes or is able to take care only

of some things, on which account He would be either weaker or more malevolent than true piety would tolerate. Furthermore, Epicurus' argument that the idea of God's existence originated from appearances in dreams or from observation of natural phenomena is circular, resting as it does on a concept of human happiness, which in turn relies on the concept of a perfect god.

Whether God exists, then, is simply not apprehensible. Nor is it possible to form any real concept of God so long as neither the common people nor the Dogmatists ascribe any agreed-upon substance, form, number, or location to the deity. So, again, it is better to suspend one's judgment. Finally, it may be noted that were religious usages and moral prohibitions valid by nature they would be recognized by everybody alike. But what different people think is good, bad, or indifferent, or about how the gods should be worshiped with sacrificial rites, dietary taboos, or reverence toward the dead, varies greatly. Still, traditional law and customs rightly incline us in our daily lives to accept piety as good and impiety as evil, on grounds that the former enjoys, if not greater certitude, at least a higher probability of truth.

Sources

Sextus Empiricus. *Against the Ethicists (Adversus Mathematicos XI).* Translated with an introduction and commentary by R. Bett. Oxford: Clarendon Press, 1997.

_____. *Against the Grammarians (Adversus Mathematicos I).* Translated with an introduction and commentary by D.L. Blank. Oxford: Clarendon Press, 1998.

_____. *Outlines of Scepticism.* Translated by Julia Annas and Jonathan Barnes. Cambridge: Cambridge University Press, 1994.

_____. *The Skeptic Way: Sextus Empiricus' Outlines of Pyrrhonism.* Translated with introduction and commentary by Benson Mates. New York and Oxford: Oxford University Press, 1996.

Bett, Richard. *Pyrrho, His Antecedents, and His Legacy.* Oxford: Oxford University Press, 2000. See esp. 94–102; 149–52.

Diogenes Laertius. *Lives of Eminent Philosophers.* Translated by R.D. Hicks. Cambridge, MA: Harvard University Press, 1972. 475–527.

Floridi, Luciano. *Sextus Empiricus: The Transmission and Recovery of Pyrrhonism*. New York: Oxford University Press, 2002.

Hallie, Philip P., ed. *Scepticism, Man, and God: Selections from the Major Writings of Sextus Empiricus*. Translated by Sanford G. Etheridge. Middletown, CT: Wesleyan University Press, 1964.

Long, A.A., and D. Snedley, trans. *The Hellenistic Philosophers*. Vol. 1: Translations of the principal sources with philosophical commentary. Cambridge: Cambridge University Press, 1987.

Long, George. "Sextus Empiricus." In *A Dictionary of Greek and Roman Biography and Mythology*. Vol. 3. Edited by William Smith. New York: AMS Press, Inc., 1967. 813–14.

Stumpf, Samuel Enoch. *Socrates to Sartre. A History of Philosophy*. New York: McGraw-Hill Book Company, 1982. 115–19.

Smart, Ninian (1927–2001)

Smart was born in Cambridge, England, the son of Scottish parents who returned to Glasgow when the father received an appointment there as a professor of astronomy. Most of his early education was received at the Glasgow Academy. He was brought up as a Scots Episcopalian Christian. This placed him outside the religious establishments of both Scotland and England, and probably contributed to the cross-cultural interests he would later show in his study of religion. At the end of World War II the eighteen-year-old Smart was drafted into the British Army and assigned to its Intelligence Corps. He spent the first year of his military service trying to learn Chinese by studying Confucian texts. The army then sent him to Sri Lanka (Ceylon) where most of the local soldiers he was expected to train belonged to the region's dominant religion of Buddhism, on which account he and his fellow officers recruited a Buddhist monk to serve as their unit's chaplain. This contact with other of the world's great religions had a profound impact upon his own religious faith, and he came to identify himself as a Buddhist-Epicopalian, partly, he said, to annoy those people who think that any one religion has a corner on the truth.

Upon returning to England in the late forties he enrolled at Oxford University, met the woman into whose Italian Catholic family he would later marry, and studied languages, history and philosophy. He found the then prevailing philosophical analysis of language lacking in an appreciation for the cultural context and linguistic plurality he had himself encountered while serving abroad, and to that extent inadequate for understanding the uniqueness of every religion's talk of divine revelation. This prompted him, in the many lectures he would later give around the world, or in the countless books and articles he would subsequently write while teaching at Birmingham, London, Lancaster, California, and other universities, to emphasize a comparative study of religion, with its survey of the whole spectrum of doctrines and practices to be found in various cultures, as being essential to any philosophical clarification of the nature and truth of religious utterances. He also played a pivotal role in establishing programs in the academic study of religion at both the university and lower levels of education. "Depending on the sort of person one is," he said, the exploration of other religions can deepen one's own religious experience. His own study of other religions, and especially Buddhism, clearly enriched his appreciation of the Christian faith to which he adhered till death.

SMART ON RELIGION. Any attempt to produce an old-fashioned definition of religion by identifying an essential content or spirit of all religions, or by having recourse to some "empty generality" (like Tillich's "ultimate concern"), will only result in distorting all the religions in question. To discourage such essentialist attempts at a definition of religion and to allow for a more disjunctive account of religion, whereby something might count as a religion even though it lacks an item central to another religion, it might be better to speak of various religions enjoying a "family resemblance" rather than a common essence. It would be better yet to cease talking about what religion is in general and limit the discussion to what a religion is. A particular religion like Christianity will, of course, admit of many subtraditions and regional, cultural variations, but will still manifest at least seven basic dimensions: the practical and ritual; the experiential and emotional; the narrative or mythic; the ethical and legal; the social and institutional; the material; and the doctrinal and philosophical.

The last dimension involves a scheme of numinous, mystical, and incarnational propositions that can only be understood in their relation to each other and to the scheme as a whole, and can be justified respectively by appeal to awe-inspiring features of the world and life, the behavior and utterances of the mystic, and a convincing historical pattern of the incarnate person's holiness. Some secular worldviews (e.g., humanism, nationalism, Marxism) enjoy most of the same dimensions and participate in the religious search for self-knowledge or identity, but it would be inappropriate to label them real or even quasi-religions since they lack transcendental reference to the sacred beyond. With such a sense of transcendence, all the different religions can complement (rather than absorb) each other and contribute to the development of a new global *Weltanschauung* by providing a divine perspective for evaluating secular values.

Sources

Smart, Ninian. *Beyond Ideology: Religion and the Future of Western Civilization*. London: Collins, 1981.

_____. *Concept and Empathy: Essays in the Study of Religion*. Edited by Donald Wiebe. New York: New York University Press, 1986.

_____. *A Dialogue of Religions*. Westport, CT: Greenwood Press, 1981.

_____. "Methods in My Life." In *The Craft of Religious Studies*, edited by Jon R. Stone. New York: St. Martin's Press, 1959. 18–35.

_____. *Reasons and Faiths*. London: Routledge and Kegan Paul, 1971.

_____. *The World's Religions*. Englewood Cliffs, NJ: Prentice Hall, 1989.

Cunningham, Adrian. "Obituary for Ninian Smart." *The Independent* (5 February 2001), reprinted in Religion 31.4 (2001): 325–26 (The whole issue is dedicated to a discussion of Smart's contributions).

King, Ursula. "Smart, Ninian." In *Encyclopedia of Religion*. Vol. 12. Edited by Mircea Eliade. New York: Macmillan and Co., 1987, 2nd ed. (2005). 8442–45.

London, Scott. "The Future of Religion: An Interview with Ninian Smart." http://www.scott-london.com/insight/scripts/smart.html.

Long, Eugene Thomas. *Twentieth-Century Western Philosophy of Religion, 1900–2000*. Dordrecht, Boston, and London: Kluwer Academic Publishers, 2003. 475–77.

Masefield, Peter, and Donald Wiebe, eds. *Aspects of Religion: Essays in Honor of Ninian Smart*. New York: Peter Lang, 1994.

Socrates (470–399 B.C.)

While Socrates may not have been the Christ-like saint that some early Christian apologists made him out to be, neither was he the freethinking, or even atheistic, subverter of religion that he was accused of being by his contemporary critics, and then later, by Voltaire and other rationalistic champions of the Enlightenment and modern thought. What Plato, Xenophon, or even Aristophanes tell us about him suggests rather that although Socrates took reason seriously and used it to critique the religious practices of his time by associating piety so closely with the pursuit of wisdom, he was a deeply spiritual man whose religious convictions were at the heart of his moral philosophy. It is possible that already in childhood Socrates had been initiated in the Orphic religion that encouraged its followers to seek salvation through mystical communion with the deity. Its underlying religious ideas would continue to influence his thinking even after his repudiation of some of its more bizarre rituals.

Although the occasional fits of abstraction he would later experience and sometimes conclude with a prayer may have been other than mystico-religious raptures in nature, his repeated reference to the mysterious "voice" or "supernatural sign" he had been hearing since childhood would seem to suggest some sort of mystical sensitivity. So, too, with his attitude toward augury. While he never considered divination a substitute for the proper use of reason and did not hesitate during his trial to confess more reliance on his own "supernatural signs" than on "the birds," he did, according to Xenophon, have some confidence in augury, the most significant example of which — the notorious report from the Oracle of Delphi that he was the wisest of all men — precipitated the spiritual crisis he went through at or before the age of forty and clarified for himself what the gods wanted him to do as a philosopher.

In any event, the charges later brought against Socrates to the effect that he had failed to accept the gods of Athens and was replacing them with novel divinities of his own were without foundation in fact. Plato's contrasting of Socrates' profound sense of piety to Euthyphro's shallow, more superstitious view of religion hardly convicts Socrates of atheism, or even of any radical unorthodoxy. For however enlightened Socrates may have become about religion and life in general, he continued sacrificing to the traditional gods ("not dogs, birds, or stones") both at home and on the public altars of the city at the appointed festivals, and seemed to have few doubts that those same gods were perfectly wise, moral and just in their providence of this world.

SOCRATES ON RELIGION. There is a supernatural realm; there are gods, although they may not be the same as "the gods the state believes in," and they are certainly not as autocratic, amoral, ruthless, and unscrupulous in tormenting the innocent as were the gods of popular, traditional Greek religion. The gods are no less subject to rational norms (e.g., justice) than are humans. There is no double standard for the gods and man. To that extent, the gods cannot be the cause of all things, but only of good things, not of evil. Things are good, however, in and of themselves, not because the gods command them. The commands of the gods, therefore, are not arbitrary; they command what they do because that which they command is intrinsically good. Being omnipresent and on that account omniscient of all that is going on, they know best what is good for man, and use a variety of means — including some that would seem at first to be less than rational — to share with man their superior wisdom. While, therefore, reason may be one's best guide to moral decision-making, one must also take into rational account what the gods have commanded one to do through a personal *daimon*, divinations, dreams, and other supernatural channels.

Such divine revelation to individuals occurs because the gods need the help of pious human beings in order to complete their creative work toward the perfection of souls. True religion, or genuine piety, consists, therefore, not in self-serving, superstitious sacrifices for which the gods have no use, but in service to one's fellow humans through the cultivation of wisdom and virtue. Any prayer to the gods, then, is only for the sake of soliciting divine help in becoming their more attentive, ever-obedient servant — even to the point of being ready to die for their divine cause. So conceived, the divine mission of the philosopher is a practical one, having little to do with the study of the universe as a whole or with the scientific scrutiny of what causes celestial events, but everything to do with the care of souls.

Sources

Chroust, Anton-Hermann. *Socrates: Man and Myth. The Two Socratic Apologies of Xenophon*. Notre Dame: University of Notre Dame Press, 1957.

Gadamer, Hans-Georg. "Religion and Religiosity in Socrates." In *Proceedings of the Boston Area Colloquium in Ancient Philosophy*. Vol. 1. Edited by John J. Cleary. Lanham: University Press of America, 1986. 53–75.

Lefkowitz, Mary. "Comments on Vlastos' 'Socratic Piety.'" *Proceedings of Boston Area Colloquium in Ancient Philosophy* 5 (1989).

Lefkowitz, Mary. "Impiety and Atheism." *The Classical Quarterly* 39 (1945): 70–82.

McPherran, Mark L. *The Religion of Socrates*. University Park, PA: The Pennsylvania State University Press, 1996.

Taylor, A.E. Socrates: *The Man and His Thought*. Garden City, NY: Doubleday and Company, Inc., 1953.

Vlastos, Gregory. *Socrates, Ironist and Moral Philosopher*. Ithaca, NY: Cornell University Press, 1991. 157–78.

Solovyov, Vladimir (1853–1900)

The grandson of a priest, Solovyov was brought up by devout parents in the faith of the Russian Orthodox Church. But his reading of the lives of Christ by Strauss and Renan while still in secondary school inclined him to embrace atheistic materialism and socialism. Entering the University of Moscow at the age of sixteen, he had occasion to read Spinoza's *Ethics*; fascinated by the latter's idea of the "total unity" of reality, he turned back to religion. Within a few years, his interest in religion further invigorated by his study of Schopenhauer and the German Idealists, Kant, Fichte, Hegel, and Schelling, he had regained his Christian faith. After a year of studying theological and mystical literature at the Theological Academy at Zagorsk, writing a master's dissertation challenging Comte's positivist dismissal of religion and briefly teaching at the University of Moscow, Solovyov traveled to London to do research at the British Museum. While there he experienced again the vision of a "beautiful lady" he had earlier had as a nine-year-old boy attending the Orthodox liturgy, and which, after a third such mystical vision in an Egyptian desert, he interpreted as a symbol of *Sophia* or the divine Wisdom unifying the cosmos. It further inspired him to continue his exploration of the idea of total unity and to work for the regeneration of mankind through its spiritualization.

His 1880 doctoral dissertation and lectures on "God-man-hood" to an audience at the University of St. Petersburg that included Dostoevsky and Tolstoy enhanced his professorial status. Political disfavor, however, resulted in his retiring from the university and devoting the rest of his life to writing and lecturing. Public expression of his growing sympathy for reunion with the Roman Church and his disillusionment with slavophile views that identified the Kingdom of God exclusively with Orthodoxy led to his being prohibited for a time from writing on religious matters by the Russian Holy Synod. The fact that in 1896 he received the sacraments of penance and the Eucharist from a Catholic priest spawned rumors that he had actually converted to the Roman Church. But by his own account that was not the case, and there is little doubt that he died as a member of the Russian Orthodox Church, having received the Last Rites from one of its priests. Whatever his final membership, he remained convinced that it was neither the Orthodox, nor the Catholic Church, but the "universal and mystical" kingdom that constituted the "one, true Church" of Christ.

SOLOVYOV ON RELIGION. Religion is the connection of man and the world with God, the unconditional principle. The reality of this unconditional principle cannot be deduced from pure reason. It is accessible only to immediate perception or intuitive faith. But given such faith, the divine nature can be experienced, and through religious thought organized into a logically connected system. The combination of religious experience and thought has gradually given rise to the development of various stages of religious consciousness, each of which has been unique, and no one of which can be said to have been entirely false. First there arose the polytheistic nature — religions, then negative revelation (e.g., Buddhism and the experience of the unconditional as nothing), and finally positive revelation, when God is experienced as the Absolute, or the ideal fullness of all that is and the realization of truth, goodness and beauty in the unity of its own being.

As an active, productive principle reducing all multiplicity to oneness, such unity is the eternal *logos*. As the manifestation of that active principle, the resultant unity can be identified as *Sophia,* or the eternal ideal of humanity that was realized in Christ, the God-man, who in turn, as the divine life of his mystical body (the universal Church), works to overcome the egoistic proclivities of fallen man and to reunite the multiplicity of creatures into one organic whole. But because of its own internal divisions and failure to promote a moral social order, contemporary religion has lost much of its significance. Instead of being all in all, it has become only one of modern man's many interests. As such, it has no chance of fulfilling its mission of reuniting man and the world with God — at least not until the end of time, when, during the reign of the Antichrist, the few remaining Christians will bring their churches back together as a visible sign of the final divinization of humanity. In the meantime, the work of justice will often fall to unbelievers, as unwitting instruments of divine love.

Sources

Solovyov, Vladimir. *The Justification of the Good: An Essay in Moral Philosophy*. Translated by N.A. Duddington. London and New York: Macmillan, 1918.

_____. *Lectures on Godmanhood*. London: Denis Dobson Ltd. Publishers, 1948.

_____. *A Solovyov Anthology*. Arranged by S.L. Frank. Translated by Natalie Duddington. New York: Charles Scribner's Sons, 1950.

Bercken, Wil van den et al., eds. *Vladimir Solov'ëv: Reconciler and Polemicist*. Bondgenotenlann, Leuven, Belgium: Uitgeverij Peeters, 1998.

Copleston, Frederick C., S.J. *Philosophy in Russia: From Herzen to Lenin and Berdyaev*. Notre Dame: University of Notre Dame Press, 1986. 206–40.

_____. *Russian Religious Philosophy: Selected Aspects*. Tunbridge Wells, Kent, UK: Search Press Ltd.; Notre Dame: University of Notre Dame Press, 1988. 10–16; 42–47; 81–87.

Papin, J. "Solov'ev, Vladimir Sergeevich." *New Catholic Encyclopedia*. Vol. 13. Edited by W.J. McDonald. New York: McGraw-Hill, 1967. 422–24.

Spencer, Herbert (1820–1903)

Spencer's parents were both originally Methodists. But while the mother remained faithful to her Wesleyan convictions, the father, who came from a family of nonconformist Dissenters, developed at about the age of forty a preference for the Quakers and began frequenting their Sunday morning meetings. Spencer was often made to accompany his father to these meetings, and later in the evening to attend services with his mother at the Methodist church. This early exposure to religious practices made next to no impression upon Spencer. Asked later whether he had first embraced the orthodox creed before eventually doubting and rejecting it, Spencer replied that he had never been attracted to any established religion. The education he got at home from his father, and then from a clerical uncle to whom he was later entrusted, did little to awaken any religious sentiments, concentrating as it did on scientific studies to the relative neglect of history, languages, and other of the humanities.

Eschewing a university education and professorial career, he worked for four years as a surveyor for the railway companies, engaged himself over the next decade in radical journalism (espousing a *laissez faire* creed that championed rugged individualism and called for strict separation of church and state), and then, with the help of a large inheritance from his deceased uncle, spent his remaining fifty years — when not incapacitated by periodic bouts of nervous illness, acute insomnia, loneliness, and drug addiction — privately pursuing a life of scholarship and publishing the books on the evolutionary principles of philosophy, ethics, psychology, biology, and sociology, which, along with a variety of other writings, would win him international renown, but little financial reward.

Although his evolutionary explanation of the origin and historical development of the various religions identified their "consciousness of mystery" as the vital element linking them up with a scientific appraisal of natural forces, he may — according to some of his interpreters — have had little more in mind thereby than to have his own materialistic brand of agnosticism accepted as the final stage of mankind's intellectual maturation. But whatever his sense of mystery might have been, he insisted to the end (death and cremation at the age of eighty-three) that his native "creed of Christendom" was both emotionally and intellectually "alien to his nature."

SPENCER ON RELIGION. The law of the multiplication of effects, resulting from the persistence of Force operating in the material realm to constantly produce variety, applies also to the phenomenon of religion. From a rather homogenous worshiping of ancestral ghosts, based upon dream-induced experience of human duality (body/soul), primitive religion evolved into multiple forms of polytheism (as superior ancestors were apotheosized and their gravesites turned into sacred places of propitiatory sacrifices and libations), and then finally into monotheism, as military conquest and fanatical tribalism resulted in the gradual merging of scattered deities into one supreme power.

The various forms of religion that surfaced along the way were most fit for those who had to live under them. But the different modes of being they ascribed to the Ultimate Force were legitimate only as symbols that were utterly without resemblance to that for which they stood. For in the final analysis the Force generating the universe and its myriad forms is absolutely unknowable. And despite historical moments of irreligion, when religious leaders tried imposing their dogmas as the ultimate truth, religion has been steadily progressing toward recognition of Mystery as its final goal.

It is a goal shared with science, since the latter's ideas of space, time, matter, and motion are no less inexplicable than the First Cause. Far from undermining the religious consciousness of mystery, therefore, science has actually contributed to its reawakening by substituting less specific and less comprehensible agencies (e.g., gravitational pull) for the specific and comprehensible agencies (e.g., chariot of a god) previously assigned by religion in its attempt to explain one or another natural phenomenon (like the motion of the sun). The more we learn, in other words, the more mysterious reality becomes, leaving no room for anyone to claim infallibility (as political leaders do when, in rightful pursuit of the greatest good, they wrongly try to impose a state religion).

Sources

Spencer, Herbert. *First Principles*. New York: The De Witt Revolving Fund, Inc., 1958.
_____. *Social Statics*. New York: Robert Schalkenbach Foundation, 1970.
Caird, Edward. *The Evolution of Religion*. New York: Macmillan and Co., 1894. 92–95.
Collins, F. Howard. *An Epitome of the Synthetic Philosophy*. London: Williams and Norgate, 1889.
Elliot, Hugh. *Herbert Spencer*. New York: Henry Holt and Company, 1917. 216–32.
Hudson, William Henry. *Herbert Spencer*. London: Archibald Constable and Co., Ltd., 1908. 1–15; 76–87.
Kennedy, James G. *Herbert Spencer*. Boston: Twayne Publishers, 1978.
MacPherson, Hector. *Herbert Spencer: The Man and His Work*. London: Chapman and Hall, Ltd., 1900.
_____. *Spencer and Spencerism*. New York: Doubleday, Page, and Co., 1900. 189–200.

Spinoza, Baruch (1632–1677)

Compelled by the Inquisition to disguise their own religious convictions with an outward profession of Christianity, Spinoza's Jewish ancestors had fled Portugal to settle in Nantes. From there, prior to Spinoza's own birth, his father had moved to Amsterdam, where, being one of the most tolerant of European communities at the time, he was free to pursue the family's prosperous business and practice his Jewish religion openly, serving on occasion as warden of the local Synagogue. Until he was about fourteen, Spinoza attended that city's Talmud Torah school to learn Hebrew and to study the Law and the Talmud. For about the next ten years, instead of taking courses that would have prepared him for the rabbinate, he participated with his father and brother in the pursuit of business affairs and came into contact with Mennonite freethinkers who had developed a keen interest in writings by the likes of Descartes, Galileo, Kepler, and Bacon.

After the death of his conservatively religious father in 1654, he began drifting away from Orthodox Jewish practices and beliefs. Not satisfied with his reading of Jewish philosophers like Maimonides, he learned Latin from the ex–Jesuit, Francis van den Enden, and joined his religious, freethinking friends in the frequent discussion of Cartesian and other rationalistic philosophies. In 1656, after the failure of several attempts "to turn him from his evil ways," he was formally excommunicated from the Jewish community for what were described as "the horrible heresies which he practiced and taught, and monstrous actions which he performed."

In subsequent years, while supporting himself by working on optical instruments, continuing his study of Descartes, and conversing on occasion with other great thinkers of his time (like Leibniz), Spinoza began composing short treatises on his own understanding of the relation of God and Nature, the interpretation of Scripture, the freedom of science, and so on. Not only Jewish authorities, but Protestant ministers as well, accused him of atheism and convinced civil authorities to declare "sacrilegious" the sketch of his metaphysics and defense of toleration they found in his 1670, anonymously published *Theological-Political Treatise*. Fear of further reprisal caused the publication of his major work, the *Ethics*, to be delayed until after his death in 1677. Spinoza repeatedly denied being an atheist and died without ever having retracted any of his supposedly heretical views. By all accounts he had lived a simple, honest, and sober life, bearing his suffering and solitude with quiet dignity.

SPINOZA ON RELIGION. Popular religion should be tolerated to the extent that it inclines the uneducated masses to curb their lusts. But apart from its moral message, it delivers no real truth. Only a philosophical religion can adequately capture the radical unity and necessity that permeates the whole of Nature. Science can never provide an adequate knowledge of the essences of things unless it is complemented by the intuitive grasp of ultimate causality. Philosophical religion must begin, therefore, with a clear idea of God or Nature as the unique and absolutely infinite substance which is the cause of itself and whose essence, considered in and of itself (*Natura naturans*), necessarily involves its existence. As far as humans can tell, it consists — apart from certain non-substantive, adjectival *propria* like eternity and immutability — of

two infinite attributes of extension and thought. These in turn necessarily find expression in the modifications that constitute empirical nature *(Natura naturata)*.

Being neither free nor purposeful in generating the universe (except in the sense of acting necessarily in accordance with his own nature), God is best conceived, therefore, as the immanent, rather than the formal, cause of all that is, providing the latter with whatever striving they display toward preservation of their own being. Outside God or Nature, in other words, there is nothing. Everything that is exists only as a modification of the divine attributes. To that extent, whatever happens, happens by necessity, and humans have no choice but to be what they are. But by coming to know themselves as being in God and developing an intellectual love of God, they can escape enslavement to their passions and find salvation, not through some inconceivable divine grace or love, but through their own strength of mind and generosity. Although the mind cannot exist apart from the body, some part of it shares necessarily in the divine attribute of thought and to that extent can be eternal, notwithstanding the eventual death of the body.

Sources

Spinoza, Benedictus de. *The Collected Works of Spinoza*. Edited and translated by Edwin Curley. Princeton: Princeton University Press, 1985.

Barrett, Don, ed. *The Cambridge Companion to Spinoza*. Cambridge: Cambridge University Press, 1996. See esp. 13–60; 343–82.

Copleston, Frederick, S.J. *A History of Philosophy*. Vol. 4. Garden City, NY: Doubleday and Company, Inc., 1962–77. 211–69.

Dunham, James H. *The Religion of Philosophers*. Philadelphia: University of Pennsylvania Press, 1947. 180–212.

Gullan-Whur, Margaret. *Within Reason: A Life of Spinoza*. London: Jonathan Cape, 1998.

Hampshire, Stuart. *Spinoza*. Melbourne, London, and Baltimore. Penguin Books, 1953.

Hartshorne, Charles, and William L. Reese. *Philosophers Speak of God*. Chicago and London: The University of Chicago Press, 1963. 189–97.

Strauss, Leo. *Spinoza's Critique of Religion*. New York: Schocken Books, 1982.

Stumpf, Samuel Enoch. *Socrates to Sartre. A History of Philosophy.* New York: McGraw-Hill Book Company, 1982. 239–45.

Winston, David. "Spinoza, Barukh." In *Encyclopedia of Religion.* Vol. 14. Edited by Mircea Eliade. New York: Macmillan and Co., 1987. 7–11.

Wolfson, Harry Austryn. *The Philosophy of Spinoza.* Cleveland and New York: The World Publishing Co., 1958.

Suzuki, Daisetz Teitaro (1870–1966)

Suzuki was born in the Japanese city of Kanazawa, where a tremendous expansion of Pure Land Shin Buddhism since the fifteenth century had replaced the Zen Soto sect as the predominant religious force. His own family was formally registered at the local temple of the relatively rare Zen Rinzai sect. But his father (who died when Suzuki was only six) was also a Confucian, and his mother's deep interest in Buddhism also found expression occasionally in some unorthodox, Pure Land Shin practices, such as *hijibomon* (a clandestine meeting during which faith is secretly transmitted through the mercy of Amida). The mother involved Suzuki himself in this ritual when he was nine years old. Although she did not talk much about religion, she created a deeply religious atmosphere in the home, inviting a priest to chant sutras every month, lighting candles on the family altar every morning, and praying to Buddha every day. This, combined with the traumatic loss of his father and an older brother, naturally helped stir Suzuki's own interest in religion.

When he was about fifteen, some friends tried to get him to join them in their conversion to Protestant Christianity, but unable to find any answer from the Christian missionaries to his question about "who created God," he turned instead to further investigating Zen. He got no help from the uneducated priest at the local Zen temple, and a visit several years later to a Zen master in Takaoka (suggested by a math teacher who was also interested in Zen) proved "ignoble." His much beloved mother died shortly thereafter. Abandoning the teaching job he had held in nearby Mikawa, he eventually enrolled at the age of twenty-one, first at Waseda University in Tokyo, and then, prompted by his old school friend Kitarō Nishida, at the Tokyo Imperial University.

Within weeks of arriving in Tokyo he walked some thirty miles to visit Kosen Roshi, the Zen abbot of Engakuji, and was very much impressed by the man, the *sanzen* sessions he had with him about the koan *Sekishu* ("the sound of one hand") and the lectures he later heard from him. Suzuki continued studying Zen under Kosen Roshi's successor, Sōyen Shaku, and spent the next five years struggling to appreciate the koan of *mu* ("Not, or no, the negative beyond mere positive and negative") given him by Shaku. After finally experiencing *satori* at the age of twenty-seven, he devoted the remaining sixty-nine years of his long life translating, editing, writing, and lecturing in America, Japan and around the world on the significance of the Zen religion. He died while working on a book about the Zen master, Sengai. His ashes were buried in the woods behind Tokeiji Temple.

SUZUKI ON RELIGION. For all their splendor, technology and science foster indifference toward the value of the individual, reducing humans to things that can be used for industrial or mechanical purposes. And although the Western world in general appreciates the legal and political implications of individuality, its religious sense of individuality is very weak. An understanding of Zen can help the West in this regard. Rooted historically in the more practical mindset of the Chinese (as opposed to the highly speculative, supernaturalistic proclivities of the Indians), Zen teaches that to become a true individual one must be emancipated from one's sinful, mortal self and identify with the Absolute Nothingness of one's godlike Buddha-nature. Such a miracle can be expedited neither by the kind of logic taught by the ancient Greeks, which begins with the division of subject and object, nor by the kind of belief encouraged by Christianity, which rests upon a distinction between what is seen and not seen. Using "logical acumen and analytical subtlety" to seek "God" outside oneself at the end of "a long and tedious series of bifurcations and unifications" will only increase one's ignorance.

Ignorance can be overcome only through *sartori*, or, in other words, by "seeing into one's own nature as it is by itself," prior to any dichotomization between self and other, subject and object, man and God. Such a nondualistic awakening gives rise to *prajna*. Unlike "discursive, divisive and wordy" *vijnana, prajna* is a silent wisdom, an undifferentiated "consciousness of the Unconscious," or special kind of intuition that goes beyond the senses to grasp immediately the suchness (the self-identity of nothingness and non-nothingness) of reality. Ultimately, it consists of a nonconceptualized "knowing of what is unknowable," an experience of mystery in the light of which "every instant is eternity," every unreligious routine of life takes on deep spiritual significance, and every individual "is with, and is, God," the "all-embracing Whole."

Sources

Suzuki, Daisetz Teitaro. "Memories; An Autobiographical Account; Satori." In *A Zen Life: D.T. Suzuki Remembered*, edited by Masao Abe. New York and Tokyo: John Weatherhill, Inc., 1986. 3–62.

———. "Reason and Intuition in Buddhist Philosophy." In *Essays in East-West Philosophy*, edited by Charles A. Moore. Honolulu: University of Hawaii Press, 1951. 17–48.

———. *Zen Buddhism: Selected Writings*. Edited by William Barrett. New York: Doubleday, 1956.

———. *The Zen Doctrine of No-Mind*. Edited by Christmas Humphreys. York Beach, ME: Samuel Weiser, Inc., 1972.

Abe, Masao, ed. *A Zen Life: D.T. Suzuki Remembered*. With photographs by Francis Haar. New York and Tokyo: Weatherhill, 1986.

Humphreys, Christmas. *Buddhism*. Harmondsworth, UK: Penguin Books, 1976.

Switzer, A. Irwin, III. *D.T. Suzuki: A Biography*. London: The Buddhist Society, 1985.

Verkamp, Bernard J. *The Sense of Religious Wonder: Epistemological Variations*. Scranton, PA: The University of Scranton Press, 2002. 77–86.

Swinburne, Richard (1934–)

Although neither of his parents were Christian, Swinburne's earliest recollections are of having always thought and prayed in Christian terms. At the age of fifteen he was baptized in the Church of England. By the time he had completed his elementary education and military service and had enrolled as an undergraduate at Oxford University, being a Christian had become "the most important thing in [his] life." The attitudes of the modern academic world he encountered there struck him as being "basically anti–Christian." Instinctively defensive of his Christian faith, and loving to argue, he welcomed the challenge, but was very much disturbed and appalled by the "lazy indifference to modern knowledge" that had been spawned in the Church by the "sloppiness" of Kierkegaard and other Continental thinkers from whom Barth and other antirationalistic theologians had derived their philosophy.

Sensing that the greatest challenge to religion would be coming, not so much from the prevailing school of philosophy (i.e., Logical Positivism) as from the modern theoretical sciences, he spent the three years following completion of his studies of philosophy and theology using a research fellowship to broaden his understanding of the life and physical sciences. Upon discovering how science employs the "criterion of simplicity" to justify and render meaningful its theories about matters that are far beyond observation, he determined to use similar criteria, analyzed in accordance with the latest philosophical insights, to show the reasonableness of Christian theology. It was not until 1972, however, after ten years devoted to the philosophy of science at the University of Hull, that he began writing the trilogy on the philosophy of theism that he would publish over the next decade while serving as a professor of philosophy at the University of Keele.

Upon moving back to Oxford in 1985 to accept "the Nolloth Professorship of the Philosophy of the Christian Religion," he turned his attention to specifically Christian questions and, in addition to other works on the evolution of the soul and the existence of God, began publishing a tetralogy of books on human responsibility, revelation, the problem of evil, and other Christian doctrines. After retirement in 2002 he continued lecturing around the world and writing in defense of his previous publications. Although he had remained in the Church of England since baptism, and valued its sacramental worship and respect for scholarship, he wrote in 1993 that he had "never felt altogether comfortable as an Anglican," and were he to live in Russia or Greece, he would feel "more at home in the Orthodox Church."

SWINBURNE ON RELIGION. Contrary to media-driven, conventional wisdom based on the popularization of scientifically astute, but philosophically unsophisticated books, like Stephen Hawking's *A Brief History of Time*, theistic belief in the existence of a personal, infinite, omnipotent, omniscient, free, everlasting, and good God is not, intellectually, a lost cause, and religious faith is not an entirely nonrational, incoherent matter. For by using the same criteria (expectation of observable events; simplicity; coherence; lack of rival theories) employed by scientists to reach their own theories, it can be shown that belief in God's existence explains everything we observe — that there is a universe at all and that there are scientific laws operating within it, conscious animals and humans with naturally evolved, embodied souls, miracles (like the Resurrection of Jesus upon which Christianity is founded), reports of religious experiences, etc.) — and not just some narrow range of data, as when science describes the physical laws of nature merely as brute facts.

By religion is meant a systematic worshiping of God that offers salvation for oneself and others by providing: a deep understanding of the world and man's place in it; divine forgiveness; and guidance toward a happy life now and hereafter. There are five types of religious experience, depending upon whether the experience of God is mediated through: (1) an ordinary, public object (e.g., night-sky); (2) an unusual, public object (e.g., burning bush); (3) private sensations describable in normal vocabulary; (4) private sensations indescribable in normal vocabulary; (5) nonsensory intuition. Given the Principle of Credulity that one ought to believe that things are as they seem to be unless there is evidence to the contrary, such religious experiences, along with other aforementioned factors (a well-designed universe, conscious beings, etc.), do provide reliable evidence for the existence of God. Those who accept it have a duty to serve both God and man through unlimited commitment.

Sources

Swinburne, Richard. *The Coherence of Theism.* Oxford: Clarendon Press, 1977.
_____. "Could There Be More Than One God?" *Faith and Philosophy* 5.3 (July 1988): 225–41
_____. *The Evolution of the Soul.* Oxford: Clarendon Press, 1986.
_____. *The Existence of God.* Oxford: At the Clarendon Press, 1979.
_____. *Faith and Reason.* Oxford: At the Clarendon Press, 1981.
_____. *Is There A God?* Oxford and New York: Oxford University Press, 1996.
Alston, William P. "Swinburne's Argument for Dualism." *Faith and Philosophy* 11.1 (January 1994): 127–33.
Clark, Kelly James. *Philosophers Who Believe. The Spiritual Journeys of 11 Leading Thinkers.* Downers Grove, IL: InterVarsity Press, 1993. 179–202.
Long, Eugene Thomas. "Richard Swinburne." In *Twentieth-Century Western Philosophy of Religion, 1900–2000.* Dordrecht, Boston, and London: Kluwer Academic Publishers, 2003. 404–7.
Padgett, Alan G., ed. *Reason and the Christian Religion: Essays in Honour of Richard Swinburne.* Oxford: Clarendon Press, 1994.

Tennant, Frederick Robert (1866–1957)

Born in Burslem, Staffordshire, the oldest son of a wine merchant, Tennant was brought up in the orthodox religious beliefs of the Church of England. Early on, while attending secondary school at Newcastle-under-

Lyme, he showed an interest in science. Upon graduation, he received a grant to attend Cambridge University's Caius College, and there took courses in physics, biology and chemistry. He spent the year of 1889 studying mathematics at Dulwich College. During the same year he was increasingly aroused by Thomas Huxley's attack on traditional religious beliefs (via biblical criticism) to begin looking for some way to reconcile religion and the latest findings of all the different sciences. Two years later he got married and was employed to teach science at his former high school.

In addition to his ongoing scientific investigations, however, he would also devote much of his time during the next three years to the study of theology, enough in fact to qualify himself for ordination to the diaconate and priesthood in the Anglican Church. After several years of pastoral work, he was appointed curate at Great St. Mary's in Cambridge, and used the opportunity to pursue further philosophical studies under the Cambridge philosophers John McTaggart and James Ward. Soon thereafter, while continuing his ministerial work, he began publishing a number of theological treatises, along traditional Augustinian lines, on the origin and nature of sin.

On the strength of these scholarly works he was invited in 1907 to become a lecturer on the philosophy of religion at Trinity College in Cambridge. Six years later he was appointed lecturer in theology at the same school and remained in that position until his retirement in 1931. During this period of his teaching at Cambridge he became a close friend of his fellow professor James Ward and was especially influenced by the latter's work in natural epistemology and psychology. It took him another fifteen years, however, to develop the personal point of view he would publish in his major, two-volume work, *Philosophical Theology*— a work that would make him the most renowned exponent in his day of an empirical defense of theism and a significant influence on the later development of the philosophy of religion, but one also that left some Christian thinkers with the false impression that Tennant had abandoned a biblically based Judaeo-Christian tradition to align himself with traditional English deism.

TENNANT ON RELIGION. There are no *a priori*, rational, logically coercive, or deductive proofs for the existence of God. The Ontological Argument upon which rational and *a priori* theology stands or falls is obviously fallacious. Nor can religious beliefs be derived from religious experience. Contrary to what Rudolf Otto and others imply, there is no uniquely religious or mystical faculty capable of immediately grasping an object that is other than the sensory and sense-derived. Its subjects may not be aware of it, but such experiences are religious only to the extent that their object is interpreted to be numinous on the basis of theological presuppositions. If religious experience is to be validated, therefore, its "notions of the numinous, the supersensible, the supernatural, and the theistic idea of God" can only be derived indirectly from study of the sensible world, man's soul and human history.

One must start with the question about how the world, inclusive of man, is to be explained. Belief in God will be reasonable only to the extent that the idea of God's existence and attributes are found to be indispensable for explanation of the totality of our scientific knowledge about the world and man, including the existence of natural and moral evils. That the idea of God is indispensable for such an explanation is suggested by the chain of epistemological, psychological and biological facts that render the teleological argument reasonable — not in its more traditional, narrow sense of challenging Darwin's conclusion that there are proximate and mechanical causes sufficient to produce adaptations, but in its wider sense that a certain "general order of Nature," designed by a morally eternal, but temporally and providentially involved, personal God, must be posited to explain how Nature, as a whole, could, against all empirical odds, give birth through an evolutionary process to a living, intelligent, free and, therefore, moral phenomenon like man. "Nature is meaningless and valueless without God behind it and man in front."

Sources

Tennant, F.R. *The Nature of Belief.* London: The Centenary Press, 1943.

_____. *Philosophical Theology.* 2 vols. Cambridge: At the University Press, 1928 and 1930.

Bertocci, Peter Anthony. *The Empirical Argument For God in Late British Thought.* Cambridge, MA: Harvard University Press, 1938. 192–255.

Buswell, J. Oliver. *The Philosophies of F.R. Tennant and John Dewey.* New York: Philosophical Library, 1950.

Hick, John. "Tennant, Frederick Robert." *Encyclopedia of Philosophy.* Vol. 2. Edited by Paul Edwards. New York: Macmillan and Co. and The Free Press, 1967. 392–94.

Long, Eugene Thomas. *Twentieth-Century Western Philosophy of Religion, 1900–2000.* Dordrecht, Boston, and London: Kluwer Academic Publishers, 2003. 56–59.

Springer, Klaus-Bernhard. "Tennant, Frederick Robert." In *Biographisch-Bibliographisches Kirchenlexikon.* Vol. 20. Verlag Traugott Bautz, 1999. http://www.bautz.de/bbkl/. 1451–53.

Thomas Aquinas (1225–1274)

At the age of five, Thomas was offered (*oblatus*) by his noble parents to the Benedictine Abbey of Monte Cassino that lay not far from the place of his birth in Aquino. He remained there for nine years and along with lessons in elementary grammar, received his earliest instruction in the basics of the Roman Catholic faith into which he had been born. An ongoing political battle between Emperor Frederick II and the pope, in which Thomas' father and older brothers were involved as military men, eventually resulted in the abbey being occupied as a fortress and the monks being exiled. After a brief return home, Thomas was sent to a school in Naples where over the next five years he got his first exposure to the philosophy of Aristotle and, much to the chagrin of his mother, joined the Dominican Order of mendicant friars, committing himself to their life of evangelical poverty and service to the Church.

The Order sent him to study under Albert the Great, and upon the latter's recommendation had him appointed seven years later (after having been ordained a priest) to a Dominican chair at the University of Paris. Amidst the internecine academic battles between the religious orders and secular clergy, Thomas pursued his licentiate and advanced degrees in theology, lecturing all the while on Lombard's *Sentences* and various biblical texts, initiating the writing of his *Summa contra Gentiles*, and publishing significant works, like his *De Ente et Essentia* and *De Veritate*. From 1259–1268 he was back in Italy, lecturing at the papal court, preaching, teaching, completing the *Summa contra Gentiles*, and writing many other works, including parts of his *Summa Theologica*.

Upon returning to Paris he became embroiled in controversy between the Augustinian theologians (e.g., Bonaventure) and the Latin Averroists (e.g., Siger of Brabant). The attack against the latter implied doubts also about the orthodoxy of Thomas' own Aristotelian leanings, and although he was never excommunicated and was always ready to submit his theological conclusions to the judgment of the Church, a number of propositions related to his teaching were condemned by several bishops after his death. The last three years of his life were spent back in Italy, teaching and writing, until after celebrating Mass one day in 1273, he concluded that all he had written was "so much straw" by comparison to what he had seen and heard in his more mystical experiences. He died the next year, never having written or dictated another theological sentence. In subsequent centuries he was canonized and proclaimed a Doctor of the Church.

THOMAS AQUINAS ON RELIGION. Whatever its etymological roots (*relegere*: to read again; *religere*: to seek again; or *religare*: to bind), religion is concerned with the relationship of man to God as the first principle of creation and ultimate end of human life. Subjectively speaking, it is one dimension of the virtue of justice. Although man can never give God all that God deserves or add one iota to

His glory, religion is the habit which inclines humans, for the sake of their own perfection, to render to the excellence and lordship of the one God the worship and service that are His due. Objectively, it consists of interior acts of devotion and prayer and exterior acts of adoration, offerings (sacrifices, oblations, tithes, etc.), and the use of sacred things (sacraments, invocations of the Holy Name, oaths, etc.).

Although not self-evident, the existence of such a superior Being can be demonstrated. From observation of motion, efficiency, contingency, gradation, and regularity in the universe, it is reasonable to posit the existence of God as the Prime Mover, the First Efficient Cause, the Necessary, Perfect, and Intelligent Being who in the beginning of time, or perhaps from all eternity, freely created the universe out of nothing, and organized its great chain of being in such a way as to facilitate the actualization of each creature's potential in accordance with eternal and natural law. While the use of reason can help man see that God is, what He is not, or even to speak analogically about what He is, it is only through the revelations of Christ that man can discover the mystery of the Trinity, or learn of the Divine Law which directs man toward his supernatural end of beatific vision. If Jews and some members of the Greek, Roman and other pagan religions have been saved without receiving the Christian revelation, it was only because by believing in divine providence they had at least implicit faith that God would deliver mankind from the sin and evil resulting from man's freedom and the corruptibility of things.

Sources

Thomas Aquinas. *Basic Writings*. 2 vols. Edited by Anton C. Pegis. New York: Random House, 1945.

_____. *Commentary on Aristotle's Metaphysics*. Translated by John P. Rowan. Notre Dame: Dumb Ox Books, 1995.

_____. *On the Truth of the Catholic Faith: Summa Contra Gentiles*. 4 vols. Garden City, NY: Doubleday and Company, Inc., 1956.

_____. *Summa Theologiae*. Vol. 39. Latin text and English translation. England: Blackfriars; New York: McGraw-Hill Book Company; London: Eyre and Spottiswoode, n.d.

_____. *Truth (De Veritate)*. 2 vols. Translated by Robert W. Mullingan. Chicago: Henry Regnery Company, 1952.

Copleston, Frederick, S.J. *A History of Philosophy*. Vol. 2, pt. 2. Garden City, NY: Doubleday and Company, Inc., 1962–77. 20–155.

Curran, John W. "The Thomistic Concept of Devotion." *The Thomist* 2 (1940): 410–43; 546–80.

Falardeau, E.R. "Religion, Virtue of." *New Catholic Encyclopedia*. Vol. 12. Edited by W.J. McDonald. New York: McGraw-Hill, 1967. 270–71.

Gilson. Etienne. *History of Christian Philosophy in the Middle Ages*. New York: Random House, 1954. 361–83.

McInerny, Ralph. *St. Thomas Aquinas*. Notre Dame: University of Notre Dame Press, 1982.

Stumpf, Samuel Enoch. *Socrates to Sartre. A History of Philosophy*. New York: McGraw-Hill Book Company, 1982. 168–92.

Wallace, W.A., and J.A. Weisheipl. "Thomas Aquinas, St." *New Catholic Encyclopedia*. Vol. 14. Edited by W.J. McDonald. New York: McGraw-Hill, 1967. 102–15.

Thoreau, Henry David (1817–1862)

Thoreau inherited his "quick-witted spirit and passionate love of nature" from his mother, the daughter of the Rev. Asa Dunbar. She had Thoreau baptized into the Unitarian Church of Concord by its pastor, the Rev. Dr. Ezra Ripley. But as his friend Ralph Waldo Emerson would later write, Thoreau "was a born protestant" in the sense of being a fiercely independent and original thinker. After graduating from Harvard in 1837 and serving a few years as a schoolteacher back in Concord, he quietly severed his ties with Ripley's church, justified his refusal to pay the church tax by signing a statement to the effect that he was not a member of any congregational body, and stopped attending any church services. At about the same time he read Emerson's *Nature* (along with works by Goethe and Virgil), moved into Emerson's house, and by his own account became something of "a mystic, a transcendentalist, and a natural philosopher."

Various biographers have suggested that

Thoreau had come to embrace a pantheist view of reality. Others, however, have argued that, while Thoreau was certainly no orthodox theist (given his emphasis upon the immanence and temporality of God), labeling him a pantheist fails to do justice to his idea of God as Transcendent Creator, and that his position might best be defined, therefore, as one of "panentheism." Be that as it may, Thoreau remained, as Emerson noted, "a person of a rare, tender, and absolute religion."

However petulant his remarks about organized religion and its priests might have been in his subsequent writings, he never doubted the importance of "holy living." "Without religion of some kind" he thought (according to Emerson) "nothing great was ever accomplished." He did not think, however, that a Bible-based, Judaeo-Christian *Weltanschauung* was the only or even the best account of Nature's wonders. In *A Week on the Concord and Merrimack Rivers* he would suggest, for example, that Zeus, as described in the Orphic fragments he had come across in Proclus's commentary on Plato's *Timaeus,* might be preferable to Jehovah, given the former's closer identification with nature and his less exclusively male features. He also became fascinated by the sacred books of ancient China, Persia, and India, concluding that the ethics they espoused were fully comparable to Mosaic law. When asked by his aunt on his deathbed whether he had made his peace with God, he replied, "I did not know we had ever quarreled."

THOREAU ON RELIGION. A science that enriches the understanding, but robs the imagination by ignoring the symbolism of things, knows things merely mechanically, and therefore knows nothing. Close observation of natural phenomena is essential to the pursuit of knowledge, but excessive scientific preoccupation with details to the exclusion of a sense of wholeness blinds one to the real Nature (the divine element) beneath the surface of things. But if science can be an obstacle to discovery of the God lurking in Nature, so too can institutional religion. There is much wisdom to be found in the sacred scriptures of various nations (especially in the *Bhagavad Gita* or in the writings of the Buddha). And it might even make sense to try collecting them all into one "Scripture of mankind," on the assumption that the gods are of no sect and side with no man. But by trying to come up with cut-and-dried schemes of the universe, and using fear to impose them in the form of fixed creeds, Christianity and other institutionalized religions suppress that homage of the infinite, incomprehensible and sublime which constitutes the very basis of religion.

Nature (and the transcendent God to which it points) is ultimately ineffable. Its mysteries can never be put into words. True religion, therefore, is that which is never spoken. It reaches its climax in the mystical, inward hearing of the kind of silence encountered at the pond on a moonlit night or walking alone through snow-covered woods. It is this intercourse with Nature, when God himself culminates in the infinite stillness of the present moment, that gives birth to the imagination and the religious sentiment. It brings with it an indescribable, infinite, all-absorbing, divine heavenly pleasure, an ecstatic sense of elevation and expansion. There needs no stronger proof of immortality. But such eternal bliss is open only to the pure of heart, who establish their divine being by dying daily to their animal past through obedience to the higher laws of Nature, even and especially when they contradict the laws of man.

Sources

Thoreau, Henry David. *The Selected Works of Thoreau.* Cambridge edition. Boston: Houghton Mifflin Company, 1975.
_____. "Selected Writings." In *The Spirituality of The American Transcendentalists*, edited by Catherine L. Albanese. Macon, GA: Mercer University Press, 1988. 233–343.
Dickens, Robert. *Thoreau: The Complete Individualist.* New York: Exposition Press, 1974.
Emerson, Ralph Waldo. "Biographic Sketch." In Henry David Thoreau, *Walden.* New York: Walter J. Black, 1942. 1–23.
Hodder, Alan D. *Thoreau's Ecstatic Witness.* New Haven and London: Yale University Press, 2001.

Krutch, Joseph Wood. *Henry David Thoreau*. [New York]: William Sloane Associates, 1948.

Richardson, Robert D., Jr. *Henry Thoreau: A Life of the Mind*. Berkeley: University of California Press, 1986.

Salt, Henry S. *Life of Henry David Thoreau*. Edited by George Hendrick, Willene Hendrick, and Fritz Oehlschlaeger. Urbana and Chicago: University of Illinois Press, 2000.

Schofield, Edmund A., and Robert C. Baron, eds. *Thoreau's World and Ours*. Golden, CO: North American Press, 1993.

Verkamp, Bernard J. *Senses of Mystery: Religious and Non-Religious*. Scranton, PA: University of Scranton Press, 1997. 88–95.

Wagenknecht, Edward. *Henry David Thoreau*. Amherst: The University of Massachusetts Press, 1981.

Wolf, William J. *Thoreau: Mystic, Prophet, Ecologist*. Philadelphia: A Pilgrim Press Book, 1974.

Unamuno y Jugo, Miguel de (1864–1936)

Unamuno had a rigorous Catholic upbringing. In his mid-teens, while still going to Mass daily and receiving communion monthly, he engaged in a bit of bibliomancy and got the impression of being called to the priesthood. Young love for his future wife, Conceptión, kept him from accepting. During his first two years at the University of Madrid he continued practicing his Catholic faith, but then gave it up when he could find no rational foundation for it. While trying, without much success, to launch a professorial career after reception of his doctorate in philosophy, he would periodically and briefly return to the practice of Catholicism, once for the sake of sparing his wife and mother any further grief, and again in 1896 when his third child was born with severe meningitis. Suspecting on the latter occasion that he was being cursed by God for his apostasy, he fell into deep depression, brooding over death and contemplating suicide. He withdrew to a Dominican monastery and tried to recover his faith by participating in Holy Week ceremonies. But it was to no avail. "God remained silent," he later observed, and he was left with his doubts.

Returning to Salamanca where he had earlier begun teaching Greek and would eventually become rector, he started reading the works of Protestant liberal theologians, like Kierkegaard, Ritschl and Harnack, who played up the role of faith as an act of the will. For the remaining four decades of his life, incessantly punctuated by intermittent academic appointments and dismissals on political grounds, he struggled, in a steady stream of novels, plays, and philosophical essays, to develop the torturous dialectic of his doubt and will to believe into a tragic sense of human existence.

Still despairing of his ability ever to find logical justification for religious beliefs, he concluded that even if no rational proof could be found for what religion promises about life after death, one should nonetheless live in such a way as to convince others that one deserves to live forever, and out of love for one's fellow humans (who may need religion to buffer themselves against daily vicissitudes), refrain from imposing one's own doubts upon them. Whether this was enough to keep him within the Catholic fold remains a matter of debate.

UNAMUNO Y JUGO ON RELIGION. Mankind has reached God through a sense of divinity. The latter arose out of a feeling of dependency on, and the subjective personalization of, the mysterious forces of nature. The divinization of these forces was simply their humanization, the only difference between gods and men being that the former were thought of as being immortal. Monotheism evolved from man's sense of divinity as a warlike, monarchical and social God. Upon being made ethical by the Judaic prophets, this one god was individualized, and then, when taken possession of by philosophy, was defined by reason (i.e., idealized) and converted into a mere idea (the logical God, the *ens summum*, the *primum movens,* the Supreme Being). The traditional proofs of the existence of God all refer to this God-Idea, and hence prove nothing more than the existence of this idea of God, a dead thing (i.e., individualized to the point of depersonalization).

The Christian Gospel by contrast reveals God as a living person with whom man can communicate through the feeling of love. Whether this personal God is a substantial being, existing independently of our consciousness and desire, is impossible to prove. But to submit to reason and no longer to wish in our heart that there is such a God, is a terrible and inhuman thing. For confronted with the painful fact of death and possible extinction, man is filled with dread at the prospect of going from nothingness to nothingness, and hungers for personal immortality. This tragic thirst for eternal life can only be appeased by the kind of absurd, religious faith in the Risen Christ and Beatific Vision (the final joyful ecstasy of ceaseless learning) genuine Catholicism protects, not by a pathetic quest for fame or some sorry counterfeit for immortality like "eternal recurrence." Perhaps, only those, like Don Quixote, who thus long for immortality, and live their lives accordingly in pursuit of truth, beauty and goodness, deserve to experience it. In any event, we must not so act as to deserve a fate of nothingness.

Sources

Unamuno, Miguel de. *The Agony of Christianity.* Translated by Kurt F. Reinhart. New York: Frederick Ungar, 1956.
_____. *Essays and Soliloquies.* New York: Alfred A. Knopf, 1925.
_____. *Tragic Sense of Life.* Translated by J.E. Crawford Flitch. [New York]: Dover Publications, 1954.
Alluntis, Felix, O.F.M. "Miguel Unamuno: The Tragic Sense of Life." In John K. Ryan, ed. *Twentieth-Century Thinkers.* Staten Island, NY: Alba House, 1967. 307–29.
Brown, Kendall W., and Patrick S. Roberts. "Unamuno y Jugo, Miguel de." In *World Philosophers and Their Works.* Vol. 3. Edited by John K. Roth. Pasadena, CA, and Hackensack, NJ: Salem Press, Inc., 2000. 1917–24.
Ilie, Paul. *Unamuno: An Existential View Of Self and Society.* Madison, Milwaukee, and London: The University of Wisconsin Press, 1967.

Vico, Giambattista (1668–1744)

Naples was still a stronghold of Roman Catholicism at the time Vico was born, the son of a poor bookseller. At his baptism in the church of St. Januarius he received his Christian name, Giovanni Battista. Despite a life-threatening fall during his childhood that triggered, by his own account, a "melancholic and irritable" disposition, his rational powers remained intact, and he pursued his early studies on his own or under the direction of the Jesuits, who controlled Naples' educational system. Under one of them, a Father Ricci, he developed a passing interest in the scholastic metaphysics of Duns Scotus and Suarez. While later studying law, history, and classical antiquity, he continued reading the likes of Plato, Aristotle, Epicurus, Tacitus and Descartes (preferring by far the moral and historical vision of Plato and Tacitus over that of the other three).

In 1699 he married and began a forty-year tenure as professor of rhetoric (not of law, as he wanted) at the University of Naples. All the while he remained true to his Roman Catholic heritage, at one time even discontinuing annotation of a treatise by Grotius on grounds that it would be unbecoming of a Catholic to enhance the work of a supposed heretic. Like the "wise man" he describes in his *Orations,* he was himself someone who believed in revelation and tried to live his life in accordance with Christian morality as it was being taught by Catholic authorities. But although he was a Roman Catholic, who would go out of his way sometimes to insist that his own thoughts were in harmony with the Catholic faith, and take pride in the fact that his masterpiece (*The New Science*) had originated in Catholic Italy rather than in Protestant England, Germany, or Holland, his was not a Roman Catholic philosophy in any strict sense.

He certainly was a religious and Christian thinker, and his distaste for individualism, or his appreciation of authority and common sense, may well have been colored by his Roman Catholicism. But the primary inspiration for his philosophical and legal ruminations came not so much from Christian theology or even the Bible, as it did from the likes of Plato and Cicero. His mission as a philosopher, he thought, was to demonstrate the Platonic truth of God as the eternal source of all reality. Consistent with his belief in divine providence, he bore his life-long poverty, the grievous illness of one daughter, the criminal delinquency of one of his sons, and the relative disregard of his work by contemporaries, as a test of his faith. He died while trying to sing one of David's psalms.

VICO ON RELIGION. Bayle was wrong to conclude (on the basis of false reports of travelers) that there has ever been a nation of atheists. For all nations originated in some religion. Already the very first stage of civilization — the patriarchal, family stage — was based upon and shaped by religion to such an extent that it can also be called "the age of the gods." Although the ancient gentiles, due to the original fall of the founders of mankind, lacked the kind of special divine assistance the Jewish people would later enjoy, and had not yet achieved the full use of their reason, they were nonetheless able to exercise the poetic imagination with which divine providence had endowed all human beings. Filled with wonder and fear of the awful powers of nature, and sensing their own finiteness and an innate desire for immortality, they imagined the sky, the sea, and other natural phenomena to be a divine animate body that caused things to be as they were (thereby anticipating the rational argument against skepticism that there must be a creator of all that men do not themselves create).

Eventually, and especially during the subsequent "age of heroes" when the original poetic imagery became embedded in a matrix of mythology, a plurality of gods were imagined to reflect the various forces of nature and were named Zeus/Jove, Poseidon/Neptune, and so on. However idolatrous it may have been, it was their sense of community with, and fear of, these gods that tamed the wild and egoistic native proclivities of the gentiles and inclined them to develop the structures of social life. The ascendancy of reason during the third stage of civilization ("the age of men") threatened to replace religion with philosophy. But the inherent skepticism of the latter caused a

relapse into barbarism, triggering the first of many more cycles of social development and decay through which human history would henceforth pass, under the religious influence ultimately of a Christianity that keeps its poetic imagination subject to reasoning inspired by God's own word.

Sources

Vico, Giambattista. *Autobiography*. Translated by Max Harold Fisch and Thomas Goddard Bergin. Ithaca and London: Cornell University Press, 1975.
_____. *The First New Science*. Edited and translated by Leon Pompa. Cambridge and New York: Cambridge University Press, 2002.
_____. *New Science*. 3rd ed. Translated by David Marsh. London and New York: Penguin, 1999.
_____. *On the most ancient wisdom of the Italians*. Translated by L.M. Palmer. Ithaca: Cornell University Press, 1988.
_____. *Selected Writings*. Edited and translated by Leon Pompa. New York: Cambridge University Press, 1982.
Capronigri, A. Robert. *Time and Idea: The Theory of History in Giambattista Vico*. New Brunswick, NJ: Transaction Publishers, 2004.
Collingwood, R.G. *The Idea of History*. London, Oxford, and New York: Oxford University Press, 1956.
Copleston, Frederick, S.J. *A History of Philosophy*. Vol. 6, pt. 1. Garden City, NY: Doubleday and Company, Inc., 1962–77. 179–89.
Flint, Robert. *Vico*. Edinburgh and London: William Blackwood and Sons, 1884. (Ann Arbor, Michigan, and London: University Microfilms International, 1981).
Lion, Aline. *The Idealistic Conception of Religion: Vico, Hegel, Gentile*. Oxford: The Clarendon Press, 1932.
Pompa, Leon. *Vico: A Study of the New Science*. New York: Cambridge University Press, 1990.

Voltaire (Arouet, François Marie) (1694–1778)

Voltaire was baptized a Catholic in the parish of Saint-André-des-Arts. His father was a well-placed attorney with a relatively indifferent, bourgeois attitude toward Jansenism. Although Voltaire would later express some concern about the unjust persecution of some

Jansenists, his early education by the Jesuits left him feeling nothing but contempt for the fanatically rigorous and ascetical brand of Jansenism his older brother, Armand, embraced after being sent to the Jansenist-oriented, Oratorian school of Saint-Magloire. Voltaire claimed to have been sexually abused by a number of his Jesuit instructors, but was full of praise for the "unrewarded and indefatigable pains" the majority of them had taken in their effort to discipline his intellect.

A trip to Holland in his early twenties, and then (after several brief incarcerations in the Bastille for scurrilous political writings) to England ten years later, left him impressed (as he states in his 1734 *Lettres Philosophiques*) at the ability of diverse religious sects to tolerate each other's freedom of thought. The trip to England also nurtured the deistic leanings his earlier readings had spawned. For the next twenty-five years, however, while engaged in intense literary and scientific work in Mme. du Châtelet's castle and airing his deistic views in the friendly company of Prussia's King Frederick, he refrained — apart from isolated, anticlerical jibes against religious superstition — from openly attacking traditional Church doctrine.

After finding relative security in Geneva and Ferney, however, and being outraged by the 1755 Lisbon earthquake and the Calas/Sirven affairs, he began launching an attempt to "crush the infamy" of what he considered to be ecclesiastical (both Catholic and Protestant) obscurantism and persecution. He openly repudiated the efficacy of the sacraments (notwithstanding his own occasional reception of communion), and rejected traditional beliefs in the Trinity, the Incarnation, original sin, predestination, or anything that went beyond adoration of God as the Supremely Intelligent Designer of the universe. In his final years he also devoted much of his time trying to refute the atheism of Baron d'Holbach and others. Over the protests of a skeptical archbishop of Paris, Voltaire's deathbed confession of Catholic faith was enough to get him a burial plot at the Abbey of Scellières where his nephew was abbot.

VOLTAIRE ON RELIGION. If God did not exist, it would be necessary to invent him, for while there are virtuous atheists, no civilized race can survive without the idea of a God who rewards and punishes secret crimes. Furthermore, all of nature itself cries out to us that God exists, giving rise to a natural religion at whose core is also an innate sense of morality. Astonishing natural phenomena initially triggered the idea of god as a supernatural master to whom sacrifice had to be offered as a way of protecting one group from another. The beauty and order of nature eventually reinforced this primitive notion by rightly inclining humans to think that, notwithstanding earthquakes and other physical and moral evils (like the shameful, ecclesiastical execution of Jean Calas) or the lack of historical progress, there must be some conscious intelligence providently designing and ruling our world — a Supreme Being, that is, who is equally good and powerful. But it would be presumptuous to think that we can understand why or how God acts.

True religion, therefore, has nothing to do with any incomprehensible metaphysics such as has spawned so many ridiculous dogmas (e.g., Trinity, Incarnation, Predestination) in Christianity. It consists rather in free adoration and justice, or as the good man Jesus taught us, in loving God and in loving one's neighbor as oneself. The cruelest enemy of such pure worship is the superstitious belief in a God of Vengeance despicable, power-hungry priests have ruthlessly imposed upon the masses down through the centuries. Every effort must be made to crush it! But so long as citizens (be they Turk, Jew, or Christian) do not disturb the public order, they should be free to believe whatever their enlightened or denuded reason dictates. In fact, the multiplicity of religions, as evidenced in England, is the best cure of intolerance. If it is erroneous to think that religion will make us happy not only now but in the next life also, belief in human immortality is certainly one of the more beautiful errors.

Sources

Voltaire. *Candide and Other Writings*. New York: The Modern Library, 1956.

Copleston, Frederick, S.J. *A History of Philosophy*. Vol. 6, pt. 1. Garden City, NY: Doubleday and Company, Inc., 1962–77. 31–38; 190–95.

Durant, Will, and Ariel Durant. *The Age of Voltaire*. New York: Simon and Schuster, 1965. See esp. 715–54.

Mason, Haydn T. *Pierre Bayle and Voltaire*. London: Oxford University Press, 1963.

Vial, F. "Voltaire." *New Catholic Encyclopedia*. Vol. 14. Edited by W.J. McDonald. New York: McGraw-Hill, 1967. 743–45.

_____. *Voltaire: A Biography*. Baltimore, MD: The Johns Hopkins University Press, 1981.

Wade, Ira O. *The Intellectual Development of Voltaire*. Princeton: Princeton University Press, 1969.

Von Hügel, Friedrich, Baron (1852–1925)

Von Hügel's father was an Austrian diplomat who, though generally indifferent to religion, still counted himself a member of the Catholic Church. His mother, thirty-seven years younger than her spouse, was a Scotch Presbyterian who converted to Roman Catholicism while von Hügel was still a young child. He had good reason, then, to claim later that he was "a born Catholic." In making that assertion he had added the prayer that he would also "live and die a Catholic." And he did, but not without going through a teenage crisis of faith and a lifetime of painful struggles to maintain the right not only to think, but also and especially "to think his religion," notwithstanding its institutional, authoritarian structure.

Although, while growing up in Brussels and England without any formal education, he had made his First Communion at the age of fifteen, and at seventeen had read a book by Cardinal Newman that impressed him with the Church's "intellectual might and grandeur," it was not until he was faced at the age of eighteen with a combination of his father's untimely death and an illness of his own (which left him half-deaf for life) that he decided, upon the advice of a Viennese priest,

to take his Catholicism more seriously by embracing wholeheartedly its ascetical dimension of longsuffering, as symbolized by the Cross of Christ. After burying his father in Vienna, von Hügel returned to England, soon thereafter married Lady Catherine Herbert (a convert to Catholicism who would bear him three daughters), and proceeded, with constant encouragement from friends (Norman Kemp Smith, George Tyrrell) and spiritual advice from the saintly Henri Huvelin, to initiate a lifelong study of Biblical criticism and the philosophy of religion.

This work eventually got him embroiled in the Catholic Church's so-called Modernist Crisis, during which he was attacked from both sides for being either too supportive of modern scholarship or too ready to retreat from the battle. But he had always considered his scholarly endeavors only one aspect of his overall pursuit of God through an often frustrating, dynamic balancing of the institutional, intellectual, and mystical dimensions of religion, and no doubt reckoned his subsequent lecturing (as founder of the London Society for the Study of Religion and Gifford Lecturer) and writing about the mystical element of religion, God, and eternal life, consistent with the same. In his latter years he would profess his enduring belief that, for all its authoritarian and obscurantist foibles, the Catholic Church still possessed far greater supernatural depth than Protestantism, and "more still than the quite unattached moderns."

VON HÜGEL ON RELIGION. Critical realism rightly implies that while religion is inconceivable without some human subject apprehending its Object, the reality and presence of the latter is independent of its apprehension. While, therefore, any and every religion is constituted in part by the institutional form whereby its members can anticipate eternal life through membership in a corporate body, and is further constituted by the creedal, catechetical, and theological formulas that can withstand the inevitable questioning and doubts of its maturing members, its most important constituent — "the central characteristic of all religion worthy of the name"—is the immediate experience of the Given, the Reality of God.

This latter constituent is called the "mystical element of religion" because although the immediate apprehension of it yields an intuitive knowledge that is vivid and of such emotional and moral impact as to incline all religious people to adoration and some rare souls (like Catherine of Genoa) to the heroic height of sanctity, such knowledge remains dim and ultimately beyond conceptualization by even the best of theologies (i.e., those enlightened by modern biblical and historical criticism). Triggered by sensible apprehensions of creatureliness (of weakness, instability, and dependence more than of evil, suffering or sin), it consists (contrary to all projectionist or illusionist explanations of religion by the likes of Feuerbach) of an anticipatory sense of the presence of a noncontingent, nonanthropomorphic Otherness—an infinite, superhuman and supreme Isness, whose good and creative personality Catholicism (better than any other historical religion) reveals in its teaching about the divine love and suffering of the God-Man, Jesus. It is with this experience of God as the source of all beauty, goodness, and truth, and not with the thought of merely prolonging this earthly life, that the specifically religious desire of immortality begins and ends, not unlike the trustworthiness of a little dog being put to sleep by its beloved master.

Sources

Von Hügel, Friedrich, Baron. *Essays and Addresses on the Philosophy of Religion* 1 and 2. London and Toronto: J.M. Dent and Sons, Ltd.; New York: E.P. Dutton and Co. Inc., 1928.

_____. *The Eternal Life: A Study of Its Implications and Applications.* Edinburgh: T. & T. Clark, 1912.

_____. *The Mystical Element of Religion as Studied in Saint Catherine of Genoa and Her Friends.* 2 vols. London: J.M. Dent and Sons; New York: E.P. Dutton and Co., 1923.

_____. *Readings.* Selected by Algar Thorold with an introductory essay on his philosophy of religion. London and Toronto: J.M. Dent and Sons, Ltd.; New York: E.P. Dutton and Co., Inc., 1928.

_____. *The Reality of God and Religion and Agnosticism.* Edited by Edmund G. Gardner. London and Toronto: J.M. Dent and Sons Ltd.; New York: E.P. Dutton and Co., Inc., 1931.

_____, and Norman Kemp Smith. *Letters.* Edited by Lawrence F. Barmann. New York: Fordham University Press, 1981.

Barmann, Lawrence F. *Baron Friedrich von Hügel and the Modernist Crisis in England.* Cambridge: At the University Press, 1972.

_____. "Friedrich von Hügel as Modernist and as more than Modernist." The Catholic Historical Review 75 (1989): 211–32.

_____. "The Modernist as Mystic: Baron Friedrich von Hügel." *Journal for the History of Modern Theology* 4 (1997): 221–50.

Cock, Albert A. *A Critical Examination of von Hügel's Philosophy of Religion.* London: Hugh Rees, n.d.

Whitehead, Alfred North (1861–1947)

Whitehead's paternal grandfather and uncles had provided him with good examples of how life could best be lived in accordance with Christian (i.e., Anglican) faith. His own father was appointed by Archbishop Tate (a close family friend) curate of several large, but mostly rural, parishes in southern England and came to be highly respected for the practical, "humanizing and kindly" influence he had on his parishioners. Daily life at the public school Whitehead attended included bible study, morning prayers and evensong. At nineteen, he enrolled at Cambridge, and like all students (except Roman Catholics and Nonconformists) was expected to attend chapel services at least two days of the week, and twice on Sundays.

Elected a member of the elite university discussion club known as "the Apostles" that included nonbelievers, Whitehead heard many arguments in favor of atheism, but consistently voted his belief in God and immortality "of some sort." He was still a loyal Anglican, contributing a substantial amount of his own earnings to its Foreign Missions. But there was also much talk about the relative merits of Roman Catholicism, and over the next decade Whitehead himself, while reading and visiting Cardinal Newman, seriously considered shifting his religious commitment from the Anglican to the Roman church and even toyed with the thought of becoming a monk. Whether because of his preoccupation with romancing his future wife (as Russell claimed), or because of misgivings about papal infallibility generated by his reading of church history and reinforced by the diminishing authority of Newtonian physics, or because of the moralistic, theological overemphasis upon an omnipotent God, he did not make the move. Instead, over the next twenty-five years he became a defiant agnostic.

After the death of his son in World War I, however, his desire to find religious meaning was rekindled by the thought that apart from religion, human life is but "a flash of occasional enjoyments lighting up a mass of pain and misery." Abandoning agnosticism, he began developing his own philosophical theism. He especially appreciated the Christian emphasis upon love, and showed some preference for Unitarianism, but true to his conception of religion in terms of "what an individual does with his own solitariness," he refrained from joining any particular church. Upon his death, a service was held in Harvard's Memorial Church, and his ashes were scattered in its graveyard.

WHITEHEAD ON RELIGION. To explain how formless "process" (creativity) — the ultimate fact of experience — gives rise to actual entities and their societal organization through the concretion of infinite possibilities (eternal objects), it is necessary to posit a principle of limitation called God. It is the primordial nature of God to envisage the infinite possibilities and to present them to actual entities as relevant lures toward novel determinations of being, and then, as such entities perish, to preserve their value forever as his own ever-developing, consequent nature. The real object of religious worship, therefore, is a God conceived metaphysically as the completed ideal harmony underlying the passing flux of things. But dominated by collective emotion and ritual, religion in its primitive phase was essentially an authoritarian, provincial, and pragmatic social phenomenon, with its primary

goal being the preservation of the social body by appeasement of a mythological, hostile God. Only when it was rationally purified of its collective trappings did religion become what it is supposed to be, namely, "what the individual does with his own solitariness."

Inspired by the likes of Prometheus, Mohammed, Buddha, or Christ on the Cross, genuinely religious people experience God as a Companion in the struggle against evil who lures the solitary individual into actualization of personal freedom and responsibility. The social detachment and forgetfulness of self resulting therefrom leads to a recognition that one's own life is worth living only to the extent that it is merged with the essential rightness of the objective universe. Such loyalty to the world expresses the intuition of sacredness underlying an appreciation for the interrelatedness of everything and for the significance of every detail to the total picture of the universe. Although conduct is not the main point of religion, it is an inevitable by-product, and preserved in the consequent nature of God and the cosmic order, its value will afford the individual his best chance of immortality.

Sources

Whitehead, Alfred North. *Adventures of Ideas*. New York: The Macmillan Company, 1933.

_____. *Process and Reality*. Edited by David Ray Griffin and Donald W. Sherburne. New York: The Free Press, 1978.

_____. *Religion in the Making*. Cleveland and New York: The World Publishing Company, 1966.

_____. *Science and the Modern World*. New York: The Free Press, 1967.

Bixler, Julius Seelye. "Whitehead's Philosophy of Religion." In *The Philosophy of Alfred North Whitehead*, edited by Paul Arthur Schilpp. Evanston and Chicago: Northwestern University Press, 1941. 487–511.

Cobb, John B. *A Christian Natural Theology Based on the Thought of Alfred North Whitehead*. Philadelphia: The Westminster Press, 1965.

Cobb, John B. "Whitehead, Alfred North." In *Encyclopedia of Religion*. Vol. 15. Edited by Mircea Eliade. New York: Macmillan and Co., 1987. 380–81.

Crosby, Donald A. "Religion and Solitariness." In Victor Lowe, *Alfred North Whitehead: The Man and His Work*. Vol. 2: 1910–1947. Baltimore and

London: The Johns Hopkins University Press, 1985. 149–69.

Ford, Lewis S., and George L. Kline, eds. *Explorations in Whitehead's Philosophy*. New York: Fordham University Press, 1983.

Hartshorne, Charles. *Whitehead's Philosophy: Selected Essays, 1935–1970*. Lincoln, NE, and London: University of Nebraska, 1972. See esp. 63–110; 193–99.

Johnson, A.H. "Some Conversations with Whitehead Concerning God and Creativity." In Lowe, *Whitehead*, Vol. II. 3–13.

Lawrence, Nathaniel. "Ethics, Aesthetics, and Philosophical Theology." In *Alfred North Whitehead, Essays On His Philosophy*, edited by George L. Kline. Englewood Cliffs, NJ: Prentice-Hall, Inc., 1963. 168–78.

Lowe, Victor. *Alfred North Whitehead: The Man and His Work*. Vol. I: 1861–1910. Baltimore and London: The Johns Hopkins University Press, 1985; Vol. II: 1910–1947. Edited by J.B. Schneewind. Baltimore and London: Johns Hopkins University Press, 1990.

William of Ockham (c. 1235–1349)

Little is known about Ockham's first years. He joined the Franciscans at the age of fourteen and began his early education in their house of studies at Southwark, in the diocese of Winchester. Its Archbishop Winchelsey ordained him a subdeacon circa 1303–06. The fact that Ockham later sought from the bishop of Lincoln a license to hear confessions would seem to suggest that he was also ordained to the priesthood, although there is no evidence of pastoral activity on his part. After studying theology at Oxford and while pursuing advanced degrees in that discipline, he lectured (at both Oxford and Southwark) on the Bible and the *Sentences* of Peter Lombard, and during the subsequent decade wrote some of his major commentaries on Lombard and Aristotle.

That he never became a *magister regens* was mainly due to the accusation of heresy raised against him by Oxford's chancellor, John Lutterell. Summoned by the Avignon pope, John XXII, and found guilty, but never formally condemned, for a number of his propositions, Ockham subsequently became involved with the Franciscans' minister general, Michael of Cesena, in an argument against the pope about papal authority, the beatific vision, and evangelical poverty. After charging the pope with heresy on the latter matter, and fleeing Avignon to seek refuge at Pisa with an archenemy of the pope, Emperor Ludwig of Bavaria, Ockham and his superior were both excommunicated in 1328.

Ockham's alienation from church officials worsened over the next twenty years as he (along with Marsilius of Padua) went to the defense of the emperor in the dispute over the proper balance of secular and spiritual power. But all the while he claimed to be a faithful Catholic, ready and willing to submit to any genuinely legitimate ecclesiastical authority. And there is no evidence that by raising serious philosophical issues he had in mind to undermine the Church's dogmas, or to align himself with his Order's more radical wing. In any event, with the death of Emperor Ludwig in 1347, Ockham apparently made some attempt to reconcile himself with the Church. Whether he ever signed the papal formula of submission that would have required retraction of some of his earlier views is not known. After dying as a victim of the bubonic plague he was buried in the choir of the Franciscan church in Munich. This would seem to suggest that his excommunication had in fact been lifted.

WILLIAM OF OCKHAM ON RELIGION. Universals are nothing but words; as natural or conventional signs, they have logical significance, but no existential import, not even in the mind of God. Only singulars really exist. Thus, while one religion may resemble another because each, in and of itself, is a form of worship whereby God is paid the reverence that is His due, there is no common nature of religion that produces their resemblance. They resemble each other simply by virtue of what they are as distinct entities. So, too, in regard to the church. It may be said to be universal, but not in the sense of existing apart from the totality of individuals that are its members. The universal church is simply the communion of all believers from the time of the apostles to the present who have enjoyed the certitude of the Catholic faith. It cannot be identified with any one or another of its members, be it the pope, a college of bishops, or a particular church like that of Rome or Constantinople. It is rather Christ's Mystical Body, which Christ, as its Head, might preserve in the faith of a single individual believer.

God's power being absolute, it is not inconceivable that God could have chosen or can still choose to save individuals in a way other than the established system of salvation represented by Christianity's sacramental order and its ethical dictates of eternal, natural, and positive law. But the latter do express God's free choice, making it likely that rather than arbitrarily introducing a new morality or extraordinary means of grace, He will be true to the order He has established and reward those who adhere to it with salvation. There are limits, though, to what reason can tell us about God. It might hint at the existence of a Prime Efficient Cause, but given the lack of any intuitive or abstractive cognition thereof, it cannot prove whether such a Prime Cause is unique, free, infinite, or omnipotent. So too with other religious matters, like the existence and fate of the human soul. In the end, we have only faith upon which to rely for certitude.

Sources

William of Ockham. *Philosophical Writings*. A selection edited and translated by Philotheus Boehner, O.F.M. Edinburgh, London, and Melbourne: Thomas Nelson and Sons, Ltd., 1962.

Adams, Marilyn McCord. *William Ockham*. Vol. II. Notre Dame: University of Notre Dame Press, 1987.

Copleston, Frederick, S.J. *A History of Philosophy*. Vol. 3, pt. 1. Garden City, NY: Doubleday and Company, Inc., 1962–77. 56–133.

Courtenay, William J. "Nominalism and Late Medieval Religion." In *The Pursuit of Holiness in Late Medieval and Renaissance Religion*, edited by Charles Trinkaus and Heiko A. Oberman. Leiden: E.J. Brill, 1972. 26–58.

Freddoso, Alfred J. "Ockham on Faith and Reason." In *The Cambridge Companion to Ockham*, edited by Paul Vincent Spade. Cambridge: Cambridge University Press, 1999. 326–49.

Gál, G. "William of Ockham." *New Catholic Encyclopedia*. Vol. 14. Edited by W.J. McDonald. New York: McGraw-Hill, 1967. 932–35.

Gilson. Etienne. *History of Christian Philosophy in the Middle Ages*. New York: Random House, 1954. 489–99.

Hambly, Gavin R.G. "William of Ockham." In *World Philosophers and Their Works*. Vol. 3. Edited by John K. Roth. Pasadena, CA, and Hackensack, NJ: Salem Press, Inc., 2000. 1419–22.

Klocker, Harry, S.J. *William of Ockham and the Divine Freedom*. Milwaukee: Marquette University Press, 1996.

Leff, Gordon. *William Ockham*. Manchester: Manchester University Press; Totowa, NJ: Rowman and Littlefield, 1975.

Matson, Wallace I. *A New History of Philosophy: Ancient and Medieval*. Vol. 1. San Diego: Harcourt Brace Jovanovich, Publishers, 1987. 245–47.

Wisdom, John (1904–1993)

Wisdom was the son of an Anglican clergyman and grew up in various rectories in and around Suffolk County. After primary education at the Aldeburgh Lodge School, he was enrolled at Monkton Combe School in Bath, a private institution with a long history of providing instruction in the Christian faith and promoting basic Christian values. At the age of seventeen he began his undergraduate studies at Cambridge. There he got his first exposure to careful philosophical analysis from professors G.E. Moore and C.D. Broad, obtaining the highest honors on one part of his tripos in the then so-called Moral Sciences (philosophy) and graduating in 1924 with a B.A. degree.

After working five years with the National Institute of Industrial Psychology, he was hired to teach philosophy at St. Andrew's University. He returned to Cambridge in 1934 to lecture in philosophy and to finish work on his M.A. Soon thereafter he was elected a fellow of Trinity College. Several decades later he succeeded to the chair of philosophy formerly held by Wittgenstein and became renowned for the lively, Socratic, and often humorous lectures he delivered. He retired from Cambridge University at the age of sixty-four, but then taught for four years more at the University of Oregon, before returning to live out his retirement years in Cambridge.

While publishing many books and articles throughout all these years (often under the influence of Wittgenstein's philosophy of language) about the reductive or nonreductive nature of philosophy, he also retained a keen interest in religion, not only writing about it, but sometimes also (according to his friend Renford Bambrough) attending Sunday morning church services. He left the impression of being enthusiastic about such services. But he also applied to his experience of religion the notion he had earlier developed about how philosophical "paradoxes" or "perplexities" should be welcomed because of their power to illuminate one's sense of reality and the way one conducts one's life. Bambrough reports, for example, that while silently walking back from a church service one Sunday morning in Ireland, Wisdom suddenly exclaimed, with long pauses between his words: "Isn't ... Christianity ... *fantastic*?" But then, to the consternation of those accompanying him who might have wanted a clearer indication of where he really stood on the practice of religion, he added, after a similar and longer pause, "And yet ... and yet...." Predeceased by his second wife, he died in a Cambridge nursing home and was buried with a private ceremony.

WISDOM ON RELIGION. Given the advance in scientific knowledge, disagreement between theists and atheists about what god or gods exist is no longer the kind of experimental issue it once was when the prophet Elijah's prayer supposedly brought down fire from the heavens to make his case. It is now recognized that questions about whether there is a God who made the world and looks after it, whether God became incarnate in Jesus, and so on, belong to a family of obscure questions that simply admit of no inductive or deductive answers, since God is by definition a spirit that cannot be seen or heard. Contrary to what some philosophers have rather courageously claimed, this does not mean, however, that because such questions cannot be settled

by empirical observation or in the deductive manner used in mathematics and logic, they are unreal, meaningless, worthless, and merely verbal, emotive, or nonsensical questions. Nor does it imply, therefore, that the dispute between theists and atheists is any more idle than would be a dispute between two individuals agreeing on all the relevant facts about whether a gardener has been seen attending a beautifully arranged but weed-infested garden, while still arguing about how to respond to the garden as a whole.

Just as in legal arguments, or in arguments about the aesthetic quality of one or another painting, or about the love that one individual might have for another, so in the dispute between theists and atheists, even if all the facts have been established, there remain meaningful questions about the patterns in which the facts are arranged and how one set of acts is connected with or disconnected from another. By combining such a technique with the readily acceptable, psychoanalytical observation of hidden forces of good and evil, light can be shed on certain patterns of human reactions that give substance to religious beliefs. This will keep questions about the existence of God or the devil within the scope of rational thought, and generate a new awareness of what we have always known — a new way of experiencing the facts as being of religious significance.

Sources

Wisdom, John. "Gods." *Proceedings of the Aristotelian Society* 45 (1944–45): 185–206.

_____. *Paradox and Discovery.* Oxford: Basil Blackwell, 1965. (Essays: "The Logic of God," 1–22; "Religious Belief," 43–56).

Ayers, Michael. "Wisdom (Arthur) John Terence Dibben." *Oxford Dictionary of National Biography: From the earliest times to the year 2000.* Vol. 59. Edited by H.C.G. Matthew and Brian Harrison. In association with The British Academy. 2004. 827–28.

Bambrough, Renford, ed. *Wisdom: Twelve Essays.* Oxford: Basil Blackwell, 1974.

Barker, Stephen F. "John Wisdom." In *World Philosophers and Their Works.* Vol. 3. Edited by John K. Roth. Pasadena, CA, and Hackensack, NJ: Salem Press, Inc., 2000. 1981–89.

Diamond, Malcolm L., and Thomas V. Litzenburg, Jr., eds. *The Logic of God: Theology and Verification*. Indianapolis: The Bobbs-Merrill Company, Inc., 1975. 151–55.

Dilman, İlham, ed. *Philosophy and Life: Essays on John Wisdom*. The Hague, Boston, and Lancaster: Martinus Nijhoff Publishers, 1984.

_____. *Studies in Language and Reason*. Totowa, NJ: Barnes and Noble Books, 1981. 85–135.

Hick, John. *Philosophy of Religion*. 3rd ed. Englewood Cliffs, NJ: Prentice-Hall, Inc., 1983. 95–97.

London Times, "Obituary," December 13, 1993, 17.

Phillips, D.Z. "Wisdom's Gods." *The Philosophical Quarterly* 19 (1969): 15–32.

Richmond, J. *Theology and Metaphysics*. London: SCM Press, 1970. 63ff.

Thomson, Judith Jarvis. "Wisdom, (Arthur) John Terence Dibben." *Encyclopedia of Philosophy*. Vol. 8. Edited by Paul Edwards. New York: Macmillan and Co. and The Free Press, 1967. 324–27.

Wittgenstein, Ludwig (1889–1951)

After the Napoleonic decree of 1808 required Jews to take a surname, Ludwig's paternal great-grandfather adopted the name of his employers, the German aristocratic Seyn-Wittgensteins, and subsequent generations generally disengaged themselves from the Jewish community. Like all of his seven brothers and sisters, Ludwig was baptized into the Catholic faith and sometimes (as he later confessed) tried to conceal the fact that he was more Jewish than Aryan.

He claimed to have lost his religious faith as an adolescent while studying at the same Realschule in Linz attended by Hitler, and initially shared the hostile attitude toward religion of his teacher and fellow professor at Cambridge, Bertrand Russell. On several occasions he stated that he could not possibly bring himself to believe all the things that (Catholics) believe, and rejected all attempts to prove the existence of God and other Catholic beliefs by philosophical arguments. As an Austrian soldier in World War I, however, he came across Tolstoy's *Gospel in Brief* and claimed to have been "kept alive" by its em-

phasis upon practical simplicity and the inner life as protection against all external vicissitudes. And even after reading Nietzsche's *The Antichrist* he remained convinced that in providing the example of Christ's dignified suffering, Christianity offered the "only sure way to happiness." He admitted to friends that, however hard it sometimes was, he prayed a lot and, except for his "fundamental deficiency," would have preferred becoming the kind of priest who might, instead of babbling theological nonsense, read biblical stories to children (as he would later have a chance to do while teaching at a grade school in the mountain village of Trattenbach). He even considered becoming a monk.

Russell thought his favorite student had become something of a mystic. Wittgenstein in turn had come to loathe Russell's vitriolic attacks on religion, and tried steering him back to Christianity. This contributed significantly to the cooling of their friendship. Wittgenstein never practiced his Catholicism in any traditional way. He in fact admitted that he was not religious, but was inclined to see everything from a religious perspective. As he lay dying of cancer, at peace with his own conscience, several of his Catholic friends, recalling Wittgenstein's own request for their prayers, summoned the "nonphilosophical" priest (Father Conrad) with whom they had earlier put him in touch, to administer the last rites of the Catholic Church. He was given a Catholic burial the next day at St. Giles's Church in Cambridge, England.

WITTGENSTEIN ON RELIGION. Frazer's dismissal of primitive religion as "bad science" is symptomatic of the arrogant, corrosive assumption of modern culture that science can explain everything and is the goal toward which all cultural evolution has been progressing. But religion is not scientific in nature. Quite to the contrary, to believe in God means precisely that the facts of the world are not the end of the matter, and that life has a meaning beyond anything explicable by science. To try to base religion on science is to reduce it to superstition. Nor can religion be based upon metaphysical wisdom. The perennial attempt to explain the contingency of this world by reference to a Necessary Being treated God as just another item in the world, something about which one could talk. But if the word "God" makes any sense at all, it is only as a limit or terminus to all explanation. "God" simply designates "the world as a limited whole" or "how things stand," that is Fate (that which has been decreed, and is good precisely because it has been decreed).

To avoid talking nonsense or trivializing this mystical meaning and value of life, it is best to pass over it in silence. But what cannot be spoken can and does show itself in religion. It includes various forms of life (hoping, feeling certain) that involve the use of a language (prayer, myths/rites, hymns) with its own set of rules, not to justify factual propositions, but to draw a picture (Last Judgment, Eye of God) of what deeply affects its members and regulates their lives as they face death and other critical situations. Unlike wisdom that is "cold, grey ash covering glowing embers," religious faith is a passion that can change and redeem one's life, inclining one, for example, to seek immortality in the timelessness of the moment. And although it may be nigh impossible to be a religious person in the modern world, the decline of religion is no cause for rejoicing.

Sources

Wittgenstein, Ludwig. *Culture and Value*. Oxford: Blackwell Publishers, 1998.
_____. *Lectures and Conversations on Aesthetics, Psychology and Religious Belief*. Oxford: Blackwell Publishers, 1966.
_____. *Notebooks, 1914–1916*. Edited by G.H. von Wright and G.E.M. Anscombe; translated by G.E.M. Anscombe. Chicago: The University of Chicago Press, 1979.
_____. *On Certainty*. Oxford: Blackwell Publishers, 1977.
_____. *Philosophical Investigations*. Oxford: Blackwell Publishers, 1953.
_____. *Remarks on Frazer's Golden Bough*. Translated by A.C. Miles. Doncaster: Byrnmill Press, 1979.
_____. *Tractatus Logico–Philosophicus*. Translated by D. Pears and B. McGuinness. London: Routledge and Kegan Paul, 1961.
Barrett, Cyril. *Wittgenstein on Ethics and Religious Belief*. Oxford: Blackwell Publishers, Ltd., 1991.
Clack, Brian R. *Wittgenstein, Frazer and Religion*. Houndmills, Basingstoke, Hampshire and New York: Palgrave Publishers Ltd., 1999.
Finch, Henry Le Roy. "Wittgenstein, Ludwig." In *Encyclopedia of Religion*. Vol. 15. Edited by Mircea Eliade. New York: Macmillan and Co., 1987. 428–30.
Goodman, Russell B. *Wittgenstein and William James*. Cambridge: Cambridge University Press, 2002.
Gudmunsen, Chris. *Wittgenstein and Buddhism*. London and Basingstoke: The Macmillan Press, Ltd., 1977.
Hodges, Michael P. *Transcendence and Wittgenstein's Tractatus*. Philadelphia: Temple University Press, 1990.
Hudson, W. Donald. *Wittgenstein and Religious Belief*. London: The Macmillan Press, Ltd., 1975.
Malcolm, Norman. *Wittgenstein: A Religious Point of View?* Ithaca: Cornell University Press, 1994.
McGuinness, Brian. *Wittgenstein: A Life, Young Ludwig 1889–1921*. London: Duckworth, 1988.
Phillips, D.Z. *Wittgenstein and Religion*. Houndmills, Basingstoke, Hampshire and London: St. Martin's Press, 1993.
Sherry, Patrick. "Is Religion a 'Form of Life?'" *American Philosophical Quarterly* 9, no. 2 (April 1972): 159–67.
Smart, Ninian. *Philosophers and Religious Truth*. London: SCM Press Ltd., 1964. 163–82.
Zemach, Eddy. "Wittgenstein's Philosophy of the Mystical." *Review of Metaphysics* 18 (1964): 38–57.

Xenophanes (c. 580–480 B.C.)

Xenophanes was a native of Colophon, a small town in the region of Ionia where Greek philosophy was first getting started and many an Ionic temple could be found housing Apollo and other of the Olympian gods immortalized by Homer and Hesiod. He lived there for twenty-five years until he was forced to flee when the small town was captured by the Persians. Many of his remaining sixty-seven years were spent wandering from one Greek community to another in Sicily and southern Italy, composing and reciting poetry along the way.

Whether he was ever the teacher of Parmenides or the founder of the Eleatic school of thought is doubtful, but he certainly was a serious philosopher. He prided himself on being a wise man, claiming on one occasion that his "wisdom is better than the strength of men and horses." His assertion that nothing could be known about the gods or about anything else of which he was speaking may only have implied a distinction between opinion and knowledge, but even that would have taken philosophy a major step beyond the absolutist posturing of his Ionian predecessors. It did not, however, make him a skeptic, for in other passages he definitely states that in time humans can make progress in their understanding of the gods and reality in general.

At the time Xenophanes was living (and for many centuries thereafter) the gods of Homer and Hesiod were still being worshiped; on the assumption that their actions could not be judged by human standards of morality, they remained "objects of cult" and a focus for popular religious beliefs and practices. That Xenophanes attacked the anthropomorphic nature and immorality of such deities does not mean that he was an atheist. He was not necessarily a monotheist either, declaring as he did that the one god is the "greatest of gods," but he certainly did believe in the existence of God. He imagined this god being totally different from human beings, and (contrary to accusations of his being a pantheist) as the lord of the universe. And unless he is to be dismissed as a hypocrite, in the light of the advice he gave to others about the need to preface their festive celebrations with prayer, hymns, and other acts of spiritual purification, it would seem that he himself did occasionally pray and participate in some religious acts of worship. He died at a very advanced age, apparently without ever having attracted any disciples.

XENOPHANES ON RELIGION. Contrary to claims of divine inspiration by some, the gods did not, and never will, reveal all things to mortals, either by direct revelation, or by divinatory portents. As a result, humans are left to seek the truth themselves, hoping to grow in knowledge, but fully aware that even were they to chance upon the truth they would never know it. No one has ever, or will ever, know the whole truth about the gods. Many of the names given in the past to the gods were merely personifications of natural phenomena (e.g., Iris, in reality, is a rainbow). Images of the gods simply mimic how humans conceive of themselves, as if the gods are born, wear clothes, or have a voice and a body. Thus, while the Ethiopians picture their gods as snub-nosed and black, the Thracians describe theirs as having light blue eyes and red hair. If cattle, horses, or lions were able to draw, they would no doubt make the gods look like themselves! Worst of all in this regard were Homer and Hesiod, who attributed to the gods all sorts of things that are reprehensible among humans (e.g., theft, adultery, deceit).

Table talk about such fictions of old or about the furious conflicts of the ancient gods is either useless or harmful to civic virtue. The gods should rather be held in high regard, and especially the one god who is greatest among gods and men. Alike in all parts or not, this one god is certainly not like mortals in body or in thought. Lacking any separate sense organs, It sees, hears, and thinks with the whole of Its being. Its vision, unlike the narrow perspective of mortals, is comprehensive, effortlessly setting all things in motion, while remaining immobile Itself. Before launching into their festive banquets it would behoove the glad-hearted participants, therefore, to try to match the physical cleanliness of their surroundings with a display of spiritual purity by first hymning the god with reverent words and pure speech, pouring a libation, and praying for the power to do what is right (e.g., avoiding drunkenness and excessive luxury), whether or not such behavior will result in the transmigration of the soul after death.

Sources

Xenophanes. *Fragments*. Text and translation with a commentary by J.H. Lesher. Toronto: University of Toronto Press, 1992.

Barnes, Jonathan. *Early Greek Philosophy*. Harmondsworth, UK: Penguin Books, 1987. 93–99.

De Young, Ursula. "The Homeric Gods and Xenophanes' Opposing Theory of the Divine." http://ablemedia.com/ctcweb/showcase/deyoung5.html.

Jaeger, Werner. *The Theology of the Early Greek Philosophers*. Oxford: At the Clarendon Press, 1948. 38–54.

Kerferd, G.B. "Xenophanes of Colophon." *Encyclopedia of Philosophy*. Vol. 8. Edited by Paul Edwards. New York: Macmillan and Co. and The Free Press, 1967. 353–54.

Kirk, G.S., J.E. Raven, and M. Schofield. *The Presocratic Philosophers: A Critical History with a Selection of Texts*. Cambridge: Cambridge University Press, 1990. 163–80.

Lesher, J.H. *Xenophanes of Colophon: Fragments: A Text and Translation with a Commentary*. Toronto: University of Toronto Press, 1992.

Melchert, Norman. *The Great Conversation*. Boston: McGraw-Hill, 2002. 14–18.

Wheelwright, Philip, ed. "Xenophanes." In *The Presocratics*. New York: The Odyssey Press, Inc., 1966. 31–39.

Zeno of Citium (336/5–263 B.C.)

Zeno's father was a merchant. On one sea voyage to Athens and back to his hometown, the Phoenician-Greek city of Citium in Cyprus, he is said to have brought to his son the Socratic dialogues. Zeno supposedly devoted himself to their study until he was in his mid-twenties, when, following the advice of a local oracle, he decided to go to Athens. The ship he took wrecked, but he survived, apparently arriving in Athens penniless and with his usual gloomy demeanor, dark complexion, and the slight deformity of his body probably exacerbated by his experience at sea.

Adopting the calm and rational lifestyle he had read about in Xenophon's remarks about Socrates, he turned to the further pursuit of wisdom, studying the metaphysical ruminations of Heraclitus, the radical adiaphorism of Crates the Cynic, the logical methodology of Stilpo the Megarian, the poetic insight of the Academic Polemo, and some Aristotelian ideas from a possible association with Theophrastus, before finally, perhaps in reaction to what he considered to be the amoral views of Epicurus, proceeding to give his own lectures on the Painted Porch from whose Greek name (*Stoa Poikile*) his school of thought would derive its historical appellation. During his long tenure as head of the school he produced multiple writings (of which only the titles and fragments cited by followers remain).

He disliked crowds and declined Athenian citizenship (to remain loyal to his native country), but there is no evidence to suggest that he was totally disengaged from Athens' political and religious activities. Notwithstanding his downplaying of the Homeric/Hesiodic pantheon or his questioning the wisdom of building temples for the gods or making images of them, he did not attack all aspects of the popular religion. One of his arguments for the existence of God was in fact based upon what he calls the "reasonableness of honoring the gods." And according to Diogenes Laertius, all the Stoics, in addition to their emphasis upon "right reason," were of the view that good people are "acquainted with the rites of gods," "know how to serve the gods," and are "worshipers of God" by virtue of the purity of their lives and the sacrifices they offer to the gods. Furthermore, despite an element of theoretical Pantheism, there is also a more emotional side to Zeno's thought that leaves room for conceiving of God as something of a father figure to whom one might relate on a more personal level. Finally, had Zeno not respected and participated in some of the city's religious practices it would be hard to explain why its officials and citizens held him in such high confidence and esteem, honoring him as they did when he died (or killed himself) by affording him a "golden crown and public burial in the Cerameicus."

ZENO OF CITIUM ON RELIGION. The deities variously named by Hesiod in his *Theogony* are not divine beings in any literal sense. They are simply the names given to dumb, inanimate objects for allegorical purposes. But the heavenly bodies and other natural phenomena which they symbolize might, along with the intelligent *daimons*, be worthy of reverence, to the extent of manifesting God or Zeus as the Active Principle of Reason or Fate at work in our material universe. That the cosmos is in fact endowed with Reason follows from the twofold assumption that nothing is superior to the cosmos, and that anything endowed with reason is superior to that which is without reason.

Although the common notion of God might be at least virtually innate, in the sense that humans have a natural tendency to form such a notion, all human knowledge ultimately rests on sense perception. And what the senses reveal to us is that Reality consists of one living, materialistic Whole that is constituted by two indestructible principles, one passive, the other active. The former is indeterminate Matter. The latter is the ethereal, fiery Mind that breathes into matter the spermatic forms contained within itself, giving rise to the four elements from which all other things are eventually formed to constitute the Active Principle's body. At times — in a sequence of events that can also be called Fate — the whole universe is dissolved by fire, and then reformed into a new world, with the same things reappearing in the same, but reinvigorated, relations. Humans originated out of one such creative event. Endowed with rational souls, they are also free. Rationally discerning the direction of Fate, they can choose either to cultivate a virtuous attitude of indifference toward all external matters and accept the hand that Fate has dealt them, or they can fight against it. Those who embrace Fate will find some peace of mind until the next universal conflagration. The others will be pulled along anyway, like a dog tied to a moving wagon.

Sources

Arnim, H.F.A., ed. *Stoicorum Veterum Fragmenta*. 4 vols. Lipsiae: in aedibus B.G. Teubneri, 1921.

Bevan, Edwyn. *Later Greek Religion*. London and Toronto: J.M. Dent and Sons, Ltd.; New York: E.P. Dutton and Co., 1827. 1–9.

Brandis, Christian A. "Zenon." In *A Dictionary of Greek and Roman Biography and Mythology*. Vol. 3. Edited by William Smith. New York: AMS Press, Inc., 1967. 1313–17.

Diogenes Laertius. *Lives of Eminent Philosophers*. Vol. 2, no. 9. Translated by R.D. Hicks. Cambridge, MA: Harvard University Press, 1972. 110–263.

Copleston, Frederick, S.J. *A History of Philosophy*. Vol. 1, pt. 2. Garden City, NY: Doubleday and Company, Inc., 1962–77. 129–44.

Frede, Dorothea. "Theodicy and Providential Care in Stoicism." In Dorothea Frede, and Andre Laks, eds. *Traditions of Theology: Studies in Hellenistic Theology, Its Background and Aftermath*. Leiden and Boston: Brill, 2002. 85–118.

Hallie, Philip P. "Zeno of Citium." *Encyclopedia of Philosophy*. Vol. 8. Edited by Paul Edwards. New York: Macmillan and Co. and The Free Press, 1967. 368–69.

Hunt, Harold A.K. *A Physical Interpretation of the Universe: The Doctrine of Zeno the Stoic*. Carlton, Australia: Melbourne University Press, 1976.

Inwood, Brad, ed. *The Cambridge Companion to the Stoics*. Cambridge and New York: Cambridge University Press, 2003.

Saunders, Jason L. *Greek and Roman Philosophy after Aristotle*. New York: The Free Press; London: Collier-Macmillan Limited, 1966. 59–132.

Sedley, David. "The Origins of Stoic God." In Dorothea Frede, and Andre Laks, eds. *Traditions of Theology: Studies in Hellenistic Theology, Its Background and Aftermath*. Leiden and Boston: Brill, 2002. 41–84.

Index